Also in the Variorum Collected Studies Series:

PIERRE LEGENDRE
Ecrits juridiques du Moyen Age occidental

JANE E. SAYERS
Law and Records in Medieval England

C. R. CHENEY
The English Church and its Laws, 12th-14th centuries

C. R. CHENEY
The Papacy and England, 12th-14th centuries

STEPHAN KUTTNER
The History of Ideas and Doctrines of Canon Law in the Middle Ages

STEPHAN KUTTNER
Gratian and the Schools of Law, 1140-1234

ANDRÉ GOURON
Etudies sur la diffusion des doctrines juridiques médiévales

ROBERT FEENSTRA
Le droit savant au Moyen Age et sa vulgarisation

BRIAN TIERNEY
Church Law and Constitutional Thought in the Middle Ages

MARCEL PACAUT
Doctrines politiques et structures ecclésiastiques
dans l'Occident médiéval

JEAN GAUDEMET
La formation du droit canonique médiéval

JEAN GAUDEMET
Eglise et société en Occident au Moyen Age

CHARLES MUNIER
Vie conciliaire et collections canoniques en Occident, IVe-XIIe s.

RENÉ METZ
La femme et l'enfant dans le droit canonique médiéval

KARL F. MORRISON
Holiness and Politics in Early Medieval Thought

DONALD R. KELLEY
History, Law and the Human Sciences
Medieval and Renaissance Perspectives

Law and Jurisdiction in the Middle Ages

Walter Ullmann
(29.xi.1910 – 18.i.1983)

Walter Ullmann

Law and Jurisdiction in the Middle Ages

Edited by
George Garnett

VARIORUM REPRINTS
London 1988

British Library CIP data

Ullmann, Walter, *1910-1983*
Law and jurisdiction in the Middle Ages. —
(Collected studies series; CS283).
1. Europe. Law, *ca.* 1000-1500
I. Title II. Garnett, George
340.5′5

ISBN 0-86078-231-X

Published in Great Britain by Variorum Reprints
20 Pembridge Mews London W11 3EQ

Printed in Great Britain by Galliard (Printers) Ltd
Great Yarmouth Norfolk

VARIORUM REPRINT CS283

CONTENTS

This volume contains xviii + 332 pages

PUBLISHER'S NOTE

The articles in this volume, as in all others in the Collected Studies Series, have not been given a new, continuous pagination. In order to avoid confusion, and to facilitate their use where these same studies have been referred to elsewhere, the original pagination has been maintained wherever possible.

Each article has been given a Roman number in order of appearance, as listed in the Contents. This number is repeated on each page and quoted in the index entries.

PREFACE

Five years after his death, the appearance of a fifth volume of Walter Ullmann's essays calls for no *captatio benevolentiae*. In the prefaces to earlier volumes he often seemed to assume that each would be the final one in the series; but his output had been so vast that there always remained a few essays which had somehow been squeezed out, and which merited re-publication in order to render them accessible to a wider audience. As the supplementary bibliography of his publications — printed below — indicates, this rate of production continued in high gear until the end. So this volume consists of a number of valuable early essays, previously excluded and sometimes half-forgotten in the crush, together with pieces published after the other volumes had been compiled. Despite the gap of over forty years between the earliest and latest items, and the obvious development in his thought, they all reveal a remarkable continuity of approach in analysing the topics broadly covered by the title of this volume. An explanation of this approach may best be attempted biographically: to adapt one of his favourite aphorisms, we have to show what he was in order to understand what he became.

While still at school at Horn in Lower Austria he had developed strong interests in ancient history, particularly its constitutional aspects, and was very tempted to read classical philology at university. But eventually he opted for law instead. This decision proved to be crucial to his later development as an historian. It meant that he was not primarily taught those philological techniques which had formed the groundwork for the academic study of history since the time of Lorenzo Valla, except in so far as they impinged on his Roman law studies. Rather, he was trained to be a practising lawyer. At the University of Vienna he was inspired by the Romanists; but after he moved to Innsbruck in 1931 it was the criminal lawyers who captured his enthusiasm. He became particularly interested in the broad issue of crime as a social phenomenon, reflecting the sociological emphasis in the legal teaching he had received, and in a related area of criminal law: the elements of *mens rea*.

After graduating J.U.D. at the end of 1933, he began to work in the criminal departments of a district court; partly in the one concerned with pre-trial preparation, and partly in the senate which functioned as a court of appeal in criminal cases decided by the lower courts of the district. The former involved detailed investigation of crimes, and necessarily brought him face to face with the seamier side of social reality; the latter entailed the drafting of judgements giving the reasons why a particular appeal was to be allowed or dismissed, and was much more theoretical in character. At first his academic activities were confined to part-time teaching of criminal law procedure and civil law. But he was soon appointed as an unpaid assistant to Ferdinand Kadečka, the professor of criminal law at Vienna; and he embarked on research, choosing a topic which combined his two main undergraduate interests: the legal aspects of criminal psychology. He steeped himself in the works of Freud, Jung, and their followers. Modern psychological theory was, however, only one line of attack; another was to investigate some of the sources of modern jurisprudential thought on the topic by reading what scholars of earlier generations had written about it. He worked his way back to von Feuerbach, then from Beccaria to the seventeenth-century jurist Carpzow. By following up references cited by early modern lawyers, he eventually began to struggle with the postglossators.

It had already become apparent that his subject was almost limitless in scope, and would have to be trimmed in some way. His reading of the postglossators was the catalyst for another crucial decision. He realised that late medieval concepts of *mens rea* were quite distinct from modern ones; they would be of little use in a juristic analysis of modern criminal psychology. At this crossroads he chose to follow his new medieval interests rather than to drop them and to pursue the increasingly unmanageable subject which addressed itself to the sort of problems with which he had to deal every day at work. Like some postglossator himself, he had initially attempted to use earlier legal thought as a tool in the analysis of contemporary legal problems. But, unlike them, he had come to realise that this could not be done without wrenching it from its historical context and distorting it in order to make it fit entirely alien circumstances. Here his training in Roman law in particular, and also in legal history and modern history, economic theory and practice — all of which had formed parts of his undergraduate course — stood him in good stead. It informed his understanding of law. Law was not a series of static concepts distinct from society; it did not form an entity in itself; it had to be viewed as a function of society, a product of the factors which shaped social life. Nothing could have been further from the Austinian concept of law. So when he began to work for his *Habilitation* on the medieval doctrine of criminal attempt, he did so not in order to facilitate an understanding of modern doctrine, except in the very general sense of discovering some of its distant antecedents. He was trying to understand it in its own, medieval terms. And because of his views on the character of the law, such an understanding could only emerge from a much wider investigation of medieval society. The precise and objective character of law — in the sense that it addressed itself to external, verifiable actions — meant that it could provide a more reliable probe into medieval beliefs and assumptions than any other form of evidence. He had become an historian.

So, by the time of the *Anschluss*, the essential elements in his approach had already been formed. This is not the place to tell the story of his obstinate refusal to compromise his professional principles in the slightest degree when dealing with Nazi criminals, or to take an oath to the Führer; of his being a marked man for the Gestapo, and consequently having to go half underground; and of his flight to England through Gemany, orchestrated by Count Johannes Sarnthein, a friend in high places whose name makes him sound like a character from the Vienna Opera where Ullmann had worked as an extra in his student days. Suffice to say that he arrived in England in the late summer of 1938 — penniless, with his suitcase stuffed with precious notes and books rather than clothes. Initially he had hopes that the Western powers would stand up to Hitler and that he might be able to return to Austria in the fairly near future. But after Munich he stopped grasping at these straws. He refused to be dubbed a German citizen, and returned his passport to the German Embassy in London. He had already corresponded with H.D. Hazeltine, Downing Professor of the Laws of England at Cambridge, and with David Daube of Caius, and they arranged for him to be partially supported by a charitable committee while he worked on the postglossatorial collections in Cambridge libraries. During 1938–9 he lived a precarious, hand-to-mouth existence as it became apparent that war was approaching. Immersion in his academic work was his only refuge and solace from the pains of exile: there was, of course, not the slightest possibility that he might pursue his legal career in England, since he knew nothing of English common law. That decision was made for him. Although he had come to Cambridge with the intention of continuing to read for his *Habilitationschrift*, the incomparably rich collections which he found in the Wren Library of Trinity College in particular also led to numerous excursions and diversions into other aspects of postglossatorial thought. In addition to the more famous authors, he became particularly interested in a neglected fourteenth-century scholar — Lucas de Penna. What attracted him was the unusual way in which Lucas used theological and philosophical writers like Thomas Aquinas and John of Salisbury in his analysis of the last three books of the Code. For Ullmann, this showed that Lucas recognised that law was not an entirely distinct subject of intellectual inquiry; it could only be properly understood in relation to a much wider body of scholarship and belief. In other words, he saw Lucas as sharing his own understanding of the character of law. Lucas was self-consciously explicit about the sort of connections which Ullmann tried to detect in the other postglossators. Lucas' thought was to provide him with the subject of his first book, significantly entitled *The Medieval Idea of Law as represented by Lucas de Penna.*

This was only published after the war. But already, in the essays which appeared during it, the expansion of his interests into the wider ramifications of postglossatorial thought and beyond is evident. In particular, Lucas stimulated a life-long interest in the works of John of Salisbury; and he was inspired by C.N.S. Woolf's great book on Bartolus to begin to look in detail at the political theories of the medieval civilians. Obviously he could not make much progress in new areas of research while serving in the Army Pioneer Corps; but he did manage to write up a considerable amount. Indeed, he was twice threatened with courts martial for neglecting his duties in the sanitary fatigue in order to do so: Bartolus was more interesting than toilets. After he had been discharged, however, and returned to the position as a schoolmaster which his Cambridge connections had found for him just before the outbreak of war, he was able both to complete his book on Lucas and to embark on new projects. It was while searching through Baldus' commentaries on the Code that he came across the jurist's *consilium* of 1378 on the legality of Urban VI's position. This was precisely the sort of thing which inspired him with enthusiasm: the application of abstract juristic thought to the analysis of particular events. That these events were of great political importance meant that a study of them would readily mesh with his developing interest in the points where political life and legal logic met. Thus his second book — on the origins of the Great Schism — was planned before the first was completed. The new project represented a fresh departure in another sense: it was his first real foray into medieval canon law and papal history. Yet he continued to draw directly on his experience as a practising lawyer: Baldus' *consilium* reminded him of his former duties in the appeals-senate of the district court where he had worked, and he decided that he would attack his historical problem in the same way as if he had been drafting a judgement in court. There could be no clearer example of the way in which his legal training continued to inform his approach to history, or better indication of why his writing sometimes betrays the thrilling intensity and immediacy of a protagonist in the debate, rather than an historian looking back over the centuries.

By the time he had been forced to flee from Austria, he had become an historian. By the time he was given his first university post — at Leeds, in 1947 — he was already thoroughly embroiled in the political theories of the medieval canonists. In 1948 he used these researches as the basis for his Maitland Lectures at Cambridge, under the title 'Medieval Papalism'. The future was mapped out and the framework of his intellectual formation was complete. Many of the essays in this volume give snapshots of the process of formation; some of them are the fruits of his last years. All of them have in common an approach to history which reveals the mind of someone trained to be a practising lawyer adapting that training to historical analysis.

*
* *

Thanks are due to Elizabeth Ullmann and to Ralph Ullmann for helping me to decide which essays to include in this volume. I am further indebted to Elizabeth for undertaking the laborious task of obtaining permission to re-publish the essays from their respective publishers, and to those publishers for granting permission so readily. Peter Linehan cast the gimlet eye of an experienced editor over the bibliography, and improved its presentation substantially. He, Richard Brent, and Melissa Dalziel have helped me to clarify the thoughts I attempt to express in the preface. For the obscurities that remain I alone am responsible. Shelley Lockwood has probably done more than any of us, in compiling the index. It was largely at the enthusiastic instigation of Eileen Turner and John Smedley that the project was ever undertaken; the latter deserves special thanks for the way in which he has pursued it to its conclusion, bearing with my inefficiencies with an exemplary patience.

GEORGE GARNETT

Magdalene College, Cambridge
April, 1988

SUPPLEMENTARY BIBLIOGRAPHY
of the Writings of Walter Ullmann

A continuation of that compiled by Peter Linehan in B.Tierney and P.A.Linehan, eds., *Authority and Power. Studies on Medieval Law and Government presented to Walter Ullmann on his Seventieth Birthday* (Cambridge, 1980), pp.255-74, nos.1-384.

1928

'Ein leistungsfähiges Zweiröhrengerät', *Radio-Woche*, V (1928). p. 5.

1944

'The influence of John of Salisbury on the Medieval Italian Jurists', *EHR*, LIX (1944), pp. 384-92.

1980

385 *Radici del Rinascimento* (Rome-Bari, 1980) [Italian translation of no. 349].

386 *Jurisprudence in the Middle Ages*, Collected Studies IV (London, 1980).

387 'Personality and Territoriality in the *Defensor Pacis*: The Problem of Political Humanism', *Medioevo: Rivista di Storia della Filosofia Medievale*, VI (1980), pp. 397-410.

388 *Review* of I.S.Robinson, *Authority and Resistance in the Investiture Contest. The Polemical Literature of the Late Eleventh Century* (Manchester-New York, 1978), *Catholic Historical Review*, LXVI (1980), pp. 616-18.

389 *Review* of R.A.Fletcher, *The Episcopate in the Kingdom of León in the Twelfth Century* (Oxford, 1978), *EHR*, XCV (1980), pp. 197-8.

390 *Review* of K.J.Leyser, *Rule and Conflict in an Early Medieval Society: Ottonian Saxony* (London, 1979), *JEH*, XXXI (1980), pp. 348-51.

391 *Review* of G.Melville, ed., *Secundum Regulam Vivere: Festschrift für P.Norbert Backmann, O.Praem.* (Windberg, 1978), *JTS*, n.s. XXXI (1980), pp. 247-9.

392 *Review* of J.Richards, *The Popes and the Papacy in the Early Middle Ages 476-752* (London, 1979), *JTS*, n.s. XXXI (1980), p. 298.

393 *Review* of R.Sommerville, *Pope Alexander III and the Council of Tours (1163). A Study in Ecclesiastical Politics and Institutions in the Twelfth Century* (Berkeley and Los Angeles, 1977), *JTS*, n.s. XXXI (1980), p. 299.

394 *Review* of H.J.Sieben, *Die Konzilsidee der Alten Kirche* (Paderborn-Munich-Vienna, 1979), *JTS*, n.s. XXXI (1980), pp. 623-7.

395 *Review* of A.Patschovsky, *Quellen zur Böhmischen Inquisition im 14. Jahrhundert* (MGH, Quellen zur Geistgeschichte des Mittelalters, XI) (Weimar 1979), *JTS*, n.s. XXXI (1980), pp. 641-4.

396 *Review* of E.Türk, *Nugae Curialium: le règne d'Henri II Plantagenet (1154-1189) et l'éthique politique* (Geneva, 1977), *Revue Belge de Philologie et d'Histoire*, LVIII (1980), pp. 231-3.

397 *Review* of M.Dykmans, *Le Cérémonial papal de la fin du Moyen Age à la Renaissance*, vol I: *Le Cérémonial papal du XIII siècle* (Brussels-Rome, 1977), *Revue Belge de Philologie et d'Histoire*, LVIII (1980), pp. 753-6.

1981

398 *Gelasius I. (492-496): Das Papsttum an der Wende der Spätantike zum Mittelalter* (Stuttgart, 1981).

399 'Calvin and the Duty of Guardians to Resist: a Further Comment', *JEH*, XXXII (1981), pp. 499-501.

400 *Review* of L.De Giovanni, *Chiesa e Stato nel Codice Teodosiano: Saggi sul Libro XVI* (Naples, 1980), *JEH*, XXXII (1981), p. 256.

401 *Review* of P.O.Kristeller, *Renaissance Thought and its Sources*, ed. M.Mooney (New York, 1979), *JEH*, XXXII (1981), pp. 355-6.

402 *Review* of J.Gilchrist, ed. and trans., *The Collection in Seventy-Four Titles: a Canon Law Manual of the Gregorian Reform* (Toronto, 1980), *JEH*, XXXII (1981), pp. 521-2.

403 *Review* of D.Williman, *Bibliothèques ecclésiastiques au temps de la Papauté d'Avignon*, vol I (Paris, 1980), *Nottingham Medieval Studies*, XXV (1981), pp. 84-8.

1982

404 'On the Medieval Origins of the Renaissance', in *The Renaissance: Essays in Interpretation to Eugenio Garin* (London, 1982), pp. 33-82 [= English version of no. 374].

405 'Medieval Monarchy', *Sewanee Mediaeval Colloquium Occasional Papers*, no. I (Sewanee, Tennessee, 1982), pp. 19-59.

406 'Zum Papstwahldekret von 1059', *Zeitschrift der Savigny-Stiftung für Rechtsgeschichte*, kanonistische Abteilung, LXVIII (1982), (Festschrift Stephan Kuttner) pp. 32-51.

407 'Public Law as an Instrument of Government in Historical Perspective: New Rome and Old Rome in the Light of Historical Jurisprudence', *Diritto e Potere nella Storia Europea. Atti del Quarto Congresso Internazionale della Società Italiana di Storia del Diritto: in Onore di Bruno Paradisi* (Florence, 1982), pp. 37-52.

408 'Grundfragen des mittelalterlichen Papsttums', in M.Kerner, ed. *Ideologie und Herrschaft im Mittelalter* (Darmstadt, 1982), pp. 207-40 [a revised version of pp. 9-41 of no. 184].

409 'Politisches Denken und politische Organisation', in *Propyläen Geschichte der Literatur: Literatur und Gesellschaft der westlichen Welt*, vol II, *Die mittelalterliche Welt* (Berlin, 1982), pp. 11-38.

410 *Review* of P.A.McShane, *La Romanitas et le Pape Léon le Grand. L'apport culturel des institutions impériales à la formation des structures ecclésiastiques* (Montreal, 1979), *Catholic Historical Review*, LXVIII (1982), pp. 92-4.

411 *Review* of M.Laufs, *Politik und Recht bei Innozenz III. Kaiserprivilegien, Thronstreitregister und Egerer Goldbulle in der Reichs- und Rekuperationspolitik Papst Innozenz' III.* (Cologne, 1980), *Catholic Historical Review*, LXVIII (1982), pp. 286-9.

412 *Review* of D.Wyduckel, *Princeps legibus solutus: Untersuchung zur frühmodernen Rechts- und Staatslehre* (Berlin, 1979), *EHR*, XVCII (1982), pp. 402-3.

413 *Review* of C.Jeudy and J.Quillet, eds., *Marsile de Padoue: Oeuvres Mineures* (Paris, 1979), *EHR*, XCVII (1982), pp. 406-7.

414 *Review* of *Untersuchungen zu Kloster und Stift*, ed. Max-Planck-Institut für Geschichte (Göttingen, 1980), *EHR*, XCVII (1982), pp. 884–5.

415 *Review* of S.Kuttner and K.Pennington, eds., *Proceedings of the Fifth International Congress of Medieval Canon Law, Salamanca 21–25 September 1976* (Vatican City, 1980), *JEH*, XXXIII (1982), pp. 119–22.

416 *Review* of M.Brecht, ed., *Text, Wort, Glaube: Studien zur Uberlieferung, Interpretation und Autorisierung biblische Texte. Kurt Aland gewidmet* (Berlin–New York, 1980), *JEH*, XXXIII (1982), pp. 323–4.

417 *Notice* of K.Baus, *From the Apostolic Community to Constantine*, with an introduction by H.Jedin; K.Baus, H.-G.Beck, E.Ewig and H.J.Vogt, *The Imperial Church from Constantine to the Early Middle Ages*; F.Kemp, H.-G.Beck, E.Ewig, and J.A.Jungmann, *The Church in the Age of Feudalism* (reprinted London, 1980), *JEH*, XXXIII (1982), p. 487.

418 *Review* of G.Alberigo, *Chiesa conciliare: Identità e significato del conciliarismo* (Brescia, 1982), *JTS*, n.s. XXXIII (1982), pp. 611–16.

1983

419 *Historia del pensamiento político en la Edad Media* (Barcelona, 1983) [Spanish translation of no. 320].

420 *Review* of U.Horst, *Die Kanonessammlung Polycarpus des Gregor von S.Grisogno: Quellen und Tendenzen* (Munich, 1980), *EHR*, XCVIII (1983), p. 402.

421 *Review* of R.Elze, *Päpste-Kaiser-Könige und die mittelalterliche Herrschafts-symbolik* (London, 1982), *JEH*, XXXIV (1983), pp. 124–5.

422 *Review* of M.Ascheri, *I consilia dei giuristi medievali: per un repertorio-incipitario computerrizato* (Siena, 1982), *JEH*, XXXIV (1983), p. 153

423 *Review* of W.D.McCready, ed., *The Theory of Papal Monarchy in the Fourteenth Century: the* Tractatus de Causa Immediata Ecclesiastice Potestatis *of Guillaume de Pierre Godin* (Toronto, 1982), *JTS*, n.s. XXXIV (1983), pp. 338–41.

424 *Review* of A.García y García, ed., *Constitutiones Concilii quarti Lateranensis una cum Commentariis Glossatorum* (Vatican City, 1981); and K.Pennington, ed., *Johannis Teutonici Apparatus Glossarum in Compilationem Tertiam*, vol I (Vatican City, 1981), *JTS*, n.s. XXXIV (1983), pp. 654–8.

1984

425 *Review* of P.Weimar, ed., *Die Renaissance der Wissenschaften im 12. Jahrhundert* (Zurich, 1981), *EHR*, XCIX (1984), pp. 150–1.

1985

426 *Principios de gobierno y política en la Edad Media* (Madrid, 1985) [reissue of no. 255].

1986

427 'Königs- und Papstherrschaft im Spiegel der Bistumsbesetzungen: Skizze einer Rechtsideologie', in K.Ebert, ed., *Festschrift Nikolaus Grass zum 70. Geburstag dargebracht von Fachkollegen und Freunden* (Innsbruck, 1986), pp. 407–22.

428 'Alexander III and the Conquest of Ireland. A Note on the Background', in F.Liotta, ed., *Miscellanea Rolando Bandinelli, Papa Alessandro III* (Siena, 1986), pp. 371–87.

1988

429 *Law and Jurisdiction in the Middle Ages*, Collected Studies V (London, 1988).

Forthcoming

430 'Der Wiedergeburtsgedanke in der Staatslehre des Mittelalters', in H.Temporini and W.Haase, eds., *Aufstieg und Niedergang der römischen Welt*, part III (Berlin).

431 'Kirchengeschichte und das Recht als Ausdruk der ekklesiologischen Ganzheit', *Grundfragen der kirchengeschichtlichen Methode-Heute. Internationales Symposion des römischen Instituts der Görres-Gesellschaft* (Rome).

I

PUBLIC LAW AS AN INSTRUMENT OF GOVERNMENT IN HISTORICAL PERSPECTIVE: NEW ROME AND OLD ROME IN THE LIGHT OF HISTORICAL JURISPRUDENCE

In historical jurisprudence too little attention has been paid to public law as such and still less attention to public law as an instrument of government. And yet, no government at any time could (and can) exist and function without its being able to rely on public law as the vehicle through which it could (and can) effectively direct, order and guide society under its control. What I would like to do on the present occasion is to raise a few questions and points intimately linked with historical jurisprudence in order to stimulate discussion and further research into this much neglected topic which stands in close proximity to the *utilitas publica*.

Indeed, the very concept of *utilitas publica* appears to be an appropriate handle with which to explain one of the most conspicuous contingencies in which the *ius publicum* of Ulpianic provenance[1] played a crucial role. For the measures which Constantine the Great initiated in order to give the Christians freedom

[1] Dig. 1.1.1.2. On the passage cf. M. Kaser, *Zur Methodologie der römischen Rechtsquellen*, « Sitz. Ber. d. österreichischen Akademie der Wissenschaften », Phil.-Hist. Kl. 227, 1972, esp. p. 44, n. 75 and p. 56; see further idem, *Römisches Privatrecht*, II, 2nd ed., München 1975, p. 53, n. 7. The Princeps had the ' cura et tutela rei publicae universa ', see further G. Grifò, *Ulpiano*, in *Aufstieg und Niedergang der römischen Welt*, ed. H. Temporini, II.15, Berlin 1976, pp. 708-789. For general orientation cf. G. Dulckeit-F. Schwartz, *Römische Rechtsgeschichte*, 6th ed. by W. Waldstein, München 1975, p. 258 ff.

and a licit standing within the Roman commonwealth were upon a final analysis based on the *ius publicum*.[2] In fact, Constantine's governmental measures cannot be understood without taking into account the role played by public law. In its pristine and original shape it embraced the *sacra*, the *sacerdotes* and the *magistratus*. In his function as sole emperor he had quite evidently at his disposal the interpretation, manipulation, application and modification of the *ius publicum*, and since the Christian body had *sacerdotes* as administrators of the *sacra*, the emperor in his governmental capacity clearly had the right to exercise jurisdiction over them, especially as the Christians considered themselves as a *corpus* entirely in consonance with the Roman law as well as with Pauline doctrine. Hence the legal presuppositions were at hand: the Christians constituted a body which had hitherto been proscribed and which, by virtue of its own strong monocratic structure, could profitably be harnessed to the interests of the Roman common weal: the *utilitas publica* virtually suggested the measures enacted by Constantine. He turned the illicit *corpus* into a *corpus licitum*,[3] in order to harness it to his over-all governmental aim of the *regeneratio imperii Romani*. As such the Christian body quite obviously came within the precincts of the Roman *ius publicum*, which Constantine skilfully wielded as an instrument of his government in the interests of a rebirth or a renewal of the Roman empire.[4] The *ius publicum* was virtually tailored for the occasion, because two of its three constituent parts pronouncedly applied to the *Corpus* of the Christians.

---

[2] For some details see W. ULLMANN, *The constitutional significance of Constantine the Great's settlement*, in *Scholarship and Politics in the Middle Ages* (Collected Studies, III), London 1978. See further A. EHRHARDT, *Constantin d. Grossen Religionspolitik*, « Zeitschr. d. Savigny Stiftung f. Rechtsgeschichte, Rom. Abt. », 72, 1955 pp. 127-190. For the background see F. AMARELLI, *Il « De mortibus persecutorum » nei suoi rapporti con l'ideologia coeva*, « Studia et Documenta Historiae et Iuris », 36, 1970, pp. 207-264.

[3] For this see also A. EHRHARDT, *Das Corpus Christi und die Korporation im römischen Recht*, «Savigny Z., Rom. Abt. », 79, 1953, pp. 299-347; 71, 1954, pp. 25-40. In this context cf. also J. VOGT, *Zur Frage des christlichen Einflusses auf die Gesetzgebung Konstantins d. Gr.*, in *Festschrift für Leopold Wenger*, II, München 1944, p. 119 ff., esp. p. 127 ff.

[4] Cf. the inscription on Constantine's statue: EUSEBIUS, *Vita Constantini* I.40, ed. F. Winkelmann in *Die griechischen christlichen Schriftsteller*, Berlin 1975, pp. 36-37. See also E. PETERSON, *Theologische Traktate*, München 1955, pp. 88 ff.; H. DÖRRIES, *Das Selbstzeugnis Kaiser Konstantins*, « Abhandlungen der Akademie d. Wissenschaften zu Göttingen », Phil.-Hist. Kl., 3. Folge, no. 34, 1953, p. 215 f.

That the Christians now fully welcomed the steps taken by Constantine, went without saying, but their internal squabbles quite clearly prevented them from playing the part which Constantine had allocated to them and which he expected from them. A divided and quarrelling body was of no use to any Ruler who wished for unity within his realm. It was in this very context that the *ius publicum* came to assume a major role. He, not yet a Christian, summoned councils, and notably the ecumenical council to Nicaea, in which the theological and dogmatic controversies were to be thrashed out.[5] In this measure alone the efficacy of public law showed itself plainly: the requirement of public peace and the public interest alike presupposed a united body that was capable of assisting the imperial designs, and it could do so only if it had a commonly agreed doctrine and programme. Organisation, management and administration of the Council lay entirely in the hands of the imperial commissions and committees. The substantive decisions, however, were taken solely by the 318 participants. The decrees did not acquire general validity in law until the imperial government had sanctioned them. This requirement was likewise based upon the *ius publicum*, because both the *sacra* and the *sacerdotes* were involved, and they were involved as fully constituted and structural parts of the Roman empire.

It was on the occasion of the Nicaean Council that Constantine made, according to his biographer, the statement in an address to the assembled bishops that he was the ἐπίσκοπος τῶν ἐκτός whereas they were the overseers of a different order.[6] This statement was of fundamental importance, not only in regard to the delineation of imperial power, but also, and perhaps even more so, in respect of the extent and scope as well as of the applicability of the *ius publicum* in relation to the Christian *Corpus*.[7] The sense

[5] Some details in my *art. cit.* (above n. 2), at p. 10 ff.

[6] EUSEBIUS, *Vita Constantini*, ed. cit. (above n. 4) IV.24, p. 128 lines 21-22: ʽἀλλ' ὑμεῖς μὲν τῶν είσω τῆς ἐκκλησίας. ἐγὼ δὲ τῶν ἐκτός ὑπὸ θεοῦ καθεσταμένος ἐπίσκοπος ἄν εἴην'

[7] For the interpretation of this famous expression cf. my *art. cit.* (above n. 2); F. VITTINGHOFF, *Eusebius als Verfasser der Vita Constantini*, « Rheinisches Museum für Philologie », n.s., 96, 1953, p. 330 ff.; A. H. M. JONES, *Constantine and the conversion of Europe*, Harmondsworth 1972, p. 194 ff.; J. STRAUB, *Kaiser Konstantin als* ΕΠΙΣΚΟΡΟΣ ΤΩΝ ΕΚΤΟΣ in his *Regeneratio Imperii*, Darmstadt 1972, pp. 119-133. See further, J.-M. SANSTERRE, *Eusèbe de Césarée et la naissance de la théorie « césa-*

of this statement was that what concerned the external activites and matters of this body, came within the orbit of public law and therefore within imperial jurisdiction. Thereby the *ius publicum* acquired a far larger sphere of applicability than it hitherto had had. Taking into account the *utilitas publica*, it stands to reason that the Ruler had in fact the duty to apply the public law to this Christian body,[8] with the important consequence that its protection became a structural element of public law and government. Herein one may well discover the origin of what later came to be seen as the tutorial function of the Ruler.[9] The consequence was clear: public law not only embraced the external manifestations of the Church (understood as the *congregatio fidelium*) but also their foundations, that is, in the present context, the faith. Protection of the faith – not its fixation, formulation or contents – came to be included within public law. It was barely two generations afterwards that the Ruler called himself the *cultor divinae religionis*, was designated as *custos fidei* and acted as a *defensor fidei*.[10]

This is assuredly one of the most fascinating epiphenomena in historical jurisprudence: the Ruler, himself the sole monarchic legislator, who took no part in the elaboration and making of religious dogmas or doctrines or matters pertaining to the *Interna*, because they belonged to the faith and religion in the strict meaning of the term, extended his protective hand to precisely these *Interna* which manifested themselves in the *Externa*, such as administration, organisation, and so forth. The actual development in the course of the fourth century showed that the hopes of the imperial government to preserve the unity of the very body which was to assist the recovery of the empire, were far from being realized. Strife, quarrels, debates of an interminable

---

ropapiste », « Byzantion », 42, 1972, pp. 131-185; 532-594; P. G. CARON, *Constantine le Grand,* ἐπίσκοπος τῶν ἐκτος *de l'église romaine,* « Rev. internationale des droits de l'antiquité », 22, 1975, pp. 179-188, who considers that the *ius gentium* should be brought to bear upon the interpretation.

[8] For the maintenance of public order within the *Res Romana* was committed to the Princeps, cf. on this also W. ULLMANN, *Über die rechtliche Bedeutung der spätrömischen Kaisertitulatur*, in *Scholarship* (cit. above n. 2), Ch. 2, p. 31 f.

[9] See W. ULLMANN, *The Carolingian Renaissance and the Idea of Kingship*, London 1969, pp. 122 f., 177 ff. Hence the king had the *tutamentum regni.*

[10] For some details of these functions cf. my *art. cit.* (above n. 8) at notes 8, 9, 28, 31, 32. The examples could easily be multiplied.

character divided the ecclesiastical exponents of dogma – and the original intention to utilize the liberated Christians in the service of the empire was quite clearly not fulfilled. Hence the employment of compulsory measures or what Caspar has once so felicitously called the « Politik der Zwangsunion » [11] came to the fore. By imperial measures – again wholly based on the public law which proved itself capable of an ever widening field of application – the division of the various Christian factions was to be brought to an end, so that there was unity and not unsettling strife and discord. The end of this development was the imperial rescript *Cunctos populos* by Theodosius the Great on 27 February 380, signed also by Valentinian and Gratian, by which the Christian religion was imperially decreed to be the solely legitimate religion within the empire. It constituted a landmark in constitutional no less than in juristic respects.[12]

The basis was quite obviously the public law – and the aim was the promotion of the common good, the *utilitas publica*. It stood in fact on the same level as the convocation of councils or any other item of the *Externa*. Moreover, imperial jurisdiction was now constitutionally greatly extended: deviation from faith became a public crime and hence to be dealt with by the imperial courts. And not the least important consequence of this decree was the constitutionally sanctioned imperial control of the clerical body which was directly attributable to the tenor of the rescript. For its over-all effect was the coalescence of Roman empire and Christendom: it was the union of *Römerreich* and *Christenreich*. The two entities had become identical. They were the two sides of the same coin. There was a « coincidence », that is, one constitutional unit where previously there had been two public bodies. By virtue of the prevailing monarchic principle the imperial government was evidently the legislative organ, with the qualification, however, that it confined itself to the strictly external matters of the Christian body. In other words, *Cunctos populos* was, seen from the historical and evolutionary angle, merely an extension of the Constantinean distinction between the *Externa*

---

[11] E. Caspar, *Geschichte des Papsttums,* I, Tübingen 1930, p. 167 ff.

[12] C. Theod. XVI.1.2. The faith to be adhered to was the one propounded and interpreted by the present pope Damasus. See further C. Just. I.1.1. For the background see Ch. Pietri, *Roma Christiana: Recherches sur l'église de Rome, son organisation, sa politique, son idéologie de Miltiade à Sixte III,* Roma-Paris 1976, pp. 849 ff.

and the *Interna*. Hence convocation of general councils, appointments of higher ecclesiastics or their translations, were within the orbit of the *Externa*, and so was jurisdiction, especially in criminal matters as far as they affected the public good.[13] Ecclesiastical administrative and organisational matters touching upon public life, came within the purview of the public law. Protection was understood in the widest sense and included the conferment of privileges and immunities upon the Christian body. There is ample, though too little noticed, legal evidence for the enshrinement of the Constantinean distinction in an enactment of the late fourth century. Arcadius and Honorius issued a law on 20 August 399, according to which matters of religion (i.e. *Interna*) were to be the preserve of the bishops gathered in an assembly, whereas other issues were to be adjudged according to the public law.[14]

From the purely juristic standpoint very little had in fact changed as a result of Constantine's and his successors' measures, including Theodosius'. What has received far too slight attention in modern research is the intitulation of the emperors in the fifth century.[15] It is true that after *Cunctos populos* the emperors could not and did not call themselves *Pontifex maximus*, but their function as *pontifex* appears to have been kept, as a number of instances would go to show: the emperor as the *pontifex inclitus* was, certainly by the mid-fifth century, the title used to indicate precisely what Constantine had meant by the *Externa*. The acclamation by the synodists in the Council of Chalcedon (451) – τῶι ἱερεῖ, τῶι βασιλεῖ – followed the same pattern.[16] That did not mean that they saw in the emperor a « priest »; they considered him an organ that dealt with external matters of the Church. The acclamations in fact are first-rate evidence of the synodists'

---

[13] See P. E. Pieler, Art. *Gerichtsbarkeit*, « Reallexikon für Antike und Christentum », 9, 1977, pp. 471-487 (with exhaustive literature).

[14] C. Theod. XVI.11.1: ' Quotiens de religione agitur episcopos convenit agitare; ceteras vero causas, quae ad ordinarios cognitores vel ad *usum publici iuris* pertinent, legibus oportet audiri '. Cf. also *ibid.*, XVI.2.23, according to which criminal proceedings against clerics were to be dealt with by the ordinary, that is, civil courts.

[15] For the following cf. *art. cit.* (above n. 8).

[16] *Acta Conciliorum Oecumenicorum*, ed. E. Schwartz, II.1.2, Berlin 1933, no. 20, p. 157 line 29. In the Latin translation: sacerdoti imperatori.

awareness of the ever-present Constantinean distinction enshrined as it was in the just-mentioned law. None of the synodists – and they constituted a veritable élite of learned bishops – thereby implied that the emperor possessed charismatic qualities or was entitled to administer sacraments. The old *pontifex* reappeared without the specific priestly – internal – attributes which Christianity had conferred upon him.

There is one more point that deserves mentioning in this context, because it too carries over, so to speak, an ancient feature into a period in which it may at first sight have seemed inappropriate. It may be recalled that during the imperial regiment the Rulers' designation was characterized by the prefix *Divus* (Hadrianus, Severus, etc.).[17] This divinisation of the Ruler made perfect sense at the time, but was wholly out of place within a Christian framework. Here again it is noteworthy that, to mention just a few examples, the *Novellae* of Theodosius II were promulgated under the title « Liber legum Novellarum *divi* Theodosii ».[18] Thus, the second *Novella* is headed: « De confirmatione legum novellarum *divi* Theodosii A. »,[19] whereas in the body of the *Novella* itself he refers to « *divorum* retro principum constitutiones »[20] and singles out in an earlier *Novella* the « lex *divae* memoriae Constantini »[21] whose « consilium » was *divinum*.[22] In another *Novella* (of 12 September 439) he mentions that « *divinis* sensibus die noctuque » he cared for the good of mankind.[23] But exactly the same feature is to be found in the *Novellae* of his Western colleague, Valentinian III, whose collection of *Novellae* bears the title « Liber Novellarum *divi* Valentiniani ».[24] Indeed, all the collections of the fifth-century emperors bear this

---

[17] See A. Wlosok (ed.) *Römischer Kaiserkult*, Darmstadt 1972. For the continuation in Byzantium see H.-G. Beck, *Das byzantinische Jahrtausend*, München 1978, p. 79 f.

[18] Ed. Th. Mommsen and P. M. Meyer, Berlin 1905.

[19] *Ibid.*, *Nov.* 2 dated 1 October 447, p. 6.

[20] *Ibid*, line 2 f.

[21] *Nov.* 5, p. 13 lines 7-8.

[22] *Ibid.*, p. 14 lines 11-12. In the speech addressed to the senate in 438 concerning the publication of the Codex Theodosianus the emperor referred to Constantine ' et post eum *divi* principes nosque tulimus (leges) ' (C. Theod., *ed. cit.*, p. 2, lines 6-7).

[23] *Nov.* 16, p. 37 lines 4-5.

[24] *Ibid.*, p. 73.

prefix.[25] Yet it would be quite erroneous to say that the earlier divinisation was revived. Here the same considerations and explanations apply as in the case of the *pontifex*-title. These designations and intitulations lead compellingly to the conclusion that despite his incorporation into the Christian body by virtue of baptismal rebirth,[26] the Christian Ruler's function continued as heretofore and was based on the classical *ius publicum* as defined by Ulpian. Of the three constituent parts indubitably the *sacra* and the *sacerdotes* suggested themselves as suitable objects of the public law. It cannot and does not cause any surprise that the *leges* were *sacratissimae* [27] and that the *utilitas publica* always stood in the foreground, sometimes invoking the *necessitates publicae*.[28]

Here is the point which requires special emphasis. At no time during the period under review did the papacy or any other ecclesiastical authority raise any objection to the imperial application of the Roman public law in regard to the *Externa*, such as the convocation of councils, etc., in the function of the emperor as *custos fidei*. As a matter of fact, it was the papacy which frequently used this very designation as a sign of honour and distinction.[29] What is of no lesser interest is that the imperial chancery used in the Arengae of imperial laws the very terminology which the papacy had employed, certainly since Damasus-Siri-

---

[25] Cf. Maiorianus, p. 156 ff.; Marcianus, p. 181 ff.; Severus, p. 199 ff.; Anthemius, p. 203 ff.

[26] Baptismal rebirth effected the incorporation into the body of the Church: natural man was reborn (*renatus*) and became a *nova creatura* as a result of this regeneration (*regeneratio*), the result of the working of divine grace. Baptismal rebirth had eminently and pronouncedly legal effects: the *homo novus* entered a society in the making of which he had no share, nor did he have any share in the making of its norms or laws. He thus became a *sub/ditus*. For some details see W. ULLMANN, *Individuo e Società nel Medioevo*,* Roma-Bari 1974, pp. 4 f., 85, 93 ff., 104, 108; ID., *Law and Politics in the Middle Ages*, London-Cambridge 1975, pp. 39, 269 ff.; *Medieval Foundations of Renaissance Humanism*, London 1977, p. 14 ff. (where the biblical and patristic passages will be found). The work by O. HEGGELBACHER, *Die christliche Taufe als Rechtsakt nach dem Zeugnis der frühen Christenheit*, Fribourg 1953, is fundamental. * See *The Individual and Society in the Middle Ages*, London 1967, pp. 7, 12, 101, 123-4, 128.

[27] About the great semantic difference between *sacer* and *sanctus* see *art. cit.* (above n. 8) at p. 34 f.

[28] Theodosius II, *Nov.* 7, of 20 January 439, p. 17, lines 1-2, and frequently.

[29] Cf., for example, Leo I to the emperor in Constantinople in *Acta* (cit. above n. 16) II.4, p. 88, lines 34 f.; pp. 102-103; further *ibid.*, no. 103, p. 110, lines 27 ff.; cf. also Pope Simplicius writing to Zeno in *Collectio Avellana* (ed. *Corpus scriptorum ecclesiasticorum latinorum* XXXV), no. 66, p. 147 line 5; etc.

cius, by referring to the Pauline « inter ceteras sollicitudines »,[30] and it was the *amor publicus* which prompted the emperor to act in the way he did.[31] The conclusion is inescapable: the emperor presided over an historical entity and acted on historical premisses by employing the age-old public law. After all, nobody had ever impugned the view that the empire in the East continued uninterruptedly the Roman empire, as the very appellation of its capital – *iunior Roma* or *Nea Roma* – persuasively shows. From this followed necessarily that it also had inherited the *ius publicum* of ancient parentage, which to all seeming was tailored for the purposes of any monarchic government. And from the Constantinopolitan perspective Rome had assumed the position of a museum piece – she was the *senior Roma*. The historical development was unchangeable. The empire whose capital was Constantinople, was the Roman empire pure and simple which, by imperial decree, had adopted Christianity. But from the governmental standpoint nothing in the substance of the empire had changed. It was seen as an historic unit of which Christianity was an important adjunct. By virtue of the monarchic government the *ius publicum* remained entirely at the disposal of the emperor to be used in the interests of the *res Romana* in Ulpianic terminology.[32] In a word, law was in conformity with the Roman substance of the empire which is the same as saying that law was in conformity with history.

Like all general councils, so also was the last one of Christian antiquity, that of Chalcedon, convoked by the emperor to put an end to the christological disputes.[33] Although the council almost unanimously adopted the formula of Pope Leo I's legates, the decision did not subsequently meet with the approval of all schools of thought in the provinces and was fiercely opposed in

---

[30] Cf. II Cor. 11.28; etc. An analytical comparison between papal and imperial terminologies in their enactments is long overdue, especially the utilization of the Bible. H. v. FICHTENAU, *Arenga*, Vienna 1957, touched on this problem which was only peripheral to his main concern.

[31] Theodosius II, *Nov.* 3, p. 7 lines 7-8, combining the two terms.

[32] Dig. 1.1.1: 'Ius publicum est, quod ad statum rei Romanae spectat'. About the truncated text in the Institutes cf. F. WIEACKER, *Textstufen klassischer Juristen*, « Abhandlungen der Akademie der Wissenschaften zu Göttingen », Phil.-Hist. Kl., 3. Folge, no. 45, 1960, p. 206, n. 135, and 213. Cf. also Gaius, *Inst.* II.2.

[33] Leo I in fact implored the emperor to summon the council: *Acta*, cit. (above n. 16) II.4, p. 27 lines 4-6.

some quarters. The details are here of no concern. What is of concern is that as a consequence the empire was severely shaken by unrest, disorders and outbreaks of violence, notably in Alexandria. It was a veritable social upheaval, such as was not to be seen again until the religious dissensions and wars in sixteenth- and seventeenth-centuries Western Europe. No government worthy of its name could look upon this situation with equanimity, especially as this contingency coincided with the collapse of the empire in the West, where after Valentinian's murder there was chaos. To this must be added the external threats on the frontiers of the empire in the East. The government was bound to take measures to eradicate the causes of this ruinous internal disruption, so that peace should be restored, the very peace which the religious and dogmatic quarrels had so gravely and alarmingly destroyed.

In order to pacify the warring factions in the empire and to bring about accord and harmony, the imperial government resorted to – how could it do otherwise? – the one means at its disposal: that of the law. « Sacred » matters – the *sacra* – were at stake and the *sacerdotes* themselves were fighting each other which was a situation which no government could tolerate. And the instrument lay at hand, the public law which focused precisely on these two objects. Hence the emperor, Zeno, issued an edict – composed by the patriarch of Constantinople, Acacius – which was intended to be a compromise solution of the factious issues. The Henotikon (482) [34] was to restore the internal peace by a formula which was assumed would be acceptable to all parties. In the present context there is no need to go into the complicated details of this imperial law which has rightly been called a « kaiserliches Glaubensedikt ».[35]

However well intentioned it was and however much it revealed the emperor's concern for the *res Romana*, the Henotikon while achieving an immediate result in the East, had apparently unforeseen far-reaching and fundamental effects in the West: it

---

[34] Ed. by E. SCHWARTZ, *Codex Vaticanus gr. 1431: eine antikaldonische Sammlung aus der Zeit Zenos*, Abhandlungen der Bayerischen Akademie der Wissenschaften », 32, fasc. 6, 1927, pp. 52-54; Latin text pp. 54-56, also in Liberatus, *Breviarium* c. 17 (ed. *Acta* cit., above n. 16) II.5, p. 127 line 18 to p. 129 line 2.

[35] E. CASPAR, *op. cit.* (above n. 11) II.35.

was challenged by the papacy in Rome, and challenged it was on the basis of the very principles which the imperial government had hitherto carefully preserved and observed. There was no doubt that the Henotikon was an imperial law that laid down the faith and dealt with dogma and doctrine, in a word decided a purely theological conflict. It dealt a blow to the basic issues which Chalcedon was supposed to have settled. The finely balanced decision of the Council was rudely upset by the Isaurian warrior. It was for the first time that an emperor issued an edict of faith. He had thereby crossed the frontier that lay between the *Externa* and the *Interna* which so far no emperor had disregarded.[36] It was a serious measure which was dictated by circumstances and the general imperial duty to act in the interests of the internal peace.

By the eighties, however, the papacy had at its disposal a formidable arsenal of ammunition with which it could, as it did, accept the challenge and deal with it. Firstly, by then the papal tenet of primacy had been worked out fully and been given its final shape by Leo the Great, according to which the monocratic principle was applicable within the Christian *corpus* which on the papacy's reasonings included the Eastern half as well: the pope as successor of St. Peter was to be the *princeps* who possessed the *principatus* over the whole ecclesiological unit, the Church understood as the *congregatio fidelium*. The Leonine primatial thesis stood the test of time.[37] Its constituent elements were the Bible, juristically interpreted, and the monarchic concept of rulership. In all relevant respects papal primacy was the exact counterpart of the imperial monarchy, a feature which explains the numerous borrowings and loans and accomodations made by the Roman Church. Secondly, by the eighties the papacy was entirely under the control of (the later pope) Gelasius, one of the ablest and most astute jurists who occupied the papal-petrine office. He realized fully the significance of the transgression by Zeno who by his enactment and without any consultation of qualified

---

[36] With the exception of the usurper Basiliscus who issued on his own authority a decree against Chalcedon which he withdrew shortly afterwards. The texts are ed. by Schwartz, *op. cit.* (above n. 34) pp. 49-51; the revocation *ibid.* p. 52. The interlude lasted only a few months: Zeno drove him out of Constantinople.

[37] For an analysis cf. W. ULLMANN, *The Church and the Law in the earlier Middle Ages*, in *Collected Studies* I, London 1975, Ch. 4.

ecclesiastics set aside the carefully preserved line of demarcation between the *Externa* and the *Interna*.

The papacy under Felix III replied by denying the validity of the Henotikon and itself challenged the patriarch of Constantinople as well as the emperor by excluding the former and his followers from the Christian community.[38] It was an unprecedented step – the Acacian Schism was the first serious rift between the *senior Roma* and the *iunior Roma*, between Old Rome and New Rome, epitomizing Western and Eastern Christendom and its leadership. This rift became permanent in the separation of the East from the West. Precisely because of the developed papal primatial position, the complexion of the body of Christians had assumed sharp juristic contours. The allegory of *caput* and *membra* – inherent in the organological or corporational thesis –[39] contributed greatly to the juristic conception. All fitted perfectly into the framework of Roman law as well as into that of the Bible, particularly the Pauline letters. By issuing the Henotikon the imperial government laid itself wide open to an effective protestation on the part of the papacy which on its part denied the imperial legitimation to issue a law of the kind of the Henotikon by plainly declaring that the emperor had arrogated to himself an *alienum ius*.[40] And to make himself absolutely clear, Felix-Gelasius asserted that « non legibus publicis » but by the pontiffs and bishops was the Christian community to be ordered and dogmas fixed.[41] For in this community « imperatores christiani subdere debent executiones suas ecclesiasticis praesulibus, non praeferre ».[42] Thereby the papacy claimed for its own part the very leadership of the ecclesiological body which Zeno had assumed in his Henotikon.

---

[38] The judgment edited by E. SCHWARTZ, *Publizistische Sammlungen zum acacianischen Schisma*, « Abhandlungen der Bayerischen Akademie der Wissenschaften », N.F. 16, 1934, pp. 6 f., 76.

[39] For this see now T. STRUVE, *Die Entwicklung der organologischen Staatsauffassung im Mittelalter*, Stuttgart 1978, p. 36 ff.

[40] This passage is in SCHWARTZ, *ed. cit.* (above n. 38) p. 35 lines 34-38: '... non sibi vindicet (scil. imperator) *alienum ius et ministerium* quod alteri deputatum est, ne contra eum tendat abrupte, a quo omnia constituta sunt ... '.

[41] *Ibid.*, p. 36 lines 1-3: ' Non *legibus publicis*, non a potestatibus saeculi, sed a pontificibus et sacerdotibus omnipotens Deus ... voluit ordinari et discuti receipique de errore remeantes '.

[42] *Ibid.*, p. 36 lines 3-4.

What was the juristic significance of this papal offensive? It signified a view fundamentally different from that of the imperial government concerning the character of society over which government was to be exercised, and the law to be administered. It is essential to bear in mind here that since *Cunctos populos* one and the same entity could be looked at from two entirely different angles. It could be seen as merely the empire which happened to be Christian. It could also be seen with equal justification as an ecclesiological unit which happened to be the (Roman) empire. It stands to reason that the kind of public law to be applied differed markedly according to whether it was to be applied to an entity which was primarily an empire or an entity that was primarily an ecclesiological unit. For the core of the empire was its historic continuity and around this core the Christian religion had found a secure place of prominence that was nevertheless subsidiary to the empire ideology. In thought as well as in time the historical element had priority in the empire. It was by imperial legislation that Christianity had been, so to speak, grafted upon the (historically grown) empire and this became the latter's most important attribute and adjunct. On the other hand, the core of the ecclesiological unit was, for the papacy, the Christian religion and its corporate manifestation. What was here decisive was not historicity, but religion, and (as the medieval development in the West was to show plainly) history became an attribute and adjunct of religion. In a word, what was of primary concern in the East, was of secondary concern in the West, and vice-versa.

Differently expressed, the empire was nothing but an historic, earthbound unit. Corporate Christendom was an emanation of divinity within which the papacy claimed to have the headship and the function of a *gubernator*. What the papal challenge fixed upon was not so much the abstractions of « empire » or « church », but – and in this lies an advance of hitherto hardly appreciated dimensions in juristic respects – upon the kind of society itself and the bonds which held it together. Law – so the argument of the papacy can be summarized – did not concern itself with abstract entities, but with living and real societies, and it was above all the character of society which determined the kind of law to be applied. It will readily be seen that the papacy in the eighties and nineties of the fifth century drew the last ounce out of *Cunctos populos* issued exactly a hundred years earlier.

The society upon which the papacy rivetted attention was Christian and hence its essential fabric and texture were of a kind that was basically different from a merely historic entity, such as the Roman empire was. Consequently, law must be – according to papal argumentation – related to society: at all times law was a relative idea, depending upon the substance of society and its underlying cosmology. It was this argument that was crucial in the present context. The *ius publicum* of ancient provenance was, according to papal reasoning, inapplicable to serve as an instrument of government within an ecclesiological unit, as the papacy viewed contemporary Christendom. The papacy denied the applicability of this most hallowed basic law which at first sight seemed well-nigh impregnable and exactly tailored to the needs of the imperial government. For, and this is a consideration which should long ago have merited attention, the *sacra* and the *sacerdotes* in the definition of Ulpian's were assuredly not identical with their contemporary fifth-century namesakes. There was a deep chasm: linguistic identity does not also imply identity in meaning. Hence, quite apart from the emperor's crossing the frontier and betaking himself into the realm of the *Interna*, quite apart from his intervening in one of the most sensitive dogmatic areas, the *ius publicum* as hitherto understood and interpreted was inapplicable as a vehicle through which the emperor could govern. The Ulpianic notion of the *ius publicum* had not changed, but the meaning of two of its three constituent parts had. It was indeed an *alienum ius* for the imperial government and therefore quite illegitimate in the hands of the emperor. Law to be a valid regulatory factor had to be in conformity with the society to which it was to apply, not in conformity with history. Indeed, by acting as he did, Zeno (and following him the Emperor Anastasius) had ceased to be a *custos fidei*, and had become an opponent of the true faith as fixed by Chalcedon. On these grounds too the papacy held that the emperor had forfeited the right to issue any law relating to faith or dogma.

The papal remonstration culminated in the thesis of the intimate connection between government, law and society. It was in response to the challenge of the East that the papacy came to propound this triad which reflected the corporate or organological theory – as much Roman as it was Pauline – in practical juristic terms. In this triad all three elements were closely interrelated. On the other hand, the imperial government adhered, for perfectly valid historical and constitutional reasons, to the view that the entity under its control was the Roman empire, the cementing bond of which was the *Romanitas* of a more or less indistinct kind. Paradoxically, the imperial government in the fifth century remained apparently unaware of the deep implications which *Cunctos populos* had for the very character of the empire itself. Before 380 there was a more or less effective *Romanitas* which brought about some cohesion of the empire, but afterwards it had to share the role of a cohesive force with *Christianitas* so that the combination of mutually exclusive forces could hardly yield promising or fruitful results. From the strictly constitutional standpoint the imperial stance was justifiable – it was a stance that was to be kept for exactly a millenium. Similarly, the stance of the papacy was justifiable, as it fixed its attention upon the internal living fabric of the ecclesiological unit which (for the papacy) was one indivisible whole: the wholeness standpoint with its teleological and functionalist sequels makes the papal theme understandable.[43]

What needs emphasis is that it was an imperial law which initiated the process of integration and coalescence of *Römerreich* and *Christenreich*, and it was another imperial law exactly hundred years later which tore asunder this union – in each instance it was the *ius publicum* that was the operational instrument of government which played a most decisive role. It can be asserted with confidence that the concept of the *ius publicum* in its Ulpianic form, though not in its original meaning was to become as significant in the West as it was in the East. The concept was transmitted to the Western world in its unadulterated shape through Isidore of Seville[44] and was eventually incorporated in Gratian's Decretum.[45] This development only goes to show the historic significance of public law and its relativity: it is substan-

[43] For these matters see W. ULLMANN, *Jurisprudence in the Middle Ages*, in *Collected Studies*, IV, London 1980, Ch. 3, p. 49 ff.

[44] *Etymologiae*, ed. W. M. Lindsay, Oxford 1911, V. 8. The Lemma runs: 'Quid sit ius publicum' whereupon follows Ulpian's definition.

[45] GRATIAN, *Decretum*, Dist. 11, c. 1.

tially related to the character of society and its underlying ideological premisses. The historic separation of the East from the West – as paramount today as it was 1500 years ago – bears witness to the momentous role played by public law. The Acacian Schism was certainly not the cause of this global estrangement but merely occasioned it. The Schism brought to the fore two mutually exclusive views of society. Au fond the Acacian Schism was a purely legal issue within the realms of the *ius publicum* which by virtue of the different conceptions of society was given a correspondingly different meaning in the East and in the West.[46]

---

[46] By way of postscript attention may be drawn in this context to a later use of the Roman public law. The commonly adopted theocratic standpoint in the European Middle Ages made it extremely difficult for the king to defend his position against the papal attacks, since he had virtually nothing with which he could, within the ecclesiological framework, effectively answer the arguments of his opponents. The recourse to the ancient Roman *ius publicum* in its pristine shape began in the early twelfth century. The scientific study of Roman law opened up wide vistas in precisely this respect (cf. W. Ullmann, *Medieval Foundations of Renaissance Humanism*, cit. chapters 1-2). The coinage of the adage *Rex in regno suo est imperator* by no lesser man than Azo in the late twelfth century (for this see *Jurisprudence*, cited above n. 43, Ch. 7) and its adoption in virtually all kingdoms is highly significant. For thereby the kings claimed to have the same power as the late Roman emperor had which had particular relevance to the *sacerdotes*. This marked the initial stages of the process of secularization (cf. *Medieval Foundations*, p. 30 ff.). In this way the autonomy of the king could be fully and effectively maintained – the old proprietary church system had proved itself far too vulnerable as a defence against papal attacks, so that the sluices were opened up for the *Rezeption des römischen Rechts*. Seen from this perspective there can be little doubt that the much discussed *Rezeption* was a logical offshoot of this development. It is high time that its problems were seen against a wider background which takes into account the antecedent evolution in political humanism. See now W. Ullmann, *Radici del Rinascimento*, Roma-Bari 1980, pp. 43 ff., 73 ff. (Traduzione italiana del *Medieval Foundations*).

II

KÖNIGS– UND PAPSTHERRSCHAFT IM SPIEGEL DER BISTUMSBESETZUNGEN

Skizze einer Rechtsideologie

Die vielschichtigen Forschungen des hochverdienten und international anerkannten Jubilars, dessen unverbrüchliche Freundschaft für mich ein unschätzbares Gut bedeutet, ermutigen mich, ihm in äußerst gedrängter, weil räumlich beschränkter, bloß skizzenhafter und deshalb notwendigerweise vereinfachender Form einige Anregungen zur rechtshistorischen Forschung anzubieten.

I.

Noch zu allen Zeiten war es ein Kennzeichen monarchischer Herrschaft, daß sie sich auf alle die Gemeinschaft berührenden lebenswichtigen Interessen erstreckte. Welcher Art diese Interessen waren (und sind), hing (und hängt) von der Substanz, dem Wesen, der Gemeinschaft ab, von den die Gemeinschaft tragenden und explicite oder implicite erklärten Axiomen, Maximen und Voraussetzungen. Eine Zusammenfassung dieser lebenswichtigen Interessen hat der spätrömische Jurist Ulpian gegeben. Danach erstreckte sich das öffentliche Recht auf die Sakralangelegenheiten, deren Verwalter (die *sacerdotes*) und den öffentlichen Dienst *(magistratus)*. In ihrer präzisen Fassung besitzt diese Begriffsbestimmung des öffentlichen Rechts wohl Gültigkeit und Anwendbarkeit in der Spätantike, der mittelalterlichen und auch z.T. der modernen Lebensordnung. Anläßlich des von Kaiser Konstantin d.Gr. einberufenen ersten allgemeinen Konzils zu Nicäa behauptete er von sich selbst, daß er der „Aufseher" oder oberste Sachwalter für die äußeren Angelegenheiten der Kirche sei, während die Bischöfe die obersten Sachwalter der inneren Angelegenheiten der Kirche seien, also jener, die den Glauben, die Lehre, das Dogma berührten. Mit dieser konstantinischen Scheidung in die *Externa* und *Interna* trat nicht nur eine neue Begriffsbestimmung auf den Plan, sondern auch eine für die monarchische Herrschaftsform sehr bedeutsame Anwendung des öffentlichen Rechts. Für das Recht als solches hat stets der äußere Rahmen der Lebensordnung als Bezugsobjekt gegolten. Mit dieser inneren Seite des Christentums, worauf die konstantinische Scheidung gemünzt war, hatte die monarchische Herrschaft nichts zu tun. Die Funktion des Herrschers in einem christlichen Gemeinwesen war vornehmlich die *defensio ecclesiae,* womit sich zwingend enge Beziehungen zu den kirchlichen Organen ergaben. Diese Überlegung macht verständlich die herrscherliche Sorge um die Bischöfe als die öffentlichen Sachwalter des christlichen Glaubens, eine Sorge, die sich nicht selten in Aufsichtsmaßnahmen und Eingriffen der herrscherlichen Macht äußerte, vor allem bei der Besetzung der wichtigeren Stühle. Damit erklärt sich auch die

Maßnahme Justinians in seiner Novelle VI, worin er seine besondere Sorgfalt und Fürsorglichkeit für die höhere Geistlichkeit kundtat. Eine kurze Überlegung macht klar, daß das Interesse des Reiches diese herrschaftliche Schutz- und Sorgepflicht gebot und daß diese auch zum Teil aus dem öffentlichen Recht floß, wodurch sich die herrscherlichen Machtbefugnisse erheblich erweiterten[1)].

Es ist von Bedeutung, daß sich eine ganz ähnliche Stellung der mittelalterlichen Herrscher gegenüber den Bischöfen erkennen läßt, obwohl man jedenfalls im früheren Mittelalter kaum von einer Beeinflussung römischrechtlicher Grundsätze sprechen kann. Auch hier konzentrierte sich die herrscherliche Sorgepflicht für die Bischöfe vornehmlich in ihrer Funktion als Organe, denen die Wahrung und Verbreitung des Glaubens oblag. Die Schutzpflicht war in der deutschrechtlichen Munt enthalten, womit sich die römische *Manus*[2)] unschwer verband, so daß der Herrscher als *Tutor regni* erstand und seine Schutzherrschaft sich in der *Tuitio* oder der *Tutela* äußerte. Sachlich wurde die nicänische Verfassungsnorm niemals in Frage gestellt, doch blieb deren tatsächliche Beobachtung im Laufe der Zeit weit zurück. Was man allenthalben beobachtet, war nämlich das Recht des Herrschers, die Wahl zu bestätigen, was sich aus der Schutz- und Sorgepflicht wohl erklären läßt, die im Rahmen des öffentlichen Rechts ihre Manifestation erhielt[3)]. Aus dem Genehmigungsrecht des Herrschers konnte sich leicht ein Ernennungsrecht entwickeln, obwohl, wie betont, die nicänische Satzung stets in Kraft blieb. Maßgeblich war das Wort des Herrschers, wie sich aus dem Capitulare Pippins (i. J. 744) ergibt[4)]. Auf den Sprachgebrauch wird sogleich zurückzukommen sein. Das lebhafte Interesse der Herrscher an den Bischofsbesetzungen hielt Schritt mit der öffentlichen Bedeutung der Bischöfe, die sich stetig steigerte und die noch erhöht wurde durch die mannigfachen Privilegien, Immunitäten und die damit verbundenen Rechte der Bischöfe. Um die Wende des 8. zum 9. Jahrhundert waren die Bischöfe fest in den öffentlichen Rahmen eingespannt. Nach bestätigter Wahl oder Ernennung des Bischofs verfügte der Herrscher die Konsekration[5)].

---

1) Diese Entwicklung begann bald nach dem Erlaß des kaiserlichen Edikts von 380: Cod. Theod. XVI,2,21; Cod. Just. I,1,1. Deshalb beriefen die spätrömischen Kaiser die großen Kirchenversammlungen ein (Nicäa, Konstantinopel, Ephesus und Chalcedon), wozu sie auch von den Päpsten gebeten wurden; vgl. etwa Leo d.Gr. in: W. ULLMANN, Gelasius I.: Das Papsttum an der Wende der Spätantike zum Mittelalter, Stuttgart 1981, S. 79 f. Zum Hintergrund vgl. noch DENS., unten, A. 18.

2) L. WENGER, Hausgewalt und Staatsgewalt im römischen Altertum, in: Misc. Francesco Ehrle (= Studi e Testi Bd. 38), S. 1–38, hier 24.

3) Vgl. etwa im westgotischen Reich das 12. Konzil von Toledo anno 681, c.5, mit der königlichen Erklärung (P.L. Bd. 84, Sp. 475 und 482 f.). Desgleichen das 13. Konzil anno 683, ebda. Sp. 502–506.

4) „Idcirco constituimus per consilio . . . et ordinavimus per civitates legitimos episcopos; idcirco constituemus super eos archiepiscopus Abel et Ardobertum, ut ad ipsos vel iudicia eorum de omne necessitate ecclesiastica recurrant . . . “ (MG Capit. I, 12, c.3, S. 29, erlassen am 2. März 744). Die Schreibweise folgt dem Original. Daß trotz einer Wahl durch Klerus und Volk der Herrscher konstitutiv auftrat, ergibt sich aus dem Bericht der Ann. Regni Francorum, ad a. 823: Lothar I. setzte seinen Bruder Drogo zum Bischof von Metz ein, wobei der Sprachgebrauch sehr aufschlußreich ist: „Drogonem fratrem eius . . . Mettensi ecclesiae clero eiusdem urbis consentiente atque eligente rectorem constituit, eumque ad pontificatus gradum censuit promoveri“ (MG SSRRGG 1950, S. 161).

5) Diese Maßnahme ist schon in den Marculf-Formeln zu finden: 1,5 sowie 1,6 und 1,7.

Mit dieser Stellung des Bischofs steht völlig in Einklang die eindringliche Forderung der Pariser Synode aus dem Jahre 829, daß der Herrscher nur „taugliche und tüchtige Männer" bestimmen sollte[6]. Die im 9. Jahrhundert abgehaltenen Konzilien spiegelten die Rechtslage wider. Rechtserheblich war die Entscheidung des Königs. Sollten sich die Briefe Leos IV. und Stephans V. als echt erweisen[7], legten sie ebenfalls rechtserheblichen Wert der herrscherlichen Entscheidung bei, worin man eine *prisca consuetudo* erblickte[8]. Bedeutungsmäßig und wesentlich für das Verständnis des Sprachgebrauchs ist die von Hugo von Flavigny überlieferte Äußerung Adrians II.[9], daß die französischen Bischöfe nur jene konsekrieren sollten, die der Kaiser dazu bestimmt hatte[10]. Es fällt auf, daß man bei Pseudo-Isidor keinerlei Widerspruch gegen die allseits anerkannte rechtserhebliche Entschließung des Herrschers bei Bistumsbesetzungen findet. Es war auch in dieser Zeitspanne, daß sich die Erteilung des Wahlrechts durch den Herrscher an bestimmte Körperschaften, wie Klöster, Kapitel, Gemeinschaften usw., zu entwickeln begann[11], um dann im 10. und 11. Jahrhundert einen Hauptbestandteil der Diplomata zu bilden. Sie sind ein treffliches Spiegelbild der tatsächlichen und rechtlichen Lage. Sie wird bestätigt von Johannes X., dessen Wortlaut sich mit dem üblich gewordenen vollends deckt. Er rügt den Kölner Erzbischof, weil er sich über die alte Gewohnheit hinweggesetzt hatte, dergemäß niemand anderer als der König „episcopatum conferre debeat"[12]. In ganz ähnlichem Sinne äußerte sich derselbe Papst gegenüber Karl d. Einfältigen[13]. In gleichen Wendungen ließen sich die Chronisten vernehmen[14]. Ein Blick auf das zeitgenössische angelsächsische Reich genügt, um zu zeigen, daß dort der Sprachgebrauch und dessen Sinngehalt vollends mit

---

6) MG Concilia 2,2, c.22 f., S. 627.

7) JL 2613 und 3446. Da die Stellen aus der Coll. Brit. stammen, ist Vorsicht geboten; siehe die bei Gelasius (wie A. 1), S. 218, A. 3 zit. Literatur. Die Nichterwähnung der beiden Stücke bei R. Schieffer, Die Entstehung des päpstlichen Investiturverbots für den deutschen König (MG Schriften 28), Stuttgart 1981, erklärt sich wahrscheinlich aus seinen Zweifeln an der Echtheit dieser Schreiben.

8) Siehe auch Gratian, Dist. 63, c.16 (Leo IV.) und c.18 (Stephan V.).

9) JL 2922. Hugo von Flavigny, Chronicon, MG SS Bd. 8 (1848), S. 354, Z. 23–25.

10) Die Stelle lautet: „Defuncto autem beato Nicholao cum imperante Ludovico [II.] successisset Adrianus, et litteras misisset Galliarum episcopis, ut non alios ordinarent episcopos, nisi quibus praefatus imperator episcopatum concederet". Vgl. noch JL 2923.

11) Vgl. P. Hinschius, Das Kirchenrecht der Katholiken und Protestanten in Deutschland, 2, Berlin 1878, S. 521, A. 11.

12) JL 3564, anno 921: „... cum prisca consuetudo vigeat, qualiter nullus alicui clerico episcopatum conferre debeat ..."; R. Schieffer (wie A. 7), S. 25 f. bemängelt die „schmale Überlieferung".

13) JL 3565: „... prisca consuetudo et regni nobilitas censuit, ut *nullus* episcopum ordinare debuisset *absque regis iussione*".

14) Vgl. etwa Rodulfus, Gesta abbatum Trudonensium (999–1107), MG SS 10, S. 254, Z. 19–22: „Adhuc enim imperator hoc in toto regno suo *iure antiquo* possidebat, *ut* absque dono eius *nullus* in eo *constitueretur episcopus*". Dazu Schieffer (wie A. 7), S. 23 A.O. Vgl. noch Thietmar, Chronicon, hrsg. v. R. Holtzmann, MG SSRRGG, Berlin ²1955, Buch 1, Kap. 26, S. 33, Z. 36 u. S. 35, Z. 1 ff.: „Arnulfus ... omnes episcopatus in hiis partibus constitutos sua distribuere manu singularem habuit potestatem"; ferner ebda. 5, 44, S. 270, Z. 31 f. Zahlreiche weitere Beispiele bei Hinschius (wie A. 11), 2, S. 530, A. 9 und A. Hauck, Kirchengeschichte Deutschlands, 3. Tl., 8. unveränderte Aufl., Berlin–Leipzig 1954, S. 53 f.

den angeführten Beispielen übereinstimmte. So legte der König Mitte des 11. Jahrhunderts fest, daß er den Episkopat konzediert hatte [15]. In den angelsächsischen Diplomata kommt klar zum Ausdruck das Mandat des Königs, den von ihm ernannten Bischof zu konsekrieren [16].

Man kann wohl sagen, daß die Besetzung der Bischofsstühle vom 9. bis zum 11. Jahrhundert auf dem Wege der herrscherlichen Ernennung erfolgte [17]. Der Sprachgebrauch war überall fast identisch. Der Herrscher vergibt, bestimmt, weist an, konzediert, ernennt den künftigen Bischof. Daß dieses Verfahren von höchster Stelle gebilligt wurde, muß ebenso gewürdigt werden wie die Abwesenheit eines ernsthaften oder gar nachhaltigen oder nachdrücklichen Widerspruchs [18]. Es soll beachtet werden, daß die Bestellung oder Ernennung des Bischofs keinerlei erst durch die nachfolgende Konsekration erworbenen spezifisch sakramentalen Bischofsrechte und -privilegien berührte, also Eucharistiefeier, Ordinations-, Weiherechte, Absolution, Exkommunikation usw. M.a.W., die herrscherliche Ernennung war eine Maßnahme im Rahmen der äußeren Dinge (der *Externa*) der Kirche, in nichts sich unterscheidend von der Einberufung der Konzilien durch die Herrscher, wie sie seit dem späten 8. Jahrhundert bis ins späte 9. üblich war. Hier wie dort waren die *Externa* der Bezugspunkt der herrscherlichen Maßnahmen. Aus juristischer Sicht verlieh die Ernennung gleichsam ein *ius ad rem* hinsichtlich der Weihe, durch welches der Ernannte dann das *ius in re* der Bischofsgewalt erlangte. Man könnte hier wohl nach dem Muster von Heinrich Mitteis von einem stufenweisen Vorgang sprechen. Mithin handelte es sich um eine Maßnahme, die sich in der Übertragung von Rechten öffentlicher Natur an den (künftigen) Bischof erschöpfte. Sie waren rein jurisdiktioneller Art, die historisch begründet war, denn vermöge ihrer Bildung, Herkunft, Ansehen und Autorität hatten die Bischöfe eine stetig steigende Bedeutung im öffentlichen Leben erlangt und waren unentbehrliche Glieder der öffentlichen Ordnung geworden, die der Herrscher mit entsprechendem rechtlichen Zubehör ausstattete. Durch den Einbau in das Lehenswesen wurde die öffentliche Stellung des Bischofs kräftig gestärkt, weil die Verbindung des Herrschers als Lehensherr und des Bischofs als Lehensmann lebenswichtige Rechte und Verpflichtungen schuf [19].

Beachtung verdient ferner, daß Rechtsverhältnisse zwischen Herrscher und Bischof nicht nur geschichtlicher und ideeller Abkunft, sondern vor allem erdverbunden, und zwar im buchstäblichen Sinne waren. Die dem Bischof übertragenen Rechte waren territorial anwendbar

---

15) Anglo-Saxon Writs, hrsg. v. F.E. HARMER, Manchester 1952, Nr. 50, S. 231: „... ego [Eduardus] notifico uobis, quod ego *concessi* Waltero episcopo istum episcopatum [i.e. Hereford] hic uobiscum et omnia uniuersa illa que ad ipsum cum iusticia pertinent ... " (folgt Pertinenzklausel); ferner Nr. 64, S. 277 für Wells: „Sciatis nos *dedisse* Gisoni presbytero nostro episcopatum ... cum omnibus pertinenciis ... ", ebenso für Winchester, Nr. 109, S. 397.

16) Vgl. etwa Nr. 19, S. 545. Das gleiche gilt für Frankreich; siehe HINSCHIUS (wie A. 11), 2, S. 538–540.

17) Siehe die zahlreichen Belege bei HINSCHIUS, S. 530, A. 9, bis S. 531, A. 4; siehe auch andererseits G. WEISE, Königtum und Bischofswahl im fränkischen und deutschen Reich vor dem Investiturstreit, Berlin 1912, für Bischofswahlen (im Gegensatz zu Ernennungen), S. 59 ff. und S. 111–113.

18) SCHIEFFER (wie A. 7) bemerkt, daß sich die Investitur buchstäblich zwanglos aus der Autorität des Königtums ergab. Zum Hintergrund vgl. noch W. ULLMANN, Medieval Monarchy (Sewanee Medieval Colloquium, Occasional Papers Nr. 1), Sewanee 1982, S. 28 ff.

19) Dazu SCHIEFFER (wie A. 7), S. 15 f.

und verankert und ebenso territorial beschränkt. Sie bezogen sich auf den territorial begrenzten Diözesansprengel. Territorialgewalt deckte sich mit Diözesangewalt. Die schon erwähnten wichtigen obrigkeitlichen Rechte wurden später ergänzt durch das Heeresaufgebot, den Burgbann, alles Verhältnisse, die im Lehenswesen begründet waren. Alle diese Rechte waren samt und sonders ausschließlich jurisdiktioneller Natur. Der Ernannte wurde mit der Wahrnehmung öffentlicher Rechte im Diözesansprengel betraut. Diese obrigkeitlichen Funktionen hatten weder mit einem kirchlichen Ordo zu tun noch mit einer Weihe oder einem geistlichen Stand. Der Bischof war der Mann, der das Vertrauen des Herrschers genoß. Die Betreuung mit diesen Funktionen entstammte der herrscherlichen Schutzpflicht gegenüber dem Königreich, dessen *Tutor* er war und das ihm von Gott anvertraut worden war. Indem der König die Bischöfe beschützte, beschützte er das Königreich selbst. Darin manifestierte sich die *Tuitio* des Herrschers.

Hier ergibt sich eine verblüffende Ähnlichkeit mit der Rechtsstellung des erwählten Papstes, der noch nicht konsekriert (oder ordiniert) worden war, jedenfalls seit 1059. Auch er hatte die vollen Rechte, soweit sie in den Bereich der *Externa* fielen, jedoch keinerlei Befugnisse im internen Bereich[20]. Man kann hier von einer praktischen Verwirklichung der konstantinischen Scheidung in *Externa* und *Interna* sprechen. Nach mittelalterlicher Anschauung gehörte das öffentliche Recht unzweifelhaft in den Rahmen der *Externa.* Daß man mit der Sache, wenn auch nicht notwendigerweise mit der Quelle vertraut war, läßt sich nachweisen. Da ist z.B. Paschasius Radbertus zu nennen[21], aber vor allem das Krönungsgebet, das aus dem 9. Jahrhundert stammte[22] und in fast alle Krönungsordines einging, beginnend mit dem römisch-deutschen Pontificale aus der Mitte des 10. Jahrhunderts und das sich im Pontificale Romanum bis in unsere Tage erhalten hat. „Accipe coronam regni... non ignoras, ita *ut,* sicut *nos in interioribus* pastores rectoresque animarum intelligimur, *tu quoque* in *exterioribus* verus Dei cultor... ecclesiarum Christi defensor . . . semper appareas“[23]. Man kann vielleicht verstehen, warum sich gegen die herrscherlichen Verfügungen im öffentlichrechtlichen Bereich kein Widerspruch geregt hat.

---

20) Einzelheiten bei W. ULLMANN, Romanus pontifex indubitanter efficitur sanctus: DP. 12 in retrospect and prospect, in: The Church and the Law in the earlier Middle Ages, Collected Studies, Bd. 1, London 1975, S. 229 ff., bes. S. 241 ff.; DERS., Zum Papstwahldekret von 1059, in: ZRG 99 (1982), Kan. Abt. 68, S. 32–51.

21) Paschasius RADBERTUS, Epithaphium Arsenii, hrsg. v. E. DÜMMLER, Abhandlungen der Preuss. Akad. d. Wiss., Phil.-Hist. Kl., Berlin 1900, S. 62: „Primo considerari oportet *intus divina,* tum *exterius humana,* quia procus dubio his duobus totius ecclesiae status administratur ordinibus“. Er warnt allerdings vor einer Überspannung (S. 63 f.) der Übertragung öffentlichrechtlicher Dienste an Bischöfe, weil für sie sonst Gefahren bestünden.

22) Siehe C. ERDMANN, Forschungen zur politischen Ideenwelt des Frühmittelalters, Berlin 1951, S. 88, Nr. 3.

23) Le pontifical romano-germanique du dixième siècle, hrsg. v. C. VOGEL und R. ELZE (= Studi e Testi Bd. 226), Città del Vaticano 1963, Nr. LXXII, 22, S. 256; Pontificale Romanum CLEMENTIS VIII ac URBANI VIII . . . BENEDICTO XIV recognitum, ed. Venetiis 1836, S. 146.

Jetzt, wo wir uns den Blick geschärft haben, können wir ermessen, welche Bedeutung der symbolischen Übergabe der obrigkeitlichen Rechte an den ernannten (oder erwählten) Bischof zukommt. Hier verdient vor allem der Stab Beachtung. Es soll besonders unterstrichen werden, daß der Stab keinerlei Berührungspunkte mit den spezifisch bischöflichen Rechten und Würden hatte[24]. Schon längst war der Stab als Zeichen der Gerechtigkeit und Gerichtsbarkeit bekannt, mithin Symbol der Jurisdiktion, weshalb er auch bei der Königskrönung selbst im 9. Jahrhundert ein wichtiges Insigne mit der entsprechenden Doxologie bildete[25]. Auch der Stab ging in das römisch-deutsche Pontificale ein[26]. Die Überreichung des Stabes symbolisierte die Übertragung der in ihrem Ursprung herrscherlichen, d.h. obrigkeitlichen Rechte durch den Herrscher selbst an den (künftigen) Bischof. Bezugspunkt des Stabes waren die Gerechtsame des Bischofs im öffentlichrechtlichen Bereich[27]. Damit erklärt sich auch unschwer, warum nach dem Tode des Bischofs sein Stab an den König zurückgegeben wurde[28]. Es handelte sich hier um einen symbolischen Heimfall dieser öffentlichrechtlichen Befugnisse. Der Bischofsstab andererseits hatte mit dem Königsstab nichts gemein. Jener war das *signum sacri regiminis,* dieser versinnbildlichte die Übertragung obrigkeitlicher Rechte. Die Scheidung in *Externa* und *Interna* steht auch hier klar vor Augen[29]. Daraus ersieht man, daß die zeitliche

---

[24] Man muß sich fragen, welches andere Symbol zur Verfügung gestanden hätte, um den Jurisdiktionsakt unmißverständlich auszudrücken, denn das sonst gebräuchliche richterliche Schwert als Symbol war doch wohl denkbar ungeeignet.

[25] ERDMANN (wie A. 22), S. 88, Nr. 4: „Accipe virgam virtutis ... ". Die Ausdrücke virga, baculus, ferula waren meist sinngemäß gleichbedeutend; dazu vgl. Th. KLAUSER, Der Ursprung der bischöflichen Insignien und Ehrenrechte, Krefeld [2]1953, S. 17, A. 20 ff. Nach dem Konzil von Aachen (anno 816) (MG Concilia 2, 5, S. 412, Z. 17–19) „teneant [scil. episcopi] in manu baculum et virgam, baculum videlicet, quo aliorum virium imbecillitates spiritaliter sustentent, virgam vero, que vitia delinquentium zelo rectitudinis feriant". Dazu bemerkte KLAUSER (A. 21): „Der eine Stab wird demnach doppelt gedeutet, als Stütze und als Rute". Wie sich sogleich zeigen wird, wurden später im römisch-deutschen Pontificale die beiden (baculus und virga) getrennt: Der Baculus als „Stütze" verblieb dem Bischof, während die Virga als „Virga virtutis atque aequitatis" das herrscherliche Insigne wurde.

[26] Pontificale Romanum-Germanicum (wie A. 23), S. 256.

[27] Daß der Stab im 9. Jh. vom Herrscher tatsächlich überreicht wurde, ist einwandfrei nachweisbar; siehe die Vita Rimberti, hrsg. v. G. Waitz, MG SSRRGG, Hannover 1884, c.11, S. 90: „Susceptusque ab eo [scil. Ludwig d.D.] honorifice, cum pontificalis baculi *iuxta morem* commendatione episcopatus est sortitus dominium". Dazu HAUCK (wie A. 14), S. 52, A. 4; SCHIEFFER, S. 12, A. 18. Häufig erwähnt wird auch die ferula, die vom Herrscher überreicht wurde; vgl. etwa Chronicon Breve Bremense, MG SS Bd. 7, S. 391, Z. 9 (Konrad I.): „Sanctus Unni pallium suscepit a papa Ioanne, *ferulam* a Conrado rege". Hier sei auch betont, daß sich der Gebetstext bei der Überreichung des Bischofsstabes von dem des königlichen Stabes sehr unterscheidet: Der Bischofsstab war *sacri regiminis signum;* siehe römisch-deutsches Pontificale (wie A. 23), S. 222, Z. 5 ff., wovon bei der Überreichung des Stabes an den König (siehe ebda., S. 256, Z. 21 ff.) keine Rede ist.

[28] HINSCHIUS (wie A. 11), 2, S. 535; HAUCK (wie A. 14),S. 53 f. Es bleibt zu untersuchen, ob nicht die Rückgabe des Richterstabes nach Beendigung der Amtszeit auf ähnliche Erwägungen zurückgeht; vgl. K. AMIRA, Der Stab in der germanischen Rechtssymbolik, Abhandlungen der Königl. Bayerischen Akad. d. Wiss., Phil.-Hist. Kl. Bd. 25 (1909), S. 102.

[29] Vgl. L. EISENHOFER, Handbuch der Liturgik, Bd. 1, Freiburg 1932, S. 466 f.; DERS.,Grundriß der Liturgik des römischen Ritus. Neu bearb. v. J. LECHNER, Freiburg [5]1950, S. 109. Auch die Herkunft des Bischofsstabes war verschieden von der des Königsstabes. Jener geht wahrscheinlich auf orientalische

Abfolge bei der Besetzung des Bistums die Rechtsstellung des Bischofs ebenso klar widerspiegelt wie die Rückgabe des Stabes. Die hoheitliche öffentlichrechtliche Stellung ging zeitlich seiner bischöflich-sakramentalen Stellung voraus[30]. Bemerkt sei, daß die Königskrönung in der Thronsetzung den feierlichen Abschluß bildete, begleitet von dem höchst eindrucksvollen Gebetstext „Sta et retine", während der rein sakramentalen Bischofskonsekration nichts dergleichen entsprach[31].

Der Zusammenhang erfordert entsprechende Würdigung der Formel, die der Herrscher bei der Übergabe des Stabes gebrauchte — *Accipe ecclesiam.* Diese Formel, an der sich der nachmalige Streit gleichsam entzündete[32], stellt sich bei näherer Analyse als ein einprägsamer Ausdruck dar, der, wie alle Kurzformen, mehrerer und daher auch mißverständlicher Deutungen fähig war. Die Formel bedeutete nicht, daß der König im buchstäblichen Sinne eine Kirche vergab, sondern daß die dem Herrscheramt entstammenden und mit der Bischofskirche verhafteten öffentlichen Rechte nunmehr ihren persönlichen Träger gefunden hatten[33]. Wie kein König „Priester" im ordentlichen Sinn war und daher auch keine Konsekration oder Ordination vornehmen konnte, so konnte er auch keine Kirche als Anstalt vergeben[34]. Der Ausdruck *Accipe ecclesiam* bedeutet nichts anderes als die Übertragung der mit der Bischofskirche verbundenen und auf den Diözesansprengel beschränkten öffentlichen Rechte, die kein Metropolit oder Bischof zu vergeben in der Lage war[35].

Vorbilder zurück und ist klar nachweisbar in den späteren Konzilien von Toledo. Zur Herkunft des Königsstabes siehe K. Amira (wie A. 28), S. 111 ff. Unannehmbar ist die Ansicht, daß der König ein geistliches Amt verliehen hätte; vgl. etwa Hauck (wie A. 14), S. 56, und viele andere. Die Übertragung der hoheitlichen Rechte hätte genau so gut an einen Laienfürsten erfolgen können, und in der Tat war der „Bischof" in diesem Stadium noch kein Bischof und wurde es erst kraft der Konsekration.

30) Das war in der Tat der Schwerpunkt der scharfen Opposition Humberts und Damianis. Siehe Humberts Schrift Adversus Simoniacos, in LdL Bd. 1, S. 205, Z. 7 ff. und für letzteren vor allem P.L. Bd. 133, Sp. 219 ff., der die Doppelstellung ganz besonders wirkungsvoller Kritik unterzog.

31) Zur einfachen *sella episcopalis* im römisch-deutschen Pontificale (wie A. 23) siehe dieses, ed. cit., S. 207, Nr. 9, die die bischöfliche *cathedra* war. Die von Hinschius angeführten Zeugnisse (2, S. 537, A. 1) dürften wohl mit *inthronizare* das Besteigen der *cathedra* meinen. Damit würden in der Tat übereinstimmen Anselm, Collectio canonum, hrsg. v. F. Thaner, Innsbruck 1906—15 (Nachdruck 1965), VI, 44, S. 291 und Deusdedit, Die Kanonessammlung, hrsg. v. V. Wolf v. Glanvell, Paderborn 1905, VI, 113, S. 241. Die genaue Entwicklung der bischöflichen Thronsetzung bedarf noch der Klärung.

32) Vgl. dazu noch Z. N. Brooke, Lay investiture and its relation to the conflict of empire and papacy, in: Proceedings Brit. Academy 1939, S. 219 ff., hier S. 223 f.

33) Das bringt ein angelsächsisches Diplom sehr klar zum Ausdruck, das im Anschluß der Bestellung des Bischofs durch den König hinzufügt: „... et omnia uniuersa illa que ad ipsum [episcopatum] cum iusticia pertinent...", ed. cit. (wie A. 15), Nr. 50, S. 231. Bei Damiani war diese Sinngebung Zielscheibe des Spottes, Sp. 221 A. Für ihn handelte es sich unzweifelhaft um Simonie.

34) Die Figur des *Rex-Sacerdos* wird nur gegen den Hintergrund der Scheidung in *Externa* und *Interna* und des öffentlichen Rechts ulpianischer Prägung verständlich. Zum Hintergrund vgl. Ullmann, Gelasius I. (wie A. 1), S. 84 ff. Sehr zu Recht betonte P. Classen, Das Wormser Konkordat in der deutschen Verfassungsgeschichte, in: Vorträge und Forschungen Bd. 18, Sigmaringen 1973, S. 417, daß kein König je beanspruchte, sakramentale Weihen vorzunehmen.

35) Man kann nicht umhin, Bedenken anzumelden gegen die Ansicht von Hauck (wie A. 14), S. 54 (und auch anderen): „Die Worte Accipe ecclesiam, ..., drückten wirklich das aus, was geschah: er [der König] übergab dem [?] Bischof die Kirche, ...".

Um das Bild abzurunden, bedarf es noch einer Erwähnung des Ringes. Sowohl beim König als auch beim Bischof war der Ring ein *signaculum fidei,* und es scheint, um im Rahmen der Doxologie zu bleiben, die Funktion des Ringes bei beiden ein sichtbares Zeichen des Schutzes gewesen zu sein, den der Bischof seiner *sponsa* angedeihen lassen sollte, während der König die Aufgabe hatte, als *auctor* (d.h. Gewährsmann) *et stabilitor* (d.h. standhafter Verteidiger) *christianitatis et christianae fidei* aufzutreten. Höchst bezeichnend ist allerdings, was immerhin im gegenständlichen Zusammenhang schon längst hätte erkannt werden sollen, daß bei der Königskrönung weder der Stab noch der Ring irgendeine förmliche Weihe empfingen, während bei der Bischofskonsekration für beide Zeichen die entsprechenden Weihegebete vorgesehen waren[36]. Daß diese Unterschiedlichkeit kein Zufall war, ist einleuchtend und bestätigt den Sinngehalt der königlichen Übertragung der Hoheitsrechte an den künftigen Bischof vollends, ganz abgesehen von dem schon erwähnten Unterschied in der Bezeichnung des Bischofsstabes als ein *sacri regiminis signum*[37].

Gerade in diesem Zusammenhang scheint der durchgängige Sprachgebrauch sowohl in den Diplomata als auch in den erzählenden Quellen eine mißverständliche Auslegung bei Späteren veranlaßt zu haben. Da ist zu nennen die sehr häufige Verwendung des *episcopatum dare,* daneben *constituere, concedere, tradere, contradere* usw. Alle diese Ausdrücke sind Kurzformen, die leicht irreführen können[38]. Die Opposition Humberts und Damianis, um nur zwei prominente Reformer zu nennen[39], gegen die zeitgenössische Übung konzentrierte sich nicht nur auf das Wort, ohne dessen sachliche Bedeutung abzuwägen, sondern läßt auch alle Erwähnung der im Krönungszeremoniell aufscheinenden Symbolik vermissen. Diese spricht doch eine deutliche und ganz und gar unmißverständliche Sprache, die von geistlichen Würdenträgern stammte und ins römisch-deutsche Pontificale (wie auch in die ihm folgenden Pontificalien) einging und gleicherweise bei der Bischofskonsekration Anwendung fand. Die Forschung hat m.a.W. von der zeitgenössischen Nichtbeachtung der Krönungsordines und deren historischen Erkenntniswert für die Problematik des großen Kampfes keine Kenntnis genommen. Dieses

---

36) Vgl. die Weihegebete für den Bischofsring und -stab bei der Konsekration des Bischofs im römisch-deutschen Pontificale (wie A. 23), S. 220 f. und das Fehlen der Benediktionen im Krönungsordo, S. 256. Hervorgehoben sei, daß der Ring schon bei den Pharaonen als Zeichen der Königswürde benutzt wurde; siehe Gen. 41, 42, wo der Ring Pharaos an Josef übergeben wurde.

37) Ähnliches galt für den angelsächsischen Ordo der sog. 2. Rezension im 11. Jh.; siehe L. Wickham Legg, English Coronation Records, London 1901, S. 18. Als Investitursymbol scheint der Ring erst viel später aufzutreten, wahrscheinlich nicht vor Heinrich III., wie Schieffer (wie A. 7), S. 11, A. 16,vorsichtig urteilt. Es bleibt noch zu erwägen, ob nicht der Ring mit dem Diözesanterritorium in Verbindung gebracht wurde und die Verklammerung des Bischofs mit der Diözese versinnbildlichte. Denn außerhalb des Diözesansprengels besaß der Bischof keine Rechte. Der Ring kann sehr wohl als Verfestigung des (künftigen) Bischofs gedacht gewesen sein. Zum Ring als liturgischem Symbol siehe Klauser (wie A. 25), A. 30.

38) Man vgl. etwa den Eintrag in den Gesta episcoporum autisiodorensium, MG SS Bd. 13, S. 400, Z. 26 ff.: „... rex ... divina preordinante clementia, consilio ... domno Herifredo cum summa reverentia nominando pastoralem confert baculum atque ad Senonensem urbem dirigit ordinandum" (29. August 887).

39) Vor einer Überschätzung von Humberts Einfluß warnt Schieffer (wie A. 7), S. 41 ff.

Schweigen der Zeitgenossen, allesamt hochbegabte, geistig rege und sprachgewandte Männer, dürfte wohl einfach auf Unkenntnis beruhen. Historisch und bedeutungsmäßig stehen die Pontificalien auf gleicher Stufe mit den Diplomata und dem Statutarrecht. Sie drücken in der Doxologie und im Symbolismus aus, was diese in der Rechtssprache festlegten. Die Integration der Doxologie und des Symbolismus in den Forschungsbereich der Historiker und Rechtshistoriker könnte wohl manches „abgestandene" Problem in neuem Lichte erscheinen lassen. Dieses Postulat einer erweiterten historischen Forschungsgrundlage ist ein dringendes Bedürfnis[40].

Welches Fazit läßt sich aus diesen Überlegungen ziehen? Was auf den ersten Blick beeindruckt, ist, von ganz wenigen Modalitätsschwankungen abgesehen, eine bis in die Spätantike zurückreichende gesamteuropäische Erscheinung, die in dem Bestimmungsrecht des Herrschers gipfelte. Er war es, der Bischofswahlen genehmigte, billigte oder bestätigte oder den künftigen Bischof bestellte und dessen Konsekration anordnete. Es zeigt sich hier eine höchst beachtenswerte Angleichung an die spätantike Verfassungslage, wobei allerdings zu bemerken ist, daß diese Angleichung nicht das Ergebnis rationaler Deduktionen oder Nachahmung war, sondern sich auf unreflektierte und durch die Faktizität bedingte Übung stützte. Das herausragende Kennzeichen war die Ausübung monarchischer Herrschaft, die das Verfügungsrecht über das öffentliche Recht begrifflich enthielt und sich spezifisch in dem endgültigen Bestimmungsrecht des Herrschers hinsichtlich der höheren Geistlichkeit äußerte. Gerade weil die Bischöfe (und Äbte) zu den wichtigsten Tragpfeilern der Gesellschaft gehörten, mußte der Herrscher ihnen seine besondere Aufmerksamkeit zuwenden, wenn er seine Pflicht als *Tutor regni* erfüllen wollte. Die Auswahl der Bischöfe folgte Grundsätzen und Motiven, die im Wesen des Königtums als einer gewordenen, historisch sich entwickelten und natürlich gewachsenen Gemeinschaft lagen. Diesem Wesen entspricht, daß der Bischof zuerst Fürst war, und in zweiter Linie Bischof. M.a.W., die Auswahl läßt sich aus dem Wesen, der inneren Substanz der Gemeinschaft und ihrer Art erklären, d.h. aus dem Interesse des Königreichs, innerhalb dessen der Erwählte oder Ernannte seine Funktionen ausüben sollte. Die öffentlichrechtlichen Funktionen orientierten sich an dem Charakter der gewordenen Gemeinschaft, womit die für alle öffentliche Ordnung gültige Triade von Gemeinschaft, Herrschaft und Recht und die notwendige Harmonie der drei sie konstituierenden Elemente ihre praktische Anwendung gefunden zu haben schienen. Die Bestätigung lieferten der Symbolismus und die Doxologie anläßlich der Königskrönung.

II.

Heinrich IV. hatte offenbar wenig Verständnis für die den Kampf auslösenden und bestimmenden Kräfte und Ideen. Mit seiner Berufung auf Gewohnheit, Übung, Herkommen, die für

---

[40] Man begegnet heutzutage manchmal einer Abneigung gegen geschichtlich unanfechtbare Themen und religiös bedingte Leitbilder. In einer solchen Abkehr will man fortschrittliche Geistesgesinnung kundtun. In Wahrheit ist sie kein Fortschritt, sondern ein Rückfall in längst überwundene, weil geisttötende Geschichtsschreibung, die alles Verständnis für geschichtlich belangvolle Zusammenhänge vermissen läßt und in Kleinkrämerei ausmündet.

ihn unantastbare Richtlinien waren, glaubte er die Angriffe Gregors VII. parieren zu können. Die Entgegnung Gregors war knapp und schneidend: „Dominus non dixit, Ego sum consuetudo, sed dixit Ego sum veritas“[41]. Dieser Satz drückte einzigartig klar aus, was man wohl als Weltanschauung im buchstäblichen Sinne bezeichnen darf. Er enthielt ein Programm, das eine Gesellschafts-, Herrschafts- und Rechtslehre umfaßte. Im Grund war die Weltanschauung das Ergebnis der Besinnung — vielleicht der Wiederbesinnung — auf das Wesen der ekklesiologischen Gemeinschaft wie sie das 5. Jahrhundert geprägt hatte und auf die sich die gelehrten, weitblickenden und scharfdenkenden Persönlichkeiten der Reformer beriefen. Der Rückgriff zeigte mit erschreckender gedanklicher Deutlichkeit die Kluft, die sich auftat zwischen einer Gemeinschaft, die sich auf natürlichem Boden entwickelte, den Gesetzen des natürlichen Wachstums folgte und in welcher natürliche, unreflektierte Einsicht, natürliches Verständnis und natürlich-menschliche Beurteilungskriterien maßgeblich waren, und auf der anderen Seite einer Gemeinschaft, die nichts mit Natur zu tun hatte, sondern nachweisbar auf die Bibel und daher leicht verifizierbar auf eine göttliche Stiftung zurückging, ihren Wesensinhalt der göttlichen Stiftung entnahm und den göttlichen (nicht menschlich gesetzten) Normen unterstand. Hier galt nicht natürlich-menschliche Erkenntnis oder Einsicht, sondern das Wissen und die Befähigung, die göttlichen Normen authentisch zu erklären, denn die christliche Religion war noch niemals eine intuitive oder natürliche Religion gewesen[42].

Berücksichtigt man diesen Ausgangspunkt der gregorianischen Partei, dann fällt es nicht schwer, einen eklatanten Widerspruch zwischen der königlicherseits verfolgten Gesellschafts-, Herrschafts- und Rechtslehre und der päpstlich postulierten zu erkennen. Die Bischöfe waren als Nachfolger der Apostel die Verkünder und Wahrer der christlichen Normen und Lebensordnung. Andererseits lag in der hergebrachten Ordnung der monarchische Grundsatz, der sich auf bloßes Herkommen und die Gewohnheit stützte, offen zutage — es war der König, der die Auswahl der Bischöfe genehmigte oder sie einfach bestellte. Der Widerspruch zwischen den beiden Gesellschaftsauffassungen wird völlig klar, wenn man bedenkt, daß der König es war, der die Tauglichkeit des Bischofs prüfte und sich daher dabei von Grundsätzen und Beweggründen leiten ließ, die schon gar nichts mit dem bischöflichen Amt als solchem gemein hatten.

Die gregorianische Kampfansage machte unzweideutig die Disharmonie klar. Darin liegt der tiefe Sinn der immer wiederkehrenden Aussage Gregors von der Notwendigkeit der *concordia* und der Verurteilung der *discordia,* die das überkommene Herrschaftssystem kennzeichnete, weil es dem Wesen der Gesellschaft durchaus nicht entsprach. Eine ekklesiologische Gemeinschaft — die Kirche als die *congregatio fidelium* — konnte nur von ekklesiologisch ausgewiesenen Sachwaltern als Funktionsträger geleitet werden, aber hatte der König als Laie die Eignung, über deren Tauglichkeit zu befinden? Klaffte hier nicht ein unüberbrückbarer Wider-

---

41) JL 5277. Zum Hintergrund vgl. Joh. 14,6; G.B. LADNER, Two Gregorian letters, Studi Gregoriani 5 (1956), S. 225 ff., wo die Wurzeln aufgezeigt werden. Dazu noch SCHIEFFER (wie A. 7), S. 161, A. 250.

42) Grundlegend war die ambrosianische Thematik; dazu Gelasius I. (wie A. 1), S. 10 ff., insbes. die Diastase von *discere* und *docere.*

spruch? In der Rückschau erkannte man die Dissonanz zwischen königlicher und päpstlicher Gesellschafts-, Herrschafts- und Rechtslehre. Denn der Zweck aller Herrschaft ist die Verwirklichung der Axiome, Grundsätze und Voraussetzungen, auf denen die Gemeinschaft ruht, und zwar mit Hilfe des erzwingbaren Rechts. Deshalb müssen die drei die Triade konstituierenden Teile miteinander harmonisieren. Aber es war gerade der Mißklang, der in so schriller Weise in Erscheinung trat und auf den die Reformer mit allem Nachdruck hinwiesen.

Das Zünglein an der Waage war der Episkopat. Sowohl Papst als auch König mußten der Bischöfe sicher sein, um ihre Herrschaft ausüben zu können. Ohne Kontrolle des Episkopats war es unmöglich, die herrscherliche Stellung wirksam zur Geltung zu bringen, und das galt für den Papst wie für den König. Daraus erklärt sich die Betonung der Legitimation, die beim Papst keinerlei Schwierigkeit bereitete — es war die Primatialgewalt. Der Primatialgedanke stand nunmehr an vorderster Stelle, weil er sich aus der Schrift ableitete, in der die Stiftung der neuen Gesellschaft *uno ictu* mit der Herrschaftsform niedergelegt worden war. Andererseits besaß der König niemals eine so leicht beweisbare Legitimation, vermochte er doch bloß auf das Herkommen und die Übung zu pochen. Die Abfolge der Bistumsbesetzungen zeigte klar die entsprechenden Grundsätze. Für den König war der Bischof zuerst Reichsfürst, weshalb die Konsekration nachfolgte. Für den Papst war der Bischof Kirchenfürst, weshalb die Konsekration den Vorrang hatte vor der Übertragung der Regalien[43] des öffentlichen Rechts. Nach päpstlicher Ansicht sollten die Regalien zu einem Attribut der Bischofsgewalt werden[44]. Mit der ihm eigenen Sicherheit des Ausdrucks machte Gregor VII. die Stellung des Herrschers in einem ekklesiologischen Rahmen sehr klar, indem er behauptete: „Non ultra putet [scil. Henricus] sanctam ecclesiam sibi subiectam ut *ancillam,* sed prelatam et *dominam*"[45]. Um diese Kontrolle über die Bischöfe zu sichern, verpflichtete er die Bischöfe zum Bischofseid und zur sog. *Visitatio liminum apostolorum.*

Aus juristisch-historischer Sicht ersieht man in dem bitter durchgefochtenen Investiturstreit nicht nur einen Kampf um das richtige Recht[46], sondern um das Ringen von zwei buchstäblich grundverschiedenen Weltanschauungen. Kein Wunder, daß ein Zeitgenosse sich verlauten ließ: „... universus noster Romanus orbis contremuit"[47]. Keinem zeitgenössischen König — noch auch seinen Vorgängern — wäre es je in den Sinn gekommen, daß das Königtum kein

---

43) Zum Begriff der Regalien vgl. W. ULLMANN, The Growth of Papal Government in the Middle Ages, London ³1970, S. 408 ff., mit weiterer Literatur; vgl. noch P. CLASSEN (wie A. 34), S. 427 f.

44) Trotz der reichen Literatur zum Wormser Konkordat will es scheinen, daß noch manche Frage ungeklärt ist; z.B., wie weit war nach voraufgegangener zwiespältiger Wahl der König an die folgende Wahl des Metropoliten und seiner Suffragane gebunden? M.a.W., mußte er — trotz vielleicht berechtigter Einwände — den ihm nicht genehmen Elekten die Regalien übergeben, obwohl das Reichsinteresse dagegen sprach? Welche Rolle spielte in diesem Kräftespiel die *pars sanior?* Die Schwierigkeiten dürften sich lösen, wenn dem ekklesiologischen Grundgedanken Rechnung getragen wird.

45) Register 4, 3, hrsg. v. E. CASPAR, in: Epistolae Selectae, 2. unveränderte Auflage, Berlin 1955, S. 298, Z. 36 ff.

46) Das habe ich zu zeigen versucht in: „Von Canossa nach Pavia", Nachdruck: The Papacy and political ideas in the Middle Ages, Collected Studies Bd. 2, London 1976, S. 283 ff.

47) BONIZO von Sutri, Liber ad amicum, LdL Bd. 1, S. 609.

eigenständiges, historisch gewordenes, auf natürliche Art entstandenes und entwickeltes Gebilde gewesen wäre. Ebenso natürlich war für den König das monarchische Herrschaftsamt. Gewiß hatten die Bischöfe schon vermöge ihrer bischöflichen Stellung herausragende Bedeutung im Königreich, aber gerade deshalb hatte der König ein lebenswichtiges Interesse an den Bistumsbesetzungen, die er fest in der Hand zu halten entschlossen war, weil er sonst seiner eigenen Herrschaft nicht mehr sicher gewesen wäre und seine Pflicht als *Tutor regni* nicht erfüllt hätte. Daß die Herrscher das Christentum sehr ernst nahmen, läßt sich aus den zahlreichen Privilegien, Schenkungen usw., erkennen, vor allem aber aus der königlichen Titulatur — er war der *Rex Dei gratia,* eine wörtliche Entlehnung paulinischer Terminologie (I. Kor. 16,23). Er war ja auch eine *persona ecclesiastica,* und der deutsche König war ein *rex canonicus*[48], der Kanonikate an mehreren Kirchen besaß. Bei seinem Tode fiel die Herrschermacht zurück an die Quelle, der sie entstammte[49]. Gedanklich war also der Herrscher selbst fest in den religiös-ekklesiologischen Rahmen eingebaut. Der nicht selten erhobene Vorwurf — damals und auch bei Späteren — gegen den König, er sei ein Feind der Kirche, ist eine arge Entstellung der geschichtlichen Wahrheit. Was des Herrschers öffentliche Herrschaft anlangte, hielt er sich strikte an die *Externa,* wie es in der Tat der Krönungsordo von ihm verlangte[50]. Kein einziger mittelalterlicher Herrscher hatte sich jemals mit Lehre, Dogma, den *Interna,* befaßt (er hatte dazu auch weder die Neigung noch die Eignung).

Trotz alledem erstand dem König im Reformpapsttum ein Widersacher, der die Ausübung der monarchischen Herrschaft des Königs schärfstens bestritt, die sich überwiegend in den Bistumsbesetzungen kundtat. Vom ekklesiologischen Standpunkt war diese Manifestation der monarchischen Herrschaft unannehmbar und unzumutbar. Vom ekklesiologischen Blickwinkel waren die Rollen von König und Bischof präzise verkehrt. Dem Reichsfürsten solle nicht ein Kirchenfürst folgen, sondern umgekehrt sollte die Reihenfolge sein — dem Kirchenfürsten solle der Reichsfürst folgen. Es ging im Investiturstreit um nichts weniger als um eine Umwertung der bisherigen Wertskala, wie dies in seiner treffenden Art Gregor selbst ausgedrückt hatte, indem er den Exorzisten höher stellte als den Herrscher, weil jener an Macht diesen bei weitem übertreffe[51]. Entscheidend in diesem ekklesiologischen Gemeinwesen waren nicht die öffentlichen Rechte in der Form von Markt-, Münz- usw. Rechten, sondern jene, die das Wesen der ekklesiologischen Gesellschaft berührten, worüber nur die qualifizierten Amtsträger zu befinde hatten. Die Dissonanz zwischen Gemeinschaft und Herrschaft wurde hier so zum Angelpunkt der gregorianischen Angriffe. Entscheidend war die Erkenntnis der Reformer vom Wesen des Königtums als eines bloßen Teiles der universalen ekklesiologischen Gemeinschaft, der der Papst vorstand. Was in einer natürlich erwachsenen Gemeinschaft rechtens war, mußte nicht auch rechtens in einer ekklesiologischen sein. Recht kann daher zum Un-Recht werden.

---

48) Dazu J. FLECKENSTEIN, Rex canonicus, in: Festschrift P. E. Schramm, Wiesbaden 1964, Bd. 1, S. 57 ff.

49) W. ULLMANN, Principles of Government and Politics in the Middle Ages, London ^{4}1978, S. 133.

50) Siehe oben bei A. 23.

51) Reg. 8, 21, ed. cit., S. 555, Z. 10 ff.: „... maior potestas exorciste conceditur ... quam alicui laicorum causa secularis dominationis tribui possit".

Und das ist die Bedeutung der oftmaligen Berufung auf die *iustitia* bei Gregor[52]. Es galt daher als eine unabdingbare Voraussetzung des Reformpapsttums, daß Kontrolle der die ekklesiologische Gemeinschaft tragenden Sachwalter nicht unter Königsherrschaft stehen durfte. Darin Machtstreben und Anmaßung des Papsttums zu erblicken, ist völlig abwegig. Der Papst folgte grundsätzlichen Lehren und Voraussetzungen, die ihren letzten Urgrund in der Bibel hatten.

Auf praktischer Ebene zielte das Reformpapsttum auf die Zurückdrängung des Laientums sowie die Leugnung des monarchischen königlichen Herrschertums ab. Mittel des Kampfes waren die bis ins patristische und spätrömische Zeitalter zurückreichende Literatur, Konzilschlüsse usw. Die führenden Vertreter verstanden diese Werkzeuge mit Wucht und Geschick zu verwenden, während das Königtum im Grunde nichts anderes besaß als gewohnheitsmäßige Übung. Die Lage des Königs war umso schlimmer, als er ja von Gottes Gnaden Herrscher war, worin man ein Paradox von großer Tragweite erblicken kann. Kein anderer Begriff war so theologisch geschwängert als jener der *gratia.* Es mutet tragisch und naiv zugleich an, daß sich Heinrich auf die Salbung und seine Eigenschaft als *Christus Domini* berief[53]. Ganz zum Unterschied von der Bischofssalbung kam der königlichen Salbung kein *character indelebilis* zu. Es überrascht durchaus nicht, daß man sich auf Ambrosius besann — „imperator enim intra ecclesiam, non supra ecclesiam est"[54] — oder Isidor von Sevilla anrief, wenn auch meist nur aus zweiter Hand[55].

Ein ganz besonderes Kennzeichen der Ekklesiologie war ihre Universalität. Universal war die Sprache, die Religion, der Ritus — wesentliche Voraussetzungen und Grundlagen ekklesiologischer Ansprüche. Schon begrifflich stand das Königtum dem universalen Gedanken fern. Als ekklesiologische Körperschaft verlangte das Christentum nach universaler Geltung, die man nur durch einheitliche Führung gewährleistet sah. Damit stimmte vollends überein die seit Gregor VII. und Urban II. sich anbahnende Erweiterung der römischen Synode zu einem Plenarkonzil. Es gibt kaum ein besseres Zeichen des Selbstverständnisses des Papsttums als die universalen Lateran-Synoden. Sie schufen universal geltendes Recht unter päpstlichem Vorsitz. Körperschaftlich manifestierten sie das von Gregor so häufig postulierte *universale regimen* des Papsttums und dessen *universalitas regiminis.*

Der immer wiederkehrende Appell Gregors an das Recht — worin in der Tat die Stärke des Papsttums und die Schwäche des Königtums lagen — entfachte paradoxerweise wenig später ideelle Kräfte auf der königlichen Seite, die das Antlitz Europas verändern sollten. Die Berufung auf das Recht wurde auf der Königsseite — nicht zu Unrecht — als Herausforderung empfunden und wurde damit zum auslösenden Moment. Die Wirkung war unvorhergesehen[56].

---

52) Vgl. Growth of Papal Government (wie A. 43), S. 273 f., 283 u.ö.

53) „Me quoque, qui licet indignus inter christos ad regnum sum unctus, tetigisti, quem sanctorum patrum traditio soli deo iudicandum docuit nec pro aliquo crimine, nisi a fide, quod absit, exorbitaverim, deponendum asseruit"; Die Briefe Kaiser Heinrichs IV., hrsg. v. C. ERDMANN, Kritische Studientexte Bd. 1, Leipzig 1937, Nr. 12, S. 16, Z. 21 ff.

54) Dazu Ambrosius, wie A. 42.

55) Sententiae, 3, 51, 3: „Sub religionis disciplina saeculares potestates subiectae sunt".

56) Noch zu Lebzeiten Gregors begann die Berufung auf das römische Recht in der Schrift des Petrus CRASSUS; darüber Growth (wie A. 43), S. 382 ff. und in art. cit. (wie A. 46), S. 276 ff.

Als römischer Kaiser hatte der deutsche König allen Grund, das römische Recht in seiner überlieferten Form sein eigenes zu nennen. Ein römischer Kaiser ohne römisches Recht ist ein Unding. Und in der überlieferten Kodifikation hatte ganz besondere Bedeutung und Anziehungskraft jene Ulpian-Stelle, die der Benutzer in der ersten Lex des ersten Titels im ersten Buch der Digesten fand. Diese Begriffsbestimmung[57] des öffentlichen Rechts diente als Bestätigung und Bekräftigung der Herrschermacht. Noch zu allen Zeiten stand das öffentliche Recht zur Disposition des monarchischen Herrschers, und in diesem Zusammenhang war es geradezu auf die strittigen Fragen zugeschnitten, d.h. die Kontrolle über die Bischöfe, die den *sacerdotes* zugerechnet wurden[58]. Der Rückgriff auf das römische Recht macht verständlich, warum sich seit Heinrich V. der deutsche König ständig *Rex Romanorum* vor der Kaiserkrönung nannte[59]. Es war aber auch zur Zeit dieses Nachfahren Heinrichs IV., daß das Rechtsstudium in Bologna aufblühte. War doch Irnerius, der große Meister, sein Ratgeber. Bedeutungsvoll ist auch die Tatsache, daß die ersten zünftigen Lehrer des römischen Rechts sowie ihre Schüler allesamt dem Laienstand angehörten. Die Anwendung und das Eindringen ins römische Recht glichen zu einem nicht geringen Teil die Verluste aus, die der Herrscher im Zuge des Investiturstreits erlitten hatte.

Mit dieser frühen ideellen Rezeption des römischen Rechts auf herrscherlicher Ebene verband sich auf öffentlichem Gebiet die steigende Bedeutung der Ministerialen im Laufe des 12. Jahrhunderts, womit die Bischöfe im gleichen Maß an Boden zu verlieren begannen. Vor allem begann sich die Zentralgewalt unter Friedrich I. mit Hilfe der Ministerialen zu konstituieren. In der Tat kann er auch als Beispiel dienen für einen Herrscher, der das römische Recht und Reich sich zum Muster nahm und damit eine wesentliche Strukturänderung der Herrschaft selbst anbahnte[60]. In der folgenden Generation wurden den Landesherren (den *domini terrae*) bedeutsame obrigkeitliche Funktionen und Rechte übertragen, woraus sich eine Verlagerung der Zentralgewalt auf die Landesherren ergab[61].

Abgesehen von den kräftig emporstrebenden Territorialgewalten etwa in Frankreich und England, erkennt man schon im 12. Jahrhundert im sizilischen Königreich den Keim der nachmaligen Formel des *Rex in regno suo est imperator.* Der Sinn der Formel, der eine große Zukunft beschieden sein sollte, war nicht etwa eine Nachahmung oder Usurpation des mittelalterlichen Kaisers auf seiten eines Königs, wie häufig behauptet wird[62], sondern der Anspruch des Königs, dieselbe Funktion in seinem Königreich auszuüben, die der spätrömische Herrscher auf Grund des *ius publicum* hatte. Im Klartext hieß dies die Sicherung der Kontrolle über die *sacerdotes.* Eine solche Kontrolle konnte sich umso leichter im sizilischen Königreich auswirken, als dort das Legatenprivileg Urbans II. und Paschalis' II. diese Entwicklung tatsächlich ge-

---

57) Siehe oben S. 407.

58) Zum schillernden Begriff des *Sacerdos* vgl. Gelasius I. (wie A. 1), S. 196 ff.

59) Zum folgenden vgl. op. cit. (wie A. 46), S. 281 ff. Ferner Dies ortus imperii, ebda., Kap. 8.

60) Ebda., S. 289 ff.

61) K. Kroeschell, Deutsche Rechtsgeschichte Bd. 1, Reinbek 1972, S. 287.

62) In neuerer Zeit machte E.E. Stengel, Kaisertitel und Souveränitätsidee, Deutsches Archiv 3 (1939), S. 1 ff., das mittelalterliche Kaisertum zum Mittelpunkt seiner Ausführungen.

fördert hat[63]. Es war jedoch nicht nur in Frankreich[64] und in England[65], wo diese Formel weiteste Verbreitung fand[66], sondern auch in Deutschland, wo sie gleichfalls nicht verfehlen konnte, diese Anziehungskraft auszuüben, und zwar im Rahmen der Territorialgewalten.

Der Unterstützung, die das römisch ausgerichtete öffentliche Recht der Landesherrschaft gewährte, scheint die Forschung wenig Beachtung zu schenken. Der „Dux Cliviae in territorio suo papa est" oder der englische Heinrich VIII., der sich imperiale Befugnisse zuschrieb, sowie die Einrichtung des *Placetum regium* oder der *Recursus ab abusa*[67], der in Frankreich Eingang fand, lassen unschwer den entfernten Hintergrund des *ius publicum* klassischer Prägung erkennen. Freilich beschränkten sich die Maßnahmen noch immer auf die *Externa,* aber die Versuchung lag nahe, herrscherliche Ansprüche auf die *Interna* auszudehnen, wie der landesherrliche Anspruch auf das *ius reformandi*[68] zu zeigen schien. Es ist daher in diesem Zusammenhang aufschlußreich, auf die Ähnlichkeit mit der spätrömischen Situation zu verweisen, als der Herrscher das Henotikon, ein Glaubensedikt, erließ. Hier wie dort war das Ergebnis eine Kirchenspaltung, und das bedeutete Zerfall der ekklesiologischen Gesamtheit. Das landesfürstliche *Cuius regio, eius religio* bringt die territoriale Hoheit auf dem Boden der *Interna* zum Ausdruck. In verschiedenartiger Gestaltung und Einkleidung sowie unter verschiedenen Etikettierungen kam die Thematik des öffentlichen Rechts mit elementarer Wucht zum Durchbruch — in der spätrömischen Kaiserzeit wie auch in der anbrechenden Neuzeit Europas. Es geht hier um eine Rechtsideologie, die in variierenden Vor- und Kennzeichen sich mit dem ekklesiologisch verbundenen Herrschaftsgedanken auseinanderzusetzen versuchte. Die Kulisse lieferte der dem hellenistischen und paulinischen Speicher entstammende Ganzheitsgedanke des Christentums, wie ihn die mittelalterliche Lehre verstanden hatte.

Man kann nicht umhin, auf das Paradox aufmerksam zu machen, daß das stets als universal gegoltene römische Recht die Zerbröckelung und schließliche Auflösung der universalen Staatlichkeit förderte und die Einzelstaatlichkeit mächtig vorantrieb, die in eine Vielstaatlichkeit ausmündete und vor allem eine bis dahin geeinte Kirche in zwei feindliche Lager schied. Im Bereich des öffentlichen Rechts zeigt die Entwicklung von der Spätantike über das Hochmittelalter bis zur frühen Neuzeit einen Verlauf, in welchem sich These und Antithese ideologisch in juristischer Gestaltung auseinandersetzten. Mögen diese paar skizzenhaften Beobachtungen die Forschung anregen, den Einfluß des römischen Rechts aus bisher vielleicht ungewohnter

---

63) Dazu J. DEÉR, Der Anspruch der Herrscher des 12. Jhs. auf die apostolische Legation, Archivum historiae pontificiae 2 (1964), S. 117 ff.

64) Siehe F. ERCOLE, L'origine francese di una formula, in: F. ERCOLE, Da Bartolo all' Althusio, Florenz 1932, S. 152 ff.

65) Wie das englische Parlament i.J. 1533 sich äußerte: „This realm of England is an empire".

66) Azo, der große Bologneser Jurist, prägte wahrscheinlich den Ausdruck; siehe W. ULLMANN, Jurisprudence in the Middle Ages, Collected Studies Bd. 4, London 1980, Kap. 7.

67) R. GÉNESTAL, Les origines de l'appel comme d'abus, Paris 1951.

68) Der listige Pierre DUBOIS bemerkte schon anfangs des 14. Jhs.: „Hat sich nicht auch Moses mit Sakralangelegenheiten befaßt, als er Recht setzte?" (DUBOIS' Denkschrift für den französischen König Philipp IV., hrsg. v. E. BOUTARIC, in: Notices et extraits 20 (1865), Teil 2, Nr. 30, S. 181.

Perspektive zu prüfen, um damit zugleich einen Beitrag zu leisten zu einem besseren Verständnis der Rezeption des römischen Rechts in deutschen Landen[69].

[69] In seiner feinen, geistvollen Art, aber aus völlig anderer Sicht, hat Heinrich MITTEIS einmal geschrieben: „Die Rezeption hatte im Namen des Reiches begonnen und sie wirkte im Effekt gegen das Reich und für die partikularen Mächte; die großartige Staatskonzeption des römischen Rechtes kam nicht mehr der Reichsgewalt zugute, sie stärkte vielmehr die fürstliche Souveränität innerhalb des Reiches“: Renaissance, Humanismus und Rezeption in Deutschland, in: Die Rechtsidee in der Geschichte, Weimar 1957, S. 559.

III

Zum Papstwahldekret von 1059

I. Das unter Vorsitz von Papst Nikolaus II. in der römischen Synode im April 1059 erlassene Papstwahldekret (PWD) hat im modernen Schrifttum einen sehr kräftigen Widerhall gefunden. Die Literatur beschäftigt sich allerdings überwiegend, wenn nicht ausschließlich mit dem sog. Königsparagraphen und in weitem Abstand mit dem Anteil, den die verschiedenen Kategorien von Wählern bei der Wahl des neuen Papstes hatten. Dagegen scheint eine andere Bestimmung desselben Synodaldekretes, soweit sich überblicken läßt, nahezu gar keine Beachtung gefunden zu haben. Es handelt sich um den § 8 des PWD: Sollte aus irgendwelchen Gründen der Erwählte an der Thronbesteigung verhindert sein, so besitzt er nichtsdestoweniger als Papst die volle Herrschaftsbefugnis. *Is qui electus est in apostolica sede iuxta consuetudinem intronizari non valeat, electus tamen sicut papa auctoritatem obtineat regendi sanctam Romanam ecclesiam et disponendi omnes facultates illius, quod beatum Gregorium ante consecrationem suam fecisse cognoscimus*[1]).

---

[1]) Die maßgebliche Ausgabe in MGH Const. I, 540; die Wibertinische Verfälschung hat diese Bestimmung unverändert übernommen, ebd. S. 542—543. Nachdruck in Carl Mirbt, Quellen zur Geschichte des Papsttums und des römischen Katholizismus, 6. Aufl. hg. Kurt Aland, Band I, Tübingen 1967, S. 279. Die Berufung auf Gregor d. Gr. wird erwähnt von Petrus Damiani, Disceptatio synodalis, MGH Libelli de Lite, I, 79 Z. 33—35. Die Kenntnis dürfte auf den Bericht bei Gregor von Tours zurückgehen, siehe seine Historia Francorum, Lib. X, c. 1, ed. MGH Scriptores Rerum Merowingicarum, I, 477f. (407). Zwischen Gregors Wahl und Konsekration verliefen in der Tat gute sechs Monate. Die richtige Erklärung bei Erich Caspar, Geschichte des Papsttums, Band II, Tübingen 1933, S. 374f. Vgl. noch Walter Stuhlfath, Gregor I. der Große: Sein Leben bis zu seiner Wahl zum Papst nebst einer Untersuchung

Überblickt man die Literatur seit der Mitte des neunzehnten Jahrhunderts, so zeigt sich eine kaum verständliche Vernachlässigung dieser Synodalbestimmung. Hier sollen nur einige Beispiele aus dem Schrifttum angeführt werden. Das groß angelegte Werk von George Phillips enthält bloß ein Resumé der Verordnung und kommt sogar zu dem Schluß, daß sie ohne Bedeutung war[2]). In ganz lakonischer Weise befaßt sich Paul Hinschius in seinem grundlegenden und noch immer unübertroffenen Werk mit dieser Bestimmung und schreibt wenig weiterführend: „Nicht minder war die Bestimmung von Bedeutung, daß der Gewählte auch schon vor seiner Inthronisation zur Ausübung der päpstlichen Jurisdiktionsrechte befugt sein sollte“[3]). Obwohl sich P. Scheffer-Boichorst ex professo mit dem PWD beschäftigte, geht er mit keinem Wort auf diese immerhin wichtige Verfügung ein, sondern beginnt sogleich mit dem Königsparagraphen und schließt auch damit ab[4]). Bei den Neueren liest man ebenfalls recht wenig darüber. So zum Beispiel bei F. X. Seppelt, der den Einfluß Hildebrands stark in den Vordergrund rückt, aber bloß den Inhalt der Verordnung wiedergibt, ohne auf deren Bedeutung einzugehen[5]). Auch Johannes Haller resumiert mit seiner ihm eigenen darstellerischen Kraft die Bestimmung, die er, wie das ganze PWD, freilich zeit- und

---

der ältesten Viten, Heidelberg 193, S. 58f. Zu dieser Berufung auf Gregor I. bemerkt Hans Georg Krause, Das Papstwahldekret und seine Rolle im Investiturstreit, Studi Gregoriani, Band VII (1960) S. 82, daß man mit den historischen Belegen großzügig schaltete und eine Latitüde im Gebrauch der Termini entwickelt hatte. Daß unter Inthronisation auch die Konsekration oftmals mitverstanden wurde, zeigt Michel Andrieu, Le pontifical romain au moyen âge, Band II, Città del Vaticano 1940, S. 274. Der Begriff der Inthronisation war im elften Jahrhundert « encore inusité dans les ordines et les documents liturgiques ». Eine Mitwirkung des deutschen Herrschers in der Form eines Zustimmungsrechts würde die Bestimmung des § 8 sinn- und zwecklos machen. Die in § 6 erwähnte Konzession bezieht sich auf die Verleihung der Kaiserwürde, um die der König beim apostolischen Stuhl nachsucht.

[2]) George Phillips, Kirchenrecht, Band V, Regensburg 1875, S. 791ff., vgl. auch S. 810; ders., Lehrbuch des Kirchenrechts, Regensburg 1871, S. 204, wo sich nicht einmal ein dürftiges Resumé findet.

[3]) Paul Hinschius, Kirchenrecht der Katholiken und Protestanten, Bd. I, Berlin 1869, S. 261.

[4]) Paul Scheffer-Boichorst, Die Neuordnung der Papstwahl durch Nikolaus II., Straßburg 1897.

[5]) Franz-Xaver Seppelt, Geschichte der Päpste, Bd. III, München 1956, S. 39.

ortsbedingt auslegt, d. h. auf die Wahl Nikolaus' II. bezieht, die nachträglich durch das PWD sanktioniert werden sollte. Das PWD sei eine Neuerung gewesen[6]). Mit keiner Silbe wird dieser Bestimmung gedacht bei Willibald Plöchl[7]) und bei Hans Erich Feine[8]). Es ist in der Tat nicht leicht zu erklären, warum man diese Bestimmung so gering achtet[9]), denn sie enthält geradezu diametral entgegengesetzte Auffassungen hinsichtlich der Königsrechte vor der Krönung (genauer:

---

[6]) Johannes Haller, Das Papsttum: Idee und Wirklichkeit, Bd. II, Urach 1965, S. 234: „... es war Neuerung und zwar Neuerung mit bestimmtem, augenblicklichem Zweck". Ganz ähnlich schon Albert Hauck, Kirchengeschichte Deutschlands, Nachdruck der 8. Aufl., Bd. III, Leipzig 1954, S. 685. Übereinstimmend Krause (wie Anm. 1) S. 84, 114; Friedrich Kempf, Pier Damiani und das Papstwahldekret von 1059, Archivum Historiae Pontificiae 2 (1964) S. 73—89, hier S. 73—74 („legalisiert"; von einer Legalisierung sprach schon Karl Hampe, Deutsche Kaisergeschichte in der Zeit der Salier und Staufer, 10. Aufl., hg. Friedrich Baethgen, Heidelberg 1949, S. 37). Überzeugend und mit guten Gründen wird diese oberflächliche und unkritische Ansicht verworfen von Dieter Hägermann, Untersuchungen zum Papstwahldekret von 1059, ZRG Kan. Abt. 56 (1970) 157—193, hier S. 169ff.

[7]) Willibald M. Plöchl, Geschichte des Kirchenrechts, Bd. II, Wien—München 1955, S. 77.

[8]) Hans Erich Feine, Kirchliche Rechtsgeschichte, 5. Aufl., Köln—Graz 1972, S. 273, 318.

[9]) Vgl. noch Johannes Baptist Sägmüller, Lehrbuch des katholischen Kirchenrechts, 4. Aufl., Bd. I/4, Freiburg 1925, S. 488. Unergiebig ist die Schrift von Jesus Hortal Sanchez, De initio potestatis primatialis Romani pontificis: Investigatio historico-iuridica a tempore sancti Gregorii Magni usque ad tempus Clementis V (Analecta Gregoriana, Bd. CLXVII, 1968) S. 30, der die Bestimmung wörtlich zitiert, aber ihre Bedeutung nicht erkennt. Die Bestimmung des PWD wird berücksichtigt von Robert L. Benson, The Bishop-Elect: A Study in Medieval Ecclesiastical Office, Princeton 1968, S. 41—46, der sie im Rahmen seiner Untersuchung über die Rechtsstellung des erwählten, aber noch nicht konsekrierten Bischofs behandelt. Aus der älteren Spezialliteratur seien erwähnt, C. J. Hefele, Das Dekret über die Papstwahl von Nikolaus II., Theologische Quartalschrift 60 (1878) S. 257—293 (behandelt den Königsparagraphen); H. Grauert, Das Dekret Nikolaus' II. von 1059, Historisches Jahrbuch 1 (1880) S. 501—602 (S. 559 wird die Bestimmung kurz erwähnt im Zusammenhang mit der Immantation); Ders., Papstwahlstudien, ebd. 20 (1899) S. 236—425 (hatte keine Ursache auf die Bestimmung einzugehen, da er über simonistische Wahlen abhandelte); Anton Michel, Papstwahl und Königsrecht oder das Papstwahl-Konkordat von 1059, München 1936, übergeht die Bestimmung; Ders., Das Papstwahlpaktum von 1059, Historisches Jahrbuch 59 (1939) S. 291—357 beschäftigt sich mit Humbert als dem Verf. des PWD.

vor der Salbung) — blieb doch der erwählte König bis zur Salbung *princeps designatus*[10]).

Das moderne Schrifttum, wovon nur Proben aus führenden und wichtigen Darstellungen gegeben wurden, steht freilich nicht allein da. Denn schon ein flüchtiger Überblick über die ältere Dekretistenliteratur[11]) läßt eine ganz ähnliche Dürre in der Auseinandersetzung und Exegese des § 8 des PWD erkennen. Weder in der Summa des Paucapalea noch in dem Stroma des Rolandus[12]) findet sich irgendeine Erläuterung der Verfügung, die man bei Gratian vollständig im Wortlaut und an prominenter Stelle liest[13]). Es steht auch nicht viel besser mit den den beiden erwähnten Werken Paucapaleas und Rolandus' zeitlich

---

[10]) Vgl. etwa den sog. Frühdeutschen Ordo für die Königskrönung (spätes 9. oder frühes 10. Jh.), hg. Carl Erdmann, Forschungen zur politischen Ideenwelt des frühen Mittelalters, hg. Friedrich Baethgen, Berlin 1951, S. 84, Nr. 6f. Vor allem ist der maßgebliche Mainzer Ordo von ca. 950—960 zu berücksichtigen, siehe Le Pontifical Romano-Germanique du dixième siècle (Studi e Testi, Bd. CCXXVI, 1963), hg. Cyrille Vogel — Reinhard Elze, S. 247 Nr. LXXII Abschn. 6 und S. 248 Abschn. 7.

[11]) Von den vorgratianischen Sammlern scheint nur Ivo von Chartres das ganze PWD seiner Panormia einverleibt zu haben, Lib. III, c. 1 (Migne, PL 161 Sp. 1127—1129). Von den Zeitgenossen nahm Anselm von Lucca nur die beiden einleitenden Paragraphen (§§ 1 und 2) aus der Synodica Nikolaus' II., mit welcher die Beschlüsse der Synode (1059) bekanntgegeben wurden (MGH Const. I, 547), in seine Sammlung auf: Anselmi Collectio canonum, hg. Fridericus Thaner, Innsbruck 1915 (Nachdruck Aalen 1965), Lib. VI, c. 12, S. 273, während er das PWD in der gekürzten (und geänderten) Form, in welcher es in der Synode im April 1060 veröffentlicht wurde (MGH Const. I, 551, c. 4), in seiner Sammlung hatte (ebd. c. 13, S. 273—274). Genau dasselbe gilt für die fast gleichzeitige Sammlung Deusdedits: Die Kanonessammlung des Kardinals Deusdedit, hg. Victor Wolf von Glanvell, Paderborn 1905, Lib. I, c. 168 und 169, S. 107. Offenbar hatte Polycarp die beiden Kapitel (I, 4, 4 und 5), siehe Uwe Horst, Die Kanonessammlung Polycarpus des Gregor von S. Grisogono, München 1980, S. 58f.

[12]) Die Summa des Paucapalea über das Dekret Gratians, hg. Johann Friedrich Schulte, Gießen 1890, ad Dist. 23, S. 22, erwähnt die Bestimmung nicht. Die Summa Magistri Rolandi Bandinelli nachmals Papstes Alexander III., hg. Friedrich Thaner, Innsbruck 1874, S. 6 führt aus, daß das Kapitel über die Wahl des Papstes handelte. Zweifel an der Identität des Verfs. werden angemeldet von John T. Noonan, Who was Rolandus, in: Law, Church and Society: Essays in honor of Stephan Kuttner, ed. K. Pennington — R. Somerville, Philadelphia 1977, S. 22—48, der die Meinung vertritt, daß ein Zeitgenosse und Namensvetter Rolands der Verf. gewesen sei.

[13]) Dist. 23, c. 1: In nomine Domini.

nahestehenden Summen. Die sog. Summa Coloniensis zitiert in paraphrastischer Art die Bestimmung, indem der Verf. ausführt: *Quod autem aliter electus verus papa dici et esse debeat, declaratur ibidem his verbis ...*, woran sich der Wortlaut anschließt. Noch dürftiger ist die sog. Summa Parisiensis, deren Verf. einige Bemerkungen über den Königsparagraphen macht, insbesondere über den Begriff des darin ausgesprochenen *personaliter*, aber über die Papstrechte vor der Thronbesteigung nichts aussagt[14]).

Einen sehr wichtigen Schritt nach vorne machte der Bologneser Rufinus in seiner Summa zum Dekret Gratians, die in den späten fünfziger Jahren des zwölften Jahrhunderts entstand[15]). Was die Ausführungen dieses großen Summisten besonders anziehend macht, ist die von ihm vorausgeschickte Bemerkung, daß die Bestimmung im PWD Gegenstand von Kontroversen bildete, aber nicht hinsichtlich des Papstes in seiner päpstlichen Funktion, sondern hinsichtlich eines erwählten Bischofs. Er verlagert das Problem auf die bischöfliche Rechtsstellung vor Empfang der Konsekration. *Solet queri si in electione confirmatus ante episcopalem unctionem usque adeo plenam auctoritatem possideat, ut quemadmodum episcopus consecratus deponere valeat*[16]). Man könnte wohl behaupten, daß die Bestimmung des PWD auch die bischöfliche Stellung miteinbegriff, aber obschon an sich möglich, ist dies unwahrscheinlich, weil die Bestimmung ausdrücklich von der Inthronisation des erwählten Papstes sprach, während sich Rufinus auf die Konsekration, d. h. die bischöfliche Salbung bezog.

Nichtsdestoweniger verdient die Aussage Rufinus' Beachtung, weil sie unschwer auf die Rechtsstellung des Bischofs von Rom übertragen werden konnte. Er legt weiterhin dar, daß die bischöfliche *plena potestas* sich nur auf die Verwaltung — die *administratio* — erstreckt, aber keine *auctoritas dignitatis* vor der Weihe enthält. Dem entspricht, daß der *Electus* ohne bischöfliche Weihe zwar das *ius administrationis* besitzt, das sich beispielsweise in der Suspension von Klerikern offenbart.

---

14) Summa Elegantius in iure divino seu Coloniensis, hg. Gérard Fransen-Stephan Kuttner, Monumenta iuris canonici, series A, Corpus Glossatorum, Bd. I, 1, New York 1969, Pars tertia, c. 25, S. 125. Die Summa Parisiensis, hg. Terence P. McLaughlin, Toronto 1952, S. 23f.

15) Rufinus, Summa Decretorum, hg. Heinrich Singer, Paderborn 1902, S. 50; Entstehungszeit ebd., S. CXVIf. und Stephan Kuttner, Repertorium der Kanonistik (Studi e Testi, Bd. LXXI, 1937), S. 131f.

16) Ad Dist. 23, c. 1, S. 52.

Eine förmliche Absetzung allerdings bedarf der *plenitudo auctoritatis*, die der Bischof aber erst vermöge der Konsekration erhält[17]). Mit anderen Worten, der noch nicht geweihte Bischof kann die Ausübung der im Ordo gelegenen Rechte untersagen — das Wesen der bloß zeitweiligen Suspension —, aber ist nicht befugt, auch die Rechte selbst zu entziehen — das Wesen der Deposition. Es läßt sich nicht bestreiten, daß die Ausführungen Rufinus' trotz ihrer beschränkten Anwendbarkeit auf die fraglichen Papstrechte in die juristisch bedeutungsvolle Richtung wiesen. Der von ihm stark abhängige Stephanus Tornacensis beginnt seine Erklärung der Verfügung mit den aus ihr entlehnten Worten, wobei auch er die Inthronisation durch die Konsekration ersetzt, so daß der erwählte Papst *ante consecrationem habet potestatem regendi ecclesiam et omnes facultates disponendi*, schwenkt aber sogleich ein und lehnt sich fast wörtlich an Rufinus an, indem er zwischen dem bischöflichen (und nicht päpstlichen) Suspensionsrecht und dem Recht der Absetzung unterscheidet. Nichtsdestoweniger setzt er einen nicht unwesentlichen Punkt hinzu: Die aus dem Ordo fließenden Rechte kann der bloß Gewählte nicht entziehen *quia nec dare valet, quod tantum ex consecratione sua habet*[18]).

Bei Huguccio läßt sich eine mächtige Vertiefung und Ausweitung der Thematik erkennen. In seiner leider noch immer nicht edierten Summa zum Dekret geht er ohne alle Umschweife auf den Kern der Sache ein. Er stellt anfangs die Frage, ob der erwählte Papst, der noch nicht Bischof ist, Kleriker absetzen, suspendieren, an sie Delegationsrechte übertragen und im Besonderen sie exkommunizieren kann[19]). Mit der

---

[17]) *Dicimus, quod plenam potestatem habeat quoad administrationem, non dignitatis auctoritatem, et ideo iure plene administrationis potest aliquos ab administratione procurationum, vel ordinum suspendere, quod tamen non sine presentia capituli sui, cui capitulo episcopi mortuo licet itidem facere. Deponere autem, id est exauctorrare non potest, qui plenitudinem auctoritatis nondum habet, quam ex sola consecratione est certissimum evenisse.* Zu dieser Stelle siehe noch Benson (wie Anm. 9), S. 58, Anm. 4, und zur Lehre Rufinus' ebd. S. 57—89, bes. S. 64—71, hinsichtlich des bischöflichen Amtes.

[18]) Er fährt fort mit den Worten von Rufinus: *Habet enim electus potestatem administrationis, non auctoritatem dignitatis*, siehe Die Summa des Stephanus Tornacensis über das Decretum Gratiani, hg. Johann Friedrich Schulte, Gießen 1891, S. 35; vgl. noch S. X—XI.

[19]) Huguccio, Summa zum Dekret, Inc.: „Ad decorem sponsae", HS. Pembroke College, Cambridge, Nr. 72, fol. 132rb, ad Dist. 23, c. 1: *Ecce papa est electus et nondum episcopus, potest deponere vel degradare* (MS: delegare) *clericos,*

ihm eigenen Selbstsicherheit erklärt er kurz und bündig, daß er eine allgemeine Lehre aufstellen wolle — *generalem faciam doctrinam.* Der Papst, der noch nicht zum Bischof geweiht ist, kann Alles rechtmäßig im Rahmen der Jurisdiktion unternehmen, nichts jedoch, was im Bereich des Ordo liegt. Er kann daher absetzen, degradieren, exkommunizieren, suspendieren, Pfründen verleihen oder entziehen, und so weiter[20]). Ein solcher Papst kann jedoch unter anderem weder Weihen erteilen noch das Chrisma weihen, Altäre oder Kirchen konsekrieren. Denn die ersteren Rechte gehören dem Jurisdiktionsbereich an, für die letzteren wird der entsprechende Ordo vorausgesetzt[21]). Mit dieser „allgemeinen Lehre" hat Huguccio in der Tat neuen, aber festen Boden betreten[22]). Die Frage, ob die voraufgehende Lehre, wie sie von Rufinus *et eius sequaces* vertreten wurde, Huguccio dabei behilflich war, mag wohl auf sich beruhen. Tatsache bleibt, daß vermöge seiner präzisen und einleuchtenden Doktrin seine Ansicht Allgemeingut in der Kanonistik wurde und sich bis tief ins fünfzehnte Jahrhundert hinein behauptete, wie sogleich zu zeigen sein wird. Daß die Rechtsstellung des Papstes vor seiner Thronbesteigung im allgemeinen von geringem Interesse für die Dekretisten und Dekretalisten gewesen zu sein scheint, geht aus dem Schweigen der Glossa ordinaria zur Bestimmung hervor. Sie hat zwar einen langen Eintrag über die Frage, wie sich die bischöfliche Stellung des Papstes von jener

---

potest suspendere vel excommunicare? Zu dieser Stelle siehe noch Benson (wie Anm. 9), S. 118–120.

[20]) *Omnia potest, quae sunt tantum iurisditionis, sed non illa, quae sunt ordinis; potest ergo deponere, degradare, excommunicare, suspendere, praebendas dare et auferre et huiusmodi.* Zur Bedeutung der Stelle für den bischöflichen Ordo siehe Benson, S. 121ff.

[21]) Er fährt fort: *Sed non potest clericos ordinare, crisma conficere, altaria vel ecclesias consecrare, et huiusmodi. Prima enim potius sunt iurisditionis quam ordinis.*

[22]) Vermerkt sei, daß dieser Sätze und Beispiele von der Glossa ordinaria ad X 1, 6, 15 (Transmissam) wörtlich übernommen und mit einigen Zusätzen vermehrt wurden, wie etwa im Bereich der Jurisdiktion die Eidesleistung des Vasallen *(iuramenta recipere a vasallo ... investire)*, im Bereich des Ordo *benedicere virgines.* Der Erwähnung bedarf noch, daß Innozenz III. in X 1, 6, 28 von der Annahme ausging, ein Erzbischof, der noch nicht das Pallium eingeholt hatte, weder ein Konzil berufen noch Kirchen einweihen, Kleriker ordinieren, Bischöfe konsekrieren, das Chrisma weihen dürfe. Diese Erklärung hat auch bei den Exegeten keine einhellige Billigung gefunden, wie die Glossa ordinaria ad loc. zeigt. In der Tat ist die Gleichstellung einer Konzilsberufung mit den anderen Maßnahmen bemerkenswert.

anderer Bischöfe unterscheidet, aber über das gegenständliche Problem äußert sie sich nicht. Trotz des gewiß nicht überwältigenden Interesses der Kanonistik[23]) scheint nichtsdestoweniger der Krönung des Papstes noch anfangs des vierzehnten Jahrhunderts rechtserhebliche Bedeutung von manchen Seiten beigemessen worden zu sein, wie sich aus einer Dekretale Klemens' V. ergibt. Diese Fragestellung hatte selbstverständlich bei weitem nicht die grundlegende Bedeutung wie die Synodalbestimmung von 1059. In der klementinischen Dekretale wird klipp und klar dargelegt, daß der Papst auch vor der Krönung Dispensationen, Provisionen und Reservatrechte und alle anderen Gnadenerweise vergeben kann und bedroht mit Exkommunikation jene, die diese Papstbefugnis leugnen[24]). Mit dieser Dekretale wurde die bloß deklaratorische Bedeutung der Papstkrönung unterstrichen.

Es soll allerdings festgehalten werden, daß nach dem Bericht des so belesenen, das voraufgegangene Schrifttum stets berücksichtigenden und für uns Heutige so wertvollen Archdiakons Guido de Baysio, der ältere Zeitgenosse Huguccios, Bazianus — nicht zu verwechseln mit dem Zivilisten Bassianus —, eine Lehre entwickelt hatte, die in genau dieselbe Richtung wies, die Huguccio anzeigte und wie sie, worauf noch zurückzukommen sein wird, schon vorher von der Praxis geübt wurde, wozu freilich die Bestimmung des PWD den Anstoß gegeben haben könnte[25]). Dem Bericht Guidos zufolge soll Bazianus gelehrt haben — es sind nur Bruchstücke seiner Glossen erhalten[26]) — daß die im Synodaldekret erwähnten *facultates* keinerlei Rechtsmaßnahmen im Rahmen der Spiritualia ein-

---

[23]) Vgl. etwa Innozenz IV., Super libros quinque decretalium, Francofurti 1570, X 1, 6, 15, fol. 46 Nr. 1: *Electus ... statim potest administrare res ecclesiasticas ecclesiae suae in temporalibus et spiritualibus.* Es ist nicht sicher, daß sich diese Aussage auch auf den Papst bezieht. Andere auf den Bischof sich beziehende Aussagen bei Benson (wie Anm. 9) S. 193, 194—196.

[24]) Extravagantes communes 5, 10, 4 (Quia nonnulli).

[25]) Die Möglichkeit, daß die Entwicklung umgekehrt verlief, kann keineswegs ausgeschlossen werden. Der gesamte Problemkreis ist ein bisher vernachlässigtes Forschungsgebiet.

[26]) Johann Friedrich Schulte, Geschichte der Quellen und Literatur des canonischen Rechts, Bd. I, Stuttgart 1875, S. 154ff.; Alphonsus van Hove, Prolegomena ad Codicem Iuris Canonici, 2. Aufl., Mechlin-Rom 1945, S. 428. Seine Glossen sind meist nur aus Zitaten Späterer bekannt. Über ihn vgl. Filippo Liotta, Baziano, Dizionario biografico degli Italiani 7 (1965) S. 313—315, mit sehr reicher Literatur. Das Dictionnaire de Droit Canonique hat keinen Eintrag.

schlossen. Die Befugnis dazu werde erst durch die Weihe erlangt[27]). Im Anschluß daran fügt Guido de Baysio die Bemerkung hinzu, daß die päpstliche Kanzlei die Rechtsstellung des Papstes zwischen Wahl und Konsekration (Krönung) in der besonderen Art des Siegels zum Ausdruck bringe. Es ist die sog. Halbbulle (die *bulla dimidia*), die bloß die Köpfe der beiden Apostel darstellte ohne Namensnennung des Papstes, obwohl er seinen Papstnamen schon in den amtlichen Urkunden und Schreiben verwendete[28]). Abgesehen von der Terminologie läßt sich ein wesentlicher Unterschied zwischen den Thesen Huguccios, den der Archidiakon ganz entgegen seiner Übung hier nicht zitiert, Bazianus' und Guidos selbst nicht erkennen[29]).

---

[27]) Siehe sein Rosarium, ed. Venetiis 1577, Dist. 23, c. 1, fol. 27vb, Nr. 14: *Facultates: dicunt quidem, ut Ba., quod non habet potestatem disponendi spiritualia, nisi postquam ordines et insignia receperit, quod sit specialiter in coronatione.*

[28]) Er fährt fort: *Et haec potest esse ratio, quare papa ante coronationem tantum media bulla utitur, videlicet cum capitibus apostolorum, dumtaxat sine nomine proprio, licet statum post electionem et immantationem nomen suum designet.* Ob dies auch noch für das ausgehende 15. Jh. zutrifft, wie Antonius de Sancto Georgio im Anschluß an Zabarella lehrt, mag offen bleiben, siehe die Stelle unten Anm. 30. Zur Sache vgl. Paul Maria Baumgarten, Das päpstliche Siegelamt beim Tode und nach der Neuwahl des Papstes, Römische Quartalschrift 21 (2) (1907), S. 32ff., hier S. 37ff.; ferner Harry Bresslau, Handbuch der Urkundenlehre, 2. Aufl., Leipzig 1912 (Nachdruck 1960), S. 570, der annahm, daß die Praxis der Halbbulle mit Innozenz III. aufkam. Seine Vermutung wird zur Gewißheit, denn Innozenz selbst äußerte sich darüber in einem Schreiben vom 3. April 1198, siehe Die Register Innocenz' III., hg. Othmar Hageneder — Anton Haidacher, Band I, Graz 1964, Nr. 82, S. 121, Z. 18—25: *Quoniam insolitum fuit hactenus ut sub dimidia bulla ad tot et tam remotas provincias littere apostolice mitterentur ... universas litteras, que ab electionis nostre die usque ad sollempnitatem consecrationis sub bulla dimidia emanarant, parem cum illis firmitatem optinere decernimus, que in bulla integra diriguntur.* Gregor X. schrieb die Verwendung der Halbbulle sowie die entsprechende Datumzeile des noch nicht geweihten Papstes ausdrücklich vor, siehe Marc Dykmans, Le cérémonial papal de la fin du moyen âge à la Renaissance, Band I: Le cérémonial papal du XIIIe siècle, Bruxelles—Rome 1977, S. 161, Nr. 8: *Idem vero electus, in quocumque ordine fuerit, si scribat aliquas litteras alicui ante suam consecrationem, bullari faciet ipsas litteras cum illa parte bulle, in qua sunt capita apostolorum ex una parte, ex altera vero erit plana, cum non sit consecratus in papam.*

[29]) Er beruft sich auf den Speculator, der aber an der von Guido hier zitierten Stelle sich nicht mit dem Problem befaßt, sondern über prozeßrechtliche Themen abhandelt: siehe Guilielmus Durantis, Speculum iuris, ed. Basileae 1574, Lib. II, part. 1, De rescriptis, c. 9 § Ratione autem, fol. 419a. Dazu siehe noch Benson, S. 117, Anm. 3.

Die Thesen Bazianus' sowie die ihr verwandten Huguccios wurden noch im fünfzehnten Jahrhundert nicht nur als herrschende Lehre dargestellt, sondern wurden gleichsam zum eisernen Bestand der Rechtsdogmatik erhoben in der maßgeblichen und einflußreichen Summa des Johannes de Turrecremata, der buchstäblich die Ansichten der beiden Kanonisten des zwölften Jahrhunderts nach Guido ausschreibt[30]).

II. Einen überzeugenden Beweis für die Wirksamkeit des PWD, wenigstens in dem hier interessierenden Bereich, und dessen Anwendung liefert der Beginn des Pontifikats Gregors VII., der selbst als der Diakon der römischen Kirche (er wurde Archidiakon am Ende des Jahres) entscheidend an dem Zustandekommen des PWD beteiligt war. In höchst selten anzutreffende Weise begegnet man hier der Umsetzung des abstrakten Rechtssatzes in konkrete Gestalt und zwar durch eine an der Rechtssetzung selbst mitwirkenden Persönlichkeit. Was hier noch in Rechnung zu stellen ist, war der Namenswechsel, der gleichsam vom PWD als selbstverständlich vorausgesetzt worden war. Als solcher bezeichnete der Namenswechsel — nach dem Muster des Namens, der dem Täufling gegeben wurde oder nach dem Vorbild der Ordensnamens beim Eintritt ins Kloster — eine Wiedergeburt. Der eben erwählte Papst beginnt als Nachfolger Petri ein neues Leben, weshalb er seinen Taufnamen ablegt und als äußeres Zeichen seiner nunmehrigen Funktion einen neuen Namen empfängt. Damit wird eindeutig dargetan, daß der *Electus* eine herrscherliche, und das heißt hier petrinische Gestalt annimmt. Das läßt sich bei Hildebrand sehr eindrucksvoll nachweisen.

Wie bekannt, bekleidete Hildebrand zur Zeit seiner Wahl keinen höheren Rang als den eines Diakons. Wie das offiziöse Protokoll klar

---

30) Johannes de Turrecremata, Super Decretum, ed. Venetiis 1578, Dist. 23, c. 1, Nr. 19—20, p. 215. Genau dieselbe Darstellung findet sich noch bei Antonius de Sancto Georgio, dem sog. Praepositus (ob. 1509) in seinem Werk Super distinctionibus, ed. Lugduni 1522, ad Dist. 23, c. 1, Nr. 23—24, fol. 91ra, wo er auch über den Streit berichtet, ob Absetzung und Degradierung zum Jurisdiktionsbereich gehörten, wie Huguccio lehrte, oder ob sie in den Bereich des Ordo fielen. Unter Berufung auf Gratian, De poenit., Dist. 1, c. 31 (Verbum) wurden diese Maßnahmen nicht in den Jurisdiktionsbereich einbezogen, allerdings mit dem Vorbehalt: *nisi dicamus istud speciale in papa* (was auch von Huguccio stammte). Hier erklärt er weiter (Nr. 19, fol. 90va): *Dicit Zabarella quod spiritualia administrat* (scil. papa) *nisi postquam ceperit coronas et insignia quod fit quando coronatur. Et haec est ratio, quare papa ante coronationem utitur dimidia bulla, videlicet cum capitibus apostolorum et ab alio latere est plana sine nomine.*

herausstellt, wollten und approbierten die Wähler Hildebrand als Papst Gregor[31]), und als solcher begann er sogleich auch als Papst zu handeln, d. h. im Sinne des PWD *regere*. Er wurde zum Priester am 25. Mai geweiht und erhielt die Bischofsweihe am 30. Juni. Der Beginn dieses Pontifikats macht in völlig eindeutiger Weise klar, was das PWD in seinem § 8 ausdrückte. Vergleicht man nämlich Gregors amtliche Schreiben, die er zwischen Wahl und Konsekration erließ, mit den nachfolgenden, dann läßt sich kein Unterschied wahrnehmen. Die ersten zwölf Schreiben im Register enthalten herrscherliche Anordnungen — er befiehlt, untersagt, ordnet an, entsendet Legaten, fordert Bericht, macht Rechte des römischen Stuhles auf bestimmte Gebiete geltend[32]), gibt Anweisungen, trifft Entscheidungen usw., mit einem Wort, diese zwölf Schreiben tragen genau dieselben herrscherlichen Charakterzüge wie jene nach der Bischofskonsekration.

Nichtsdestoweniger gibt es — ganz im Sinne der Synodalbestimmung im PWD — einen sehr wesentlichen Unterschied zwischen diesen ersten zwölf Schreiben und den nachfolgenden. Gregor nennt sich *in Romanum pontificem electus* und verwendet in der Intitulatio eine Grußformel, die an sich jedem Christen zusteht: *salutem in Christo Jesu*[33]). Unmittelbar nach der Konsekration verwandelt sich seine Grußformel in die übliche: *salutem et apostolicam benedictionem*. Es ist demnach klar, daß die Erteilung des apostolischen Segens nicht zu jenen Papstrechten gehört, die das PWD im Sinne hatte. Darüber hinaus liefert Gregor VII. noch eine weitere Erkenntnis. Es sei daran erinnert, daß er im Dictatus Papae 23 vom Papst als einem *sanctus* sprach. Diese Eigenschaft hat er nach dem wohlüberlegten und durchdachten Satz[34]) nur dann, *si canonice fuerit ordinatus*. Betont sei hier, daß sich diese Bedingung nicht in der Vorlage der Stelle fand, sondern hier zum ersten Male auftritt. Die *ordinatio canonica* war nicht die Wahl, sondern die Weihe des Papstes zum

---

31) Das Register Gregors VII., hg. Erich Caspar, MGH Epistolae selectae, 2. Aufl. Berlin 1955, Reg. I, 1, S. 2: *Nos ... Heldibrandum videlicet archidiaconum, quem ammodo et usque in sempiternum et esse et dici Gregorium papam et apostolicum volumus et approbamus.*

32) Z. B. Reg. I, 7.

33) Darauf verwies ich in anderem Zusammenhang schon vor einigen Jahren, vgl. The Church and the Law in the earlier Middle Ages, Collected Studies, Band I, London 1975, Kap. XI, hier S. 247ff.

34) Über den Hintergrund und die voraufgehende Entwicklung vgl. loc. cit. (vorige Anm.), S. 241ff.

Bischof[35]). Was Gregor mit dem *sanctus*-Charakter des Papstes auszudrücken versucht, ist der Besitz der vollen apostolischen Gnadengewalt[36]). In der erst später aufkommenden Terminologie bedeutet daher die „Heiligkeit" des Papstes nichts anderes als den Vollbesitz der (bischöflichen) *potestas ordinis*[37]). Es gibt selten in der Geschichte des Rechts Zeugnisse, die so unzweideutig wie hier die Übersetzung des abstrakten Rechtssatzes in konkrete Gestaltung darlegen.

Nur Leichtfertigkeit, die an Unwissenschaftlichkeit grenzt, könnte behaupten, daß es sich hier um nichts anderes handelt als um „bloße" Formalitäten, denen keine oder nur geringe sachliche Bedeutung zukommt. Ganz im Gegenteil, diese Verfügung im PWD entfaltet ihre Wirksamkeit bis auf den heutigen Tag[38]). In dieser Bestimmung bringt das PWD das Selbstverständnis des Papsttums zum Ausdruck. Und darin liegt seine tiefe Bedeutung. Das Papsttum verstand sich vorwiegend als Herrschaftsinstitution, weshalb auch ein Laie Papst werden konnte, kann und auch wurde. Was das PWD vor allem klarstellt, ist die scharfe Trennung der Jurisdiktionssphäre von jener, die den Ordo betrifft. Damit findet die päpstliche Herrschaftsidee selbst ihre Kundgebung. Dies erklärt aber auch, wie es kommen konnte, daß Jurisdiktionsrechte an Laien übertragen werden konnten, die dann als päpstlich Beauftragte oder Legaten fungierten. Am Ausgang desselben elften

---

[35]) Das stand schon im Liber Diurnus, form. 57, hg. Theodor Sickel, Wien 1889, Nachdruck 1966, S. 46—47: De ordinatione pontificis.

[36]) Unterstrichen von Bonizo in seinem Liber ad Amicum, Libelli de Lite, I, S. 601, Z. 9ff.

[37]) Dazu vgl. noch Anselm von Lucca, Collectio canonum (wie oben Anm. 11), Lib. VI, c. 2, das die Rubrik trägt: *Ut sanctum esse nemo dubitet quem apostolicae dignitatis apex iuste attollit* (S. 266). Über die Vorlage und Einzelheiten siehe loc. cit. (Anm. 33), S. 249ff.

[38]) CIC, c. 219: *Romanus pontifex, legitime electus, statim ab acceptata electione obtinet, iure divino, plenam supremae iurisdictionis potestatem.* Schon Pius X. in seiner *Vacante sede apostolica* (25. Dez. 1904) Nr. 88, legte nieder, daß der eben Gewählte *verus papa* sei und *plenam absolutamque iurisdictionem supra totum orbem acquirit.* Sollte der Gewählte noch nicht Priester oder Bischof sein, müsse er sobald wie möglich ordiniert und konsekriert werden (Nr. 90, 106). Dazu vgl. noch Benedetto Ojetti, Commentarium in codicem iuris canonici, Band II, 2, Rom 1929, S. 42: ein gültig gewählter Laie erhält mit Annahme der Wahl alle Leitungsgewalt in der Kirche. Dazu siehe noch Eduard Eichmann, Lehrbuch des Kirchenrechts auf Grund des Codex Iuris Canonici, hg. Klaus Mörsdorf, Band I, Paderborn 1949, S. 325; August Hagen, Prinzipien des katholischen Kirchenrechts, Würzburg 1949, S. 97.

Jahrhunderts hat Urban II., wie allgemein bekannt, den normannischen Herrscher Siziliens, Roger I. und dessen Nachfolgern den Status eines päpstlichen Legaten verliehen[39]). Selbstverständlich ist die Ausübung von Jurisdiktionsgewalt nicht an einen kirchlichen Ordo gebunden, weshalb die in den Jurisdiktionsbereich fallenden Rechte an Laien übertragbar waren.

Die Bedeutung des PWD, wenigstens soweit sie sich aus dieser Bestimmung ablesen läßt, erschöpft sich keineswegs im Selbstverständnis des zeitgenössischen Papsttums. Man ist allzu leicht geneigt, päpstliche Verfügungen oder auch Synodalbestimmungen, die vom Papsttum angeregt wurden oder an denen es entscheidend mitwirkte, aus der augenblicklichen Situation zu erklären oder als Augenblicksentscheidungen anzusehen. Meist setzen sie jedoch einen langen Reifungsprozeß voraus, der sich dann in ein paar knappen, prägnanten Sätzen zusammenfassen läßt, die ihrerseits wieder über die tiefe Bedeutung hinwegtäuschen können. Und genau dies war der Fall hier beim PWD, das hinsichtlich der Papstrechte im § 8 sicherlich nichts wesentlich Neues statuieren wollte, sondern die dem Papsttum eigentümliche und von ihm schon längst verfochtene Herrschaftsthese kurz und bündig ausdrückte.

Denn das PWD — wenigstens in Beziehung zum § 8 — bildet nicht nur eine Brücke zum geltenden Recht im zwanzigsten Jahrhundert, sondern auch und vielleicht vorwiegend eine Brücke zur Vergangenheit. Es ist in der Tat fest in den rechtshistorischen Rahmen eingespannt. Eine genauere Analyse des Begriffs der Jurisdiktionsrechte verdeutlicht, daß deren Substanz per definitionem sich auf Maßnahmen beschränkt, die nicht den Glauben, die Sakramente, Dogmen usw. angehen. Diese Maßnahmen haben zum Objekt bloßes äußeres Verhalten — solches, das sich in Handlungen manifestiert, die greifbar konkret sind, ganz zum Unterschied von den Maßnahmen, die einen Ordo mit der von ihm vermittelten Gnade und dem entsprechenden Charisma voraussetzen. In dieser scharfen begrifflichen Abgrenzung — in ihrer ganzen Bedeutung

---

[39]) JL 5706, bestätigt von Paschalis II., JL 6562 vom 1. Okt. 1117. Dazu siehe Paul Fridolin Kehr, Italia Pontificia, Band VIII, Göttingen 1935, S. 251, Nr. 81; Josef Deér, Der Anspruch der Herrscher des 12. Jahrhunderts auf die apostolische Legation, Archivum Historiae Pontificiae, 2 (1964) S. 117ff., hier S. 139ff.; R. A. Schmutz, Medieval representatives, legates, nuncios and judges delegates, Studia Gratiana, Band XV (1972), S. 443ff.; Walter Ullmann, Jurisprudence in the Middle Ages, Collected Studies, Band IV, London 1980, Kap. V, S. 174ff. und Kap. VI, S. 531ff.

zuerst bloßgelegt von Huguccio — trifft man allerdings auf eine frappante Ähnlichkeit, wenn nicht sogar Parallelität mit dem konstantinischen Schema. Wie erinnerlich, grenzte Konstantin d. Gr. die *Externa* von den *Interna* ab, indem er sich selbst als einen ἐπίσκοπος τῶν ἐκτός bezeichnete, d. h. ein Organ, das die Oberaufsicht über die äußeren Dinge (der Kirche) innehatte, wie etwa Berufung von allgemeinen Konzilien, Gerichtsbarkeit, Festsetzung von öffentlichen Feiertagen usw., während den Bischöfen die Oberaufsicht über die inneren Angelegenheiten (der Kirche) zukommen sollte, worunter er eben Glaubenssachen, Religionsedikte, kurzum Dogmen und Lehren verstand[40]). In Paranthese sei vermerkt, daß kein spätrömischer Kaiser für die dogmatisch-innere Sphäre der Kirche Interesse gezeigt hatte. Das geschah erst während der Regierungszeit von Kaiser Zeno und Anastasius am Ende des fünften Jahrhunderts aus Anlaß der Veröffentlichung des Henotikon (482). Vergleicht man nun die in § 8 des PWD enthaltenen Jurisdiktionsrechte, die dem noch nicht geweihten Papst zustehen, so springt die sachliche Verwandtschaft mit den konstantinischen *Externa* sofort in die Augen und damit auch die sich von ihnen abhebenden *Interna*, die zum Gegenstand haben die Sakramente, Dogmen, die Religiosität als solche, kurzum das religiöse Innenleben des Christen, das unzertrennlich mit der Gnade verknüpft ist. Diese wiederum kann nur durch die dazu ausgewiesenen Organe vermittelt werden, die den für die Gnadenerweise notwendigen kirchlichen Ordo besitzen[41]). Jurisdiktion im richtig verstandenen Sinne ist in der *potestas ordinis* nicht enthalten.

Diese Erkenntnis besagt selbstverständlich nicht, daß sich die Verfasser und Interpreten des PWD an das konstantinische Schema anzulehnen versuchten. Daß dieses nichtsdestoweniger bekannt war, läßt sich recht überzeugend aus dem Text des Krönungsgebetes anläßlich der Königskrönung nachweisen. Im Mainzer Ordo von ca. 960, der übrigens in das römisch-deutsche Pontifikale eingegangen war, spricht

---

[40]) Konstantins herrscherliche Stellung gegenüber der Kirche ruhte auf deren Charakter als öffentlich anerkannter Körperschaft, weshalb das *ius publicum* in seiner Ulpianischen Formulierung zum Zuge kam. Einzelheiten über den Körperschaftscharakter bei Albert Ehrhardt, Das Corpus Christi und die Korporation im spätrömischen Recht, ZRG Rom. Abt. 70 (1953) S. 299ff., und 71 (1954), S. 21ff., bes. 37ff.; Walter Ullmann, Scholarship and Politics in the Middle Ages, Collected Studies, Band III, London 1978, Kap. I.

[41]) Es handelt sich um die von der Doktrin später entwickelte Unterscheidung des *forum externum* vom *forum internum*. Die begriffliche Bestimmung *forum* ist an sich kennzeichnend.

der Coronator beim Aufsetzen der Krone folgende Worte: *Accipe coronam regni* ... ut, sicut nos in interioribus *pastores rectoresque animarum intelligimur*, tu quoque in exterioribus *verus Dei cultor* ... *defensor regnique* ... *semper appareas*[42]). Also auch hier genau dieselbe Scheidung der *Externa* von den *Interna*, und es ist sicherlich nicht zu gewagt zu behaupten, daß jedenfalls bei der Interpretation des § 8 die (später übliche) Scheidung der *potestas iurisdictionis* von der *potestas ordinis* der früheren Scheidung in *Externa* und *Interna* nahesteht. Die Auslegung der Stelle bei den mittelalterlichen Kanonisten unterstützt die hier vorgetragene Auffassung sehr erheblich.

III. Läßt sich eine allgemeine Regel aus diesen Feststellungen ableiten? Die Frage kann nur im positiven Sinne beantwortet werden. Der im § 8 getroffenen Verfügung muß symptomatische Bedeutung beigemessen werden. Der das Papsttum tragende Herrschaftsgedanke ist, genau wie das konstantinische Schema, im monokratischen Grundsatz verwurzelt. In der juristischen Struktur des Herrschaftsgrundsatzes besteht kein Unterschied zwischen dem (heidnischen und späteren christlichen) Kaiser und dem Nachfolger Petri. Beiden Herrschern ist gemeinsam das ihnen zur Verfügung stehende Herrschaftsmittel, und das ist das Recht. Der Grundsatz der herrscherlichen Rechtssetzung fließt beim Papst aus dem ererbten petrinischen Amt, das von allem Anfang an als eine *gubernatio* verstanden wurde. In der Tat war der Kaiser ebenso ein *gubernator* wie der Papst, obgleich Grund und Zweck der *gubernatio* vollends verschieden waren.

Der grundsätzliche Unterschied zwischen beiden liegt in dem Wesen der von ihnen beherrschten Gesellschaft oder Körperschaft. Für den Kaiser war sie das römische Reich schlechthin, das eine natürlich entwickelte und historisch gewordene Dimension besaß, weshalb auch der über sie herrschende Kaiser sogleich beim Herrschaftsantritt die volle monokratische Funktion innehatte. Anders beim Papsttum. Der Papst beherrschte die eigenständige öffentliche Körperschaft der Gläubigen

---

[42]) Dazu Ullmann (wie Anm. 39) Kap. XII Anm. 24. Dieser Gebetstext findet sich auch unverändert in dem kurialen Zeremonienbuch des 14. Jahrhunderts, siehe Bernhard Schimmelpfennig, Die Zeremonienbücher der römischen Kurie im Mittelalter (Bibliothek des deutschen Historischen Instituts in Rom, Band XL) Tübingen 1973, Nr. XIV b, 17, S. 178. Derselbe Krönungstext mit gleichem Wortlaut ist enthalten in dem bis in dieses Jahrhundert gültigen Pontificale Romanum, ed. Venetiis 1836, S. 147.

— die *congregatio* (oder das *corpus*) *fidelium* — verstanden als die Kirche oder die Christenheit. Diese hatte kein natürlich sich selbst entwickelndes und entfaltendes Wesen, denn sie ging auf eine spezifische göttliche Stiftung zurück, woraus sich der fundamentale Gegensatz zu einem Kaiserreich (oder auch Königreich) sogleich von selbst ergab. Die für die Kirche geltenden Normen und Grundsätze waren letzten Endes göttlichen Ursprungs. Deshalb gehörte zum Inbegriff der vollkommenen Leitung dieser Körperschaft noch eine zusätzliche Gewalt, die buchstäblich geistlich war und im Ordo ihren sichtbaren Ausdruck fand.

Mit anderen Worten, das Herrschaftsmittel, das Recht, bedarf im Rahmen der Papstherrschaft noch einer Ergänzung, weil sie nicht nur (wie die kaiserliche oder königliche Herrschaft) die äußeren *(Externa)*, sondern auch die inneren *(Interna)* Dinge umfaßte. Es lag im Wesen dieser Körperschaft begründet, daß neben die Jurisdiktionsgewalt noch die *potestas ordinis* zu treten hatte. Für die volle Entfaltung der *congregatio fidelium* ist daher die Gnadenspendung wesentlich, und diese wiederum hat zur Voraussetzung den entsprechenden Ordo. Als Gemeinschaft oder Körperschaft der Gläubigen hebt sich die Kirche, wie gerade dieser Zusammenhang zeigt, buchstäblich fundamental in Ursprung, Entstehung und Zielsetzung von einem weltlich fundierten Reich ab, das als solches keine spezifisch qualifizierten, d. h. geweihten Gnadenvermittler nötig hat. Daraus erklärt sich unschwer der Unterschied in der herrscherlichen Stellung des (christlichen) weltlichen Herrschers und des Papstes. Das Papsttum war eben eine Herrschaftsinstitution sui generis. Erst in der Ausübung der Doppelfunktion, der *potestas iurisdictionis* und der *potestas ordinis*, manifestiert sich der päpstliche Herrschaftsgedanke in seiner Fülle und Vollendung[43]). Man kann in diesem

[43]) Angesichts der gewiß sehr erheblichen Bedeutung des § 8 des PWD, der an sich nur festhält, was jedem Papst vermöge seiner erbrechtlichen Stellung *(haeres beati Petri)* zusteht, ist es ein dringendes Forschungsanliegen, die vielen mittelalterlichen Päpste, die keinen höheren Rang als den eines Diakons zur Zeit ihrer Wahl hatten, gründlich zu untersuchen, wie sie ihre Funktionen zwischen Wahl und Konsekration (Thronbesteigung) ausübten. Einige Hinweise auf die Probleme op. cit. (oben Anm. 33), S. 251 Anm. 82. Zu den dortigen Bemerkungen über Innozenz III. wäre jetzt hinzuzufügen, daß nach der nunmehr maßgeblichen Edition seines Registers zwar das Protokoll und Eschakotoll auch noch nicht erstellt werden können, aber dem Inhalt gemäß in mindestens 22 Schreiben, die mit Sicherheit vor dem 22. Februar 1198, seinem Konsekrationstag, abgefertigt wurden, genau dieselben Anordnungen, Befehle, Vorschriften usw., erteilt werden, kurz Rechtsmaßnahmen enthalten, die sich in nichts von den folgenden

Zusammenhang von einer notwendigen Verklammerung dieser beiden *potestates* sprechen. Die erstere genügt zwar zur zeitweiligen Ausübung der päpstlichen Herrschaftsfunktion — wie das PWD niederlegte — aber zur Vervollkommnung des päpstlichen Herrschaftsamtes bedarf es noch des entsprechenden Ordo, der hier der bischöfliche war. Symbolisch drückte sich diese Vorläufigkeit oder Unvollständigkeit der Papstfunktion in der Halbbulle aus, wie Lehre, Praxis und Gesetzgebung beweisen[44]).

Das Selbstverständnis des Papsttums, das sich aus dem PWD ablesen läßt, äußert sich auch noch auf andere Weise. Sehr richtig wurde schon vor Jahren die Frage gestellt, warum sich der Papst seit der Mitte des elften Jahrhunderts nicht mit seinen liturgischen Abzeichen begnügte[45]). Die Antwort dürfte nicht schwer sein, vorausgesetzt, daß man das Wesen des Herrschaftsobjekts genügend berücksichtigt. Noch zu allen Zeiten waren Gesellschaft, Herrschaft und Recht miteinander verzahnt. Mit der Lenkung der Kirche als autonomer, öffentlicher Körperschaft aller Christen, einschließlich der Kaiser und Könige, war der Rechtsnachfolger Petri betraut, der sich in zeitgenössischer Art auch als deren

---

unterscheiden. Sehr wahrscheinlich gehören die ersten 26 (Nr. 23 ist bloße Notiz) in diesen Zeitraum zwischen 8. Januar und 22. Februar, denn erst ab Nr. 28 wird das Datum diplomatisch richtig wiedergegeben *(Datum Laterani V Kal. Martii, pontificatus nostri anno primo):* Die Register (wie Anm. 28), Nr. 1—28. Vor allem muß für die Zeit vor 1059 das Translationsverbot für Bischöfe in Rücksicht gestellt werden, auch wenn man sich nicht immer daran hielt. Zum Translationsverbot vgl. Gratian, C. 7, qu. 1, c. 25 (aus dem Konzil von Antioch 341; vgl. Ecclesiae occidentalis monumenta iuris antiquissimi, ed. Cuthbertus Hamilton Turner, tom. II, Oxoniae 1907, S. 294, 295) und c. 31 (aus Leo d. Gr., vgl. JK. 411, PL 54 Sp. 1261). Siehe ferner die römische Synode unter Vorsitz Stephanus III. i. J. 769, die sich mit der Papstwahl befaßte: *Oportebat ut haec sacrosancta domina nostra Romana ecclesia iuxta quod a beato Petro institutum est, rite ordinaretur et in apostolatus culmen unus de cardinalibus presbiteris et diaconibus consecratur* (MGH Concilia I, 86). Der von Jean Mabillon herausgegebene Ordo Romanus VII (PL 78 Sp. 1006) (eine Privatarbeit) schreibt vor, nur ein Priester oder Diakon sei zu wählen, *nam episcopus esse non poterit.* Die im Text versuchte Erklärung könnte sich für das Verständnis des noch immer viel zu wenig erforschten Symbolismus der königlichen, kaiserlichen und päpstlichen Krönungsordines vielleicht als nützlich erweisen.

[44]) Die im Text vorgetragene Ansicht deckt sich vollauf mit der Interpretation von Rufinus und Stephan von Tournai sowie Bazianus, siehe oben Anm. 17, 18, 27. Für die Halbbulle siehe oben bei und in Anm. 28.

[45]) Siehe Hans-Walter Klewitz, Die Krönung des Papstes, ZRG Kan. Abt. 30 (1941), S. 96ff., hier S. 115.

Herrscher auszuweisen hatte. Diese Notwendigkeit erkennt man schon im werdenden Papsttum, als der Papst nach römischem Vorbild für sich den *principatus* beanspruchte. Und im Mittelalter erfüllten Krönung und Thronsetzung dieses Erfordernis[46]). Die autonome *congregatio fidelium* mußte päpstlicher Ansicht zufolge einen Herrscher haben, der alle monokratischen Befugnisse in sich vereinigte, und dies bedeutete vor allem nach römischem Muster unter anderem die Verfügung über das *ius publicum*[47]), das weder begrifflich noch sachlich irgendwelche Schwierigkeiten bereitete. Dementsprechend mußte die herrscherliche Stellung des Papstes auch in symbolischer Gestaltung erscheinen, obwohl diese bloß Ausdrucksform der Herrschaft war. Die Triade von Gesellschaft, Herrschaft, Recht tritt damit im zeitgenössischen Rahmen in leicht erkennbare Erscheinung[48]). Mit Hilfe der symbolischen Abzeichen,

---

[46]) Deshalb waren Krönung, Thronsetzung und Konsekration auswechselbare Begriffe, wie die eben zitierten Stellen zeigen.

[47]) Das klassische Ulpianische Muster in Dig. 1, 1, 1, 2: *Ius publicum in sacris, sacerdotibus et in magistratibus consistit.*

[48]) Es ist im Rahmen dieser Miszelle nicht möglich, auf den Einfluß der zeitbedingten Faktoren einzugehen, aber der Erwähnung sind sie dennoch wert. Die Verfasser des PWD waren alle Zeugen von zwei Ereignissen, denen entscheidende Bedeutung nicht abgesprochen werden kann. Zunächst ist es die endgültige Besiegelung der Entwicklung, die im 5. Jahrhundert anhob und nunmehr den Bruch seit 1054 in formeller und materieller Hinsicht offenbar machte. Neben das Schisma trat dann zwei Jahre später der unerwartet frühe Tod Heinrichs III. Das Papsttum sah sich entledigt der von ihm als drückend empfundenen Macht der deutschen Herrscher. Dazu kam die Minderjährigkeit Heinrichs IV., und die schwache Regentschaft der Königsmutter. Genau zur selben Zeit war der feurige Kardinal Humbert mit der Fertigstellung seines großen Werkes *Adversus simoniacos* beschäftigt. An der Kurie hatten sich in diesen Jahren hellhörige und weitsichtige Männer eingefunden, die mit überragenden Kenntnissen und dem entsprechenden Rüstzeug ausgestattet, eine radikale Kursänderung im Sinne der Verwirklichung schon längst ausgesprochener päpstlicher Herrschaftsgrundsätze forderten. Nur Kurzsichtigkeit kann an dem Zusammentreffen dieser Umstände vorübergehen. Der § 8 des PWD bringt das Selbstverständnis des Papsttums in gesetzgeberischer Form zum Ausdruck. Er darf als jene Maßnahme gedeutet werden, die entscheidend die Verwirklichung der in zahllosen seit dem 5. Jahrhundert erlassenen Dekretalen, Synodalschlüssen und auch in privaten Schriften vertretenen Ansicht vom Papsttum als der die Christenheit beherrschenden Institution des Rechts, wenn nicht bestimmt, so jedenfalls mächtig gefördert hat. Und als das Führungsorgan der westlichen Christenheit, verstanden als eine allumfassende ekklesiologische Körperschaft, bedurfte das Papsttum der seine Funktion symbolisch ausdrückenden äußeren Zeichen.

wie Krönung und Thronsetzung, erhält die herrscherliche Identität des Papsttums schärfere Konturen[49]).

Wiederum anders liegt das Problem beim mittelalterlichen König, der, wie erwähnt, in den Vollbesitz seiner Herrschaftsrechte anläßlich der Salbung gelangt. Vorher war er bloßer *princeps designatus*[50]). Das ist auch leicht erklärlich. Eine Designation verleiht noch kein Recht zur Herrschaft, sondern eine bloße Anwartschaft darauf. In seinem Wesen war das mittelalterliche Königtum Gottesgnadentum, denn der König war *Dei gratia* Herrscher[51]), und dieser Gnade wird er erst teilhaftig vermöge der Salbung. Der Papst andererseits war *haeres beati Petri*, d. h. er ererbte als Rechtsnachfolger Petri dessen Amt[52]), und in dieser Funktion bedurfte seine Herrschaft keiner weiteren Ergänzung, wenn sie auch als solche bloß zeitweilige Dauer haben sollte. Die auf dem Erbrecht ruhende und daher ausschließlich juristisch faßbare Herrschaft des Papstes macht verständlich, warum die Papstkrönung und Thronsetzung vom Rechtsstandpunkt aus gesehen nur eine deklaratorische Bedeutung hatten[53]),

---

[49]) Auf ganz ähnlicher Ebene und noch schärfer profiliert liegt die universalmonarchische Gesetzgebung Innozenz' III. im 4. Laterankonzil, dessen erster Titel *De summa trinitate et fide catholica* identisch war mit dem, den Justinians erster Titel im Codex trug. Von nun ab werden alle amtlichen Dekretalensammlungen bis hinunter zu den Klementinen diese Überschrift des ersten Titels tragen. Zu dieser Erscheinung vgl. Albert Hauck, Rezeption und Umbildung der allgemeinen Synode im Mittelalter, Historische Vierteljahrschrift 10 (1907) S. 465—482, hier 468—472; vgl. noch W. Ullmann, Principles of Government and Politics in the Middle Ages, 4. Aufl., London 1978, S. 96f.

[50]) Das hat Heinrich Mitteis, Die deutsche Königswahl, ihre Rechtsgrundlage bis zur Goldenen Bulle, 2. Aufl., Brünn, 1944, klassisch gezeigt. Vgl. noch oben bei und in Anm. 10. Genau dasselbe Bild ergibt sich bei der Kaiserkrönung. Dort spricht der Ordo vom *rex (in imperatorem electus)* bis zu der Salbung und dem Friedenskuß am Hochaltar. Erst dann beginnt die vom Papst zelebrierte Messe mit dem Gebet *Deus regnorum omnium*, das zum ersten Mal den Kaiser als solchen benennt; vgl. etwa den Ordo XVIII in Ordines coronationis imperialis, hg. Reinhard Elze, Fontes iuris Germanici antiqui, Hannover 1960, S. 77, Nr. 19—20. In dem diesem Ordo wahrscheinlich voraufgegangenen Ordo XVI wird der deutsche König erst anläßlich der der Krönung folgenden Szepterübergabe durch den Papst Kaiser genannt, ebda S. 44, Nr. 41.

[51]) Siehe dazu Ullmann, Principles (wie Anm. 49), S. 117f.

[52]) Einzelheiten in Ders., op. cit. (oben Anm. 33) Kap. IV.

[53]) Mit Recht wurde die Bedeutungslosigkeit der Papstkrönung hervorgehoben von Klewitz (wie oben Anm. 45) S. 119f. Vgl. noch W. Ullmann, Growth of papal government in the Middle Ages, 3./4. Aufl., London 1970, S. 311ff. Andererseits wurde der (westlichen) Kaiserkrönung durch den Papst konstitutive Bedeu-

genau wie drüben in Konstantinopel auch der Kaiserkrönung keine konstitutive Bedeutung zugesprochen wurde. Der Bereich des päpstlich ererbten Herrschaftsrechts ist freilich fest umrissen — alles, was Sakramente, Weihen, Dogmen usw. angeht, also die *Interna*, ist davon ausgenommen. Eine öffentliche Körperschaft kann jedoch ihrem Wesen nach nur kraft des sich auf die *Externa* beziehenden Rechts gelenkt werden. Und dieser Gedanke drückte sich in der *gubernatio* der *navicula Petri* aus, wie man häufig genug in den Quellen lesen kann. Das PWD in seinem § 8 spiegelt getreulich den grundsätzlichen Charakter des Papsttums als einer vornehmlichen Herrschaftsinstitution wider.

Es obliegt der kanonistischen Forschung, die hier nur skizzenhaft angedeuteten zahlreichen und ungeklärten Probleme integral zu untersuchen und damit unsere Kenntnis vom mittelalterlichen Papsttum als Ausdrucksform monokratischer Funktion im öffentlichen Leben zu bereichern. Und diese kanonistische Forschung ist in der glücklichen Lage, auf dem breiten, sicheren und festen Fundament zu ruhen, das Stephan Kuttner in meisterhafter, unübertroffener Art erstellt hat. Kein anderer Kanonist hat uns so viele neue Erkenntnisse vermittelt. Ihm für sein Werk, das weit über die Kanonistik hinaus befruchtende Wirkung auf die gesamte Mediävistik ausgeübt hat, in dem Organ zu danken, in dem er vor genau zehn Lustren die ersten Früchte seiner Forschung vorlegte, ist eine willkommene Verpflichtung.

---

tung bis zum Erlaß *Licet iuris* Ludwigs d. Bayern und der Goldenen Bulle beigelegt.

IV

ALEXANDER III AND THE CONQUEST OF IRELAND
A NOTE ON THE BACKGROUND

In at least four separate communications Alexander III warmly approved the military conquest of Ireland by King Henry II of England. Three of these communications were issued at Tusculum and dated 20 September 1172. The one is directed to the Irish bishops and the apostolic legate in Ireland [1] in which Alexander expresses his gratification at the measures taken by Henry II who « stirred by divine inspiration » had subdued a « most undisciplined and untamed nation »; the addressees are enjoined to render all possible assistance to the king « so great a man and so devout a son of the Church » in order to maintain and preserve that land and to extirpate the filthiness of such great abominations as could be found in Ireland.[2] In the letter to the king himself Alexander points out that he was made aware of the Irish abominations by the apostolic legate, the archbishops and bishops as well as by Ralph, the archdeacon of Llandaff; the pope pays tribute to Henry for subjugating so barbarous a nation « by the working of divine grace extirpating the filthiness of these abominations ».[3] Alexander expresses his great joy about the king's success which initiated the moral improvement of the Irish, « so that they may receive the whole discipline of the Christian faith to the glory of the king's unfading crown and the health of their souls ». The pope furthermore expresses his conviction that the king had been impelled by religious fervour and had undertaken the campaign for the remission of his sins « so that he may be worthy of the

[1] *Regesta Pontificum Romanorum ab condita ecclesia ad annum post Christum natum,* ed. PH. JAFFÉ - S. LOEWENFELD, Lipsiae 1885 (reprint Graz 1956), [abbreviated *JL*], n.° 12164.

[2] Text in TH. RYMER, *Foedera, conventiones, litterae et acta publica inter reges Angliae et alios,* I. Londini 1816, 45; J.P. MIGNE, *Patrologia Latina* (abbreviated *PL*), CC, 885B - 886B.

[3] *JL* 12162. Text in RYMER, *Foedera . . . ,* I, 45; *PL* CC, 883B - 884C; GIRALDUS CAMBRENSIS, *Expugnatio Hibernica,* II, 5 ed. J. D. DIMOCK, *Opera,* V, London 1867 (Rolls Series), 317-318; ID., *De instructione principum libri III,* ed. J.S. BREWER, London 1846, 52-53; english translation in E. CURTIS - J.B. MCDOWELL, *Irish Historical Documents,* London 1943, 20. Despite the relevance for his theme this letter of Alexander III is not referred to by L. WECKMANN, *Las Bullas Alexandrinas de 1493 y la Teoria Politica del Papado Medieval. Estudio de la supremacia papal sobre islas 1091 - 1493,* Mexico City, 1949.

eternal crown ».[4] The last communication of the same date went to the king and princes of Ireland. They were bidden to hold fast to the oaths which they had taken to the king: in the interests of the Christian religion they should show themselves submissive and devoted to the king in order to win abundant favour.[5]

In addition to these letters mention must be made of a communication which is known only second-hand in the work of Gerald of Wales.[6] It cannot without further examination be accepted as an authentic rendering, and this mainly for diplomatic reasons: the king is here addressed in the second person plural which is a most unusual manner of addressing a king by the papal chancery.[7] Nevertheless, despite the doubts which the transmitted text raises, there can be no sensible reservations about the inherent veracity of the subject matter itself. For this « Privilege » substantially repeats the essence of the three letters just summarized and can be considered a formal ratihabitio. The « Privilege » thereby implicitly refers to the letter which Alexander's immediate predecessor, Pope Adrian IV, had sent to King Henry II. The most likely explanation of this entry in Gerald is that it conflates two things: Alexander's letter to Henry II[8] and the authorization of the appointment of Henry's son, John, as king of Ireland.[9] Indeed, two witnesses can be called upon to bear out the essential substance of Gerald's report.[10]

4 « Ita etiam, cooperante Domino, per te praedicta gens ad tuae sempiternae gloriae coronam immarcessibilem et suae salutis profectum, abiecta spurcitia peccatorum, omnimodam christianae religionis suscipiat disciplinam. Rogamus itaque regiam excellentiam, monemus et exhortamur ... quod laudabiliter incoepisti, tuum propensius animum robores et confortes et gentem illam ad cultum christianae fidei per potentiam tuam revoces et conserves, ut sicut pro tuorum venia peccatorum, adversus eam tantum laborem, ut credimus, assumpsist, ita etiam de suae salutis profectu coronam merearis suscipere sempiternam ». This passage, it should be noted, is suffused with allusions to, and borrowings from, prayer texts as used in the royal coronation orders.

5 *JL* 12163. Text in RYMER, *Foedera ...*, I, 45 and *PL* CC, 884D - 885B. English translation in E. CURTIS - J. B. MCDOWELL, *Irish Historical Documents*, 22.

6 *JL* 12174.

7 GIRALDUS CAMBRENSIS, *De instructione* (as. n. 3), 53-54: « Sicut a quibusdam impetratum (*scil.* hoc privilegium) asseritur aut configitur, ab aliis autem unquam impetratum fuisse negatur ». See also LOEWENFELD, ad *JL* 12174. Further JACOBUS USSERIUS (USHER), *Veterum epistolarum sylloge*, Paris 1655, 80 (from Giraldus). J.F. O'DOHERTY, *Rome and the Anglo-Norman invasion of Ireland*, in « Irish Ecclesiastical Record », 42 (1933), 133-145 at 143, has pointed out the diplomatic irregularities.

8 *JL* 12162.

9 *JL* 12174.

10 *Chronica Magistri Rogeri de Houedene*, ed. W. STUBBS, II, London 1869 (Rolls Series), 133 ad annum 1177: « Deinde venit rex Oxeneford et in generali

There are some features in these communications which warrant a few observations. Alexander is anxious to stress the rights of the Roman Church in regard to conquered Ireland because it was an island. Indeed, this is made a very special point in the letter to King Henry. Intimately linked with this is the emphasis upon the preservation and, if possible, the enlargement of the rights of the Roman Church. A cursory reading of this communication might lead to the conclusion that Henry undertook the campaign in the interests, if not of the Roman Church, at any rate of the Christian religion. The lavish praise which Henry here received from the pope is certainly remarkable when one considers that it was just 1½ years after Becket had been murdered and exactly four months after the agreement reached at Avranches on 21 May 1172 whereby the bitter conflict between king and archbiscop ended.[11] A perusal of these letters of September 1172 without the knowledge of the immediate past would not suggest the serious tension which had alienated the king and his archbishop. That the pope underscored so conspicuously the rights of the see of St Peter, may therefore be due to the very recent experience which he had with this king. On the other hand, there is nowhere any mentioning of a titledeed on the part of the king. The question must be faced: upon what basis — other than religious considerations — could Henry II have embarked upon this venture? This question brings us to the all important antecedent documentary evidence which makes abundantly clear that the initiative in conquering Ireland came from Henry himself and was conveyed to the papacy by no lesser a man than John of Salisbury.

In this context some hitherto unanswered — or even unperceived — problems must be faced. While the papal documents

concilio ibidem celebrato constituit Johannem filium suum regem in Hybernia, concessione et confirmatione Alexandri summi pontificis ». Further *Gesta Regis Henrici Secundi Benedicti Abbatis,* ed. W. STUBBS, I, London 1867 (Rolls Series), 161: « Postea praecepit ei (*scil.* Earl of Chester), ut iret in Hiberniam ad subjiciendam eam sibi et Johanni filio suo, cui eam concesserat. Perquisierat enim ab Alexandro summo pontifice quod liceret ei filium suum quem vellet coronare et regem facere de Hibernia ». Loewenfeld dated this Alexandrian letter *Quoniam* (*JL* 12174) « c. 1172 », although there is reason to think that it was issued later. O'DOHERTY, *Rome . . .*, 131, 144, has an inaccurate *JL* number (13392) and suggests the year 1175. *JL* 13392 refers to Dublin and can be dated precisely: 20 April 1179.

[11] For the terms of the compromise of Avranches see *The Letters of John of Salisbury,* ed. C. BROOKE, II, Oxford 1979, ep. 309, 752-755; it is the letter which Henry II himself wrote to the bishop of Exeter with the details of the arrangements. W.L. WARREN, *Henry II,* London 1973, 198 dryly remarks that Alexander's « reference to Henry's respect for the rights of the Church must have been greeted with astonishment if not cynicism by those who read Becket's correspondence ».

clearly show the juristic basis of the papacy's dispositions — we shall return to them briefly — these same documents contain not the slightest hint concerning any royal title-deed. This is all the more remarkable as the go-between John of Salisbury in the clearest possible terms and most explicitly mentions the title-deed upon which Henry II relied. The explanation why this matter has not aroused any interest in historical research[12] can be sought in the misunderstanding of the passage of John of Salisbury's account which uses perfectly innocuous and commonly employed juristic terminology.

The problem is simply this. At the end of the *Metalogicon* John of Salisbury remarks that he was instrumental in procuring from his papal friend Adrian IV — the English pope — a positive response concerning Ireland. The passage runs:

> Ad preces meas illustri regi Anglorum, Henrico secundo, concessit et dedit Hiberniam iure hereditario possidendam, sicut litterae ipsius testantur in hodiernum diem.[13]

With astonishing unanimity the passage is rendered in translation as if Adrian IV had conceded to Henry the hereditary possession of Ireland or had made Ireland a hereditary fee. In other words, the right of inheritance was a papal grant and consequently referred to the future.[14]

In order to understand this statement of John of Salisbury it is necessary to realize how close his relations with Adrian IV had always been, as he himself only a few lines before the passage quoted, makes perfectly plain — and in parenthesis we should note that this passage was written by John in October 1159 when Adrian was no longer alive. Indeed, John understandably boasted of his friendship with his papal compatriot and in mock modesty

[12] With the sole exception of J.A. WATT, *The Church and the Two Nations in Medieval Ireland* (Cambridge Studies in Medieval Life and Thought III), Cambridge 1970, 35, n. 1. The point was first raised by W. ULLMANN, *On the influence of Geoffrey of Monmouth in English History*, in *The Church and the Law in the earlier Middle Ages* (Collected Studies I), London 1975, Ch. 13, 257-276, at 272.

[13] *Metalogicon*, ed. C.C.J. WEBB, Oxonii 1929, IV, 42 (p. 217, lines 15-18).

[14] For instance C.C.J. WEBB, *John of Salisbury*, London 1932, 97; and following him O'DOHERTY, *Rome . . .*, 131-132; cf. also the modern translator of the whole work who goes even so far as to say that Adrian « granted and entrusted Ireland to the illustrious king of the English, Henry II, to be possessed by him and his heirs . . . », *The Metalogicon of John of Salisbury*, translated with an introduction and notes by D.D. McGARRY, Berkeley - Los Angeles 1955, 274. See also WARREN, *Henry II*, 195. For a contemporary witness see Benedict of Peterborough, cited below n. 64.

wrote of Adrian « who took pleasure in inviting me to his table and, against my will, made me have common meals and drinks with him ».[15] That John was a frequent visitor to the papal court, is a well-established fact and of quite especial significance was his sojourn with Adrian at Benevento in 1155.[16] But he also entertained very close relations with the archbishop of Canterbury, Thomas Becket, and the royal court. John was not only an acute observer of the contemporary scene, but had also close contact with the most learned personalities in England and more especially in France where Chartres was, so to speak, his intellectual home and where he later also became bishop. All these points must be borne in mind in the present context. He was one of the most penetrating and acute contemporary minds versed in ancient literature and potently endowed with intellectual capacities of quite unusual dimensions: the confidant of royalty, of high clerical circles and of the papacy, indeed a singularly unique combination.

Yet when one compares the papal letter to which he specifically refers in the passage cited, with his own text as well as with the text of Alexander's letters, one will notice the absence of the very term iure hereditario in all papal communications — assuredly remarkable, always provided that the common interpretation and translation of this terminology are correct. It is agreed on all sides — and rightly so — that Alexander's letters necessarily presuppose the letter of his predecessor in this matter, for without taking into account *Laudabiliter* they present insuperable difficulties. The execution of Henry II's plan to invade Ireland conveyed by John of Salisbury had been merely postponed in 1155 but was actually effected in 1171-1172. Whereas the terminology of iure hereditario is missing in all papal documents, they as well as John of Salisbury are in perfect harmony concerning the papal basis. John continues his statement by saying:

> Nam omnes insule de iure antiquo ex donatione Constantini, qui eam fundavit et dotavit, dicuntur ad Romanam ecclesiam pertinere.[17]

15 *Metalogicon,* IV, 42 (p. 217): « Et cum Romanus pontifex esset, me in propria mensa gaudebat habere convivam; et eundem ciphum et discum sibi et michi volebat et faciebat, me renitente, esse communem ».

16 For the significance of his sojourn at Benevento in 1155 see W. ULLMANN, *Jurisprudence in the Middle Ages,* London 1980 (Collected Studies IV), Ch. 6, 530-531.

17 *Metalogicon,* IV, 42 (p. 217, line 2).

This sentence in fact reproduces almost verbatim the statement in the letter of Pope Adrian to King Henry II — *Laudabiliter* — in which the so-called omni-insular doctrine was stated succinctly.[18] When Adrian IV informed Henry in 1155, John of Salisbury was still in his company:

> Sane Hiberniam et omnes insulas quibus sol iustitiae Christus illuxit et quae documenta fidei Christianae ceperunt, ad ius beati Petri et sanctae Romanae ecclesiae, quod tua et nobilitas recognoscit, non est dubium pertinere.[19]

There can be no doubt that jurisdiction over Ireland, because it was an island, was based on the alleged disposition by Constantine. Since Alexander's communications depend on *Laudabiliter,*[20] a few more observations are advisable. Alexander's letters convey, as already remarked, the strong impression that Henry's expedition was undertaken in order to advance the Christian religion and also the interests of the Church in general and of the Roman Church in particular. These implied motives as well as the carefully expressed omni-insular standpoint in Alexander's letter to Henry[21] assume their full significance only in connexion with Adrian's *Laudabiliter.* In itself this dependence of the Alexandrian communications of

18 For this see WECKMANN, *Las Bullas Alexandrinas . . .*, 26-44. The doctrine makes its first appearance in the pontificate of Urban II (*JL* 5448 of 3 June 1091), see WECKMANN, 37-43. The reference is to the endowment of diverse islands in the Donation of Constantine. See *Constitutum Constantini,* ed. H. FUHRMANN, *Monumenta Germaniae Historica* (= *MGH*): *Fontes Iuris Germanici Antiqui in usum scholarum,* X (1968), 86, line 206.

19 *JL* 10056. Text in *PL* CLXXXVIII, 1441; RYMER, *Foedera . . .*, I, 19. It is too little known that Peter of Blois incorporated *Laudabiliter* in his own collection of letters. See PETRUS BLESENSIS, *Epistolae, PL* CCVII, *Ep.* 226, col. 515 (Migne did not reprint it, but simply referred the reader to the letters of Adrian). This incorporation has all the greater significance as Peter of Blois was at the crucial time, that is, the early seventies, in the service of Henry II and was also chancellor of Becket's immediate successor, Archbishop Richard of Dover, from 1173. For this see C.L. KINGSFORD, *Peter of Blois,* in *Dictionary of National Biography,* XV, Oxford 1938², 932-939 at 933b. Peter assuredly realized the fundamental importance of this document to which he evidently had ready access either in the royal or in the archiepiscopal archives.

20 It is certainly of some interest that neither J. HALLER, *Das Papstum. Idee und Wirklichkeit,* III, Urach 1965, 167f., nor F.X. SEPPELT, *Geschichte der Päpste,* III, München 1956, 285-286, mention the role of Alexander III in the conquest of Ireland. See also A. GWYNN, *Ireland,* in *Lexikon für Theologie und Kirche,* V, Freiburg 1960, 754.

21 *JL* 12162: « Quia . . . Romana ecclesia aliud ius habet in insula quam in terra magna et continua, nos eam de tuae devotionis fervore spem fiduciamque tenentes, quod iura ipsius ecclesiae non solum conservare velis, sed etiam ampliare . . . ».

September 1172[22] is not at all surprising, not only because of the comparatively short interval of time, but above all because it was the later Pope Alexander III himself who as chancellor Roland under Adrian IV had been engaged in chancery business since 1153 and acted as draftsman of the official papal correspondence.[23] Both in his capacity as chancellor and as a graduate, if not also teacher, of Bologna University, he had full command of canon law — notably Gratian's *Decretum*[24] — as well as of the antecedent papal correspondence.[25] In this sense as also in other respects Adrian's and Alexander's pontificates constitute one unit. Style, diction, substance and above all the details in the relevant documents are identical. Neither the terminology nor the idea underlying the ius hereditarium nor any allusion to it occur in any of the papal communications.

The question therefore arises, in what sense and why John of Salisbury came to employ the highly technical term of the ius hereditarium, and this in so sensitive a matter. By what manner of means could the Anglo-Norman kings — or for that matter the Anglo-Saxon kings — be said to have a claim to Ireland by « rightful inheritance »? For this terminology can and does refer to an already established right of inheritance, in other words, the reference is to the past, and not to the future. From the purely juristic point of view it is quite impossible to construct a future « rightful inheritance ». The sole question at issue is the capacity of Henry as heir, because he himself has the ius hereditarium. If the intention had been to create this ius — as it is unanimously held to be the case — that is, to turn Ireland into a hereditary fee, the language would have been quite different. In other words, if

22 *JL* 12162-12164.

23 Cf. also *JL* II, 103: with the exception of three months' absence in 1157 conditioned by his celebrated attendance at the meeting in Besançon in the autumn of that year, for which see also W. ULLMANN, *The Papacy and Political Ideas in the Middle Ages*, London 1976 (Collected Studies II), Ch. 4, 108-110. Further details P. PASCHINI, *Alessandro III*, in *Enciclopedia Cattolica*, I, Città del Vaticano 1948, 740-742 at 790; P. BREZZI, *Alessandro III*, in *Dizionario Biografico degli Italiani*, II, Roma 1961, 183-189 at 184a.

24 GRATIAN, *Decretum*, Dist. 96, c. 14 which contains the *Constitutum*. The academic activity of Roland is questioned by J.T. NOONAN, Jr., *Who was Rolandus?*, in *Law, Church and Society. Essays in honor of Stephan Kuttner*, Philadelphia 1977, 22-48, who holds that the author of the *Stroma* (hitherto unquestionably ascribed to Roland) was not identical with the later chancellor and pope, but was a contemporary with the same name.

25 Especially Urban II's letters which were evidently easily available in the papal archives.

by these papal dispositions a future « rightful inheritance » had been intended, both Adrian and Alexander would have made themselves perfectly clear by stipulating that to the legitimate haeredes or rightful successores (and the like) should be accorded the same position in regard to Ireland as Henry II enjoyed on the basis of the papal « grants ».[26] It is noteworthy that in none of the documents is there mention of anybody else but Henry II personally.

The juristic impossibility of interpreting the ius hereditarium in a future sense is powerfully buttressed by the invariable usage of this terminology. Only a few instances can here be given, chosen from a great variety of sources which deal with wholly disparate conditions and topics yet, in none is there any future reference intended or implied. Without exception the reference is always to the past. In the fifth century Pelagius considered that the faith « hereditario iure descendit » from the apostles.[27] In the same fifth century the Roman synod of 19 November 465 used the term in a negative sense. The synod prohibited the designation of an episcopal successor, in order to avoid the assumption that « episcopalis honor hereditarium ius putetur ».[28] The coronation rituals in the medieval period are particularly good witnesses to the usage of the term in the past sense. There is, for instance, the enthronement formula which originally dates from the ninth century and was incorporated into virtually all medieval royal coronation orders. The beginning of this very solemn formula, said by the archbishop when performing the coronation, runs:

> Sta et retine amodo locum ... hereditario iure tibi delegatum ...[29]

Again, in a negative sense the concept appears in the so-called Aachen coronation ordo of the tenth century when the archbishop of Cologne says this prayer over the king immediately after putting the crown on his head:

26 As indeed Benedict of Peterborough writes, see the quotation below n. 64, though his view finds no support in the documentary evidence. It is nevertheless a good example of a layman's interpretation of technical juristic terminology. See also below n. 38.

27 Quoted from J. FELLERMAYR, *Tradition und Sukzession im Lichte des römisch-antiken Erbdenkens. Untersuchungen zu den lateinischen Vätern bis zu Leo dem Grossen,* München 1979, 77 at n. 225.

28 *Epistolae Pontificum Romanorum genuinae,* ed. A. THIEL, Brunsbergiae 1869, 162f, cf. also 164 and 167.

29 C. ERDMANN, *Forschungen zur politischen Ideenwelt des Frühmittelalters,* ed. F. BAETHGEN, Berlin 1951, 89.

> ... ita retine amodo locum regium quem non hereditario iure nec paterna successione ... noscas delegatum, maxime per auctoritatem Dei omnipotentis.[30]

In the same tenth century the Quedlinburg Annals refer to the death of King Henry I of Germany and the succession of Otto I:

> Henricus rex obiit 6 Non. Juli ... cuius filius Otto pacificus ... iure hereditario paternis eligitur succedere regnis.[31]

The Second Lateran Council decreed in its sixteenth chapter that nobody should claim ecclesiastical offices, churches or chaplaincies by right of inheritance.[32] The *Historia Regum* ascribed to Symeon of Durham asserted that King Henry I of England had a claim to Flanders iure hereditario.[33] Ivo of Chartres employed this terminology in no wise different from that of the writers and sources cited:

> In regem est consecratus (*scil.* Ludovicus VI), cui iure hereditario regnum competebat.[34]

And in the *Gesta Philippi Augusti* Rigord declared that Philip « Arturium militem fecit tradens ei Britanniae comitatum, qui iure hereditario eum contingebat ».[35]

Two further witnesses to the technical use of the ius hereditarium should be quoted. The one is Petrus Comestor, also of the twelfth century, who explaining the Acts of the Apostles

30 *Quellensammlung zur kirchlichen Rechtsgeschichte und zum Kirchenrecht,* ed. E. Eichmann, München-Paderborn-Wien 1925² (reprint 1968), II, 66. Cf. also the Lombard ordo of Milano, 76: « Sta et retine amodo locum, quem hucusque paterna successione tenuisti, hereditario iure tibi delegatum . . . ».

31 *Annales Quedlinburgenses, MGH, Scriptores,* III, 54, lines 35-38.

32 *Conciliorum Oecumenicorum Decreta,* ed. J. Alberigo - J. Dossetti - P.P. Joannou - C. Leonardi - P. Prodi, Bologna 1973³, 201: « Auctoritate prohibemus apostolica ne quis ecclesias praebendas, praepposituras, capellanias aut aliqua ecclesiastica officio, hereditario iure valeat vindicare aut expostulare praesumat ». This is also incorporated in Gratian, *Decretum,* C. VIII, qu. 1, c. 7.

33 Symeon of Durham, *Historia Regum,* ed. T. Arnold, II, London 1885 (Rolls Series), 282. For this work see A. Gransden, *Historical Writing in England c. 550-1307*, London 1974, 148-149.

34 *Epistolae Ivonis Carnotensis episcopi,* ed. L. Delisle, in *Recueil des Historiens des Gaules et de la France,* XV, Paris 1869 (reprint Farnborough 1967), Ep. CXIV, (p. 144B). Ivo of Chartres here justifies the consecration and coronation of King Louis VI in 1108 in this way: « Si enim rationem consulimus, iure in regem est consecratus, cui iure hereditario regnum competebat, et quem communis consensus episcoporum et procerum iampridem elegerat ».

35 Rigord, *Gesta Philippi Augusti,* ed. H.F. Delaborde, I, Paris 1882, 152.

in his *Historia Scholastica* deals with St Paul's Roman citizenship which he inherited from his father:

> Quia pater suus obsequiorum diligentiam sibi comparaverat gratiam Romanorum, et donatus est ab eis Romana libertate, ut putaretur civis Romanus ipse et haeredes sui, et sic iure hereditario habebat Paulus consortium Romanae civilitatis.[36]

The other not unimportant witness is Geoffrey of Monmouth who wrote the « bestseller » of the twelfth century. In is *History of the Kings of Britain* which will engage us presently, there is a statement that is especially important in the present context, dealing as it does with King Arthur: « The justice of his cause encouraged him, for he had a claim by « rightful inheritance » (« iure hereditario »).[37]

These examples — chosen at random — leave little room for doubt that the term and concept of the ius hereditarium consistently referred to an already existing title-deed in the shape of a right of inheritance. No witnesses can be produced who have made this term refer to the future. When this was intended, there was always a reference to successors or heirs, and the like.[38] We can go further and say that John of Salisbury himself also used this very term in the account of how *Laudabiliter* came about in exactly the right and customary sense: it referred to the past.

The correct understanding of this text presupposes that a number of points be taken into account, combined and integrated.

36 PETRUS COMESTOR, *Historia Scholastica*, cap. 101, in *PL* CXCVIII, 1710,

37 *The History of the Kings of Britain,* transl. L. THORPE, Penguin Classics, Harmondsworth 1973, 212; *Historia Regum Britanniae,* ed. A. GRISCOM, London - New York - Toronto 1929, IX, 1 (p. 433): « Commonebat etiam id rectitudo, cum tocius insule monarchiam debuerant hereditario iure obtinere». To quote one more witness from a much later time, that is, the early fifteenth century, the Florentine chancellor Leonardo Bruni, eminent humanist, legist and littérateur, says in his *Laudatio Florentinae Urbis,* ed. TH. KLETTE, *Beiträge zur Geschichte und Litteratur der italienischen Gelehrtenrenaissance,* II, Greifswald 1889, 91: « Quamobrem ad vos quoque, viri Florentini, dominium orbis terrarum iure quodam hereditario seu paternarum rerum possessio pertinet ». The implication which Bruni draws, are not at all dissimilar to those of John of Salisbury.

38 In conformity with the common opinion A. EGGERS, *Die Urkunde Papst Hadrians IV. für König Heinrich II. über die Besetzung Irlands,* Berlin 1922, 56-59 holds that *Laudabiliter* was issued to Henry and his successors, but the instances which she quotes in order to prove that a future right of inheritance was expressed, explicitly and without exception refer to « successores » or « haeredes ». For a clear instance taken from the papal chancery see *JL* 5706 concerning the conferment of legatine powers on Roger I of Sicily. The powers were bestowed on Roger « quod omni vitae tuae tempore vel filii tui Simonis aut alterius qui legittimus tui haeres extiterit... » (*PL* CLI, 506).

First, John of Salisbury always moved in circles which mattered; the passage in his *Metalogicon* is actually a good example, not of his boasting, but of his explaining how it came to pass that he was able to prompt the pope (and hence also his chancellor Roland) to grant the request of Henry.[39] The second point to be borne in mind is that John of Salisbury moved not only in papal, but also in royal circles. *Laudabiliter* itself bears witness to this: through Adrian chancellor Roland perfectly plainly states that King Henry sought the counsel and goodwill of the apostolic see, having contemplated the enlargement of the boundaries of the Church by his entering the island of Ireland, in order to subject its people to law and order and to root out the evil customs prevailing there. It can besaid with every justification that John of Salisbury acted as a messenger or intermediary of his king when he submitted the latter's plan to Adrian at Benevento in 1155.

The third point to be weighed adequately is the council held by Henry II around Michaelmas 1155 at Winchester, where the very conquest of Ireland was the topic of deliberations « cum optimatibus » and where his brother William was envisaged as a donee of Ireland, which had yet to be conquered.[40] Now this council took place in late September 1155 which brings us to the fourth point to be assessed appropriately. John of Salisbury reports that he joined Adrian IV in Apulia and stayed with the pope at Benevento for nearly three months.[41] This is a very important item. Fortunately

[39] See the passage immediately preceding the statement cited above n. 15: « Publicly and privately he, Adrian, made no secret of his friendship with me that he never missed an opportunity to open gladly his thoughts to me » (« Omnibus ille [*scil.* Adrianus] bonis flebilis occidit, sed nulli flebelior quam michi. Cum enim matrem haberet et fratrem uterinum, me quam illos artiori diligebat affectu. Fatebatur etiam publice et secreto, quia me pre omnibus diligebat. Eam de me conceperat opinionem . . . »: *Metalogicon,* IV, 42 (p. 217, lines 6-10).

[40] ROBERT OF TORIGNY, *Chronica Roberti,* ed. R. HOWLETT, IV, London 1889, 186: « Circa festum sancti Michaelis Henricus rex Anglorum habito concilio apud Wincestre, de conquerendo regno Hiberniae et Guillelmo fratri suo dando, cum optimatibus tractavit. Quod quia matri eius imperatrici non placuit, intermissa est ad tempus illa expeditio ». WARREN, *Henry II,* 195 dismisses this notice since Henry « never did much for his brothers ». He holds that the plan was really hatched by the archbishop of Canterbury, Theobald, who wished to extend his jurisdiction over the bishops of the Norse townships in Ireland. I cannot say that this argument is very convincing.

[41] *Ioannis Saresberiensis Episcopi Carnotensis Policratici Libri VIII,* ed. C.C.J. WEBB, Oxonii 1909 (reprint Frankfurt 1965), VI, 24 (p. 67, lines 6-9): « Memini me causa visitandi dominum Adrianum pontificem quartum, qui me in ulteriorem familiaritatem admiserat, profectum in Apuliam, mansique cum eo Beneventi ferme tres menses ».

the itinerary of Adrian can fairly be established. He arrived at Benevento after 31 October 1155 where his first official document was issued on 21 November.[42] There is nothing to militate against the assumption that John of Salisbury set out on his journey from England soon after Michaelmas 1155 and met the pope late October or early November. Lastly, by the year 1155 the *History of the Kings of Britain* by Geoffrey of Monmouth was well known, and especially in the contemporary literary and governmental circles. As has been shown elsewhere, there is hardly any other book which has exercised a more decisive and enduring influence upon English history than this work by Geoffrey.[43] The hero of this book was Arthur who governed a *Grossreich* in the literal sense of the term. His realm stretched from Iceland to the South and North of Europe, including Norway and the Orkney Islands, but what is of great significance in our context is that he had also subdued and invaded Ireland whose King Gilmarus was captured and who surrendered himself entirely to the conqueror. The other princes of Ireland were so stunned by these events that they followed the example of their king.[44] The implied significance of this « historical » contingency related by Geoffrey was clearly that subsequent kings had inherited the power, rule and dominions over all the territories conquered by Arthur, and they included virtually the whole of Europe.[45] As successors of King Arthur the English kings therefore had a hereditary right to these dominions, notably Ireland.

To return to John of Salisbury. No doubt is permissible about his familiarity with Geoffrey of Monmouth's *Historia*. This work was finished between 1136 and 1138 and was soon afterwards

[42] *JL* 10097. The immediately preceding document is dated San Germano, 31 October 1155: *JL* 10096. Adrian did not leave Benevento until 18 July 1136.

[43] Cf. ULLMANN, *Influence* (above n. 12), where a hitherto unknown document served as a basis to determine the influence in three specific spheres. See further C. BROOKE, *Geoffrey of Monmouth as a historian,* in *Church and Government in the Middle Ages. Essays presented to C.R. Cheney,* Cambridge 1976, 77-91 with full bibliography, 77 n. 1.

[44] GEOFFREY OF MONMOUTH, *Historia,* IX, 10 (p. 445). « Adveniente deinde sequenti estate paravit classem suam et adivit hyberniae insulam quam sibi subdere desiderabat. Applicanti autem sibi rex Gilmarus cum innumerabili gente obvios venit contra illum dimicaturus . . . nec mora captus est etiam Gilmarus et deditioni coactus. Unde ceteri principes patriae stupefacti exemplo regis deditionem fecerunt », whereupon Arthur directed his forces to the subjugation of Iceland. For Geoffrey's attention to military matters see now J.O. PRESTWICH, *The military household of the Norman kings,* in « English Historical Review », 96 (1981), 1-36 at 32-34.

[45] Indeed, this was precisely the deduction drawn in the document discussed in the study cited n. 43 at 271-272.

rendered into Anglo-Norman verse.[46] The early French version was apparently eagerly read and utilized by Wace who relied heavily on this fabulous chronicle in his work, which he finished in the crucial year 1155. And Wace, a protégé of Henry II, was actually commissioned by the king. His *Brut* was « a literary form in which the Arthurian legend made its first appearance in English ».[47] The success of Geoffrey's *Historia* was indeed striking; the list of writers in the twelfth and thirteenth centuries who relied on him or queried his findings, is long, and his influence did not end until well into the modern age. « No work before the age of the printed book attained such immediate and astonishing popularity ».[48] That John of Salisbury himself was quite apparently very well acquainted with this book can also be deduced from his being a member of the household of Archbishop Theobald of Canterbury, where he was engaged as secretary or on diplomatic missions. Particular importance must be attached to the consecration of Geoffrey as bishop of St. Asaph in February 1152 by Archbishop Theobald.[49] Furthermore, there are borrowings from Geoffrey in John's works. The designation, for instance, of a king as leo iustitiae is in actual fact used in the prophesies of Merlin as amplified by Geoffrey in his *Historia*,[50] and it recurs in John of Salisbury's *Metalogicon* where he distinguishes King Henry I (of England) by describing him a leo iustitiae.[51] Perhaps more eloquently and persuasively John of Salisbury seems to apply this designation in his *Policraticus*. In obvious dependence on Geoffrey John says:

46 For details and literature see GRANSDEN, *Historical Writing*... 203-209; further J.S.P. TATLOCK, *The legendary history of Britain. Geoffrey of Monmouth's Historia Regum Britanniae and its early vernacular versions*, Berkeley - Los Angeles 1950, 433-436; and BROOKE, 82.

47 W. LEWIS JONES, *The Arthurian Legend* in *Cambridge History of English Literature*, I, Cambridge 1907, 263. Further TATLOCK, 467-472, and R.A. CALDWELL, *Wace's Roman de Rou and the variant versions of Geoffrey of Monmouth's Historia* in « Speculum », XXXI (1936), 675-82.

48 W. LEWIS JONES, 261. Further GRANSDEN, 202: « Geoffrey was a romance writer masquerading as a historian ».

49 *Councils and ecclesiastical documents relating to Great Britain and Ireland*, ed. A.W. HADDAN - W. STUBBS, I, Oxford 1869, 360: « Anno ab incarnatione Domini MCLI (*recte*: MCLII) Theobaldus Cantuariensis archiepiscopus et totius Angliae primas sacravit Galfridum electum ecclesiae sancti Asaph in episcopum apud Lambetham ». Further literature on this point TATLOCK, 442, n. 24. By the spring of the same year John of Salisbury was at Segni in Italy see *The Letters of John of Salisbury*, ed. C. BROOKE, I, London - Edinburgh - New York 1955, 255.

50 *Historia*, VII, 3 (p. 387): « Succedet leo iustitiae, ad cuius rugitum gallicanae turres et insulani dracones tremebunt ».

51 *Metalogicon*, II, 10 (p. 78).

> Transeo ad successorum eius (*scil.* Rufus) Henricum inclitum regem qui leo iustitiae appellatus est, sicut publice notum est, non modo urbes sed et turres gallicae timuerunt.[52]

But apart from these linguistic aspects there is a most convincing passage in the *Policraticus* of John of Salisbury, the source of which can be none other than Geoffrey's *Historia.* For Brennus is here upheld as a model for English kings. It was Brennus who had invaded Italy, founded Milan, Como, Bergamo, Verona, Trent, Vicenza.[53] It was also Brennus together with his brother who had captured Rome itself.[54] Since Geoffrey's work provided as a central figure a hero of whom Normans and Saxons, Welshmen and Bretons could justifiably be proud, it is not all surprising that it was of greatest interest to a king of Henry II's calibre, ambitions and aspirations. It is therefore understandable that Henry should demonstrate a lively interest in this book with which he was familiarized by the chief patron and dedicatee of Geoffrey, Robert of Gloucester, himself sometime tutor of the young Henry II.[55] Rightly has it therefore been observed that Geoffrey's *Historia* « was of interest to Anglo-Norman aristocrats and assuredly to no one more than to Henry II and his court ».[56] That a man of John of Salisbury's standing, alertness, acuity of mind, wide intellectual and literary horizons and equally wide contacts with leading and celebrated personalities, of his time, should be conversant with this *Historia* can hardly cause any surprise. And that he had a genuine admiration and affection for Henry II at the crucial time, that is, the mid-fifties, is demonstrated by his own writing.[57] It should also be borne in mind that, according to William Fitzstephen, John of Salisbury was held in so great esteem by the king that he was sent as the royal delegate to Alexander III, in order to receive from him the pallium for Thomas Becket, the newly created archbishop of Canterbury, former chancellor of Henry II himself and the dedicatee and intimate

[52] *Policraticus,* VI, 18 (p. 48, lines 13 ff.).

[53] *Policraticus,* VI, 17 (p. 45, lines 5 ff.).

[54] *Policraticus,* VI, 17 (pp. 44-45); cf. VIII, 18 (p. 361, lines 22-24). The editor, C.C.J. Webb, had already noted the dependence of John of Salisbury on Geoffrey; see editorial notes ad locos.

[55] TATLOCK, 467.

[56] TATLOCK, 467-468.

[57] ULLMANN, *Jurisprudence,* ch. 6, 535.

friend of John himself.[58] This assuredly was a singular distinction bestowed on John of Salisbury.

The only plausible conclusion which can be drawn from John of Salisbury's statement concerning Ireland is that he acquainted Pope Adrian IV with the intention of Henry II to invade Ireland which was the king's by right of inheritance. The reason for the approach to the papacy was to obtain confirmation, endorsement and encouragement rather than permission to undertake the military measures. As already mentioned, *Laudabiliter* makes a special point in calling attention to the king's seeking papal counsel and favour.[59]

Here it is apposite to emphasize that John's passage has a very strong juristic complexion. He advisedly employs the term p o s s i d e r e which is certainly not identical with ownership.[60] In actual fact this crucial passage of John is very well thought out and fully explains the essential character of the transaction. For his statement « ... et dedit Hiberniam iure hereditario possidendam » is immediately followed by: « Nam omnes insule de iure antiquo ex donatione Constantini ... dicuntur ad Romanam ecclesiam pertinere ».[61] In actual fact the « nam » expresses the acknowledgment of the Roman Church as the owner of islands in which capacity it must evidently have the right to countenance measures affecting them. The sovereignty of the papacy over islands manifested itself concretely in the right of infeudation. Indeed, this is precisely what John of Salisbury himself in the very next sentence tells us:

> Anulum quoque per me transmisit aureum, smaragdo optimo decoratum, quo fieret i n v e s t i t u r a i u r i s in gerenda

58 *Vita sancti Thomae Cantuariensis archiepiscopi et martyris auctore Filio Stephani,* ed J.C. ROBERTSON in *Materials for the History of Thomas Becket,* III, London 1877, cap. 25 (p. 36): « Alexander papa tertius pallium misit per clericum eius Johannem Salesberiensem ». See further *Vita sancti Thomae Cantuariensis archiepiscopi et martyris auctore Wilielmo Cantuariensi,* ed. J.C. ROBERTSON in *Materials ...,* I, London 1875, cap. 8 (p. 9): « Consecratus vero infra tres menses consecrationis suae ad exponendam fidem suam palliumque suscipiendum (quia in propria persona proficisci non potuit) mittens ad Montes Passulani civitatem pallium transmissum accepit ». In RADULPHUS DE DICETO, *Opera Historica,* ed. W. STUBBS, I, London 1876, 307 there is a marginal note according to which John of Salisbury was accompanied by four others on this mission that is, the abbot of Evesham, the treasurer of York, a monk of Canterbury and Jordan of Chichester. See on this also WEBB, *John of Salisbury,* 104.

59 Though unaware of the background WARREN, 196, had the right reaction to *Laudabiliter*: « It reads more like an attempt to encourage a hesitant king ».

60 Property or ownership must be clearly and sharply distinguished from mere possession, as Ulpian had taught generations of jurists, *Dig.* XLI, 2, 12, 1: « Nihil commune habet proprietas cum possessione ».

61 *Metalogicon,* 217-218.

> Hibernia. Idemque adhuc anulus in cimiliarcho publico custodia iussus est.[62]

This is entirely in conformity with Henry's possession of Ireland and the papacy's ownership. There is no need to stress that all manuscripts have g e r e n d a which in the context is not identical with r e g e n d a. With this tallies also Henry's later request for permission to install his son John in Ireland which was easily comprehensible within a feudal framework.[63]

John of Salisbury's statement concerning the royal hereditary right was in the nature of a comment or an explanatory remark, in order to interpret Henry's intentions and to make clear why he approached Adrian in the first instance. What mattered to the papacy was not a royal title-deed — the papal silence on this score is significant[64] — but its own claim to ownership derived from a somewhat liberal interpretation of the *Constitutum Constantini.* It is certainly not without consequence that it was in relation to an island (Lipari) just off the coast of Sicily that Pope Urban II inaugurated the omni-insular doctrine,[65] and that, as has been shown, John of Salisbury was particularly well informed about Sicilian and related matters.[66] In all likelihood John presented the case originally in such a manner which called for papal collaboration, since nominally

[62] *Metalogicon,* 218, lines 2-5.

[63] For the relevant statements see above n. 10.

[64] There is a piece of evidence which has not, as far as I am aware, received the attention which is due to it. The author known as Benedict of Peterborough for the year 1171 has an entry which flatly contradicts Adrian's and Alexander's dispositions and makes Alexander say the very thing which he together with his predecessor had studiously avoided: « Praedictus rex Angliae misit nuncios suos ad Alexandrum summum pontificem cum litteris archiepiscoporum et episcoporum Hyberniae ad confirmandum s i b i e t h a e r e d i b u s s u i s regnum Hyberniae sicque factum est. Nam summus pontifex auctoritate apostolica confirmavit e i e t h a e r e d i b u s s u i s regnum illud et eos inde i n p e r p e t u u m reges constituit », *Gesta Regis Henrici Secundi Benedicti Abbatis,* ed. W. Stubbs, I, London 1867, 28. The author was said to be well acquainted with internal governmental matters, cf. Grandsden, 223-224. It was clearly secondhand information which he had obtained. O'Doherty 142, refers to this statement and comments: « This is indeed a strong interpretation of the documents (i.e. of *JL* 12162-4); nevertheless it could hardly be regarded as unfair description of them ». The really essential point escaped this savant.

[65] *JL* 5448, dated 3 June 1091, *PL* CLI, 329C - 330D: « Cum universae insulae secundum instituta legalis (regalis?) iuris sint, constat profecto quia religiosi imperatoris Constantini privilegio in ius proprium beati Petri eiusque successoribus omnes occidentales insulae condonatae sunt ». Similarly *JL* 5449 in relation to Corsica (28 June 1091) with the significant addition that the « statuta legalia i u r i s p u b l i c i » related to the island (*PL* CLI, 330D - 331D).

[66] Cf. Ullmann, *Jurisprudence,* ch. 6, at 530-535.

Ireland was Christian but had, so to speak, badly strayed from the path. The links between it and the Roman Church were certainly extremely tenuous. A successful invasion and subjection of the island would therefore give effect to the inherent rights of the Roman Church as the owner. Having been now accomplished, the campaign could be, as it certainly was, presented to Alexander III as an undertaking in the interests of the Christian religion. That Alexander emphasized the ecclesiastical rights so strongly is comprehensible: he was chancellor when these rights were disregarded in Germany; he was pope when these same rights came under severe attack by Frederick I in Germany and by Henry II himself in the conflict with Becket; and as the draftsman of *Laudabiliter* he was of course perfectly familiar with the subject-matter itself; as pope now in 1172 he could effectively drive home the claims of the papacy in regard to the ownership of islands.

This important transaction has profoundly shaped the course of history virtually down to the present day. And the case is not without some piquancy. Despite the lapse of some seventeen years the chief personages were still the same, though each in a different capacity. The chancellor had become pope and could rely on the document produced in his former capacity; the much reviled king had now become a pious and magnificent prince as well as a devoted son of the Church acting as a Christian warrior. What was common to both king and pope was the reliance on fiction, and each was totally unaware of the truth of the matter. Both had become victims of fabricated history.

V

FREDERICK II'S OPPONENT, INNOCENT IV, AS MELCHISEDEK

The seventh centenary of Frederick II's death (1) is an extremely fitting occasion to probe a little into the development of ideologies which guided his enemy, Innocent IV, which eventually brought Frederick to his knees, and effectively contributed to the destruction of the medieval idea of a universal empire. The drama that unfolded itself at Lyons in the oppressive, sultry mid-July days of 1245 was the culmination of Roman papal policy: in a most spectacular manner the world was shown the function of the pope as the leader of (Western) Christendom who disposes empires, deposes emperors and orders the constitutional agency to proceed to the election of a candidate who might possibly acquiesce in the acknowledgment of papalist aims. The hierocratic idea had indeed achieved a resounding victory at Lyons: the pope, the master of the world, had become the embodiment of an idea. The first half of the thirteenth century is a particularly good example of the relentless force that lies in ideas, which, once they have taken a firm hold on the minds of individuals, impel the latter to actions quite regardless of the consequences involved. Society was still conceived, in the first half of that century, as a *Respublica Christiana,* but what was the role of the emperor in this society? What Frederick II, as a Ghibelline, claimed was his leadership of that Christian commonwealth; what the curia, on the other hand, claimed was the papal, sacerdotal leadership of the same organism. Frederick II appears as the personification of the idea that the government of that Christian commonwealth

(1) 13 December 1250. The present writer desires to apologize for the lack of detailed references and other deficiences, as this contribution had to be written within a very short time.

is entrusted to him: in his flaming protests from 1239 onwards the idea emerges with ever increasing clarity that the conception of the Church, with which his opponents operated, was a distortion of the original meaning: appealing to the princes he says: « Vos ergo... nec solum nobis, sed ecclesiae, quae congregatio est fidelium omnium, condolete » (2). It was as a spokesman of this Christian commonwealth that Frederick attempts to raise his protest against the papalist system (3). The popes, on the other hand, also operated with the idea of a Church; with the idea, that is, that since the *Respublica Christiana* was essentially and intrinsically a Christian union which was nothing else but a « congregatio fidelium », hence a universal Church, its leadership was in their hands, not in those of a layman. This latter idea gained a temporary victory at Lyons, where the effective leadership of the popes was vigorously and visibly asserted. Both pope and emperor therefore quarrelled for the government of one and the same body (4): but each followed different patterns of thought and

(2) *Mon. Germ. Hist., Const.*, vol ii, p. 298; the resuscitation of the idea of the Church as a « congregatio fidelium » appears, with Frederick, already in the communication of 3 Decembre 1232: « ecclesia, quae congregatio fidelium dicitur », HUILLARD-BRÉHOLLES, *Historia Diplomatica Federici II*, vol. iv., p. 409; on this see F. GRAEFE, *Publizistik in der letzten Epoche Kaiser Friedrichs II*, p. 26; HELENE WIERUSZOWSKI, *Vom Imperium zum Nationalen Koenigtum*, p. 179; the idea is also in canon law, *Decretum, De Consecrat., dist.* i, c. 8, C. XXIV, q. i, c. 18. Some early canonists held identical views about the « ecclesia », see my *Medieval Papalism*, p. 214. The glossator of the *Compilatio Quinta*, Jacobus de Albenga, commenting on Frederick II's decree (*Comp.* V, I, i. 2) says: « Debet enim imperator vocari ad concilium, quando quaestio fidei agitari debet... et merito vocandi sunt laici quando tractatur certa causa fidei et matrimonii, quia quod omnes tangit, ab omnibus comprobari debet », MS Brit. Museum, Royal II C. VII, fol 246 rb. Frederick II's decree was not embodied in the *Gregoriana*, but was resuscitated by Boniface VIII in the *Sextus*, V. ii. 18.

(3) The idea was adopted by the French publicists half a century later: « sancta mater ecclesia, sponsa Christi, non solum est ex clericis, sed etiam ex laicis, » DUPUY, *Histoire du differend etc.*, p. 21; for the general ideological background see « A Medieval Document on Papal Theories of Government » in *English Historical Review*, 1946, pp. 180 ff, R. SCHOLZ, *Die Publizistik zur Zeit Philips des Schoenen etc.*, and J. RIVIERE, *Le Probleme de l'Eglise et de l'Etat etc., passim.* For a classic expression of the idea of the Church at that time see also John of Paris's definition: « Dici potest, quod una est ecclesia, unus populus Christianus, unum mysticum corpus non quidem in Petro vel Lino, sed in Christo, qui solus est, proprie et maxime caput ecclesiae, a quo est distributa utraque potestas distincta quoad diversos gradus, » *De Potestate Regia et Papali*, cap. XVIII, p. 230, of the edition by Dom J. Leclercq, 1942.

(4) For the preceding century the conflict is very well expressed by F. HEER, *Aufgang des Abendlandes*, 1950, p. 614: « Es ist der Kampf um die irdische Repraesentation des rex regum: wer vertritt den König der Könige und seine richterliche Oberhoheit über die regna mundi auf Erden — der Kaiser oder der Papst? »

conceived this organism differently. The one stood on the firm bedrock of ancient Roman ideas, the other on the almost equally ancient tradition of the Roman curia. What Nicholas I had expressed in a cautious manner (5), what Gregory VII stormily and impetuosly tried to achieve, what Innocent III formulated as a point of programme moulded in the inflexible letter of the canon law — that was realized and translated into the chilly atmosphere of actual politics by Innocent IV. What, we must ask, did the hierocratic system that could proudly look to an impressive past, to an imperceptibly slow, but steady development, ideologically propound? What, in other words, was its chief ideological element?

Innocent IV himself, in no unmistakable terms, has told us: « The Lord Jesus Christ, as very man and very God, so remaining true king and true priest according to the order of Melchisedek... has established in the apostolic throne not only a pontifical, but also a regal monarchy, committing to the blessed Peter and his successors the government of both an earthly and celestial empire » (6). Innocent's condemnation of Frederick at the Council of Lyons points into the same direction when he made God depose the emperor (7). And as a canonist he expresses himself in very much the same terms when he declares: « Nota, quod papa deponit imperatorem, et est hoc de jure, nam cum Christus, filius Dei, dum fuit in hoc saeculo et etiam ab aeterno dominus fuit naturalis, et de jure naturali in imperatores et quoscumque alios sententias depositionis ferre potuisset... et *eadem ratione* et vicarius potest hoc ». (8).

These utterances leave no room for doubt that Innocent IV spoke in the function of a vicar of Christ, no more in that of a vicar of St. Peter. He was not indeed the first to say so, but he certainly was the first to act so in a spectacular and impressive manner. Through him spoke God and the deposition was God's work. Being no philosopher, but all the better a canonist, Innocent IV is a classic example of how much ideas become absorbed by their bearers, without their often clearly realizing where the ideas had taken their origin. « The wind blows where it listeth ». What Innocent IV put into practice at Lyons was the ancient Augustinian idea of a universal Church which, however, had been

---

(5) SEE A. HAUCK, *Der Gedanke der Weltherrschaft etc.*, pp. 15 ff, A. GREINACHER, *Die politischen Anschauungen des Papstes Nikolaus I*, the late L. HALPHEN, *Carlemagne et l'Empire Carolingien*, 1949, pp. 390-5. The argumentation of the late Johannes Haller, *Nikolaus I und Pseudo-Isidor*, pp. 121 ff., is not convincing.

(6) K. MIRBT, *Quellen zur Geschichte des Papsttums*, 4 th ed., pp. 197 f; cf. also E. WINKELMANN, *Acta Imperii Inedita*, vol. II, no. 1035.

(7) MGH, *Epistolae saeculi XIII*, vol. II, no. 124; cf. *Sextus*, II. XIV. 2.

(8) Commentary on « Ad apostolicae » at *Extra*, II. XVII, no. 6.

considerably modified in the course of time: the vehicle by which this idea of a universal Church was to be given its concrete shape was the — by that time — traditional curial theory of the pope as Melchisedek on the one hand, and of the position of the Roman Church within the universal Church on the other hand. The emperor working on the same Augustinian pattern (9) tried to realize it with the help of the Roman law that made him the « dominus » of the (Christian) world. The contest, *inter alia,* concerned also the efficacy of the means at the disposal of each of the contestants: the static Roman law in its Justinianean form had to face the dynamic and living force of the curial tradition embodied in the canon law. We are not here concerned with the problem of how the idea of the papal *Sacerdos-Rex* came to be an indispensable element in curial theory, but rather with the question, how this idea of the pope being Melchisedek, so openly and frankly acknowledged by Innocent himself, came to be the very cornerstone of curialist policy and of hierocratism altogether?

The idea of Melchisedek as combining both royal and sacerdotal power was introduced into the pattern of political thought by St. Augustine when he spoke of Christ being « verus rex et sacerdos secundum ordinem Melchisedek» (10). Christ was the head of the mystical union of all the believers in Him: the congregation of the faithful, the « populus fidelis » (11), form the universal Church at whose head Christ Himself stands: He is the « caput ecclesiae » (12), of the true, universal, that is, Catholic Church. Unity within the mystical body of Christ is the essential criterion, and salvation can be achieved only when the unity is maintained (13). But next to this universal conception of the Church at whose head Christ as true king and priest stands, St. Augustine also knows of another Church which is functional: its *raison d'être* is the administration of sacraments which are the practical means whereby salvation can be achieved, conferring as they do divine grace. The criterion for membership of this functional (or sacerdotal or institutionalized) Church is ordination (14). This sacerdotal Church constitutes an essential part of the universal Church, just as those who are not ordained, also form an essential part of the mystical body of Christ, the universal Church. Both sections, therefore, are contained in the « ecclesia universalis » at whose head

(9) H. Wieruszowski, *op. cit.,* pp. 179, 183.

(10) De Civitate Dei, XVII, 7. 17; XVIII, 35; cf. E. Bernheim, *Mittelalterliche Zeitanschauungen in ihrem Einfluss etc.,* pp. 117 f, 150 f.

(11) *De Civ. Dei,* XVIII, 14.

(12) *Ibid.* XVIII, 19.

(13) Cf. *Ep.,* 151, and *De unitate eccl.,* c. 49.

(14) See *Contra Ep. Parm.,* II. 13. (29); *Sermo* 137, c. 8.

Christ Himself stands. There can be no gainsaying the stimulating nature of Augustinian conceptions which, in fact, shaped medieval ways of thinking in general and curial ways in particular to an extent that becomes the more apparent the closer curial thought is analysed. And of this Augustinian welter of ideas none was more determinative than the Melchisedek idea. Nevertheless, it is as well to keep in mind that the primacy of the Church of Rome based on Petrine grounds, was not apparently conceded by him — « Sumus enim Christiani, non Petriani » (15). How, then, could the Melchisedek idea, with its far-reaching consequences, gain such wide, almost universal currency, so that at Lyons we find the pope acting in his capacity as Melchisedek?

We suggest that Pope Gelasius I's various literary products provided the channel which transmitted the idea into the realm of practical politics. We suggest, furthermore, that the ideas expressed by Gelasius in his writings as draughtsman of Felix III and as pope, still based as they were on Augustinian conceptions, do not, as it is commonly maintained, constitute a dualism, but what may be termed implicit hierocratism. We are well aware of the *prima facie* incompatibility between Innocent IV's above quoted dictum in which he claimed Melchisedekian powers for the pope, and the Gelasian dictum which made Christ appear as the last Melchisedek. The reason for this — no more than an apparent — incongruity is that Gelasius had not applied the theory, developed since his time, the theory of the peculiar position of the Roman Church and its head. That missing link between Gelasius and Innocent was provided by the conception of the Roman Church being the epitome of the universal Church and of the pope being the vicar of Christ. It is, therefore, our contention that the Gelasian conception of the relations between the two powers provides the basic ancestral source of hierocratism, into which needed only to be injected the idea of the Roman Church as the epitome of the universal Church in order to yield a fully developed hierocratism (16).

It cannot be within the scope of this essay to depict the background which produced the communications of Gelasius. It must suffice to state that he had inherited the claim of earlier popes, notably Innocent I and Leo I, of the primacy of the Roman Church. As head of this Church the pope occupied the « fasti-

---

(15) *Enarratio in Ps.* 44, 23. See E. Caspar, *Geschichte des Papsttums*, vol. I, pag. 340; against this St. J. Grabowski, « St. Augustine and the Primacy » in *Traditio*, 1946, pp. 89-113.

(16) For this the reader may be referred to Innocent III's *Registrum*, the passage of which is transcribed below in note 115.

gium sacerdotale », as Pope Hilarus had put it (17). On the whole, the primacy of the Roman Church was acknowleged in the West: to all intents and purposes the pope was the head of the sacerdotal Church to use an Augustinian idea. But this claim was not acknowledged in the Eastern half of the empire: the creation of the patriarch in Constantinople was indeed a formidable challenge to the Roman papal claim. And the promulgation of the *Henoticon* by Emperor Zeno, upon instigation of the Patriarch Acacius in 482, brought matters to a head: this was nothing but a « kaiserliches Glaubensedikt » (18). What it amounted to was that the *Rex-Sacerdos* conception had found a concrete and practical manifestation in the East (19). The emperor claiming to be both king and priest in one person challenged the primacy of the Church of Rome. The blatant violation of ecclesiastical discipline by Acacius entailed his expulsion in 484 (20): that was the point when the primacy of the Roman Church had now effectively been translated into practice. But the emperor, too, was taken to task by Pope Felix III who sent the following significant message to him:

> I believe that your pious majesty, which prefers obedience to your own laws to resistance to them, should also obey the heavenly decrees; and your majesty should also know that the highest rank in human things is entrusted to you, so whatever is divine should be accepted from the administrators to whom this is divinely attributed. I believe that it would be advantageous to you, without any doubt, if you let the catholic church for the time of your rulership use its own laws and if you did not allow that anybody put obstacles in the way of the freedom of the church which has restored to you the power of your kingdom. It is certain to be advantageous to you if you should be anxious to subordinate in divine affairs, according to the

(17) JAFFÉ, *Regesta Pontificum Romanorum,* no. 651; ANDREAS THIEL, *Epistulae Romanorum Pontificum Genuinae,* vol. I, p. 169, ep. 17; MANSI, *Sacrorum Conciliorum ... Collectio,* vol. XII, col. 929.

(18) CASPAR, *op. cit.*, vol. II, p. 35.

(19) Nevertheless, we should bear in mind that Leo I, at least by implication, promoted the latent *rex-sacerdos* tendencies when he praised the emperor for his « Christiana doctrina » etc., on this see CASPAR, *op. cit.*, vol. I, pp. 527 ff., epp. 116 c. l, ep. 115, c. 1 (to the emperor himself). In another respect, too, Leo unintentionally promoted the Eastern tendencies when he said that only the emperor would be entitled to summon a council; on this see W. KISSLING, *Das Verhältnis zwischen Sacerdotium und Imperium nach den Anschauungen etc.*, pp. 27 f. 34-40, 52-58; K. VOIGT, *Kirche und Staat von Konstantin bis zum Ende etc.*, pp. 78, 98.

(20) JAFFÉ, 600; Thiel, *op. cit.*, ep. 247, ep. 7; Mansi, VII, 921.

decree (of Himself), your royal will to the priests of Christ, and not to choose your own; to learn rather than to teach the holy things from those who are in charge of them; to follow the established pattern of the church, and not to prescribe to the church any laws to be followed nor dominate the church to whom, God willed, you should bow your neck in pious devotion (21).

There is indubitably a great kinship between this letter and the communication of Gelasius: this letter shows us clearly the delicate touch, the subtle phraseology and the exquisite and inimitable style for which Gelasius as pope has justly been renowned; it was as a deacon that the future pope composed this communication (22). The significance of this letter lies in its constituting a trenchant frontal attack upon the *Rex-Sacerdos* conception which, by its very nature, challenged the primacy of the Roman Church. The attack was two-pronged: resting on the Petrine power to bind and to loose, it directs the opposition to the emperor's ecclesiastical-organisational measures, as exemplified in the appointments to the sees of Alexandria and Antioch — « ecclesiae *formam* sequi, non huic humanitus sequenda jura praefigere » — as well as to the imperial fixing of dogmas or articles faith: « sacrosancta per eorum praesules discere potius quam docere » (23). The realization that Christian society was in fact ruled by two different orders, emerged in a further communication of Felix III (Gelasius) which calls attention to the peace of the « mundanum regnum » and the tranquillity « sacrarum rerum », and by so doing lifts at once the authority of the apostolic see to a higher level than that of the « mundanum regnum » (24). The ground upon which this higher dignity of the apostolic see is

---

(21) JAFFÉ 601; Thiel, *op. cit.*, pp. 249-50; Mansi, VII. 1065.

(22) Cf. THIEL, *op. cit.*, pp. 21 ff. who had already noticed the close linguistic resemblance between Felix III and Gelasius' communications. Cf. also CASPAR, op. cit., pp. 750-1 cautiously assuming that Felix's letters were drafted by Gelasius.

(23) That this letter had no result, except that Felix's name was struck off the diptychs, proves the close union between the emperor and the patriarch: THEOPHANUS, *Cronographia*, ed. C. De Boor, p. 132.

(24) J. 612; MANSI, vii. 1098; THIEL, pp. 271 f, ep. 15, c. 3: « Postulationes certe gentium barbarum, venerabilis imperator, pro quiete mundani regni publice benignus exaudis; quanto praestantius, quaeso te, praeces apostolicae sedis pro sacrarum tranquillitate rerum placatus admittas ». The pairs are significant: « quies - tranquillitas »; « postulatio - praeces » (in conjunction with « quaeso te »): « benignus - placatus »; « exaudis - admittas ».

based is that Christ puts his demands forward through St. Peter's vicar (25).

Although the evaluation of the two entities was already clearly expressed in that letter — « postulationes... exaudis; *quanto* praestantius... » — it was given its permanent classic formulation by Gelasius as pope. Operating with the primacy of the Church of Rome Gelasius not only conceived it to be the *primatus magisterii,* but also, and more important for our present purpose, the *primatus jurisdictionis.* This see, he exclaims, has the right to pass judgment on every individual church, and nobody is allowed to sit in judgment over this see (26). In the same letter Gelasius distinguishes between the « potestas regni saecularis » and the « distributio ecclesiasticarum dignitatum, » (27) and in this context not only the choice of the terms « potestas - distributio » is significant, but also the contention that the Roman Church has the *principatus* (28); we find also espressed in this letter the principle that the Roman Church cannot be judged by anyone — the forger of the « Papa a nemine judicatur » indeed was given a pontifical stimulus. The jurisdictional primacy of the Roman Church referred to the exercise of supreme jurisdiction *within* the ecclesiastical organism — and yet, there was another side to it. For there were cases in which jurisdictional powers were claimed (and exercised) over persons of the ecclesiastical organism by persons outside it. The jurisdictional primacy of Rome, in other words, referred also to the exemption of clerics from jurisdiction by non-clerics: the cases of John Talaja and Calendio were still fresh in the memory of contemporaries; both were expelled from their sees by a sentence of the emperor himself. Accordingly, the sentence on these two clerics was passed by someone outside the ecclesiastical organism, that is, outside the sacerdotal Church of Rome. The *privilegium fori* was simply an effluence of the jurisdictional primacy of the Roman Church. The intimate connexion between the emperor and the patriarch destroyed the frontiers between their relative powers that were

---

(25) c. 4: « In me enim qualicumque vicario b. apostolus Petrus et haec in illo, qui ecclesiam suam discerpi non patitur, ipse enim Christus exposcit».

(26) « ... de omni ecclesia fas habeat judicandi, neque cuiquam de eius liceat judicare judicio... ab illa (scil. Romana ecclesia) autem nemo sit appellare permissus »: J. 664; THIEL, p. 406, ep. 26, c. 10. The sense of this passage is not correctly rendered by G. MICHAUD in *Rev. internat. de théologie,* xvi, p. 47; see CASPAR, ii. 61.

(27) « Alia potestas... alia distributio... ».

(28) This term means « dignitas, auctoritas et regimen eius, quem penes est summa rerum »: J. FACCIOLATI, *Totius Latinitatis Lexicon,* s. v. principatus.

supposed to have existed as a consequence of the creation of the ecclesiastical organisation culminating in the primate at Rome: the imperial sentence was indeed the concrete manifestation of the *Rex-Sacerdos* idea.

Nevertheless, there remained a difficulty and that concerned the question, upon what grounds may a trial of a member of the ecclesiastical body not take place? Was he also to be « exempted » from the jurisdiction of the non-clerical tribunal for offences which had nothing to do with a violation of ecclesiastical discipline? Vice-versa, was he also to be subjected to the ecclesiastical tribunal for crimes that did not affect ecclesiastical discipline? That was a vital question indeed — and John Talaja and Calendio were certainly not condemned for crimes against the ecclesiastical order, but for high treason and perjury. In other words, what was the scope of the jurisdictional primacy and of the consequential *privilegium fori*? There were only two possibilities: either to regard the status of the person (without regard to the matter) or to consider the kind of offence. Gelasius chose the former. Clearly foreshadowing later hierocratic thought he says to the emperor dealing with the affair of the two bishops that the Christian emperor should let the Church observe its own rules — « ut ecclesiae sineret Christianus princeps regulas custodire » — and divine and human laws likewise hold that judgments on priests come forth from priestly council: « divine pariter leges humanaeque censerent, ut sacerdotali concilio de sacerdotibus judicia provenirent » (29). However badly the two bishops may have failed « out of worldly error » — « etsi errore humanitus accedente » — and « of whatever quality » they might have been — « qualescumque pontifices » — they may not be judged by the « saecularis potestas » (30).

This naturally represents a quite considerable advance upon hierocratism, and this view fits rather badly into the picture of Gelasius as a dualist. For obvious reasons, the question suggested itself to Gelasius, what is the meaning of a Catholic prince? This question was asked and answered by Felix III, whose draughtsman, as we know, was Gelasius as a deacon. In his letter to the oriental bishops (31) the problem is put very neatly: « Quod si dixeris: "sed imperator catholicus est"? ». The answer is that the Catholicism of the prince expresses a peculiar relation to the

(29) Thiel, *op. cit.*, p. 407.

(30) Thiel, pp. 407-8, ep. 26, c. 11. The « humanae leges » referred to may be the short-lived privilege of Emperor Constantius in 335, *Cod. Theod.*, xvi, 2, 12.

(31) J. 611; Mansi, vii, 1072; Migne, *Patr. Lat.*, vol. lviii, col. 947; Thiel, p. 292, ep. 1, c. 10.

Church, so, however, that he is the son of the Church, not its superior: « Filius est, non praesul ecclesiae ». We shall not here dwell upon the somewhat ambiguous use of the term « ecclesia » — we suggest that Gelasius deliberately used it: as a « filius » the emperor could be conceived only in relation to the universal Church; « praesul » could refer only to his relation with the sacerdotal Church — but confine ourselves to the statement that in these few words not only the inferior position of the secular power in a Christian society is clearly and exquisitively brought out, but also the intimate relationship between the universal and sacerdotal Church is hinted at in a most suggestive way. Surely, in a Christian society, matters of religion are of supreme, exclusive and fundamental importance: and these matters profoundly affecting all life in a Christian society, the emperor has not to teach, but to learn from the ecclesiastics: « Quod ad religionem competet, discere ei convenit, non docere » (32). That, we furthermore suggest, was not only an attack on the *Rex-Sacerdos* conception, but implied a reversal altogether, in so far as, in a Christian society, the scales should be turned. The privilege of his power had been conferred on the emperor for the sake of the administration of public affairs by divine ordinance: he should be content with this privilege and he should not show himself ungrateful for the disposition of the divine ruling (33). What the emperor has, in other words, is a *beneficium* divinely conferred: the very choice of the term by Felix's draughtsman is revealing (34), and points to what Gelasius considers to be the *raison d'être* of the secular power: it is a privilege that he has « potestas » at all. We shall not be surprised to find that Gelasius made Felix III say that if the secular power is Christian, it has to be subjected to the priests: « Deus... seculi potestates, quae si fideles sunt, ecclesiae suae et sacerdotibus voluit esse subjectas ». This subjection of the secular power goes, according to Felix-Gelasius, so far that even within the purview of actually managing the *beneficium,* the ecclesiastics exercise supervisory rights: « Imperatores Christiani subdere debent exsecutiones suas ecclesiasticis praesulibus ». It is surely no mere coincidence that Gelasius uses Ulpian's term « exsecutio » (legis or juris) in this context (35).

(32) *Ibid.*

(33) « Habet privilegia potestatis suae, quae administrandis publicis rebus divinitus consecutus est, et eius beneficiis non ingratus contra dispositionem coelestis ordinis nichil usurpet. »

(34) We should keep in mind that there was a fundamental difference between the « ministerium » and « beneficium »: would it be too much to interpret Cardinal Roland's words at Besançon as an echo of Gelasius' words?

(35) Dig. 43, 29, 3 pr.; Dig. 50, 16.178 (2).

This, too, manifestly points to Gelasius's idea of what is the *raison d'être* of the State in a Christian society. Ideologically there is only a small step from the conception to the use of the temporal power « ad nutum ecclesiae ».

The « Magna Charta » of medieval ecclesiastical freedom (36), as the letter of Gelasius to Anastasius has been called, moves in entirely the same direction as the letters drafted by Gelasius on behalf of Felix III (37). Begging the emperor not to consider it as arrogance when he expounds the divine scheme of things, Gelasius tells him that the sacred priestly authority and the royal power rule this world. The choice of the word « auctoritas » and « potestas » is, of course, deliberate and expresses the same idea which we found in the previous letter that was not addressed to the emperor, but to bishops: hence in this case a more careful diction was advisable.

Two observations must here be made. Firstly, the contrast between « auctoritas » and « potestas » warrants a few words. According to Roman conceptions he who has « auctoritas » has, to use Gelasius's own term, the « facultas », that is, the power to shape things creatively: the etymological derivation from « auctor » should not be overlooked. « Potestas », on the other hand, means the power to execute decrees. In the words of the Roman jurist, Paulus, « potestatis verbo plura significantur, in persona magistruum imperium » (38). Cicero's passage conveys no different meaning (39): « imperia, potestates, legationes, cum senatus creverit, populusque jusserit, ex urbe exeunte ». The Roman senate had « auctoritas », the Roman magistrate « potestas » (40). The notion « potestas » therefore means no more than mere execution which is exactly the same thought as expressed in Fe-

---

(36) A. Dempf, *Sacrum Imperium,* p. 141: « the fundamental political doctrine of the Middle Ages », P. E. Schramm, *Kaiser, Rom und Renovatio,* vol. i, p. 16; see also E. H. Fischer, « Gregor d. Gr. und Byzanz » in *Zeitschrift der Savigny Stiftung, Kanonist, Abtlg.,* 1950, p. 26.

(37) J. 632; Thiel, pp. 349 ff., ep. 12; Hinschius, *Pseudo-Isidor,* cols. 639 ff; Migne, *PL.,* vol. lix, cols. 41 ff.

(38) Dig. 50, 15.215.

(39) *De Legibus,* iii. 3.

(40) It is noteworthy how long ideas, once firmly entrenched, live: this is particularly noticeable with these two terms. Leibniz in his *Tractatus de Jure Suprematis ac Legationis Principum Germaniae* (1678) says that the emperor as head of Christendom has « auctoritas » over all the Christian States of Europe, but that the German and foreign princes have only « potestas », quoted P. Koschaker, *Europa und das Römische Recht,* p. 52, note 1, with further literature. The paper by the late R. Scholz in *Zeitschrift f. die deutsche Geisteswissenschaft* was not accessible to me. On the ideological background see also U. Gmelin, « Auctoritas, Römischer Princeps and päpstlicher Primat » in *Forschungen zur Kirchen und Geistesgeschichte,* 1938 (vol. xi), pp. 143-9.

lix III's letter. « Auctoritas » the emperor has not, since this is reserved to the priests: their « potestas », differently expressed, is an « auctoritas » because they alone have the power to bind and to loosen: by virtue of this unique « potestas » they have « auctoritas ». The distinction between « auctoritas » and « potestas » was a very ingenious weapon against the *Rex-Sacerdos* idea: but it was also more, as we shall presently see, for it was a means to turn the scales altogether and to imply, in a most delicate manner, that the true state of affairs in a Christian society was precisely the opposite.

Secondly, the « gravius pondus » also merits a few words. Why have the priests « greater weight » than the secular prince? The contrast between « auctoritas » and « potestas » alone would have given a sufficient answer, but Gelasius reasons that the « greater weight » must be attributed to the clerics, because they have to render an account before God's tribunal « pro regibus hominum ». The secular princes need the help of the priests, if they wish to achieve salvation and in this way, Gelasius suggests, the priestly account before God's tribunal will be of vital importance. They have to render an account as to how the princes have administered the *beneficium,* as to what use they have made of the *privilegia* conferred upon them by divine ordinance. That is why he had counselled through Felix III that « Christiani imperatores exsecutiones suas subdere debent ecclesiasticis praesulibus ». But all that stands in close proximity to what Gelasius thinks is the *raison d'être* of the secular power. The idea that it is a mere *beneficium*, a *privilegium* resulting in « potestas », indicates in what direction his thoughts were moving. That brings us to the interpretation of *Tractatus IV*.

We recall that, according to St. Augustine, Christ had combined royal and sacerdotal power « secundum ordinem Melchisedek ». Now it must have been obvious to Gelasius that the emperor in the East could very well be compared with Melchisedek. It was, in order to countermand this conception that Gelasius invented the idea that Christ was the last Melchisedek (41). Christ had distinguished between the offices of the two powers. In an unhistoric manner Gelasius asserts that since Christ no pontiff had usurped the title of emperor, and no emperor had attributed the title of pontiff to himself. The question is still not answered, why Christ distinguished between the « offices » of the two powers? And on the answer to this question a good deal depends. Christ was prompted to distinguish between the functions (« offi-

---

(41) *Tractatus IV*, Thiel, pp. 557 ff; Gratian, *Dist.*, 96, c. 10; J. 701; Mansi, viii. 88 ff., Mirbt, *op. cit.*, pp. 85 f.

cia ») of *Regnum* and *Sacerdotium*, because He was mindful of « human fragility ». What does the Gelasian phrase « Christus memor fragilitatis humanae ...officia utriusque potestatis discrevit » really mean? In it Gelasius expresses his idea about the *raison d'être* of the State. When we keep in mind how from early days of Christianity onwards Christian writers and thinkers insisted on contempt for the earthly, for the material, for the carnal, we shall find it easier to understand the import of this sentence. And it is no coincidence that Gelasius, in the very same context, invokes the advice of St. Paul to Timothy that « Deo militans minime se negotiis saecularibus implicaret » (42). Christ had foreseen, we follow Gelasius's reasonings, what evil consequences there would ensue if the « administrators of the divine mysteries » were to combine, like Him, sacerdotal with royal power: out of consideration for the « humana fragilitas » of the clerics He had distributed the functions of each of the two powers. For dealing with the « carnal affairs » would result in a distraction of the priests from their proper vocation which is « Deo militare ». In consideration of their human fragility Christ had taken away the care for material affairs from the clerics and handed this care over to those who were not engaged in sacerdotal pursuits. In order to preserve the clerics from « carnal inroads » — « carnalibus incursibus » (43) — Christ had « by a marvellous dispensation » given the administration of the material things to the emperor. To be sure, the emperor has thereby been given a privilege, but it amounts to no more than a *beneficium*. Correctly seen, the institution of the State was beneficial to the clerics: the empire exists for the sake of the pontiffs. In so far therefore as the priests live in the world, they must make use of the institution of the State which was precisely set up in order to relieve them from a burdensome and distractive business. The State, if we tried to express Gelasian ideas in modern terminology, was a trust conferred on the emperor by Christ for the sake of the clerics.

We need not point out that all this can have application only in a Christian society. So far from being the expression of a dualist principle, this passage manifests itself as the exposition of an implicit hierocratism. And in order to leave no room for doubt Gelasius, in this very same passage, tells us what he thinks about the hierarchical ordering within the Christian « mundus »: bearing in mind what he holds to be the *raison d'être*

(42) 2 Tim. ii. 4.
(43) The change of terms will be noticed: St. Paul spoke of « secularia negotia », Gelasius of « carnales incursus ».

of the Christian State and the clerical rendering of account for the management of this *beneficium,* we shall find only a different way of expressing his axiom that « Christiani imperatores subdere debent exsecutiones suas ecclesiasticis praesulibus » when he declares that emperors request the priests to absolve them from their sins: no inferior can absolve a superior: « Inferior quippe potiorem absolvere non potest » (44). « The secular power must not teach, but it must learn from the priests and in particular from the vicar of St. Peter what is (and what is not) divine » (45). What is, and what is not, divine, is obviously a vital question affecting Christian society. The maxims that influence public life in a (Christian) State are, by their very nature, Christian and made known by those who administer the divine mysteries: hence they have a residual supervisory right over the « exsecutiones » of the Christian emperor. Again, ideologically, there was only a small step from here to the more outspoken jurisdiction « ratione peccati ».

It will have become manifest that Gelasius still operates on the basis of Augustinian ideas, particularly on that of the universal Church, of a union of all Christians united in their faith in Christ. To Gelasius the « mundus » was still only the Christian world (46) and within this wide union the secular power had been given certain functions, in order to relieve the clerics of a burdensome and perhaps even harmful duty. There is, as yet, no indication in Gelasius's framework that the pope was anything but a vicar of St. Peter. Nevertheless, he comes very near to the conception, in itself based upon the primacy of the Church of Rome, that the *sacerdotium* (the sacerdotal Church) occupies a peculiar place within the universal Church. He certainly does not go as far as to say that the Roman Church constitutes the epitome of the universal Church, but by injecting into the sacerdotal Church the primacy of Rome as well as the latter's jurisdictional powers, Gelasius made a considerable advance towards the idea that the Roman Church, as the primatial Church, represents the whole Church. In this approximation towards the conception of the Roman Church being merely the epitome of the universal Church, Gelasius must be given the credit that is due to him (47). Natu-

---

(44) « Non imperator absolvit, sed a pontificibus poposcit absolvi », *ibidem.*

(45) J. 622; THIEL, p. 347, ep. 10, c. 9.

(46) With all due respect we cannot agree with Mgr. ARQUILLIÈRE, *L'Augustinisme Politique*, p. 72, who takes the term « mundus » far wider than we think it ought to be taken. Would the passage otherwise make sense?

(47) Reviewing the Petrine ideas of Leo I, the late CASPAR, *op. cit.*, vol. i, p. 428, very succinctly hinted at the change in Peter's position:

rally, the identical terminology — «ecclesia» for both conceptions — aided this development considerably. We have only to look ahead to see how vitally important the distinction between the two Churches in fact was, and what havoc could be wrought by the claim that the secular prince was the *brachium saeculare* of the Church, which really means that he has become the executive organ of the *sacerdotium*.

We have in fact a perfectly clear instance of how frightfully near Gelasius himself came to this conception. Passages like this — that the authority of the apostolic see is set above the whole Church (48) or that the pope had charge of the whole of mankind, « totius orbis terrarum universitatis » (49), whilst the emperor had to rule over the people of one State only — indubitably lent their weight to the later emerging idea that the Roman Church was no more or less than the epitome of the universal Church. It is assuredly no coincidence that Nicholas I, who is usually credited with being the « Father » of hierocratism, relied so heavily on Gelasius, as a glance at Nicholas's letters proves (50). What Nicholas did, was to take that step omitted by Gelasius, but so clearly indicated: to make the Roman Church the epitome of the whole Church and in this way to change the relations of the « pontifices » and the « reges » fundamentally.

And there is one more point that merits attention in this context, a point which brings Gelasius's position as the true father of hierocratism into clear relief. The pope, according to him, as head of the Roman Church speaks on behalf of the universal Church: the « auctoritas pontificum» comes to be narrowed down to an «auctoritas pontificis Romani ». This is what he himself, again in the most subtle and delicate manner, says. The Eastern opposition had complained that there had not been a synodal judgment on Acacius (51). Ironically Gelasius asks who would be qualified to sit in judgment over Acacius — would the participants of a synod not be enemies, witnesses and judges all in one?

« Petrus im ewigen Consortium der Gewalt mit Christus stehend, wird damit tatsächlich — wenn auch natürlich nicht dogmatisch in eine ähnliche Stellung gerückt, wie sie Christus selbst, als der ewig zur Rechten des Vaters sitzet, innehat ».

(48) J. 632; THIEL, p. 356, ep 12, c. 9: « Apostolicae sedis auctoritas, quod cunctis saeculis Christianis ecclesiae praelata sit universae, et canonum serie partenorum et multiplici traditione firmatur ».

(49) *Ibid.*, p. 353, c. 6: « Proinde si pietas tua unius civitatis populum negat posse componi, quid nos de totius terrarum sumus universitate facturi, si, quod absit, nostra praevaricatione deceptus ».

(50) Particularly in the model of editorial scholarship as exhibited by E. PERELS, in the *Epistolae*, vol. vi.

(51) See J. 622; THIEL, p. 347, ep. 10, c. 9.

He evades a plain, straightforward answer, but his refusal to commit the case to a synod is as significant as a plain answer would have been. « Quaero, » he says, « tamen ab his, judicium, quod praetendunt, ubinam possit agitari: an apud ipsos, ut iidem sint inimici, et testes, et judices? Sed tali judicio nec humana debent committi negotia, nedum divinae legis integritas. » (52). The implication is obvious: he, as the head of the « prima sedes », exercises supreme jurisdictional powers: he, in his function as pope, stands above all other Christians, whether laical or clerical, as the supreme judge (53). But so far it was no more than an implication.

To sum up. Still on the basis of Augustinian conceptions, Gelasius conceives of Christ as the head of the Christian world, but in his framework the sacerdotal Church, the *sacerdotium,* assumes a different complexion from that which St. Augustine had given it, and hence also the *imperium.* The latter exists for the sake of the former. The peculiarly close relationship between the *sacerdotium* and the « caput ecclesiae » is brought about by the infusion of the tenet of the primacy of the Church of Rome. Although the *raison d'être* of the *imperium* puts it on a plane entirely different from that of the *sacerdotium* and although for this reason, if for no other, Gelasius's ideas present themselves as implicit hierocratism, to him the two were still *within* the universal Church; its head was Christ Who was Melchisedek but Who had no successor combining as He did royal and sacerdotal power. But when the pope could be conceived, not as a vicar of St. Peter, but of Christ Himself, then not only a further modification in the status of *imperium and sacerdotium* was sure to emerge, but also the function of the pope as Melchisedek was bound to come. The idea that the Roman Church, by virtue of its primacy, was the epitome of the universal Church, expresses the same thought in a different way: the sacerdotal Church, in other words, was substituted for the universal Church, culminating in its apex, the Roman Church; the *sacerdotium* stepped into the place that was once reserved for the universal Church. When Christ was the head of the universal Church, it was then also His vicar, the pope. When Christ was Melchisedek combining royal and sacerdotal powers, then His vicar too held the same position on earth. When Christ, according to Gelasius, had conferred on the emperor his *beneficium* — for the reasons

(52) Thiel, *ibid.*

(53) Caspar, *op. cit.*, vol ii, p. 69, note O, already hinted at this idea inherent in the refusal of Gelasius: « Das Hierarchische musste herausspringen ».

which we attempted to show — then His vicar too could do the same: the medieval empire, then, was conferred by the pope.

This development took a long time. We tried to focus attention on the main channel through which the Melchisedek idea entered the political thought of the hierocrats, and in so doing we were to find the so-called Gelasian principle as the expression of a monistic form of Christian government, which, for convenience sake, we styled implicit hierocratism. But we should not omit to refer to other foundation of medieval hierocratism, that is, the Donation of Constantine which, properly understood, is a popularized, coarsened form of Gelasianism. The re-orientation of the papacy during the pontificate of Gregory II characterized by the sharp-hitting attack against the Eastern *Rex-Sacerdos*, by the resuscitation of Gelasianism culminating in this pope's claim that « nos habemus Christi sensum » (54) and resulting in the break with the East in 731, heralded the new tidings. The two decades following Gregory II's death must be classed as equally formative for the papacy as those of the pontificates of Felix III and Gelasius I. The remarkable *volteface* at Ponthion was the direct result of the Donation of Costantine (55). The Donation was not only, as the late Erich Caspar said, the « theoretische Generalabrechnung des Papsttums mit Byzanz » (56), but it also revealed the inner-most desires of the Roman pontiffs (57). There is no reason to doubt that the forgery was made in the papal chancery (58).

The fabricator of this document by combining the two functions of the pope — as vicar of St. Peter and as heir of the Caesars, clearly tried to make the pope appear as Melchisedek. The

(54) J. 2182, of 729; Mansi, xii. 977.

(55) See now especially L. Halphen, *op. cit.*, pp. 26-34; cf. also *idem*, « Les origines du pouvoir temporel de la papauté » in *A travers l'histoire du Moyen Age*, p. 49, n. 1. The explanation of Haller in « Die Karolinger und das Papsttum » in *Abhandlungen zur Geschichte des Mittelalters*, pp. 1-40, is too artificial to be convincing.

(56) Caspar, « Das Papsttum unter fränkischer Herrschaft » in *Zeitschrift f. Kirchengeschichte*, 1935, p. 150.

(57) P. E. Schramm, « Regnum und Sacerdotium im Austausch ihrer Vorrechte » in *Studi Gregoriani*, vol. ii, p. 414.

(58) See Caspar, *art. cit.*, p. 230 (though under Paul I), and K. Hartmann, « Grundherrschaft und Buerokratie in Kirchenstaat etc. », in *Vierteljahrsschrift f. Social und Wirtschaftsgeschichte*, 1909, pp. 146 ff. On the other hand, the adoption of the *rex-sacerdos* idea by the Carolingian power and writers may have roots identical with those of the papalist doctrine, although the infiltration of Eastern conceptions is here of great importance, see, e.g., F. Kampers, « Rex-Sacerdos » in *Historisches Jahrbuch*, 1925, pp. 496 ff., and W. Ohnsorge, *Das Zweikaiserproblem*, pp. 9 ff.

conferment of the imperial *insignia* on the pope by Costantine should make the *Rex-Sacerdos* position of the pope visible to all: « ad imitationem imperii » (59) the pope receives the imperial *insignia* (60).

This eighth-century forgery is, as it is well known, based upon the older forgery, the so-called *Legenda sancti Silvestri* (61). This story assumes a particular significance when it is borne in mind that it was fabricated during the formative period of Gelasian times (62). The contents of this forgery throw into significant light not only the frame of mind of the author, but also the atmosphere and temper of the time. Clad in hagiographical language the forged document of Constantine's conversion says (63) that the emperor had left the faith of his forefathers and then goes on to describe how on the fourth day after his conversion the emperor conferred on Silvester and the Roman Church the privilege that all priests should have their superior («caput») in the pope just like kings should be the head of the judges (64). Moreover the Silvester forger knew that Constantine, upon the request of the pope, put down his purple mantle and diadem (p. 512) as a sign of his penitence before he was actually baptized. And on the eighth day after his conversion Constantine throws himself down on the ground as a further sign of his contrition, lays his

(59) The profound investigation of PERCY SCHRAMM, *loc. cit.*, is of particular interest in this context.

(60) As so often, Innocent III is an excellent interpreter of papal history: his interpretation of the Donation was that Silvester was made Melchisedek. In his *Sermo in Festo B. Silvestri* (*PL.*, vol. ccvxii, col. 481-4) he says that Silvester was « pontificali et regali potestate sublimis. Illius quidem vicarius, qui est Rex Regum et Dominus dominantium; sacerdos in aeternum secundum ordinem Melchisedek ». And Innocent saw how Silvester practically realized his double function: « Ex auctoritate *pontificali* constituit patriarchas, primates, metropolitanos et praesules; ex potestate *regali* senatores, praefectos, judices et tabelliones instituit ». Following the Donation Innocent declares: « Romanus pontifex in signum imperii utitur regno, et in signum pontificii utitur mitra ». How a canonist of the late J. B. Sägmüller's standing could assert that the idea the pope was emperor over the occident, « blitzte in der Donatio Constantini zunächst doch nur wie in glänzender Meteor auf, um ebenso "rasch" wieder zu verschwinden » (*Theologische Quartalschrift*, vol. lxxx, p. 69) is incomprehensible.

(61) The late W. LEVISON, « *Konstantinische Schenkung und Silvesterlegende* » in *Miscellanea Francesco Ehrle*, vol. ii, pp. 181 ff., proved the dependence of the Donation on the earlier forgery; he also showed how well known the story was in Rome, in the Frankisch kingdom and in England during the 8th century, pp. 206-14.

(62) For the dating see LEVISON, *art. cit.*, pp. 181-2.

(63) We have used the text in B. MOMBRITIUS, *Sanctuarium seu Vitae Sanctorum*, ed. H. Quentin and A. Brunet, 1910, vol. ii, pp. 508-31.

(64) *Ed. cit.*, p. 513.

crown down and wets his purple mantle with his tears. The incident is extremely pregnant and suggestive: who conferred the crown on Constantine after this incident? In whose custody, so to speak, was the crown whilst Constantine was on the ground? That Constantine was emperor again after this day, nobody ever doubted: but that the crown was put back on his head by the pope was an action that suggested itself (65). Furthermore, the conferment of the imperial *insignia* on the pope was at least implied in the *Legenda;* who else, if not the pope, was their trustee during the time when Constantine rid himself of all external imperial signs? (66)

That was the « historical » background upon which the forger in the eighth century set to work to construct his papal Melchisedek (67). By virtue of having received the imperial *insignia* from the legitimate Ruler of the Roman Empire, the pope becomes the legitimate heir of the Caesars. As pope-emperor he can use the imperial *insignia* — « papa uti possit imperialibus insigniis » — and from here to chapter viii of the *Dictatus Papae* is only a small step, though Gregory VII characteristically enough inserted a « solus » (68) As regards the imperial crown, however, an observation should not be omitted. We have seen how the *Legenda* in a very suggestive way left the question unanswered who put the crown back on Constantine's head after his humiliation on the eighth day. Now, in the Donation itself, the forger asserts that Constantine had given the crown to Silvester, but that the latter refused to accept it, not because of any scruple based upon principle, but out of humility. He kept the imperial garments, but would not wear the imperial crown. What significance can this have? On his intention to create a papal Melchisedek there can be no legitimate doubt — why then does he not go the whole way and let even this last sign of imperial power pass over to the pope, so that the institution of an empire could be regarded as superfluous altogether? We think that here is the link

---

(65) G. Laehr, *Die Konstantinische Schenkung,* p. 3, drew attention to this.

(66) We cannot agree with Levison, *art. cit.*, pp. 186, 201, 214, that the *Legenda* was merely a literary example of « Christian entertainment», a tendentious novel; even Levison has to admit that the forger pursued « certain tendencies »; what were they? We think that Wattenbach's view in *Deutschlands Geschichtsquellen,* vol. ii (6th ed.), p. 490, comes nearer to the truth when he says that the forgery pursued « hierarchical purposes ».

(67) To whom indeed the *Legenda* might well have drawn his attention, see p. 519, lines 14-5.

(68) Cap. viii: « Quod solus papa uti possit imperialibus insigniis », see Schramm, *loc. cit.*, p. 413.

between the forger in the eighth century and the Gelasian principles. We have tried to explain why Christ, according to Gelasius, had distinguished between the offices and function of emperor and pope: Christ did not wish to see the combination of royal and sacerdotal power continued in the ecclesiastics, because he knew to what dangers, owing to their « fragilitas », the clerics would be exposed, if they were to care for the material, carnal things. What the Gelasian theory amounts to is that the institution of the empire is necessary, in order to relieve the clerics from the burden of having to care also for their carnal wants. And this is precisely the same idea that the forger of the Donation had in mind when he made Silvester refuse to accept the imperial crown: he still thought that an empire was necessary, so that the pope (and the *sacerdotium*) would not have to be distracted from the proper function. The pope is Melchisedek, but out of his own volition he leaves some power to the emperor. The Donation and Gelasianism are one and the same thing: the difference between them is merely that the one originated with a clumsy historically and theologically untrained bungler, and the other with a very real Roman who was a political and linguistic genius (69). In neither case had the *imperium* been conceived of as an institution that had any inherent rights: in each case the *imperium* as a Christian institution existed by virtue of the will of Melchisedek (70).

---

(69) As far as we know there was only one attempt to relate Gelasius's theory to the Donation: this attempt was made by CASPAR, *art. cit.*, pp. 143, 147, 149; he maintained that the two powers which Gelasius had nationally separated, were also locally and geographically to be separated by the forger. Cf. p. 147: « Dem Weltbild seiner Zeit — päpstliches Rom, kaiserliches Konstantinopel — gibt er eine Rechtsbasis; als Grundlage dient dabei die gelasianische Zweigewaltentheorie ». There is a « räumliche Trennung der beiden Gewalten » (pp. 147, 149). Even « des Hierarchischen » is Gelasianism.

(70) The re-creation of the empire in the West was the direct result of the Donation: did not its very model, the *Legenda*, clearly hint at the right of the pope to put the crown on the emperor once he had become a Christian? On the connexion between the coronation of Charlemagne and the Donation, see, e. g., A. BRAKMANN, « Die Erneuerung der Kaiserwürde, etc. » in *Geschichtliche Studien A. Auck Gewidmet*, p. 133, J. FRIEDRICH, *Die Konstantinische Schenkung*, p. 174, and F. SCHNEIDER, *Rom und Romgedanke*, p. 51, and CASPAR, *art. cit.*, pp. 230-1. K. EICHMANN, *Die Kaiserkroenung im Abendlande*, vol. i, p. 28, must reject any connexion because he dates the forgery much later.

That the creation of the Christian State was the work of the papal Melchisedek, esp. the one emerging in the Donation, becomes quite clear in the writings of later hierocrats, such as Honorius of Autun, « Summa Gloria » in *Libelli de Lite*, vol. iii, pp. 71 f., see G. LAEHR, *op. cit.*, pp. 48 ff. But when the ideology of hierocratism had been developed and the

The circle was closed when the development of the idea that the pope was the vicar of Christ was completed. It is not possible, within the scope of this essay, to depict the various stages by which the claim of the pope as vicar of Christ proceeded. We confine ourselves to the ninth century when ideologically the process, that had begun much earlier, was to all intents and purposes finished. At the beginning of the re-orientation of the papacy there stood the Donation of Constantine; at its end there stood another forgery, Pseudo-Isidore. That Pseudo-Isidore shaped the mind of that able papal mentor, Anastasius, is too well known to need any comment: but through Anastasius the frame of mind of Nicholas I was shaped in precisely that direction to which historical tradition and ideological development had pointed. Although the claim that the clerics function as the lieutenants of Christ, had been dormant for a very long time, it was given its great publicity and currency by Pseudo-Isidore. When Leo I had declared that he functioned as vicar of St. Peter (« cuius vice fungimur », (71) Pseudo-Isidore applies the vicariate not to St. Peter, but to Christ Himself. « Sacerdotes vice Christi legatione funguntur « (72). The clerics are the chosen people of Christ —«in sorte Domini electi » (73) — because He Himself had selected them « ad mandata divina seminanda ». (74) Or as he makes Pope Eusebius say: « Christi vicarii sunt sacerdotes, qui vice Christi legatione funguntur in ecclesia » (75). Hand in hand with this superior function of the clerics goes Pseudo-Isidore's pronounced hostility towards anything laical. The « plebs » or the « vulgar people » (76) or those individuals « malae vitae » (77) or the «perverted individuals » (78) are all tautological expressions for the

---

Melchisedek idea had been brought to its full fruition, there was of course no more need to make the Donation an exclusive basis; we very much agree with Mgr. ARQUILLIÈRE, « Origines de la théorie des deux glaives » in *Studi Gregoriani,* vol. i, p. 414: « C'était dans la logique du mouvement des esprits. La « Donation » n'était nullement nécéssaire: elle constituait seulement pour la papauté un titre supplémentaire ».

(71) *Sermo,* III, c. 4.

(72) HINSCHIUS, p. 90, ep. ii, c. 4 of Evaristus; many other passages of other popes: e. g., CLEMENT, p. 53, ep. iii, c. 57; ep. ii, c. 56, p. 52; cf. ANACLETUS, p. 79, ep. ii, c. 22; ALEXANDER, p. 95, ep. i, c. 3 and c. 5, p. 97; ANTERUS, p. 155, c. 7, etc.

(73) URBAN, p. 143, c. 1.

(74) CLEMENT, p. 43, ep. i, c. 39.

(75) p. 239, ep. iii, c. 17.

(76) EVARISTUS, p. 91, ep. ii, c. 9.

(77) PONTIANUS, p. 147, ep. i, c. 3.

(78) ANACLETUS, p. 78, ep. ii, c. 22; FABIANUS, p. 162, ep. ii, c. 13; EUSEBIUS, p. 234, ep. ii, c. 9; JULIUS, p. 473, c. 18. *Cap. Angil.*, p. 761, c. 13, etc.

lay population (79). The practical conclusion to be drawn from the difference in function between lay people and clerics is that the latter must not be subjected to the former, that is, must not be judged or even accused by the former, since an inferior cannot judge or accuse a superior. From his strict hierarchical standpoint Pseudo-Isidore has of course no difficulties in considering the primacy of the Roman Church as one of his fundamental axioms; the Roman Church is the hierarchical apex of the « ecclesia ». The primatial position of this Church entails, *inter alia,* the specific and concentrated application to the Curch of Rome of all the rights, privileges and functions which the clergy have as a whole. In other words, the Roman Church epitomizes the superior status and function of all the clerics. Whatever rights the clerics have, and that applies in particular to their power to bind and to loosen, they have from the « prima sedes » (80). The virtual exclusion of the lay population from any say in ecclesiastical-political matters entailed the assumption of powers by the clerical authority over the whole community. By shaking off the consequences of the *Rex-Sacerdos* (still at work at his time), Pseudo-Isidore approached in a suave and propagandistic manner the *Sacerdos-Rex.* The priestly order culminating in the pope as Christ's vicar was given the government of universal Christendom (81).

Familiar as he was with this fabrication no less than with genuine history, Anastasius raises the pope to the level of a vicar of God — « vicarius Dei » —, makes him the « pontifex universitatis » and apostrophizes the pope in these remarkable terms: « Vicem namque in terris possides Dei » (82). The climate of the time can also be gleaned from a casual address of the bishop of Metz, Adventius, to Nicholas I « qui vices Dei tenetis » (83). The same bishop assures the pope that he was ready to obey the pope's edicts as if he were obeying God — « veluti Deo » — « and on Whose behalf you make everything known » (84).

Thrown against the background of such ideological expressions the religious-political views of Nicholas I, a worthy successor of the really great popes, have no element of surprise in them:

---

(79) See furthemore STEPHEN, p. 186, ep. i, c. 2.

(80) See esp. ANACLETUS, p. 84, c. 34; MARCELLUS, p. 223, c. 1; JULIUS, p. 459, c. 6.

(81) For understandable reasons the forger also included Gelasius's letter in his fabrication.

(82) *MGH., Epp.,* vol. vii, p. 397.

(83) *MGH., Epp.,* vol. vi, pp. 219-20, anno 864.

(84) *Ibid.,* p. 221: « Et ecce paratus sum obsecundare edictis vestrae auctoritatis veluti Deo in cuius persona cuncta profertis ».

he was the articulate expression of the atmosphere of the time. With him the development of the idea that the pope was the vicar of Christ, hence the vicar of Him who combined royal and sacerdotal powers, found its conclusion. It was this step that was not taken — and, we suggest, could not have been taken — by Gelasius who made Christ the last Melchisedek. The numerous references to Gelasius, sometimes also without naming this authority, make it perfectly clear how much Nicholas owed to his great predecessor; other equally influential ideas were taken from Pseudo-Isidore with whom Nicholas became acquainted through his Bibliothecarius (85). Gelasianism and Pseudo-Isidore are the two ideological pillars of Nicholas I. To him, all the privileges of the clerics, that is of the *sacerdotium*, are epitomized and concentrated in the person of the pope; indeed, he possesses the fullness of power which is diffusely dispersed throughout the ecclesiastical hierarchy. Christians *qua* Christians are subject to his authority and jurisdiction, because he possesses the « sollicitudo totius ecclesiae » (86). Hence it is by virtue of his fullness of power that the pope can rightfully claim to exercise his government over all Christians (87). The privileges of the Roman Church are all the privileges of Christ Himself: « Privilegia namque Romanae ecclesiae totius sunt Christi » (88). The Roman Church represents Christ on earth: it has the « principatus divinae potestatis » (89); Christ's ordinances are alive in the Roman Church (90).

The « principatus divinae potestatis » entails that the pope speaks « on the authority of Christ »; that he promulgates his decrees on Christ's authority; that he acts as one who « vice Christi tenet »; « auctoritate summi judicis domini nostri Jesu Christi promulgamus, sancimus atque decernimus » (91); that he judges « Dei auctoritate » (92). The pope is the vicar of Christ on earth. We recall that, according to St. Augustine, Christ was the « caput ecclesiae », that is, of the universal Church, but now when the pope becomes the vicar of Christ, he automatically assumes the role of Christ on earth; by virtue of his vicariate the pope becomes also Melchisedek. That Nicholas referred so lavishly to Gelasius I and in particular quoted also from *Tractatus IV* (without naming his source) is therefore not an incongruity, but

(85) HALLER, *Nikolaus I und Pseudo-Isidor*, p. 131.

(86) *Epp.*, vol. vi., ep. 31, p. 300; ep. 90, p. 491.

(87) Ep. 88, p. 476: « Eam (scil. Romanam ecclesiam) totius jura potestatis pleniter meruisse et cunctarum ovium Christi regimen accepisse »

(88) Ep. 60, p. 371.

(89) Ep. 82, p. 433.

(90) Ep. 71, p. 398.

(91) Ep. 91, p. 521; identical wording in ep. 94, p. 545; ep. 98, p. 559.

(92) Ep. 29, p. 296.

a confirmation of the monistic view of Gelasius. How well Nicholas I had understood his great predecessor, can be seen from the almost imperceptible insertion of a single word which, however, reveals the underlying mentality of Nicholas (and the meaning of Gelasius) so clearly: the *raison d'être* of the secular Christian power, according to Gelasius, lies in that the clerics should be left free from the burdensome, distractive pursuance of « carnal », material things; the secular power was necessary if the clerics were to fulfill their sacerdotal functions. Now, Nicholas says, whilst the Christian emperors need the priests for eternal salvation, the priests, on the other hand, should make use of the imperial laws *merely* for the management of their temporal affairs. The insertion of a « tantummodo » by Nicholas strikingly reveals the frame of mind of this pope, no less than being a correct interpretation of Gelasius (93).

The « promotion » of the pope to being the vicar of Christ, hence the head of Christianity, involved naturally a change in the function of the Roman Church of which he was the head. This was conditioned by the — at that time — acknowledged claim that the Roman Church was the primatial Church. The apostolic see decrees on behalf of the universal Church. What is laid down by the Church of Rome, is observed throughout the universal Church: « Quae ab ea (scil. apostolica sede) statuta fuerint, haec universalem ecclesiam tenuisse » (94). And when Gelasius wrote that the Church of Rome had the right to sit in judgment over every individual Church, Nicholas made this into the right to sit in judgment over the *whole* Church (95). We find perhaps the neatest expression conveying the idea that the universal Church is epitomized in the Roman Church in the very crisp dictum of Nicholas: « Universa ecclesia sancta, quae apud nos est » (96). Metaphorically, too, Nicholas explains the position of the Roman Church, when he elaborates the example of the vessel (97). Let us quote the passage in full: « Ipsius vasis instar dignoscitur in se continere universorum animalium, quae homines intelliguntur, spiritualiter nationes. Suscepit *ergo* ac continet in se Romana ecclesia quod Deus universalem ecclesiam suscipere

(93) Ep. 88, p. 486. The passage of Gelasius in its formulation by Nicholas went into Gratian, *Dist.* 96, c. 6, and was attributed to Nicholas.

(94) Ep. 91, p. 523.

(95) Nicholas, ep. 90, p. 501: « sedis apostolicae de *tota* ecclesia fas habentis judicare moderamina retinemus »; Gelasius, Thiel, p. 406, ep. 26, c. 10: « sedes b. Petri apostoli... utpote, quae de *omni* ecclesia fas habeat judicandi »; here again Nicholas did not give his source.

(96) Ep. 88, p. 480.

(97) *Acts*, x. 11-12; xi. 5-6.

et continere praecepit » (98). Lastly we may refer to Nicholas's liberal interpretation of St. Augustine (99) when he uses the saint's commentary to state: « Nos divinitus.... constituti principes super omnem terram, id est, super universam ecclesiam » (100). The world, Christianity, universal Church — all these are identical terms: the pope by virtue of his position as vicar of Christ is its *princeps* (101). The Roman Church was the epitome of the universal Church: the *sacerdotium* culminating in the pope was ideologically the ruler of the Christian world (102).

We may well sense the hierocratic temper of the time when we read in one of Nicholas's letters to the Frankish bishops (103) that the (Christian) Ruler had received the *use* of the sword from the pope in order to protect the Church against infidels. When therefore Gelasius maintained that Christ Himself had conferred the secular power as a *beneficium* on the emperor, it is now the pope as Christ's vicar who hands out secular power. It is as a son of the (universal) Church that the king receives his power through the intervention of the Roman Church, that is, through benediction and unction; should this be absent, the Christian Ruler would not be entitled to use his power (104). The very terminology employed by Nicholas I, namely, the *use* of the sword reveals the kinship between him and Gelasius: Christ

---

(98) Ep. 88, p. 478. The « homines » and the « nationes » were his own interpretation, see *Acts loc. cit.* It is interesting to see how a later hierocrat, Johannes Andreae, crisply expressed the idea of the city of Rome being the epitome of the whole world: « Urbs composita est ad exemplum orbis », *Novella* ad *Sextum,* I. vi. 17. I am grateful to my pupil, Mr. B. Tierney, for this reference.

(99) *Enarratio in Ps.* 44, 17 (*PL.* vol. xxxvi, col. 513).

(100) Ep. 88, p. 475, cf. also ep. 29, p. 296.

(101) Although Greinacher's reasonings that it was the « ausgedehnte Liebestätigkeit » of Nicholas which prompted the advance of the papacy, cannot command serious respect, he neverthless comes near the truth when he says that Nicholas pushed « das Papsttum in das Zentrum der Christenheit: der Papst erscheint als der natürliche Vertreter ihrer Interessen. Die Machtstellung Karls d. Grossen beginnt auf das Papsttum überzugehen », *op. cit.,* p. 59.

(102) Characterizing « la doctrine théocratique » Mgr. ARQUILLIÈRE, *loc. cit.,* p. 516, says (though with reference to Innocent III): « C'est, en d'autres termes, la doctrine du government du monde par Dieu, au moyen de son plus haut réprésentant ici-bas, de son suprême vicaire: le pape. Les autres pouvoirs ne sont légitimes que dans la mésure où ils sont approuvés... par ce suprême hierarque ».

(103) Ep. 34, p. 305.

(104) « Sinatur omnino a Deo protectum imperium suum, quod cum benedictione et sacratissimi olei unctione sedis apostolicae praesule ministrante percepit, ad exaltationem et quietem matris suae, huius sanctae et apostolicae ecclesiae... macherae usum, quem primum a Petri principis apostolorum vicario contra infideles accepit. »

appears in His vicar. In both Gelasius and Nicholas the secular power fulfills a function that is not inherent in it, but bestowed upon it by Melchisedek; and in both cases the State exists for the sake of the clerics: in the one case to relieve them of the burden of caring for the carnal things, in the other to protect them (105). We suggest that this slight shift of emphasis concerning the *raison d'être* of the Christian State gave rise to the theory of the idoneity of the secular Ruler: for in order to be effectively protected, the Church needs a suitable secular prince. Set against such ideas and expressions Nicholas's exclamation in his letter to the emperor Michael has no obscure, but a rather distinct meaning: « Ingrati filii circa matrem vestram, ex qua imperandi fastigium vos et patres vestri ordine coelitus disposito percepistis » (106): when it is borne in mind that every Ruler at that time had some sacral-religious character and when the Roman Church was considered the epitome of the universal Church, no difficulty exists in plausibly interpreting this exclamation of Nicholas.

We sense furthermore the hierocratic temper of the time when we witness the heraldings of the theory of the two swords which symbolize the royal and sacerdotal powers (107). St. Peter, according to Nicholas's implication, had both swords: the « corporal » sword he wielded in the case of Malchus, because of the latter's disobedience; the spiritual word he used in the case of Ananias and Saphira (108). Even if the pope had claimed no more than being a vicar of St. Peter, the suggestive character of this passage and of the idea expressed in it is too obvious to need any comment. The peculiarly Nicholean suggestive character of his statements can also be observed in regard to another idea, that is, that Christ had constituted the « see of St. Peter » within the universal Church as the « greater light » of which we read

---

(105) That, incidentally, is the reason why Nicholas omitted the words of Gelasius « Christus memor humanae fragilitatis ».

(106) Ep. 90, p. 508. The interpretations of HAUCK, *op. cit.*, p. 21, and of HALLER, *op. cit.*, p. 142, note 379, tend to obscure rather than illustrate the point.

(107) Moving within the idea of the *Rex-Sacerdos*, Alcuin, it should be noted, was apparently the first to use the allegory of the two swords which, naturally, were in the possession of the king: « His duobus gladiis vestram venerandam excellentiam dextra levaque divina potestas armavit... », *MGH, Epp.* vol. iv, p. 282.

(108) It will be recalled that the hierocrats later used the same examples, see my *Medieval Papalism*, pp. 148 ff, 195, with particular reference to Alan.

in Genesis i. 16 (109). « The greater light » is the Roman Church epitomizing the whole Church: « the greater light » was day — the potentialities of this idea were indeed very great.

The chief architects of the hierocratic system and hence of the Melchisedek idea had laid firm foundations. True, it needed some more pioneering to put this into practice, but fundamentally the spade work had been done by the time of pope Nicholas I. What we read in the works of the hierocrats from Umbertine-Hildebrandine times onward rested firmly on the ancient foundations. And what we see at work from Innocentian times onwards is the execution of an impressive system that was to leave a deep impact upon the European frame of mind. The secular power had become the « brachium saeculare » of the Church: the real meaning of this hierocratic dogma was that the State had become the executive organ of, not the universal Church, but the *sacerdotium*. This was achieved by the application of the Melchisedek idea to the pope: considering that the *sacerdotium* had taken the place of the universal Church and was considered identical with the Church, we can no more be surprised about the cry of the thirteenth-century hierocrats that it would be monstrous to postulate two heads. And the hierocrats were not entirely wrong in saying so, for past ideology supported them. It is therefore quite typical of contemporary ideology that the English canonist, Alan, in his great *Apparatus,* in concise and succinct terms puts his finger on the very problem: according to him, the emperor receives his sword from the pope, because the Church forms one body and hence can have one head only: « Verius est quod gladium habeat a papa, est enim *unum corpus ecclesia,* ergo unum caput debet habere » (110). Society was one body and that body was the Church meaning the *sacerdotium* which had advanced to the position of the universal Church. Consequently, the insistent demand during the thirteenth century — « nullum imperium extra ecclesiam » — expresses the same idea in different words: society was a *Respublica Christiana,* the universal Church, at whose head stood Melchisedek in the person of the pope as the vicar of Him Who was the « verus rex et sacerdos », who, for the sake of the (Roman) Church, had translated the empire from

(109) Ep. 103, p. 611: « ...Petri eiusque successorem luculentissimam doctrinam sedemque spernentes, quem Dei filius in sancta ecclesia sua tamquam luminare majus in coelo constituit ».

(110) *Apparatus ad Comp. I,* De Appell., Si duobus, MS Badische Landes Bibliothek, Karlsruhe, Cod. Aug. XL, fol. 13 va; also in the mixed *Apparatus* on *Comp. I* (which has a few of Richard's glosses) in MS. St Peter's Abbey, Salzburg, aIX. 18, fol. 38ra.

the East to the West (111). As usual, Innocent III was clear and concise when he claimed that he had not only been given the right to rule the *sacerdotium,* but also the *imperium,* which he called the *saeculum* (112). That on the basis of this idea of the Church, over which presides Melchisedek, the electoral college like any other secular institution could be understood as having derived its constitutional rights from the pope, presented no difficulties at all (113). The pope, we hear from the mouth of Innocent III, « est sacerdos in aeternum secundum ordinem Melchisedek, constitutus a Deo judex vivorum et mortuorum » (114). And we find also with this pope an expression with which Gelasius would not have disagreed: « Romanus pontifex... non solum in spiritualibus habet *maximam,* verum etiam in temporalibus *magnam* ab ipso Domino potestatem » (115). That all this ideology was the product of not always correct interpretation and of not always genuine documents, is beside the point. What matters is that, upon the basis of Gelasianism, Pseudo-Isidore and Nicholas I, the idea had become common property that the pope was the vicar of Christ and hence was Melchisedek. That Frederick II was smitten by the living Melchisedek at Lyons finds its effortless explanation in his persistent assertion that the « ecclesia » was something different from what his great opponent conceived it to be. The essence of the conflict centred in the different ideas about what the Church was: to Frederick II the Church was the « ecclesia universalis », the congregation of all the faithful, the Augustinian conception of the mystical body

---

(111) « Nota ipsum papam imperium propter ecclesiam Romanam a graecis in germanos translatum », Johannes de Deo in his *Flores Decretalium,* (hitherto unnoticed) MS. Cistercian Monastery, Wilhering, no. 29, fol. 6va, ad *Extra,* I. vi. 34.

(112) *Registrum Innocentii,* lib. ii, c. 209; *PL,* vol. ccxiv, col. 759: « Christus... Petro non solum universam ecclesiam, sed totum reliquit saeculum gubernandum ».

(113) Cf. again Innocent III in « Venerabilem », *Extra,* I, vi, 34: « ad eos (scil. principes) jus et potestas huiusmodi ab apostolica sede pervenerit ».

(114) « Per venerabilem », *Extra,* IV, xvii, 13.

(115) *Registrum Innocentii,* lib. viii, c. 190; *PL.* vol. ccxv, col. 767. The preceding passage is equally significant: « Licet pontificalis *auctoritas* et imperialis *potestas* diversae sint dignitates, et officia regni et sacerdotii sint distincta, quia tamen Romanus pontifex illius agit vices in terris, qui est rex regum in terris et dominus dominantium, sacerdos in aeternum secundum ordinem Melchisedek, non solum... » (as text). Would one still maintain that Gelasianism is dualism when the very words of Gelasius are used by Innocent in order to declare himself Melchisedek?

of Christ; Frederick's Church was headed by Christ, the Melchisedek. To Innocent IV the Church was the *sacerdotium* that had come to supplant the universal Church; the pope as Christ's vicar was the personified Melchisedek effectively ruling the « unum corpus » of the medieval world and enacting the drama at Lyons.

VI

The Medieval Papacy, St Thomas and Beyond

Ubi unitas, ibi perfectio (St Bernard, *De consideratione*, ii. 8).

LET me begin by saying what great pleasure it gives me to be able to address your Society this evening on a subject which is assuredly of general interest and which is also of particular interest to myself. But to use a stereotyped medieval expression employed for similar occasions, '*rem non novam aggredimur*'. Perhaps no other institution, be it religious, political, social, legal, economic, and so forth, has received so much attention as the medieval papacy; it is, I think, equally true to say that no other institution has met with so many contradictory appraisals and assessments as the Roman papacy in the Middle Ages.

It is undeniable that amongst the few institutions which have survived the storms and stresses of the historical development—stretching in fact from post-apostolic times down to this very day—the papacy must of necessity assume a very special place. The papacy is in fact the only concrete and tangible link between the primitive Christian era and our present epoch. It has outlived the ancient Roman empire for some fifteen hundred years; it has witnessed the emergence, growth, prosperity, decay, destruction and disappearance of kingdoms and empires; it has witnessed the appearance, influence, fashions and abandonment of doctrines, movements and ideologies, stretching from severe christological disputes to economic collectivism, from Gnosticism, Montanism and Arianism to Communism, from the opening up of new continents to the crossing of the Antarctic; it has witnessed, in a word, the growth of the universe from the tiny Roman world to the embrace of the whole wide cosmos.

Whilst all these features are self-evident matters of fact, it is a somewhat different matter if one wishes to find an answer to the question of why the papacy in the Middle Ages exercised such overpowering influence. Why was it that in the Middle Ages the papacy initiated, developed and applied principles which were perhaps the most potent factors in the making of Europe? What was it that guaranteed the steady progress of the medieval papacy, a progress that eventually led to its emergence as the central pivot of, and dominating factor in, Europe? Despite innumerable vicissitudes; despite seemingly insuperable obstacles; despite the absence of the usual paraphernalia of ordinary governments, that is, the lack of police and armed forces; despite the apparently unbridgeable gulf between the highly developed Roman culture and outlook and the primitive outlook of the still rather crude Western nations; despite the poverty of communications; despite many other vicissitudinous circumstances, in a word, despite the absence of any *prima facie* favourable factors, the papacy reached heights of influence and status in the Middle Ages which, even in the long and checkered history of the Continent and by the standards of any other governmental institutions, can without exaggeration be classed unparalleled.

The papacy imprinted upon the face of medieval Europe its own physiognomy. For the fact that medieval Europe was Christian, was very much the result of papal influence; considering organised Christianity it is a truism to say that Christendom was very largely the outcome of papal steps, of papal initiative, of active papal participation. What actually made medieval Christendom one entity, one unit, one body, was the indisputable fact of the papacy acting as the organ of unity. The medieval popes never became weary of emphasising the generative part played by the papacy.[1] This papal assertion had a perfectly good title-deed. It was the unique directing power claimed and effectively exercised by the papacy which supplied the life-blood, which vivified the Christian body and which determined the path of Christendom. Can one seriously maintain the view that this diversified Christian body, for brevity's sake called Western Europe, consisting of so many nations, groups, and strata of vastly

[1]That is why the Roman Church was always allegorically compared with the source of a river, as early as by Innocent I (*PL*. xx. 583): '*velut de natali suo fonte*', all other churches received their 'life' from the Roman Church. Hence also the ancient designation of the latter as the *mater et caput* of all Christianity. This theme is already in the so-called *Decretum Gelasianum* (ed. E. Dobschütz in *Texte u. Untersuchungen z. altchristl. Lit.*, xxxviii, no. 4 (1912), pp. 29–31), and quoted over and over again in papal communications. Cf. also *Miss. Romanum* for 29 June (*Oratio*): '*per quos (scil. Petrum et Paulum) religionis sumpsit exordium*'.

differing cultures, outlook and development, could have presented that living organism, that inherent capacity of resistance, that resilience and that internal vigour, that sameness above all in regard to the basic assumptions of life, had it not been for the directive powers of the papacy?

The reason why the work of the medieval papacy is so differently assessed and evaluated by the papal historians is, I think, because, generally speaking, they confine themselves—and perhaps legitimately—to the mechanisms of space and time, and thereby tend to neglect the inherent principles of the institution itself. How many papal historians have tried to explain the work and aim of the medieval papacy from within itself, from its own premises, on its own ground? Why is it that such fundamental divergencies in assessment are not encountered with histories of individual kingdoms? The inadequacy of the common historical approach to the papacy shows itself also in that the history of the papacy resolves itself so very largely into a history of popes. How many papal historians have faced up to the simple papal principle, without which no satisfactory explanation of the medieval papacy can be given, the principle that no pope succeeds another pope? For every pope, according to the papal axiom, succeeds directly, and without intermediary, St Peter. Or how many papal historians have taken the trouble to reduce papal principles of action to the Bible or to see in papal statements concrete applications of Pauline dicta? What papal historians are so much inclined to do is to consider the papacy as just one more governmental institution, in no wise different from a royal government and subject to exactly the same laws of historical evolution and recognition as are applicable to the history of a kingdom or a town, and so forth. If indeed every pope succeeds another pope, then there is really no difference between him and a king who succeeds another king. If furthermore the vital distinction between the office and the person of the office holder is not given its due prominence—and mark it, that distinction was as clearly drawn as you might wish in the mid-fifth century by Leo I by styling himself the *indignus haeres* of St Peter[2]—then it is

[2]This expression comes from Leo I, cf. W. Ullmann, *Growth of Papal Government in the Middle Ages* (London, 1955), p. 8. The term *haeres* signifies the official position of the

so very easy to slip from the permanent institution to the transient person who just happened to be pope, to commit in other words a cardinal error by wiping out a distinction which was as fundamental to the institution itself as it is to its adequate understanding. The lack of attention given to such basic principles animating papal actions accounts for not only so many divergent and purely subjective assessments of the medieval papacy, but also for the quite disproportionate status given to individual popes, thereby distorting the very institution which is to be explained.

One thing, however, seems to be clear. In the Middle Ages the papacy was considered as much divine as it was earthly, and in this latter function it was of course subjected to the ordinary laws of evolution. A divine institution indeed, but one that was charged with very definite tasks and functions to be realised on this earth, that is, charged with the realisation and transmission of the divine will through appropriate means and agencies. Primarily a governmental institution, the papacy's task was to govern, to direct, to lead by issuing decrees and laws: and these decrees emanated from its inherent divine character, and are addressed to the whole Christian Church, in itself again, just as the papacy, a divine institution. Both the government and the body over which government was exercised are of divine origin, and in as much coming within a theological purview; both are at the same time here on this earth and subjected to the factual changes and movements of a less exalted order, and in as much coming within an historical purview. The papacy is—and this is what I would like to stress before this *forum*—a governmental institution *sui generis*. To put it on the level of other governmental institutions results in its unjustifiable degradation or their exaltation, depending on the angle from which you look at it. Seen from a wider viewpoint it is certainly not beyond the bounds of doctrinal comprehension to conceive the papacy as institutionalised divinity—the concept of the vicariate of Christ, admittedly a later medieval concept,

pope as heir to the full powers of St Peter, whilst *indignus* refers to the personal unworthiness of the individual pope to succeed St Peter. This is the distinction between office and personal office-holder. It was rather late, i.e. in Tudor times, when royalist theory arrived at a similar view: 'Kings are heirs, not of kings, but of the kingdom', cited from E. Kantorowicz, *The King's Two Bodies* (Princeton, 1957), p. 373; for France, s. *ibid.*

would strongly bear this out.[3] *Papa est Deus*, often enough maintained in medieval times and hardly ever understood in modern times, was to express the one 'nature' in the pope. But I am anticipating things.

The visitor to St Peter's basilica is suitably impressed by the inscription over his tomb, an inscription that bears in large letters the Petrine commission of Matthew xvi. 18: *Tu es Petrus. . . .* Appearing in a somewhat innocuous manner, this commission contains *in nuce*, so to speak, the whole programme, the basic principles of the papacy. A comparison with any other declaration would only detract from the fullness of powers committed to St Peter by Christ himself. It is futile and useless to explain this—as in fact it has been done—as the Magna Carta of the medieval papacy, and an explanation of this kind is only apt to show that he who tries to proceed in this manner admits of the limitations of his perception. Fulness of power, indeed, as proved by the unambiguous and, in its conciseness unsurpassable, wording: '*Quodcumque* ligaveris . . .' and the *quodcumque* expresses, according to the constant papal reasoning, the totality of power: neither person nor matter is excluded. What was essential in the papal view was the binding and loosing here on this earth: the binding and loosing in heaven is the automatic consequence of the binding and loosing here. The essential feature is the conduct of the Christian on this earth and in this world. This automatic consequence is of crucial importance if one wishes to understand the principles of the medieval papacy. There is, to express the same thought crudely, no superior tribunal or court of law that can control or revise or confirm the judgment of St Peter and of his successors. This is the recurrent theme in the thousands of papal communications—the pope '*non solum terrena, sed coelestia quoque dijudicat*'.[4] If we keep this principle in mind, we have taken a not inconsiderable step towards understanding the comprehensive powers of the medieval papacy. For that principle is expressed in the *claves coelorum* which are in the pope's hands. Or in the easily available juristic terminology this profound idea was

[3]About the 'christology' of the pope I hope to report separately.

[4]Innocent III in *Suppl. Register*, 89 *bis* (*PL.* ccxvii. 131); also *Reg.* ix. 73. The same expression before Innocent, made by Alexander III, *Ep.* 150, and Celestine III, *Ep.* 235 (*PL.* ccvi. 1127).

presented in the guise of the *claves juris*[5] and in the formula that the pope had been entrusted with the *jura terreni simul et coelestis imperii*.[6] In a word, the whole Christian body was for governmental purposes in the hands of the monarch, the pope.[7]

The binding and loosing power of Matthew xvi. 18 is, however, only one of the pillars of the medieval papacy: the other is John xxi. 16 f. with its threefold command of Christ to St Peter: *Pasce oves meas*. Now this command tallies perfectly with the Petrine commission and is actually the fulfilment of Caesarea Philippi: the *pascere* in this passage is derived from the Old Old Testament[8] and means the exercise of proper judicial power. Hence the insistence of the papacy from the fourth century onwards that it alone was given the power to judge, hence also the emphatic insistence that papal decrees are statements of law, and in parenthesis we may note that the very term *decretum* or *epistola decretalis* is derived from the final juristic decision, the *decernere* in a law suit—hence also the ease with which the early papacy, and therefore also the medieval papacy, could borrow notions and terms from the Roman constitution. The thing itself was entirely non-Roman; the name to signify the thing was Roman.

The pope possessed therefore the *principatus*, a succinct Roman constitutional term expressing the jurisdictional primacy of the pope. And for purposes of government this same *principatus* appeared also in the shape of a charismatically inspired but equally native Roman *auctoritas*. The pope was credited with

[5]St Peter Damian in his *Disceptatio synodalis*, ed. in *MGH., Lib. de lite*, i. 78, lines 7-8 Cf. also his poem no. 72. in *PL*. cxlv. 941.

[6]Pope Eugenius III in his *Ep*. 232, of 12 Oct. 1147, in *PL*. clxxx. 1285. The formula becomes a standing phrase, cf. Honorius III in *MGH. Epp. sel. XIII saec*., i. 163, no. 234; Gregory IX, *ibid*., p. 568, no. 672; Innocent IV, *ibid*., ii. 52, no. 71; idem, in *Acta imperii inedita*, ed. E. Winkelmann, ii. 698, p. 1035: '*Jesus Christus . . . in apostolica sede non solum pontificalem, sed et regalem* **monarchatum** *constituit, b. Petro eiusque successoribus terreni simul ac coelestis imperii commissis habenis, quod in pluralitate clavium competenter innuitur, ut per unam, quam in temporalibus super terram, per reliquam, quam in spiritualibus super coelos accepimus . . .*'. For the fourteenth century see, e.g., John XXII in *Extravagantes*, V, cap. un., and Benedict XII in *MGH. Constitutiones*, v. 256, no. 525 and p. 266, no. 546.

[7]Innocent III in *Reg*. vii. 1: '*Expresse notatur, quod Petro non specialiter aliqua ecclesia, sed* **totus mundus** *commissus fuerit*'; *Reg*. ii. 209: '*Petro non solum universam ecclesiam, sed* **totum** *saeculum gubernandum reliquit . . .* **universum** *orbem susceperat gubernandum*'. On the dependence of Innocent III on St Bernard, cf. *Growth of Papal Government*, pp. 426 ff.

[8]Ezek. xxxiv. 16 and 17: '*Ego pascam oves meas*' and '*Ego judico inter pecus et pecus*'.

these attributes because of his *direct* succession to St Peter: *cuius vice fungimur*—we function on behalf of St Peter[9]—the fulness of power was inherited by the pope. In contemporary terminology the pope was seen as the monarch, the *monarcha*, precisely because of his succeeding to the Petrine commission. The *monarchia* or the *monarchatus* of the pope was nothing else but the Petrine commission expressed in a more usual and also easily available nomenclature. It is exactly the same idea which re-appears in the pope's designation as *Rex* and *Sacerdos*: in medieval times the concept of monarchy, of the true *monos* and *archos*, was always understood to comprise both regal and sacerdotal powers. And when once the vicariate of Christ in the pope was fully developed, it was not indeed so difficult to see in the pope the vicar of the true *Rex et Sacerdos*, namely, Christ.[10] Moreover, by virtue of this vicariate of Christ the pope acted in his dual capacity, both as king and priest, and could justifiably apply to himself a number of biblical expressions,[11] notably '**Per** *me reges regnant and principes dominantur*'.[12] The application of biblical *dicta* appears to me to contain a very articulate and neat designation of Christ's true monarchy on earth. At the same time the mediatory principle was thereby given concrete shape: there is but 'one mediator between God and men, the man Christ Jesus',[13] and this truth finds its practical realisation in the vicar of the Mediator, the pope who designates himself rightly as '*inter Deum et hominem* **medius** *constitutus*'.[14]

The directive power contained in the papal monarchy related to the conduct of the individual Christian as well as of Christian

[9]Cf. II Cor. v. 10.

[10]Cf. Apoc. i. 5: '*princeps regum terrae*'.

[11]Such as Ps. xxiii. 1 and xliv. 17: '*Domini est terra et plenitudo eius orbis terrarum et universi, qui habitant in eo*'. The latter passage—'*constitues eos super omnem terram*'—is also incorporated in the *Graduale* of the *Miss. Romanum* ad 29 June. Cf. furthermore Jer. i. 10 which was also capable of papal application; also Matt. xxiv. 45 (cf. Innocent III in his second consecration sermon, *PL*. ccxvii. 653 ff. and St Bernard, *De consideratione*, iv. 1).

[12]*MGH. Const*., iv. 80, no. 105.

[13]I Tim. ii. 5.

[14]Innocent III in his sermon, *PL*. ccxvii. 658; cf. also idem in *Reg*. i. 335; the pope '*non puri hominis, sed veri Dei vicem gerit in terris*'. It is not without irony that the words quoted in the text were literally repeated by the Countess of Arundel and applied to King Henry III in 1252: '*medius inter Deum et nos constitueris*', see Matthew Paris, *Chron. maj*., v. 336, and E. Kantorowicz, op. cit., p. 162, at note 222, who has not, however, seen the Innocentian source.

rulers. The papacy considered, again basing itself upon biblical ideas, that the act of baptism worked, so to speak, a metamorphosis in the natural man. Man with all his natural appetites, aims, maxims and inclinations was transformed into a Christian which is something fundamentally different from the natural man. Baptism is a regeneration, a re-birth—the individual is re-born, has shed his characteristics as a man of nature and appears as a new creature. But since he has to live on this earth, his whole orientation, outlook, being and maxims are no longer determined by the postulates inherent in his nature, but exclusively by the postulates flowing from his participation in the divine attributes. What mattered was not the natural man,[15] but the reborn man, the Christian.[16] Baptism, on the one hand, raised the individual out of his natural surroundings, by endowing him with specific qualities so that he partook in the divinity of Christ. On the other hand, baptism was always considered an eminently legal act, by virtue of which the Christian becomes legally a member of the Church; he becomes thereby an essential link within the corporate union of Christians. This corporate union, the *corpus Christi*, the Church, is itself a divine foundation having been instituted by Christ Himself and therefore as plainly as possible a creation that has nothing whatsoever to do with nature.

These are pretty obvious topics and yet it is astonishing to see how little they are taken into account in assessing, and making accessible to understanding, the work of the medieval papacy. We must realise that the medieval papacy (and medieval men generally) were not familiar with the modern categorisation of human activities: this atomisation of our own actions is of rather recent date—the religious, social, political, economic, and so forth activities were unknown. What there was, was the Christian, and he was considered as one whole and his life judged on that basis alone. There was no splitting up of his actions into political, moral, social, religious, and what not activities: he was considered as a Christian and as nothing else. He was in a very real sense held to have been one indivisible whole—every one of his actions was thought to have been accessible to judgments by

[15] I Cor. ii. 14.
[16] I Peter i. 23.

Christian standards and norms.[17] You could not have a religiously indifferent action as you could not have an action outside the pale of the fixed Christian code. It is the totality of the individual Christian that counted, and not his political, religious, moral and what not strain, and it is the totality of powers conferred by Christ on Peter which is exercised upon man as a Christian.[18] That all this is thoroughly Platonic as well as Pauline and Augustinian goes without saying. Hence also in a very real sense it may well be said that the most conspicuous feature of the papal exercise of Petrine power was its totalitarian character—I need not say here that I use the term totalitarian with no modern overtones whatsoever, but simply as an adjective for totality—since through the efficacy of baptism the life of the Christian was now subjected to Christian standards, epitomised in the Petrine commission. It is one of the most disquieting features amongst so many who have tried to interpret the medieval papacy that this totalitarian orientation is so wantonly overlooked, that in other words the distinction between mere man and the Christian is not adduced as the basis of the explanation. For to the papacy this was one of the vital principles, without which the whole imposing edifice breaks down. To confuse the two, to interchange the man and the Christian, is to commit a cardinal error, with fatal consequences at least as far as an attempt to understand the medieval papacy goes.

Once this axiomatic principle is given its proper due, it will not be too difficult to see why the papacy insisted upon directing the whole Christian. If indeed Christianity was a force that seized

[17]Although looking at this medieval feature from an entirely different standpoint, O. Brunner, *Land und Herrschaft*, 3rd ed. (Vienna, 1943), pp. 4–5, stresses the medieval principle of *Ganzheit* and queries whether certain categories, such as '*Wirtschaft*', '*soziale Verhaltnisse*', '*geistiges Leben*', etc., were not better omitted altogether.

[18]Cf. the constant papal interpretation of Matt. xvi. 18 in the sense of a totality of power, in Gelasius I, *Tract.* IV, cap. 5, p. 562 (ed. A. Thiel, *Epp. Romanorum pontificum genuinae* (Braunschweig, 1862)): '*In "quibuscumque"* **omnia** *sunt quantacumque sint et qualiacumque sint*'; id. in *Ep.* 30, cap. 12, p. 445 (*ibid.*): '*His verbis (scil. quodcumque ligaveris) nihil constat exceptum . . . et* **totum** *possit generaliter alligari, et* **totum** *consequenter absolvi*'. Adrian II (862–72) repeats Gelasius literally, *MGH. Epp.* vi. 701, *Ep.* 4, lines 4–5; John VIII, *ibid.*, vii. 187, *Ep.* 210, lines 27 ff.: '*Divina potestate, quam accepit ecclesia Christi,* **cuncta** *solvuntur vincula, quando per pastoralem auctoritatem, quae fuerant ligata, solvuntur*'; Innocent III in *Extra*, I. xxxiii. 6: '*Nihil excipiens, qui dixit "Quodcumque ligaveris"* . . .'. It was on the basis of this totality of power that Gregory VII insisted on the *universale regimen* of the papacy, *Reg.* ii. 44, p. 180 (ed. Caspar). Cf. also Egidius Romanus, *De eccl. pot.* (ed. R. Scholz, Leipzig, 1929). i. 3. p. 9: what matters is the *totus homo.*

the whole of the individual, if indeed every one of his actions was prompted—or should have been prompted—by Christian motives and principles, then it is wholly understandable why the papacy was bound to direct the Christian's so-called temporal life. If we judge spiritual and celestial things, how much more do we decide and judge the earthly and secular, said Gregory VII in a memorable, but so heavily censored, passage which is simply a paraphrase of another profound Pauline expression.[19] What the medieval papacy did was to act as the agency that concretely applied Pauline views. The important thing is that the temporal, that is the purely mundane and transient, cannot and does not have within the Christian framework—and one must, I believe, assume that the medieval papacy acted within a Christian framework—any value in itself. Matter, to use a modern but legitimate transposition, is dead, has no meaning, no value, no purpose, no life of its own: it must be directed to some end; it receives its whole meaning from the purpose to which it is put, and that purpose can within the terms of a christocentric society only be determined by Christian norms and standards. On the basis of this teleological and self-evident point of view, life on this earth is the one essential feature in the path of a Christian, and when you recall what I have said about the automatic consequences of Petrine, i.e. papal judgments, you will realise the added significance of the comprehensive papal government. Matter or the temporal, to have any meaning at all, must serve a wholly Christian purpose. Man as a Christian and Christian society were one and indivisible: they could not be split up into different compartments. '**Omnes actiones** *christianorum sunt ordinatae ad consequendam vitam aeternam.*'

Perhaps on no other count has the medieval papacy been so severely censored as for its very active and effective concern with the so-called temporal. But the fiercer and the more self-righteous this censorious attitude is, the surer you can be that real understanding of the medieval papacy is lacking. Is it really possible—taking the wholeness of the Christian and consequently of

[19]Gregory VII in *Reg.* iv. 2, p. 295, ed. cit., and I Cor. vi. 3; cf. also id. in *Reg.* viii. 21, p. 550: '*Cui ergo aperiendi claudendique coeli data est potestas, de terra judicare non licet? Absit.*'

Christian society, the Church, as one's starting point—to distinguish between the temporal and spiritual? Who lays down the dividing line, if indeed a dividing line can be discovered? The interpreters of the medieval papacy who castigate the institution from their own modern point of view, in reality import a distinction which was not there. Or better, they attribute to the temporal, to matter, an autonomous character, precisely the feature which was so emphatically denied by the papacy—and denied on wholly Christian and biblical grounds. Why blame the papacy for doing something that was its duty to do? Or are the modern critics of the medieval papacy better and more trustworthy interpreters of the Bible than the most distinguished line of the successors of St Peter? One might almost think so. It is unfortunately also true that even amongst Catholics it is nowadays considered bad taste to refer to the medieval papacy. '*Spiritualis homo judicat omnia et ipse a nemine judicatur*' said St Paul, and the medieval popes, acting within the charge committed to them, implemented this as so many other Pauline statements.

Evidently, for purposes of government it would have been a contradiction in terms if the papacy had tried to direct, that is, to govern the Church—the *congregatio fidelium*—by mere persuasion. For governmental purposes the directive instruction, the binding rule, is indispensable, hence the importance which the papacy at all times attached to law. Law, according to papal doctrine in the Middle Ages, is merely the crystallisation of the idea of *justitia*, and since the Roman Church was held to have been the *sedes justitiae* and since, furthermore, what mattered was the Christian concept of *justitia*, who else was better qualified to pronounce upon it than the successor of St Peter possessing the *claves juris*?[20] The laws issued for the whole Christian body emanated from the monarch himself and transformed the mere idea of *justitia* into concrete and universally applicable rules of action.[21]

In implementing the principle of monarchic government the papacy also implemented another equally important principle

[20]This is of importance for the validity of customary law; the criterion was *rationabilis et justa*, i.e. accordance with divine precepts, and the Roman Church as the *sedes justitiae* could at all times override customary law.

[21]This is what I have in a different context called 'Juristic Theology'.

(again of distinguished ancestry), necessitated by the numerous functions to be performed within the vast *corpus*, the *societas christiana*, the Church. 'We are many, but not all have the same functions', said St Paul. This is the principle of division of labour. Proper directive *auctoritas*, supreme legislative power, must always remain with the papal monarch. But the important point to be borne in mind is that this principle of division of labour can adequately be applied only if the functions are allocated by the monarch. The correct appreciation of this principle presupposes what for want of a better name I call the descending theory of government: all power comes, metaphorically speaking, from above, and is transmitted to the lower organs by the pope as the monarch. I will return to this point in a moment, but I would like to stress in this context that the concept of papal monarchy does not mean that the pope himself has to do all the governing and has to perform all governmental acts by himself. Far from it: he institutes the bishops by conferring upon them the *potestas jurisdictionis*—as successors of the apostles the bishops have only the *potestas ordinis* which is of no concern to us here—and in this way the popes could again invoke the bible when they declared that the bishops were called upon to partake in the pope's plenitude of power—'*ut sis vocatus in partem sollicitudinis, non in plenitudinem potestatis*' wrote Leo I[22]—because after all the solicitude for all the churches rests upon the pope alone, another Pauline application.[23] Evidently, functions could be allotted only to those who were suitable—the principle of suitability for the office—and hence, quite apart from all other considerations, the insistence of the papacy to exercise control over episcopal appointments and the demand for episcopal obedience enforced through the episcopal oath.

Potestas jurisdictionis, the power to govern his diocese, the bishop received from the pope,[24] the effluence of the principle of division

[22]Leo I, *Ep.* 14, cap. 1. The biblical background is Luke x. 41-2.

[23]II Cor. xi. 28.

[24]This is a correct application of the vertical form of government. The episcopalists maintained that in their functions the bishops were equals of the pope and as successors of the apostles received both the *potestas ordinis* and the *potestas jurisdictionis* without the intermediary of the pope. As far as I can see there has never been an official statement by the papacy on this delicate point, and it is well known that the *Tridentinum* and the *Vaticanum* shirked clarification of this question. If my reading is correct, however, it

of labour within the sacerdotal sphere. It is exactly the same principle which is at work in the regal sphere in which for the execution of papal rulings the pope appoints a lieutenant, an auxiliary organ, a *brachium*, principally in the shape of the Roman emperor. And here, too, the principle of suitability assumes its proper place. That is why the pope was called the *speculator*[25] who metaphorically may well be compared with the conductor of an orchestra in which all the players, that is, the emperor, the kings, princes, bishops and so forth, have to play their allotted part, but in which the conductor himself alone has the full score and accordingly directs the whole orchestra.[26]

Generally speaking, the lay ruler, that is, the Christian layman who wielded public power, was according to papal conceptions just as much a member of the Church as the lowliest villein or the most exalted patriarch. With this difference, however, that he possessed power in the public sphere and had at his beck and call an army and other means of physical control. Furthermore, there existed between the lay ruler and divinity a special connection: not only was he as a member of the Church *qua* Christian subjected to the pope—in no wise different from any other Christian—but as regards his powers he was in a quite particular sense the recipient of divine favours. And it is these favours which were transmitted by the pope by virtue of the mediatory rôle. In the widest possible sense rulership was held to be a divine favour or a divine *beneficium*, a good deed, a *favor* or a *gratia*. No lay ruler had a right to rulership which was nothing else but a divine grant and a concession transmitted in the last resort by the pope.

seems that Pius XII in a rather unobtrusive manner settled this centuries-old moot point in no unmistakable terms whose significance appears to have been overlooked: '*Id tamen dum faciunt* (*scil. episcopi*), **non plane sui juris sunt, sed sub debita Romani pontificis auctoritate positi,** *quamvis ordinaria jurisdictionis potestate fruantur,* **immediate sibi ab eodem pontifice summo impertita**', *Acta Ap. Sedis*, xxxv (1943), pp. 211 f. (also in Denzinger, no. 2288); emphasis mine. In this recent papal statement we note the ancient juxtaposition of pontifical *auctoritas* and episcopal *potestas*. The introduction in the eleventh century of the formula for the bishop, '*episcopus Dei et* **apostolicae sedis gratia**' brings the correct papal standpoint towards the bishops clearly into relief. The best literary statement of an anti-episcopalist nature is that by Johannes de Turrecremata, *De pontificali . . . auctoritate* (Venice, 1563), no. 22, p. 16 verso: '*ceteri apostoli non immediate a Christo jurisdictionem acceperunt, sed* **mediante Petro** *apostolorum eorum principe*'.

[25]Biblical model: Ezek. iii. 17.

[26]This metaphor is actually suggested by Cardinal Johannes Monachus in his gloss, cf. *Growth of Papal Government*, p. 447 note O. Aug. Triumphus compared the pope with the general of an army, *S. de eccl. potestate* (ed. Rome, 1584), p. 133.

Further, this Christian lay ruler was established for a particular purpose—again the Pauline background appears: '*princeps non* **sine causa** *gladium portat*'—and that purpose (*causa*) was the extermination of those evils which struck at the very roots of Christian society. What is, and what is not, evil, in a Christian society, must obviously be determined by those who are specifically qualified to pronounce upon this theme. Vice versa: the lay ruler was by no means granted an autonomous status by the medieval papacy: he was simply the agency that eradicated evil. His was no monarchic status; his was a mere *potestas regalis*[27] and his function was purely auxiliary, having received the sword, from the pope, for the explicit purpose of combatting evil. Consequently, his laws are valid only in so far as they do not contradict evangelical or canonical decrees, as already Deusdedit[28] and Gratian had it (x. 6) or as Egidius Romanus will later demand: the laws of the kings are to be confirmed—'*confirmandae sunt*'—by the ecclesiastical authority.[29]

This conception of the lay ruler, despite the obvious disadvantages it brought him, had nevertheless also some compensatory features for him. He owed nothing to the people he ruled. The people, on the contrary, was entrusted to him by Christ. The standing phrase '*populus mihi commissus*' or the very significant prayer text on the occasion of the king's coronation, a text which has a very good pedigree, dating from the late eighth century and in use throughout the Middle Ages (and also in 1953),

> Be anointed . . . king over the people whom the Lord your **God has given you to rule and govern** . . . that by the assistance of this heavenly **grace** you may govern and preserve the **people committed to your charge** (*populus tibi commissus*),

[27]The contrast between *auctoritas* and *potestas* was sharply pointed up by Gelasius I: Christ, as true Monarch, had both—the old monarchic principle, cf. Jud. 25: *imperium et potestas*, and was in fact designated as *Imperator*, cf. E. Peterson, '*Christus Imperator*' in *Theol. Traktate* (Munich, 1951), pp. 148 ff. For Christ depicted as emperor, cf. E. Stauffer, *Die Theologie des Neuen Testaments*, 4th ed. (Stuttgart, 1948), Table 71, hence also the medieval designation of the pope as *imperator*. St Augustine, too, spoke of Christ as *imperator*, cf. *PL*. xxxvii. 1163: '*in ipso tabernaculo Imperator militavit pro nobis*', cf. Kantorowicz, op. cit., p. 72, note 68.

[28]*Libellus contra invasores* (ed. in *Lib. de lite*, ii. 352 f.), iii. 12.

[29]*De ecclesiastica potestate*, ed. R. Scholz (Weimar, 1929), ii. 10, p. 92: '*Omnes tales leges a potestate terrena editae . . . per potestatem spiritualem et ecclesiasticam confirmandae sunt. Est enim justitia res spiritualis.*'

are as clear indications of the kings freely acknowledging the divine derivation of powers and their denying any popular element in their rulership as are the standing designations: *rex* or *imperator Dei gratia, divina gratia, divina clementia, divina ordinatione*, and so forth. This is a very important point: the kings had detached themselves from the popular assembly, had emancipated themselves from the grip of the people and recognised the source of their power in Christ, and no longer in the people. This descending conception of government accorded entirely with basic Christian tenets as well as with the principles developed by the papacy itself. Rulership being a divine favour, a divine *beneficium*, a divine grace in the widest sense, the king or emperor had no right to it.

It does not need much historical imagination or doctrinal acumen to realise the vast potentialities of this papal axiom—and the papacy relentlessly drove the point home, especially after the vicariate of Christ in the pope had been fully worked out. Since Christ was *Rex et sacerdos secundum ordinem Melchisedech*, from whom all power stemmed, the pope as his vicar could claim the same position, with the consequence that rulership originated in the pope who dispensed it according to the exigencies of the time and persons. Both the language and actions of the papacy from the eleventh century onwards are evident, concise and consistent on this point, and they make it crystal clear that the popes considered themselves as the mediators of divine favours so that rulership was held to be a *favor apostolicus*. And once again the popes hammered in another Pauline theme—that the lay rulers should show themselves grateful for the favour thus received.[30] All this stands in closest proximity to the other fundamental Pauline and deeply Christian axiom: we have no inherent right to anything, and what we have, we have by the grace of God. *Gratia Dei sum id quod sum.*[31]

The papal programme derived its strength from many sources,

[30]Clearly stated by Gelasius I, in his *Ep.* 1, cap. 10: '. . . *beneficiis non ingratus* . . .' and repeated frequently by later popes; hence also the claim that the popes have to render an account of how kings have discharged the trust put in them. Biblical model: Hebr. xiii. 17. For the historical development cf. W. Ullmann in *Misc. Historiae Pontificiae*, xviii (1954), pp. 107 ff.

[31]I Cor. xv. 10.

chief amongst which is the Bible and the conception of the Church. What the medieval papacy tried to do was to translate the Bible and especially Pauline maxims into the workaday world —a gigantic undertaking. In more than one sense one can speak of the papal programme and work as the application of biblical doctrine in practice. And the entity to be governed according to these papal principles was the *universitas fidelium*, the *corpus Christi*, the Church. This was the one society; the Christian was the one individual with whom the papacy dealt. It is on this exclusively Christian level that the work of the papacy becomes accessible to understanding. The natural man as such did not enter into the vision of the papacy: why should he—was it not precisely the miraculous effect of baptism which enabled man to conquer himself, to shed his natural self, to raise himself? Within the papal programme and the traditional Christian doctrine (which again I must assume was correctly expounded by the medieval papacy) there is no room for a natural man, there is no room for a natural society, there is no room for an independent, self-sufficing, autonomous conception of the State. The corporate organic, juristic and visible union of all Christians was at once earthly and divine. It was one and indivisible.

To this closely knit, so well integrated, biblically founded and historically developed scheme of government there was no answer: true, kings and emperors, and particularly the latter, often enough attempted to impugn, not so much the essence of this programme as certain features and consequences of it. From the purely human standpoint the opposition of the lay rulers is perhaps understandable. What the anti-hierocrats were groping for was to find a basis which was the lay ruler's own: that is, they valiantly tried to discover the ground upon which the lay ruler stood, so as to fix for him a sphere of government in which he alone, autonomously and independently of the papacy, could rule. In this attempt—made in the eighties of the eleventh century—can be seen the first glimmerings of the modern idea of the State, for it was this the anti-hierocrats were groping for, but which with the means at their disposal and on their premises they never could find, since they spoke the same language, employed the same arguments and took their stand on the same Bible:

what hope could there be to combat successfully the papacy which so conspicuously derived its very life from the Bible and based all its themes on the Bible? Who stood a better chance to be accepted as an expositor of the Bible, the papacy or the king or emperor? If you want to attack your opponent you must have at least a modicum of your own ammunition, and not borrow everything from your enemy. You must above all and primarily attack the premises and bases of your opponent.

All the battles which the anti-hierocrats delivered were nothing more than skirmishes. Perhaps with the exception of Archbishop William Bona Anima of Rouen, a frontal attack upon the hierocratic premises is conspicuously absent. The attacks concerned the periphery but never the core of the programme. Thus, the Petrine commission was not impugned: what was impugned was its extent claimed by the papacy. Only those things the pope was said to be entitled to bind and to loose which he can bind and loose. And in further elaboration of this shallow and barren thesis the doctrine emerged, of which we hear for the first time in the moving communication of Henry IV in 1076, that there was a *dualitas* of government: this dualist conception of government was to be the panacea for all future generations of anti-hierocrats. It was not only this concept and programme of a dualism that was introduced by Henry IV, but also the allegory of the two swords owed its publicistic utilisation to the same opponent of Gregory VII: Christ had given one sword, the spiritual, to the pope, and the other, the temporal, to the emperor or king. One can only marvel at the *naïveté* that inspired such reasoning. This thesis tried to deny the mediatory role of the pope and to draw a line of distinction where on christocentric premises no such line could be drawn. And when you looked at the actual coronation ceremony you would have found perhaps the best reply to this Henrician scheme: just as the pallium was taken from St Peter's altar, so was the sword by the pope, who himself girded the candidate with it. Could there be a more convincing symbolism to show how and from whom the emperor received his sword, i.e. that physical means of his government which constituted his *raison d'être*? Rightly therefore has the medieval papacy condemned this dualism, because in its essence it attacked vital Christian and therefore papal principles. The height of this dualist ideology was reached when the Staufens declared that there was a dual vicariate of Christ: the emperor was the vicar of Christ the King, the pope the vicar of Christ the Priest.[32]

Another line of attack was attempted with equally little success, though with perhaps greater doctrinal significance. This school of thought hit at the device to deprive the concept of Church of its earthly connection and to present it as a mere mystical body. The *corpus Christi* was, as it were, mysticised, de-mundanised, inflated, with the result that its purely sacramental, pneumatic character came to be stressed at the expense of its earthly reality.[33] This thesis exercised a certain attraction, because of its indubitably Pauline background. If the purely sacramental aspect of the Church is stressed, then there was indeed no need for a law, for a tribunal and governmental institutions. The notion of *jurisdictio*, for understandable reasons, loses its earthly connection. The more the Church was conceived as a purely mystical body, the more it tended to evaporate into the elusive regions of other-worldliness, with the consequence that the essence of Christianity as a force that shapes and determines earthly life is apt to undergo some radical change. That the papacy could never adhere to this deflated or truncated concept goes without saying. Within a purely mystical union there was no need for a papacy or, for that matter, for any organisation at all.

On its own ground—as in fact history proves—the papal-hierocratic theme was unassailable: without difficulty the papacy could weather the storms. The danger to it lay not in its pro-

[32]Cf. e.g., Frederick I in *MGH. Const.*, i. 254, no. 183; also Frederick II in Huillard-Bréholles, *Hist. Diplomatica Frederici II*, v. 1125. Even in the fourteenth century emperors claimed the *plenitudo potestatis*, derived from this concept, e.g. Henry VII in *MGH. Const.*, iv. 308, no. 361; Louis the Bavarian, *ibid.*, v. 517, no. 653, vi. 207, no. 291; Frederick of Austria, *ibid.*, v. 372, no. 450. In the fifteenth century Antonius de Rosellis, *Monarchia* (ed. Venice, 1612), p. 273, lines 4–5, speaks of '*duo vicarii distincti ordinarii*', because '*Deus eternus duos constituit vicarios, unum in spiritualibus, alium in temporalibus*'. Even the Jeremiah passage was applied to the emperors themselves, as late as by Louis the Bavarian, *loc. cit.*, vi. 344, no. 436. It may be recalled that Bracton too styled the king a '*vicarius Dei in terris*' and one who governed in stead of Christ, cf. ed. Woodbine, ii. 20; 33; 305.

[33]It should perhaps be pointed out that the concept of *corpus mysticum* was used for the Eucharist only down to the twelfth century, s. H. Weisweiler, *Maître Simon et son group* (Louvain, 1937); and H. de Lubac, *Corpus Mysticum*, 2nd ed. (Paris, 1949), pp. 116 ff.; cf. also A. H. Chroust in *Review of Politics*, ix (1949), p. 436.

gramme; the danger lay in the introduction of principles which could fall on soil fertilised by the anti-hierocrats. What they were groping for was an autonomous and independent basis for the lay ruler—a hopeless task with the means at their disposal. It was less so, if the themes of the Philosopher were brought to bear upon the issue itself. For if it could be shown that next to the Church there was another society or body which was autonomous, self-sufficing and independent, for and on behalf of which the lay ruler acted, then indeed the matter assumes a very different complexion.

Certainly from Innocent III onwards the papacy was perfectly alert to the inherent dangers of Aristotelianism and what is of particular interest here, of its naturalism. The prohibition of Aristotelian studies by the papacy shows how keenly alive it was to the corroding assumptions of the Philosopher. The translation provided by William Mörbeke certainly provided a secure basis, and the seemingly impossible task of reconciling Aristotle with Christianity was performed by Thomas who created an ingenious synthesis of disparate elements. It was the Thomist synthesis which deprived Aristotelianism of its most harmful ingredients. In the history of ideas this synthesis was a major achievement, but precisely because it was a synthesis it contained potentially harmful germs, unless the presuppositions upon which the synthesis was erected were punctiliously adhered to.

As far as concerns my topic the gist of Aristotelian teaching is that there exists a union or a society which is the product of nature. This *human* union, called the State, is a natural product with its natural propensities, natural aims and ends. One of the characteristic features of this theme is its emphasis upon the naturalistic essence, for it is the working of nature manifesting itself in the natural man and natural society which is its hallmark. A thesis such as this, propounded as it was by the Philosopher of antiquity, could not fail to exercise great attraction and there is no gainsaying this influence in the thirteenth century—witness Siger of Brabant, Thomas's contemporary, who on an unadulterated naturalistic-Aristotelian basis developed an extreme kind of naturalism within which the natural man became the determinative principle, and for the Christian there remained hardly any room.

If there is a society, a State, which is a natural product, growing from below upwards, from the family, through the smaller communities to its comprehensive consummation, then this State, because it is a product of nature, is not only a perfect entity, but also one that is essentially *human*, consisting of nothing else but natural men: the *homo*—and not the *christianus*—becomes the central feature within this framework.

The Thomist definition of man as an *animal politicum et sociale* must therefore be seen in its correct perspective. Man is an animal and that animal is also political.[34] The concept 'political' therefore makes its unheralded and inconspicuous entry into the discussion.[35] It was not a term that could have exerted any influence on papal doctrine before this time: for the very existence of this mental category, of the 'political', presupposes the existence of some other mental categories, such as religious, moral, etc. But as I have tried to show, the papacy operated entirely on a 'totalitarian' basis, i.e. conceived man as a Christian only and viewed all his activities from the standpoint of wholeness.

But now through the introduction of Aristotelian theorems—having been worked out in immemorial times by the Philosopher and quite independent of medieval reality—a feature was introduced that was to be of enduring influence. By adopting the Aristotelian *civis*, the Aristotelian *homo* and its characterisation as an *animal*, Thomas reconciled it is true the *homo* with the *christianus*, but also opened up hitherto unknown fields of vision. Not only did the Thomist doctrine usher in a correctly understood *humanism*—and is not the pregnant Thomist term of *humanitas* a clear pointer?—with all its fructifying consequences, but he also provided, again on an Aristotelian basis, the first doctrinal elaboration of the State in the West, viewed as a creation of nature, that is as the result of the natural instinct: '**per instinctum naturae** *inditum a summo regente, qui est actor naturae*'.[36] Thereby a real and articulate kind of dualism emerged. The individual could

[34]Sometimes *homo* is also called *naturaliter sociale animal* in *De reg. principum*, i. 2 (ed. Venice, 1593), fol. 165v; or *animal naturaliter civile* and *optimum animalium* in the Comm. to the *Politics*, I lect. i, fol. 3 and 4, ed. cit.

[35]He defines political science (*politica scientia*) as *civilis scientia* wherein the accent lies upon the *civilis*, i.e. a science dealing with the *civis*, whence *civitas* and *civilitas* with their human overtones.

[36]*De reg. princ.*, i. 12, fol. 165v.

now be viewed under the aspect of Man (*homo animalis*) by nature as well as under that of the Christian by grace; there is an *et-et*, and no longer an *aut-aut*. And arising out of this fundamental dualism there was now not only the dual conception of the functions of law—the one to direct man towards God, the other towards his fellow men[37]—but also a State, self-sufficient, autonomous, standing on its own feet and master in all respects pertaining to it; being a product of nature, and nature leaves nothing imperfect, the State is therefore a perfect community,[38] a *corpus morale et politicum*.[39] Next to it there was the Church, also self-sufficient, autonomous, its own master in all respects pertaining to it, but not because it was a product of nature, but because it was a product of divinity. The one entity is subject to the natural forces of growth and evolution, the other is instituted, is founded by a divine act.

I do not think it is necessary for me to comment upon the genuine revolutionary character of this doctrine. The reconciliation is provided by the axiom that *summus regens est actor naturae*, i.e. by the efficacy of the divinised natural law.[40] The *impressio divini luminis in nobis* operates through the *lex naturalis inserta* (*in nobis*) which enables in turn man to be in the possession of the *principia naturalia* of his action. Thereby man was rescued from the oblivion to which he had so long been consigned; room was found for man within the Christian cosmology. Just as the *homo* or the *civis* was now a being in his own right with his own natural critical faculties and his own *virtus*, so now was the State endowed with its own natural ends, faculties and *virtus*. Negatively expressed, the State, being a product of nature, had nothing what-

[37]For this point cf. O. Schilling, *Die Staats und Soziallehren des Hl. Thomas von Aquin* (Paderborn, 1923), pp. 135 ff. with special reference to *Summa Theologiae*, II–ii, xc, art. 2, xcvi, art. 1.

[38]The State is '*quoddam totum perfectum*', Comm. *Politics*, II lect. ii, fol. 17; I lect. i, fol. lv: '*ultima est communitas civitatis ordinata ad per se sufficientia vitae humanae . . . ipsa est perfectissima*'; cf. also ibid., fol. 3: '. . . *illa erit perfecta communitas, quae ordinatur ad hoc quod homo habeat sufficienter, quicquid est necessarium ad vitam, talis autem communitas est civitas . . . unde manifestum est, quod civitas est communitas perfecta*'.

[39]Lucas de Penna wrote, obviously influenced by his fellow countryman, that the prince concludes with his *respublica a matrimonium morale et politicum* (Comm. ad *Cod. Just.*, XI. lviii. 7, no. 8); see on this important development E. Kantorowicz, *op. cit.*, pp. 214–6.

[40]For the concept of natural law amongst the Romanists, cf. W. Onclin, '*Le droit naturel selon les romanistes des xiime et xiiime siècles*' in *Misc. Moralia A. Jansen* (Louvain, 1948), ii. 329 ff.

soever to do with the papacy, neither in its origin nor in its establishment. On the basis of Thomist premises, and only on their basis, it was perfectly legitimate for Thomas to say that any authority, including the secular authority, has coercive power—*virtus coactiva*—in respect '*non tantum temporaliter, sed etiam spiritualiter propter conscientiam*'.[41]

This dualistic aspect, by which the natural assumes its own status as of right, is executed by Thomas with rare consistency. In order to show this, I would like to refer to a doctrine of his which has, in this context, not been properly evaluated. This doctrine concerns the virtues: you know that the seven virtues were divided into the four so-called moral (also called by Thomas political) virtues (justice, temperance, fortitude and prudence) and the three theological virtues (faith, hope and charity). Now according to the traditional doctrine, the four cardinal virtues were considered indifferent—hence not really virtues—unless the actions prompted by them were inspired by one of the three theological virtues. The four virtues had no autonomous standing and received their substance from the theological virtues. Here again Thomas made another revolutionary contribution: he considered that the four cardinal virtues in themselves produced morally valuable actions, quite irrespective of whether they were inspired by the theological virtues.

> *Actus virtutis politicae non est indifferens, sed* **de se bonus**, *et si sit gratia informatus, erit meritorius.*[42]

I do not think I need to labour the pregnant implications of a statement such as this.

But this view so succinctly expressed in Thomas's doctrine of

[41]II *Sent.* xliv. ii. 2, ed. cit., fol. 146: '*Dictum est obedientia respicit in praecepto quod servat debitum observandi. Hoc autem debitum creatur ex ordinatione praelationis, quae virtutem coactivam habet non tantum temporaliter, sed etiam spiritualiter propter conscientiam, ut Apostolus ad Romanos, XIII, secundum quod ordo praelationis a Deo descendit . . .*'

[42]Quoted from Dom O. Lottin, '*Les vertus morales acquises, sont-elles de vraies vertus? La réponse des théologiens de Pierre Abélard à s. Thomas*' in *Recherches de théologie ancienne et medievale*, xx (1953), at p. 36. Dom Lottin is the first authority to have pointed to this decisive passage. This is of course in accordance with Thomas assigning an independent status to philosophy, about which cf. Ueberweg-Geyer, *Grundriss d. Geschichte d. Philosophie*, 12th ed. (Basel, 1951), pp. 141 ff. Thomas's view of the independence of the acquired virtues was utilised polemically by John Quidort, *De eccl. pot.* (ed. J. Leclercq, Paris, 1942), c. 19, p. 234.

the virtues re-appears in exactly the same way in the context which is of direct interest to us: *Gratia non tollit naturam, sed perficit.*[43] The underlying theme here too is that for its existence, functions and working the State is in no need of grace; but if grace is brought to be borne upon the State, it will be all the better. As far as the inherent purpose of the State is concerned, that is, to provide for the *bene vivere*, the State is autonomous and self-sufficient. The consequence of this theory was that what was hitherto considered the unquestioned character of government, namely the descending theory, was now reversed. Thomas gave a great impulse to the revival of the half-forgotten ascending theory of government[44] by his concept of the *regimen politicum*, according to which the ruler is bound by the laws of the citizens.[45] His definition of democracy leaves nothing to be desired: democracy lies in the people's power, in the '*potestas populi*' in so far as '*ex popularibus possunt eligi principes et ad populum pertinet electio principum*'.[46] Power resides with the people who arrange for their government by election, so that the ruler '*personam eius (scil. populi) gerit*',[47] or still better: '*Quod rector civitatis facit, dicitur civitas facere*'.[48] The Thomist presupposition is, however, at all times that *Deus est actor naturae*, a presupposition that enables him to achieve the reconciliation. On its own premises the Thomist system was a superb masterpiece of synthesising: it erected an intellectual and all-embracing structure which moulded fundamentally divergent and contradictory elements into one consistent whole. In short, it was a balanced system.

Its applicability depended exclusively, however, upon the strict adherence to the principles of Thomas himself. Any correction or modification or reduction or a particular emphasis upon the one

[43] *S. Theol.*, I-ii. cix. 2.

[44] It is noteworthy that just at this time the Roman law principle '*Quod omnes tangit, ab omnibus approbetur*' assumed great practical importance. Equally, the ideological significance of the *Lex Regia* in Roman law gained in practical and theoretical significance, cf. e.g., Ockham, *Breviloquium de potestate papae*, ed. L. Baudry (Paris, 1937), III. xiv, p. 96; of modern literature cf., e.g., Freiherr von der Heydte, *Die Geburtsstunde des souveraenen Staates* (Passau, 1952), pp. 314 ff.

[45] In contrast to the *regimen regale* in which the king has *plenaria potestas* and acts on his own initiative and in accordance with the laws he himself has given (Comm. ad *Politics*, I lect. i).

[46] *S. Theol.*, I-ii, cv. art. 1.

[47] *Ibid.*, II-ii, lxvii. 2, ad primum: '*princeps qui curam populi habet et eius personam gerit.*'

[48] *Ibid.*, I, lxxv, art. 4 ad 1.

or the other item will inevitably lead to a very different situation. Destroy the delicate balance and you are left with explosive fragments. What Thomas did was to allow Aristotle to enter the drawing-room, strictly guarded and watched. But what if the guards were withdrawn? if no longer a watchful eye were kept on him? if he were left to himself so that his naturalist theorems could be given a free rein? Or to look at it from a different angle: was not the doctrine of the State, conceived on Aristotelian-naturalist lines, the very answer which the anti-hierocrats had been groping for during the preceding centuries? Was it not that they were presented, one might almost be tempted to say, gratuitously, with the very concept that they themselves could never discover? Was it not possible to snap the link between God and nature?[49] Is it really a mere coincidence that representative institutions in the fourteenth century developed so greatly, incorporating the idea of the ascending form of government?

It does not really need much historical imagination to put oneself into the position of Thomas's contemporaries who, perhaps not always correctly perceiving the subtle and balanced structure of the Master, would sense the inherent capabilities of the system. What proved itself of particular significance was that the naturalistic theme of the State was very soon afterwards made the main object of the French anti-hierocrats in their conflict with the papacy. The end of the thirteenth and the early fourteenth centuries witnessed the heroic stand of the papacy under Boniface VIII against the French king, Philip IV, and the literature accompanying this conflict is very strongly permeated with Aristotelian-Thomist themes.[50] The anti-hierocrats or royalists were now in the position to fight a battle with nearly equal weapons, and the first really able and successful attack on the hierocratic theme came from the pen of John Quidort. The desperate stand which Boniface adopted, however firmly rooted it was in the traditional point of view and however much buttressed it was by Thomas's

[49]This is correctly stressed by O. Brunner, op. cit., p. 153, when he says that there grew up '*seit der Spätscholastik eine Lehre von einem nicht gottgebundenen, sondern aus der menschlichen Vernunft zu deduzierenden Naturrecht, das die These vertritt, dass dieses Naturrecht kraft* **Vernunftseinsicht** *auch dann gelten würde, wenn es keinen Gottgabe*' (emphasis mine).

[50]Cf. R. Scholz, *Die Publizistik zur Zeit Philips d. Schönen* (Stuttgart, 1906), pp. 22 ff., and the as yet unpublished (Cambridge) dissertation of my pupil, Dr M. J. Wilks: *Augustinus Triumphus and the problem of authority*.

own statements, could not stem the tide. More and more was it emphasised, not indeed in accordance with Thomas, that the Church was merely a mystical body and more and more emphasis was given to the product of nature, the State. The Thomist balance was tilted. Can it be wondered at that only a few years hence Dante will operate with the *civilitas humana*—and note the overtones in the Dantesque apotheosis of the union of all men, whether Christian or not in the *universitas humana*[51]—endowing this universal body politic with autonomous character that pursues its own end,[52] and that still a few more years later that Marsiglio, again on Aristotelian-naturalist lines, will develop the theme of the concept of State and of popular sovereignty, according to which all coercive power rests with the people? It is the humans, pure and simple, who elect their own officers and their own government; it is the State which through its own and exclusively coercive laws lays down its own path, its aims and ends, because it has its own natural moral code. It is no surprise to hear Dante exclaim and applaud '*il Maestro della nostra vita, Aristotile*'. There was, as the same Dante had it on the authority of Thomas, a *duplex ordo in rebus*, and it is this double ordering which becomes the characteristic feature of late medieval thought.[53]

The *universitas civium*, the State, within barely a generation, had arisen to take its place beside the Church, conceptually the *universitas christianorum*.[54] For a mystical body there was, as Marsiglio was insistent and as John Quidort had already indicated, no need to have tribunals, courts of law, or even the law, that is,

[51]S. *Monarchia*, I. ii and iii. The idea that all men were God's creatures gave rise to the theory that the pope as vicar of Christ exercised power over all men, whether Christians or not; this was maintained before Thomas by Innocent IV and afterwards by Boniface VIII: '*Romanus pontifex super reges et regna constitutus a Deo in ecclesia militante hierarcha summus existit, et super* **omnes mortales** *obtinens principatum*', *Les Registres de Boniface VIII*, no. 4401.

[52]S. for this and the fundamental difference with Thomas, E. Kantorowiz, *op. cit.*, 463-4, 484: Dante was 'to release the "human" from the Christian aggregate of thought'.

[53]Cf. Dante, *Monarchia*, I. vi; and Thomas, Comm. *Politics*, I lect. iii. Thomas also declared that '*(ecclesia) assimilatur* **congregationi politicae,** *quia ipse populus ecclesia dicitur*', s. A. Hauck in *Hist. Vierteljahrschrift*, x (1907), at p. 474. In close proximity to the *duplex ordo* is the problem of double truth, cf. A. Maurer in *Medieval Studies*, xvii (1955), 233 ff.

[54]This separation of the Church from the State will give rise to such weird designations as (in the U.S.A.): *The Order of St Benedict Inc.*, indicating that corporational character is accorded by State legislation.

an enforceable rule of action. That within this trend of thought the question of apostolic poverty assumes added significance, seems evident.[55] Enforceable rules can come only from that entity which by nature is the State. The officers of the Church, and hence the pope, can only give counsel, can exhort, but no longer decree and enforce their decrees, so as to produce results in the social life within the State. That right appertains only to the citizens, because they naturally form the *universitas civium* with which the papacy had nothing to do.[56] The State constitutes *animalem naturam*.[57] In close proximity to Thomas, Marsiglio defines the State as a '*congregatio perfecta et terminum habens per se sufficientiae*'.[58] The government therefore as elected by the citizens '*repraesentat totam universitatem*',[59] which again is a rather concise view of the ascending form of government. Only in their capacity as Christians may the citizens follow the advice of the pope—and you note the vital dichotomy between the citizens and the Christians—but such counsel of the pope cannot display any effects in the purely mundane life, unless the sovereign people, the *legislator humanus*, has made this counsel its own and shaped it into law. This is a resounding victory of Aristotelianism—it is at the same time the dawn of the modern era. Politics and theology, enforceable law and unenforceable morals, appear henceforward as the twofold criteria, the result of the working of the *duplex ordo*. For the one, the *animalis homo* and the *societas humana* are competent, for the other the Church and the pope. The totality of the Christian was denied.

Whilst however Thomas had erected the delicately balanced structure concerning the natural and supernatural entities and had within this structure neatly delineated the scope and extent of the

[55]This connection is not seen by F. Tocco, *La quistione della povertà nel secolo XIV* (Naples, 1910). Hence also the pre-occupation by writers with the problem of *dominium* and *proprietas*. One of the charges made by Louis the Bavarian against John XXII was the latter's alleged dogmatic error to conceive of Christ as a '*rex terrenus et mundanus regnorum et principatuum dominium possidens temporale nec erat pauper* . . .'.

[56]For the denial of the papal *potestas coactiva*, s. *Def. Pacis*, II. v. 6, pp. 189 f. (ed. R. Scholz), and *passim*.

[57]*Def. Pacis*, I. ii. 3, p. 11, ed. cit.

[58]*Ibid.*, I. iv. 5, p. 19; I. iii. 4, p. 15, and 5, p. 16. The employment of the Dantesque formulation by Marsiglio, i.e. the *civitas* as a *civilitas*, should be noted: I. i. 3, p. 5; I. xiii. 4, p. 73; II. xxii. 13, p. 433, etc.

[59]*Ibid.*, I. xii. 5, p. 65.

State's authority by confining it to its natural ends, subsequent Aristotelians considerably widened the scope of the State's authority, so that by Marsiglio's time the State as the *universitas civium* came to emerge as the all-embracing entity, even to the extent of appointing and regulating the clergy, because they form part of the State, are, in other words, citizens, and for their functions and institutions dependent upon the citizenhood, the people—a theme that is again quite clearly foreshadowed by John Quidort. Once this line was taken, the next step followed logically: it is the *legislator humanus*, i.e. the sovereign people which by virtue of its own natural perfection determines the character of its own legislation and can on this same premise extend so very greatly the subject-matter of the laws.[60] The State, because a product of nature, legislates upon all matter relating to the *bene vivere* of the citizens. What, in short, constitutes *bene vivere*, is the result of the sovereign insight of the sovereign people into its own sovereign needs. Over and above all stands the popular will. God's causality in this is, if indeed it is expressed in so many words, conceived as a *causa remota*—the divine intervention fades away. And it will not be so very long before we read in the fifteenth century that the entire social life, including language, education, laws, the actual cohabitation of the citizens, the State, are human inventions made, for utility's sake, *duce naturae*.[61]

How receptive the fourteenth-century soil was for this sort of ideas, can be seen from their influence in the least expected quarter. For the ever so attractive theory that power resides with the people was with increasing, almost alarming, force applied to the Church. Although consisting of many strands, notably not always correctly understood canonistic themes and of the old force of episcopalism, the conciliar theory is very largely the application of the principle of popular sovereignty to the Church itself, with the result that residual power within the Church

[60]According to Marsiglio (I. xviii. 2, p. 121) the government '**regula** *est atque* **mensura** *cuiuslibet civilis actus*.' Emphasised terms are strongly reminiscent of Thomas's definition of law, *S. Theol.*, II-ii, xcv, art. 3.

[61]Franciscus Patricius Senensis in his *De reipublicae institutione* (ed. Paris, 1575), see, p. 13: '*Civilem societatem quam civitatem appellamus* **hominum inventum** *esse* **utilitatis gratia duce naturae**, *nequaquam mihi ambigendum esse videtur. Est enim homo sociale . . .*'.

rested with the Christians themselves who, just like the citizens of the State, elect their own officers and above all, act through the representative General Council:[62] the pope instead of being the monarch, divinely appointed, a successor of Peter and vicar of Christ, becomes now a mere representative of the *congregatio fidelium* to whom he is responsible and on whose behalf he acts.[63] The ascending theory of government had won an equally resounding victory in the ecclesiological field. During the heyday of conciliarism it could well and truly be said that Peter is built upon the Church. With all due solemnity the Council of Constance in its fourth session decreed that the Council *represented* the whole Catholic Church,[64] had its authority *directly* from Christ —'*potestatem* **immediate** *a Christo habet*—and therefore demanded obedience from everyone, including the pope: '*cui quilibet cuiuscumque status vel dignitatis,* **etiamsi papalis existat,** *obedire tenetur*'. In a word, effective coercive power comes from below, and no longer from above as a result of the mediatory role attributed to the pope. The pope is no more than a *caput secundarium* in this scheme of things and, above all, he becomes structurally a member, admittedly of some importance, of the Church itself: he stands *within* the *congregatio fidelium* and has ceased to form an estate of his own, standing outside and above the Church and therefore above the law, the very hallmark of the proper papal monarchic doctrine;[65] his earlier visible detachment from the Church gives way to his being incorporated into the

[62]The importance of John Quidort in this context has been noted by a pupil of mine, Prof. B. Tierney, *Foundations of Conciliar Theory* (Cambridge, 1955), pp. 161 ff.; cf. also E. Merzbacher, '*Wandlungen des Kirchenbegriffs*' in *Savigny Z., Kan. Abt.*, xxxix (1953), pp. 343 ff. and M. Seidlmayer in his review of Tierney's book, *ibid.*, xliii (1957), 374-88, at p. 383 f. The misunderstood Roman principle '*Quod omnes tangit*' (about which s. H. Jolowicz, 'The stone that the builders rejected' in *Seminar*, xii (1954), 40 ff.) also played its rôle. Cf. also Y. M. J. Congar in *Rev. hist. dr. fr. et étr.* xxxvi (1958), 210 ff.

[63]The designation of the pope as '**servus** *servorum Dei*', used since Gregory I, was now conveniently inverted.

[64]This is clearly modelled on Conrad of Gelnhausen's definition and function of a General Council, s. Martène-Durand, *Thesaurus novus Anecdotorum* (Paris, 1717), ii. 1215, and for some remarks cf. W. Ullmann, *The Origins of the Great Schism* (London, 1948), pp. 197 ff. Ockham in his Dialogue (Goldast, *Monarchia* Frankfurt, 1614, ii. 514) had stated that '**papa . . . a communione fidelium** *solummodo habuit* **jurisdictionem**'.

[65]Cf. Dietrich of Niem, *De modis uniendi* (ed. H. Heimpel, Leipzig, 1933), pp. 7, 12, 72 etc. Hence the Petrine powers are brought to earth, p. 39: '*Tali concilio ipse papa in omnibus tenetur obedire. Tale concilium potest potestatem papae limitare, quia tali concilio, cum representat ecclesiam, claves ligandi et solvendi sunt concessae.*'

Church, hence the easy applicability of corporation laws.[66]

I cannot leave this topic without saying a word about the increased importance now also given to the natural man. If indeed the *homo*, or seen from the political angle, the *civis*, becomes the criterion of all evaluation, it is not difficult to see why the Quattrocento shows us features which are in striking contrast with its immediate predecessors. I am sure you will appreciate the significance of the fact that the term *laicus* more and more fades into the background, and his place is taken by the *homo* or *civis*. The important feature of this so easily unnoticed change is that *laicus* is still related to the concept of Church and only within this framework makes sense and assumes meaning. For to operate with the *laicus* is to admit implicitly and logically the corollary, the *clericus*. The citizen, man, does not bear the overtones of another complementary concept; he stands alone and on his own feet.[67] It is furthermore a well-attested fact that the Middle Ages brought forth no biographies, no portraits, no pictorial representations which in any way would have mirrored the man himself: what there was, was typified and stereotyped, almost petrified, material which lacks the distinguishing mark of individuality. *Mutatis mutandis* the same may be said about the absence of *belles lettres* in which human passions, human failings and human heroism figured. Is it not significant that no one in the Middle Ages ever thought of painting a landscape? Nor was there anything approaching the rights and duties of man as man. Language always being a first-class signpost, is it not again significant that the very term of *filius naturalis*, the illegitimate son, conveys unmistakable overtones implying an inferior status? Are not, furthermore, the proverbially low hygienic conditions of the Middle Ages a rather clear pointer? What, in short, mattered was not the *homo naturalis*, natural man, with all his natural individuality, natural wants for his natural well-being, his natural proclivities, but the Christian, the baptised man, standing on an entirely different level.

[66]On this s. Tierney, *passim*.

[67]That the *civis* assumes proportions quite different from those of a *laicus*, becomes clear from a statement by Thomas, *S. Theol.*, I. lx. 5: '*Est etenim* **virituos civis**, *ut se exponat mortis periculo pro totius reipublicae conservatione*.' It would be difficult to substitute *laicus* in this passage.

How very different from the fourteenth and fifteenth centuries. In a Dante, Petrarch, Boccaccio, there is a search for the discovery of man's true nature. Why does poetry make such great strides? Why do the natural sciences leap ahead? Why is it that masters such as Jan van Eyck, Piero della Francesca, Konrad Witz, Donatello, and so forth, present us with these magnificent pictures showing the real physiognomy, the true nature of man?[68] Why is there in the fourteenth and fifteenth centuries such intense concentration upon natural man, resulting in a veritable discovery of his natural personality? From now onwards the physical contours of man become discernible. 'Art imitates Nature', Aristotle had said.[69] Man had become emancipated. The almost exclusive fixation of the attention given to natural man naturally tended to obscure the Christian. Here the fact no doubt invites attention that now also whole books came to be written on the excellence and dignity of Man—Gianozzo Manetti and Piero della Mirandolla spring to mind with the titles of their books: *De dignitate et excellentia hominis* and the *De hominis dignatate*.[70] It is again no coincidence that whilst the naturo-centric emphasis made such great progress and so rapidly, the christo-centric orientation lags behind. What there is is a regurgitation and repetition almost *ad nauseam* of well-worn themes, without the fresh breeze of the new and original. From the position of the initiator the papacy was driven into a position of accommodation and adjustment. When in 1439 there arose in Felix V the last antipope ever to claim this distinction—and he distinguished himself not very conspicuously—this fact alone, I believe, would seem to prove more convincingly than I could hope to prove by a lengthy disquisition. And in resisting certain demands made by Pius II, the Austrian emperor, Sigismund, protested against papal interference in matters of State, because this was an issue of the natural law which cannot be touched by anyone, not even the pope.[71] To a true medievalist this protestation by an emperor telling the

[68]S. the very fine observations by R. Hamann, *Geschichted. Kunst von der altchristl. Zeit bis zur Gegenwart* (Berlin, 1933), pp. 406 ff. Cf. now esp. H. Schmidinger, 'Das Papstbild in d. Geschichtschreibung des M.A.' in *Rom. Hist. Mitt.*, i (1958), at 144 ff.

[69]Aristotle, *Physics*, 194a, 20.

[70]Ed. by E. Garin (Florence, 1942).

[71]The *naturalis ratio* was invoked by the French against the papacy in the early fourteenth century in forbidding the export of bullion, gold, silver, horses, etc.

pope where papal rights begin and end, is a perturbing illustration of the turn things have taken.

You have allowed me to expound before you the perennially fascinating theme of the medieval papacy and to indicate the reasons why the institution exercised so overwhelming and overpowering an influence that it might well be called the epitome or quintessence not only of the corporate union of Christians, but also of the particular kind of Roman-Christian civilisation which we have inherited. The secret of this assuredly unparalleled success can be revealed in a very short formula—strict and ruthless adherence to principles; faithful loyalty to vital axioms; dynamic initiative on all fronts. I have furthermore tried to indicate—albeit limited by the boundaries of my perception—some of the reasons which contributed to the decline of the medieval papacy's power and status. That decline can be compared to the opening bars of the atonal symphony of the modern era. I can rarely resist the temptation to think that in our own days the ascending form of government has been rather effectively resuscitated, almost evangelised, and that we may well witness the equally effective return to the pre-Pauline *homo animalis* with all his pre-occupation for his material, natural, well-being. Where is there room for the totality of the Christian? Where is there room, even if the possibility existed, for the exercise of the totality of those powers which Christ had given to Peter:

Tu es Petrus et super hanc petram edificabo ecclesiam meam?

VII

The Development of the Medieval Idea of Sovereignty

I

THE unsuccessful attempt of the Emperor Henry VII to bring King Robert of Naples to his knees marks the last imperial effort to assert in practice the universal overlordship of the emperor over kings and princes. This episode also reveals the influence of the papal curia on the outcome of this far-reaching contest. The quarrel between Henry VII and Robert of Naples constituted a real test case of the political strength of the medieval empire. The core of the question was whether the emperor was in reality the ' dominus mundi ' as the law books so clamorously maintained : that is to say, had he jurisdictional powers and authority over the kings of the various kingdoms constituting the Holy Roman Empire, or were the heads of the kingdoms equal in their legal and political status to that of the emperor ? The first alternative was naturally the point of view of Henry VII, the second, which signified the theoretical disintegration of the empire, was the standpoint of Robert. The outcome of this contest clearly brought to light that the empire had ceased to exist as a political and homogeneous unit. Its fabric had already been profoundly shaken and Henry's attempt to assert his overlordship over Robert was the last practical attempt to maintain a position that, however much in agreement with the letter of the law, failed to suit the temper of the time. When Clement V issued his famous bull *Pastoralis cura* he succinctly gave formal expression to a current of political thought which political thinkers had entertained for some time. With this bull the political supremacy of the Holy Roman Empire over kingdoms was formally repudiated by the curia.

This struggle between emperor and king is interesting as an indication not only of the importance of political theory and speculation, but also of the vacillation and quickly changing policy of the papacy which eventually decided the issue. For whilst, in agreement with Innocent III, Boniface VIII recognized the French king's *de facto* independence of the empire, but asserted his *de jure* dependence on the empire, a few years later, Pope Clement V repudiated Innocent III's and Boniface VIII's views, and maintained, in general terms, that kings were *de facto* as well as *de jure* independent. Thus not only the French, but also the Neapolitan king were sovereign heads of their kingdoms. After the turn of the century Clement V found himself taking up an attitude which was in complete harmony with that of the vigorous assailants of Boniface VIII.

The many-sidedness of this struggle between emperor and king faithfully reflects the conflicting ideological forces prevailing at the time. On the one hand, we witness the last solemn word of the ruler of the Holy Roman Empire, which was in effect a pathetic cry for times gone by; on the other hand, there is that trend in political theory and speculation which successfully attempted the justification of the actual disintegration of the medieval empire. Robert would never have dared to go so far in his challenge of imperial prerogatives and in obvious defiance of the existing laws, had he not been backed by political theory. And it is this latter to which we owe the modern concept of sovereignty—with all its implications. This ideological movement came to an end in the second decade of the fourteenth century, soon after the victory of the king over the emperor.

Towards the end of the thirteenth century the actual weakness of the empire moved the Austrian Engelbert, abbot of Admont, to bewail this lamentable state of affairs in his *De Ortu et Fine Romani Imperii.* In the preface to his work the abbot allows us an insight into the mentality of contemporary educated men. He refers us to a conversation which he had with some prudent and mature men; the subject of this conversation turned upon the state in which the Holy Roman Empire found itself: some said that the empire was so weak, both in its juristic structure and in its actual power that it would soon cease to exist altogether; the others said that the empire rested upon force, and its absorption by its component kingdoms was only a natural development.[1]

This narrative of the abbot shows the actual state of affairs under Henry VII better than any learned disquisition. The empire as the supreme political unit came to be buried during his reign. But this funeral was far less the result of force or violence than the direct outcome of one current of political thought which, had it not been for the papal pronouncement, might never have assumed the proportions which it actually did assume.

[1] Goldast, *Politica Imperialia*, Francofurti, 1614, p. 754.

II

What Henry VII really attempted was the practical realization of the legal axiom embodied in the *Corpus Juris Civilis*, namely that theoretically the emperor was lawful overlord and supreme monarch of Europe: every king and prince was inferior to him. Now, in practice this imperial superiority meant, firstly, that the *crimen laesae majestatis* could not be committed against a king, e.g. the French or Spanish; secondly, that the only authority entitled to issue universally binding rules was the emperor, i.e. that his laws had the same binding force within, say, the French domain, as they had in Germanic lands; thirdly, that the creation of public notaries—those entrusted with drawing up documents to which full legal authority was attached—was the sole prerogative of the emperor; fourthly, that the legitimation of illegitimate children was a privilege reserved only to the emperor; fifthly, that an appeal could be made to the emperor against a sentence of a king. These five items do not of course exhaust the legal and political supremacy assumed by the emperor, but they were some of the most frequently discussed topics.

According to the law, D. 14, 2, 9 and C. I. l. 1, this supreme authority was indivisible and inalienable: [1] the emperor was 'lex animata', legality and justice personified—every human creature was subjected to his will. The universal overlordship was also recognized by the interpreters of canon law. The glossator of the *Decretum*, Johannes Teutonicus,[2] however, formulated in a succinct form an idea that proved to be of greatest importance. Commenting upon *Dist.* lxiii. 22, he declared this universal overlordship of the emperor as of right, whilst at the same time, he exemplified the words 'per singulas' in this *distinctio* by a reference to France and Spain. He set forth the idea that the emperor was 'dominus mundi',[3] and had jurisdictional authority over every king, unless a king proved to be exempted from the emperor's overlordship.[4] Apparently the famous decretal of Innocent III *Per Venerabilem*, issued in

[1] See the present writer's *Medieval Idea of Law*, London, 1946, pp. 50 ff., 179 f.

[2] Johannes Teutonicus was a pupil of Azo in Bologna, see Johannes's gloss to *Dist.* lxxxv. 4. J. F. Schulte, *Geschichte der Quellen und Literatur des Canonischen Rechts*, Stuttgart, 1877, i. 173, thinks that Johannes finished the *Glossa Ordinaria* before the Fourth Lateran Council, 1215. But F. Gillmann, *Die Entstehungszeit der Glossa Ordinaria zum Gratianischen Dekret*, Paderborn, 1920, pp. 184 ff., and S. Kuttner, 'Eine Dekretsumme des Johannes Teutonicus', in *Zeitschrift der Savigny Stiftung, Kanon. Abt.*, xxi (1932), 142, *id.*, *Repertorium der Kanonistik*, Rome, 1937, p. 93, prove that the *Glossa Ordinaria* was finished a short time after the Lateran Council.

[3] His interpretation of *Decretum*, vii. 1. 41, was identical.

[4] 'Unus est enim imperator, ut vii in apibus, quod concedo nisi probent se exemptos ab imperatore.' Cf. also the passage below, p. 5, n. 2.

1202,[1] gave legal expression to an actual state of affairs: Innocent III declared, inter alia, 'insuper cum rex (Franciae) superiorem in temporalibus minime recognoscat'.[2] This decretal opened up a wide field of controversy. One of the first juristic reactions to this decretal came from the pen of the famous canonist Alanus in 1208. In assessing the worth of his dictum we must not, however, lose sight of the fact that he was English [3] and that therefore his interpretation of this decretal may have been somewhat biased. He declared that 'unusquisque enim tantum juris habet in regno suo, quantum imperator in imperio'. In this interpretation we may well detect the germ, if not more, of the later 'rex in regno suo est imperator'.[4] But the importance of this canonistic utterance does not seem to have been fully recognized, for Bernardus Compostellanus Antiquus, in his gloss on this decretal, still distinguished between a *de facto* and a *de jure* independence. And it was this distinction, first introduced by this glossator, which became the pivotal idea of stalwart imperialists. In his gloss Bernardus said: [5] 'De facto (scil. non recognoscit), de jure tamen subest (scil. rex) Romano im-

[1] Potthast, *Regesta Pontificum Romanorum*, no. 1794.

[2] *Decretales*, iv. 17. 13; C. Mirbt, *Quellen zur Geschichte des Papsttums*, 4th edn., 1924, p. 183.

[3] And not French, as Guido Pancirolus, *De Claris Legum Interpretibus*, Leipzig, 1721, p. 124, seems to think; see Schulte, *Quellen*, i. 188, n. 7. Alanus's *Apparatus* was finished before 1209, see R. v. Heckel, 'Die Dekretalensammlungen des Gilbertus and Alanus', in *Zeitschrift der Savigny Stiftung, Kanon. Abt.*, xxix (1940), 116–357 and S. Kuttner, 'Bernardus Compostellanus Antiquus', in *Traditio*, i (1943), 289, n. 52.

[4] The whole passage runs thus: 'Et quod dictum est de imperatore, dictum habeatur de quolibet rege vel principe, qui nulli subest. Unusquisque . . . (as text) . . . divisio enim regnorum de jure gentium introducta a papa approbatur, licet antiquo jure gentium imperator unus in orbe esse deberet', quoted after J. F. Schulte, 'Die Literaturgeschichte der Compilationes Antiquae', in *Sitzungsberichte d. kaiserl. Akademie*, lxvi (1870), 89–90; cf. also J. Rivière, *Le Problème de l'Eglise et de l'Etat au Temps de Philippe le Bel*, Louvain, 1926, p. 428. Alanus's gloss is contained in his *Apparatus* on the *Compilatio Prima*, De Appelationibus, c. si duobus (in the *Gregoriana:* ii. 28. 7), and anticipated Boniface VIII's *Unam Sanctam.* An idea not unlike that of Alanus is to be found in another *Apparatus* on the *Compilatio Prima:* this *Apparatus* (MS. Lambeth Palace Library 105) is largely based on the work of the English canonist Richard de Lacy (Ricardus Anglicus, see Kuttner, *art. cit.* p. 313, n. 22). The author of this gloss maintained substantially the same as Alanus, but pointed out that the national king's powers rested upon the people, and not on those derived from an emperor: 'Patet reges multos imperatori non subjici . . . nam universitas civitatis multo magis regiam jurisdictionem et imperium conferre potest . . . rex eadem auctoritate, eadem consecratione, eodem crismate inungitur, unde (non ?) potestatis diversitas . . . item teste canone animadversionem plenam habent reges . . .', fo. 196vb, s.v. 'recognoscat'. A detailed report of this manuscript which contains large layers of glosses by Petrus Brito will be made on another occasion. It is difficult to say whether Huguccio, the great teacher of Innocent III, adhered to a similar conception. In his *Summa* he put forward a point of view that might be interpreted in this sense: 'Rex in regno suo edidit edictum, imperator constituit constitutionem, vel idem est rex et imperator, sed rex (est ?) ante imperator coronetur, et idem constitutio quod edictum', on *dist.* ii, c. 4, fo. 118ra of MS. 72, Pembroke College, Cambridge.

[5] *s.v.* 'minime recognoscat'.

perio, vii. 1, in apibus'. And to leave no doubt in the minds of his readers, he declared in his gloss on i. 6. 34:[1] 'Est autem imperator ille super omnes reges, vii. 1, in apibus, et omnes nationes sunt sub eo . . . ipse enim est princeps mundi et dominus . . . et omnes provinciae . . . et omnia sunt in potestate imperatoris, viii. quo jure.'[2] Thus, theoretically, every kingdom and king, every nation and province, was dependent in its political and juristic structure upon the empire, though, in fact, some may not have recognized this imperial superiority. This non-recognition on their part left their theoretical, legal and political inferiority untouched. This glossator's distinction between a *de jure* dependence and a *de facto* non-recognition facilitated the task of those who had to explain Innocent III's decretal desiring at the same time to uphold the banner of the emperor's universal overlordship.

The imperialist lawyers eagerly snatched at this very welcome instrument. Cynus, perhaps the most consequent and the staunchest of the imperialist lawyers, stated in his lecture on C. I. 1. 1. that the emperor was 'dominus mundi' and, therefore, 'temporaliter sub imperio omnes populi omnesque reges sunt, sicut sunt sub papa spiritualiter'.[3] He was of course well aware that there were some 'domini' who would recognize no temporal superior and to those he gave only a *de facto* independence: 'Talis dominus, qui non recognoscit superiorem, est princeps in terra sua de facto'.[4] Even as late as Paulus Castrensis this distinction between *de facto* and *de jure* independence was adduced.[5] Bartolus, who is sometimes thought of as the originator of the doctrine of national sovereignty,[6] also adhered to this distinction. Commenting upon the constitution *Ad Reprimendum*, issued by Henry VII to put into legal effect his ambitions as a true universal monarch, Bartolus came to

[1] *s.v.* 'unde'.

[2] The reference is to the famous dictum of St. Augustine in *dist.* viii, c. 1. Very similar were the opinions of the Spanish glossator and bishop, Laurentius, and of the German, Johannes Teutonicus. Their dicta were incorporated in the *Apparatus* of Tancred on the *Compilatio Tertia*, Qui filii sint legitimi, c. per venerabilem, *s.v.* 'recognoscat', fo. 193va, MS. C. III. 4 of Durham Cathedral Chapter Library: 'De facto. la. De jure tamen subest Romano imperio, ut vii in apibus. jo'. There is no indication that the Compostellan had influenced Laurentius and Johannes. But the German nationality of the latter may have had some bearing on the formation of his political views.

[3] See also his lecture on C. IV. 6. 3, and on his ideas G. Monti, *Cino da Pistoja*, Pistoja, 1924, p. 176.

[4] See his lecture on C. V. 16. 26, no. 1, as well as his lectures on C. IV. 6. 3 and C. V. 16. 25.

[5] Lecture of Paulus Castrensis on C. 1. 1. 1.

[6] H. Rehm, *Geschichte der Staatsrechtswissenschaft*, Berlin, 1896, pp. 193–5, and E. E. Stengel, 'Kaisertitel und Souveränitätsidee', in *Deutsches Archiv für Geschichte des Mittelalters*, iii (1939), 1–49, at pp. 39–40; and C. N. S. Woolf, *Bartolus of Sassoferrato*, Cambridge, 1913, pp. 154–62, 380–1.

speak of the insecurity and restlessness within the empire. The cause of this sorry state of affairs he found in that the 'imperium fuit prostratum' which gave rise to tyrannical governments and therefore to so many internal upheavals.[1] The greater part of the world no longer obeyed the emperor, and that surely was the real reason for the weakness of the empire: 'Major pars mundi non obedit principi'. But this was, he says, 'de facto, sed de jure secus'. A few lines later Bartolus said in the traditional manner, 'patet, quod imperator recte dicitur dominus mundi'. If any doubt should remain about Bartolus's position it would be dispelled by his lecture on D. 49. 15. 24, where he declared anyone who failed to recognize the overlordship of the emperor to be a heretic: 'Si quis diceret dominum imperatorem non esse dominum et monarcham totius orbis, esset haereticus'.[2] Baldus,[3] too, maintained an attitude in this question which lends support to our assumption that he too must rank amongst those who stood up for the overlordship of the emperor. In a *Consilium*, far too little appreciated, Baldus adopted the view that the emperor was 'dominus mundi': 'Contrarium dicere est sacrilegium'.[4] The fact that Baldus's view has been generally overlooked warrants the quotation of the passage in full.

> Imperator est dominus universalis. Nam in dubio omnis temporalis jurisdictio sua est et de jure ipse immobilis, id est, perpetuus manens. Habet namque imperium universa dictione qui ascendentem videt et descendentem solem et quod ex utroque latere est, id est, meridie et septentrione, et in omnibus insulis, quae usque ad oceani recessus extenduntur, et in omnem terram, quam Romanorum continet lex et catholicae ecclesiae sanctio. *Non enim idolum colimus, sed veritatem.*

Perhaps the strongest defence of the juristic universality of the Holy Roman Empire and the strongest repudiation of the specially privileged position of France accorded in Innocent III's bull *Per Venerabilem*, is contained in one of Boniface VIII's typically strong-worded utterances. When addressing the legates

[1] See Bartolus in his tract *Super Constitutione Extravaganti Ad Reprimendum*, vers. 'Fidelitates', no. 2: 'Princeps est Deus in terris . . . cum imperium fuit in statu et tranquillitate, totus mundus fuit in pace et tranquillitate, ut tempore Octaviani Augusti, et cum imperium fuit prostratum, insurrexerunt dirae tyrannides et haec fuit opusculi causa finalis . . .'.

[2] '. . . haereticus, quia diceret contra determinationem ecclesiae, contra testimonium S. Evangelii, dum dicit, exivit edictum a Caesare Augusto, ut describeretur universus orbis, ut habes Luc. 2. Ita etiam recognovit Christus imperatorem ut dominum.'

[3] See O. Gierke, *Deutsches Genossenschaftsrecht*, Berlin, 1881, iii. 639; E. Chenon, 'Le Droit Romain à la Curia Regis de Philippe Auguste à Philippe le Bel', in *Mélanges Fitting*, 1907, i. 195–212; A. Esmein, *Cours Elementaire d'Histoire du Droit Français*, Paris, 1910, p. 339; J. N. Figgis, *Churches in the Modern State*, London, 1909, p. 195.

[4] *Consilia*, tom. iii, consilium 218.

of Albert I in Rome, Boniface VIII spoke of the role of the emperor and characterized him in these words: '(Rex Romanorum) est sol sicut monarcha, qui habet omnes illuminare et spiritualem potestatem defendere, quia ipse est datus et missus ad laudem bonorum et ad vindictam malefactorum'. The king of the Romans duly elected by the seven princes, 'est promovendus in imperatorem et monarcham omnium regum et principum terrenorum'.[1] Turning to the subject of the French monarchy Boniface made this far-reaching declaration: 'Nec insurgat hic superbia gallicana, quae dicit, quod non recognoscit superiorem. Mentiuntur, quia de jure sunt et esse debent sub rege Romanorum et imperatore'.[2] As we shall presently see, this claim was in direct contradiction to the opinion of one of his predecessors, Innocent IV, as well as to that of Innocent III's decretal.

III

Let us now turn to the French political writers and jurists whose dicta, owing to the peculiarities of the French political structure, surely must be of great interest to our inquiry. Amongst the French we can discern a minority opinion, characterized by applying the *de facto* and the *de jure* distinction to France, and the majority view rejecting this distinction, either expressly or implicitly, and maintaining the *de jure* independence of the French king. This latter view became prevalent and dominated jurists as well as political writers. Perhaps the earliest representation of the minority opinion was the *Summa Feudorum* of the Marsilian Johannes Blancus who staunchly declared himself for the universal overlordship of the emperor: 'Imperator tenet a Deo imperium et potestatem seu gladium; reges vero habent regna ab imperatore'. Petrus de Bellapertica also belonged to the school of thought upholding the universal state idea. In his lecture on C. I. l. 1,[3] he stated in general terms that 'omnia sunt subjecta imperatori'. Everybody, and apparently

[1] Bull, *Patris Aeterni*, 30 April 1303, and allocution to the Sacred College the same day, see Raynaldus, *Annales Ecclesiastici*, ad annum 1303, § 2; De Marca, *De Concordia Sacerdotii et Imperii*, Paris, 1704, p. 110; *M.G.H.* IV, iv, pars i, p. 133; Woolf, *op. cit.* p. 333. Cf. also the bull of Boniface VIII, 'Nuper ad audientiam' of 15 August 1303, in *Les Régistres de Boniface VIII*, ed. G. Digard and others, iii, no. 5383 (pp. 893–4).

[2] Part of this allocution is also in *Bullarium Romanum*, Aug. Taur., 1857, tom. iv, p. 159, n. 18, where it is slightly different: 'Rex Romanorum omnes universaliter reges praecellit, et hoc dicimus signanter non obstante superbia Gallicana, qui dicunt, quod non debent subjici Romano imperio, sed mentiuntur, per gulam, quia subesse deberrt, sicut omnia alia regna'. See also Potthast, *Regesta Pontificum Romanorum*, p. 2018, no. 25234. The whole speech is also contained in A. Niemeier, *Untersuchungen über die Beziehungen Albrechts I zu Bonifaz VIII*, Berlin, 1900, pp. 114–18.

[3] Fo. 2 of the edition, Paris, 1509.

even the French king, were *de jure* dependent on, and inferior to, the emperor: 'Debetis scire quantum est de jure, omnes sunt subjecti imperio'. Nevertheless, there are some who are not subjected to the Emperor *de facto*: 'Quidam autem de facto non sunt subjecti'. Now it is interesting to note that Petrus avoided the expression 'non recognóscunt imperatorem'—used by all other writers—instead, he turned the idea of non-recognition which is surely an outcome of the will, into the objectively orientated idea of non-subjection. To those kings, then, the emperor did not wish to issue his laws—'his non vult imperator praecipere'—firstly because they were not worthy of imperial laws, just as the Greeks did not wish to hand over their laws to the Romans before they knew that the latter were worthy of them; and secondly, because the emperor must be on his guard that his commands are not made illusory by non-compliance: this idea makes it abundantly clear that Petrus considers the problem, not from the point of view of non-recognition on the part of the kings, but from that of non-subjection on the part of the emperor. The position, therefore, is reversed in Petrus: instead of a king unwilling to recognize the emperor he visualizes an emperor unwilling to enforce his commands. The expression of this thought on the part of a Frenchman is indeed remarkable.[1] Another representative of the minority opinion was Guilelmus de Cuneo. He, too, seemed to have thought, at least by implication, that *de jure* the emperor was universal overlord. He compared the French king to the Roman princeps and concluded that the same status must also be given to those who do not in fact recognize a superior: 'Idem in aliis regibus, qui de facto non recognoscunt superiorem'.[2]

The overwhelming opinion amongst the French, however, was that, neither in fact nor in theory, could the French monarch be considered inferior to the emperor. But it would be rash to conclude that the French were, so to speak, the originators of French independence and thus of French sovereignty. We must again fall back on the decretal *Per Venerabilem* of Innocent III in which the French non-recognition of a superior in temporal matters was publicly and officially postulated. The germ of the idea of sovereignty was contained in this decretal which only needed elaboration and scientific justification. There is a direct line from this decretal to the fully-fledged theory of sovereignty as we find it later with Andreas de Isernia and

[1] It appears that Cynus did not quite understand the subtlety of Petrus's reasoning. Cynus still had the phrase 'non recognoscunt' and even spoke of those 'qui resistunt', but he adopted Petrus's reasons why the emperor did not enforce his laws.

[2] Guilelmus de Cuneo, *De Diversis Officiis Digesti Veteris*, ed. Brandi, *Notizie interno a G. de Cuneo*, Rome, 1892, p. 126.

Oldradus de Ponte. Before we examine the majority view of the French, it will be advisable to see what other interpretations had been given to Innocent III's decretal. These will show that French political opinion was not as original as it is commonly supposed to have been.[1]

The idea of a universal overlordship of the emperor was effectively challenged by that current of political thought which was initiated by Innocent IV. In his commentary on *Decretales* iv. 17. 13 he interpreted the word 'recognoscat' thus: 'De facto, nam de jure subest (scil. rex Franciae) imperatori Romano, ut quidam dicunt, nos contra'.[2] There was obviously here a challenge to the gloss which introduced the distinction between *de facto* and *de jure*. With Innocent IV the French monarchy was endowed with real, legal and political independence. That this statement of Innocent IV was not an isolated one, follows from his commentary on *Decretales*, ii. 22. 15.[3] Speaking of those who have the right to institute public notaries, Innocent declared that not only the emperor (pope) can create notaries, but also those other kings who have supreme power: 'Credimus tamen, quod alii reges, qui habent supremum et merum imperium, possent idem statuere de tabellionibus, si vellent'.

Whether influenced by Innocent IV or whether acting independently, Guido de Baysio, the famous 'Archidiaconus', put forward in his commentaries on the *Decretum* a view which was hardly distinguishable from Innocent's theory. When discussing the jurisdictional powers of princes Guido maintained that, notwithstanding the general jurisdiction of the emperor, any king had the same powers within his domain. The idea that what is the emperor's is also the king's as regards his own kingdom, emerges quite clearly from this passage: 'Dicas, quod omnia sunt imperatoris quoad jurisdictiones. Sic et omnia, quae sunt in regno suo, sunt regis quantum ad jurisdictionem generalem'.[4] The king enjoys the same juristic and political status within his domain as does the emperor. In order to exemplify his general view on the powers of a king, Guido refers us to the position of the French king. This king, according to

[1] See especially F. Ercole who attempts to prove the exclusively French origin of the famous formula, see his 'L'Origine Francese di Una Nota Formola Bartoliana', in *Archivio Storico Italiano*, lxxiii, part ii (1915), pp. 241–94, particularly at pp. 285–7, and his 'Sulla Origine Francese e le Vicende in Italia della Formola "Rex Superiorem non recognoscens est Princeps in Regno suo"', *ibid.* xvi, ser. vii (1931), pp. 197–238. There is a good summary by F. Declareuil, *Histoire Générale du Droit Français*, Paris, 1925, pp. 427–41, G. de Lagarde; *La Naissance de l'esprit laïque*, ed. 1948, pp. 162-4.

[2] *Commentaria Super Quinque Libros Decretalium*, Francofurti, 1570, fo. 481.

[3] Fo. 280; see also his remarks on *Decretales*, ii. 24. 18, no. 10, fo. 285vo and in the bull *Dolentes* of 12 Oct. 1253, printed in Matthew Paris, *Chron. Maj.*, vi. 293, and Denifle, *Chart Univ. Paris*, i. no. 235.

[4] *Rosarium seu in Decretorum Volumen Commentaria*, Venetiis, 1577, ad xxiii. 8, fo. 317.

Guido, possesses supreme power over all persons living within the kingdom.[1] That was, compared with Innocent's laconic statement, already a remarkable step forward in the direction of the rex-imperator conception.[2]

The last mentioned statement can also be found in Guilelmus Durandus's *Speculum Judiciale.* Durandus, using almost the same words, placed the king on a footing equal to that of the emperor.[3] But concerned as he was with the practical application of the law, Durandus touched upon issues which had not as yet aroused the interests of others. He examined the question of whether a baron who rises against the French king would be guilty of the *crimen laesae majestatis.* He replied in the affirmative ; and the reason for his affirmative answer was that 'rex Franciae est princeps in regno suo '.[4] His statement provides not only the famous phrase, but also the clear conception of the king as ' majestas '.[5] All this was, to be sure, against the positive law as laid down in the *Corpus Juris Civilis.* Another problem intimately connected with the question of sovereignty was that of appeal against the king's sentences. Was the king last instance or was a further appeal to the emperor allowable ? The latter alternative would have affirmed the emperor's universal overlordship, whilst the former made the king what the emperor was according to the law. Durandus bluntly stated that ' a sententia lata in curia Franciae non appellatur . . . et sic ibi de facto observatur '.[6] But Durandus restricted the sovereignty of the emperor only as regards the French king ; this emerges from another passage where he declared that the emperor was ' dominus mundi '.[7]

[1] ' Unde omnes homines, qui sunt in regno Franciae, sunt sub potestate et principatu regis Franciae et in eis habet imperium generalis jurisdictionis et potestatis ', *loc. cit.* Cf. also his remarks in xii. 2. 8, fo. 228, no. 7 : ' Quaelibet regio potest sibi imponere legem, et ita Francigenae et Hispani non obligantur Romanis legibus '. To support his dictum in this passage Guido referred to ' L ', who may be the already mentioned Laurentius and who may have held differing views. But, as has recently been proved (S. Kuttner, *art. cit.* pp. 291, 309), Guido did not quote directly from the *Apparatus* of Laurentius, the tradition of which is most unsatisfactory, but from the collection of glosses, the so-called *Glossa Palatina,* discovered by Kuttner, *Repertorium,* p. 81, and *art. cit.* p. 290, n. 64. Therefore, too much weight should not be placed on Guido's reference. It should be borne in mind that the *Glossa Palatina* relied extensively on Laurentius, but also on Alanus, Vincentius and many other glossators. It was written between 1210 and 1215.

[2] A similar line of thought is in his *Commentaria super Sexto Decretalium,* I. viii. 3, fo. 41vo. There is no reference to ' L ' in this passage.

[3] See *Speculum Judiciale,* Basiliae, 1574, pars iv, partic. iii, *De Feudis,* ' De Homagiis ', § Quoniam, no. 28, fo. 320.

[4] With a reference to *Per Venerabilem.*

[5] Bodin's identical conception (*De Republica,* II. ii. 189) was therefore not as novel as it is commonly supposed to be, cf. W. A. Dunning, *Political Theories, From Luther to Montesquieu,* New York, 1919, pp. 87 ff., and J. W. Allen, *History of Political Thought in the Sixteenth Century,* London, 1942, pp. 407 ff.

[6] *Loc. cit.* no. 2.

[7] *Op. cit.* lib. ii, particul. iii, *De Appellationibus,* § Nunc tractemus, no. 1, fo. 839, where he significantly adds : ' praeter regem Franciae '.

Now, what was the attitude of the French king himself? How did he himself consider his position as regards the emperor? We are in the fortunate position of having access to an official dictum of St. Louis, made in 1254. Speaking of the application of Roman law he laid down that it was applied, not because he was bound to apply it, but because he did not want to change old established customs. There is thus no doubt that this king did not feel himself to be legally and politically subjected to the emperor.[1] Perhaps the earliest practical recognition of the juristic independence of France is to be found in a report from the year 1259. It is noteworthy that this report concerned the problem of the *crimen laesae majestatis*. A baron forfeited his privileged position by decree of the French king on a charge of this crime. In this report the consultation of jurisconsults was made the basis of the king's condemnation; they considered that the king could be made the object of this crime.[2] An almost identical view was expressed by the French jurist Johannes de Blanosco (Jean de Blanot, *fl.* about 1255). In his *Tractatus de Actionibus* he maintained that a baron who rebels against the king commits the *crimen laesae majestatis*, the reason being that 'rex in regno suo princeps est'.[3] Though belonging to a later period, it may be worth while to refer briefly

[1] Cf. F. A. Isambert, *Recueil Général des Anciennes Lois Francaises*, Paris, 1830, p. 164: 'Jura scripta, quibus utuntur ab antiquis volumus observari, non quia eorum nos obliget auctoritas seu astringet, sed quia mores eorum in hac parte non duximus immutandos'. Cf. also his exclamation: 'Car li rois ne tient de nului fors de Dieu et de lui', *Les Etablissements de Saint Louis*, ed. P. Viollet, ii. 135, and iv. 22–3. One case has so far come to light in which a French king called himself 'Imperator', and that was Louis VII of France. Cf. A. Teulet, *Layettes du Trésor des Chartes* (Inventaires et documents), Paris, 1863, i. 75, n. 141: 'Ludovicus Dei ordinante providentia Francorum imperator Augustus'. Early medieval kings were rather wont to call themselves emperors, cf. e.g., J. M. Kemble, Codex Diplomaticus Aevii Saxonici 4, no. 727 (year 1018): 'Ego imperator Kunto a Christo rege regum regiminis Anglici in insula potitus'; or *loc. cit.* 3, no. 673 (year 990): 'Famosus totius Brittanicae insulae imperator'. But too much importance should not be attached to these somewhat flamboyant expressions of power. Cf. also Bracton, iii. 9. 3, who said that the king "parem autem habere non debet, nec multo fortius superiorem'.

[2] See A. A. Beugnot, *Les Olim ou Régistres des Arrêts rendus par la Cour du Roi sous les Règnes de S. Louis (1254–1318)*, Paris, 1839, i. 460, n. iv: 'Rex consuluit plures fidei dignos et jurisperitos, qui habito consilio dixerunt, quod idem A commisit crimen laesae majestatis, et secundum jura scripta amisit jus successionis, ipse et haeredes sui'. For some more practical examples see J. R. Strayer, 'The Laicization of French and English Society in the thirteenth century', in *Speculum*, xv (1940), 76–86, at p. 82 notes.

[3] 'Baro ille, qui insurgit contra regem, videtur incidere in legem Juliam majestatis ex eo capite . . . quod directe videtur fecisse contra principem, nam rex in regno suo princeps est, nam in temporalibus superiorem non recognoscit', quoted by F. Calasso, 'Origini Italiane della Formola "rex in regno suo est imperator"', in *Rivista di Storia del Diritto Italiano*, iii (1932), 226, n. 39. Calasso tries to prove that the phrase was of purely Italian origin, just as Ercole attempts to show that the same phrase was of purely French descent. To attempt to fix the territorial origin of this idea, seems rather futile. Moreover, both these authors fail to show the influence which this particular idea exercised upon the actual events.

to Johannes Faber, another great French jurist in the first decades of the fourteenth century.[1] He asked whether kings were lawfully in a position to legitimate. This power he denied to those kings 'qui superiorem habent'. Others, however, had this right: 'In aliis dicitur idem, quod in imperatore'.[2] The juristic justification for French independence is only touched upon by Faber. In his *Breviarium in Codicem* he doubted whether the emperor was able to derive his position as a universal monarch from the 'jus commune'. Faber believed that the emperor's overlordship was confined to those lands in which his laws were respected. The emperor could not base his position on the 'jus commune extra metas suas, infra quas ei obeditur'. This affords Faber an opportunity to state in general terms that whoever possessed a limited territory for a long time ('ab antiquo') was established there by right and possessed the same powers as the emperor.[3] The reference to actual possession 'ab antiquo' is of course merely the claim, so vociferously put forward by contemporary publicists, that the French monarchy derived its legal position from prescriptive rights. We will turn to this point presently.

An interesting point of view was propounded by Petrus Jacobi, of the late thirteenth century. He claimed that the kingdom of France was not subjected, but—and this is the interesting feature of his exposition—federated, to the empire: 'Hodie vero regnum Franciae non est subjectum imperatori . . . sed est foederatum seu gentes regni Franciae sunt foederatae imperatori'.[4] Not infrequently the freedom of France from the imperial yoke was deduced from the ethymological explanation of the term 'francus', meaning free from the empire.[5]

This summary of the opinions of the French juristic writers indicates that they did not go beyond the mere denial of imperial sovereignty and the mere assertion of French sovereignty and independence. In other words, these jurists maintained the actual, political and juristic independence of France without attempting to prove the correctness of their assertions by historical or political or juristic arguments. It is true that Durandus stated in his *Speculum Judiciale* that the king was emperor in

[1] See F. Savigny, *Geschichte des römischen Rechts im Mittelalter*, 2nd edn. vi. 41–2.

[2] *Super Institutionibus*, Lugduni, 1543, tit. De Nuptiis, fo. 31, col. 2.

[3] Johannes Faber, *Breviarium in Codicem*, C. I. l. 1, no. 2: 'Nec crederem imperatorem fundatum esse de jure communi extra metas suas, infra quas ei obeditur . . . sed tu potes dicere, quod quilibet, qui habet territorium limitatum ab antiquo, sit fundatus de jure communi infra metas eiusdem ad exercendum, in qualibet parte jus, quod in toto universali exercet'.

[4] *Practica*, Lugduni, 1577, 'De Praejudiciis', fo. 45vo; see also Degressalius, *Regalium Franciae Libri Duo*, Paris, 1538, p. 316.

[5] Cf. Stengel, *loc. cit.* p. 38, and W. Berges, *Die Fürstenspiegel des hohen und späteren Mittelalters*, Leipzig, 1938, pp. 76 f.

his domain and that there was no appeal to the imperial court; it is furthermore true that Faber gave the (imperial) right to legitimate to the (independent) kings. But apart from the latter's reference to prescriptive acquisition by the French king, we find no plausible explanation of why the imperial sovereignty was non-existent. Some attempts to justify the assertion of French sovereignty can be found in the writings of the political publicists at the beginning of the fourteenth century. And, to use modern terminology, we may well classify the reasons for the independence of France given by the political writers as belonging to the social-political category, distinct from the purely legal reasons which were set forth with great acumen by jurists belonging to a quite different environment and school of thought. Let us now briefly examine the opinions of the French political writers.

IV

It will be recalled that the quarrel between Boniface VIII and Philip IV provoked a considerable quantity of controversial literature. These writings naturally deal mainly with the alleged rights of the pope in (French) temporal matters. But as there was an influential body of opinion which claimed, on the basis of the allegory of the two swords, that the pope had jurisdictional powers over the emperor and that, consequently, the French king by virtue of his dependence on the emperor, was also subjected to the pope, these political writers [1] were necessarily compelled to touch upon the problem of the political relationship between king and emperor. Nor should it be forgotten that papacy and empire, since the accommodation of Albert I with Boniface VIII, constituted a united front against the French: Albert I had recognized the dependence of his crown on the papacy, and thus presented the French writers with the political implications of this step.

The document entitled *Rex Pacificus*,[2] which attempted to

[1] About the opinions of the French politicians, such as Peter Flote, William of Nogaret, William of Plaisian, and so forth, see Helene Wieruszowski, *Vom Imperium zum Nationalen Königtum* (Beiheft 30 of the *Historische Zeitschrift*, 1933), pp. 157–64.

[2] See G. Dupuy, *Histoire de Differend d'entre le Pape Boniface VIII et Philippe le Bel*, Paris, 1655 (Preuves du differend), pp. 663–83; S. Bulaeus, *Historia Universitatis Parisiensis*, tom. iv, pp. 935 ff. and *Acta inter Bonifacium VIII, Benedictum XI, Clementem V et Philippum Pulchrum Regem Christianum* (Troyes ?) 1614, fos. 164 ff. The editio princeps is contained in the collection of tracts by Durandus, *De Origine Jurisdictionum*, Paris, 1506, 4to. On the manuscript versions, see the present writer's paper, 'A Medieval Document on Papal Theories of Government', *EHR* xli (1946), 183, n. 4. Short references to this tract, the importance of which has not yet been fully recognized, are in S. Riezler, *Die literarischen Widersacher der Paepste zur Zeit Ludwig des Baier*, Leipzig, 1874, p. 141; H. Finke, *Aus den Tagen Bonifaz' VIII*, Münster, 1902, p. 159; C. McIlwain, *Growth of Political Thought in the West*, London, 1932, p. 262; J. Rivière, *Le Problème de l'Eglise*, &c., pp. 274 ff., and R. Scholz, *Publizistik zur Zeit Philipps des Schönen und Bonifaz VIII*, p. 232.

dispose of the extravagant claims of papal supporters, touched upon this problem. The author—or authors (the document was alleged to have been drawn up by the masters of the university of Paris)—did not yet go beyond the position of Faber. The independence of France was asserted—'regnum Franciae non subest Romano imperio'—and definite territorial limits of the empire and of the French kingdom were insisted upon. The basic justification for these territorial limitations of empire and kingdom was found to be the French king's peaceful enjoyment of his possessions; the prescriptive acquisition of the king's rights was claimed to be the title for his independence. Consequently, the French monarchy had limited the territorial sovereignty of the empire. 'Sunt certi limites et fuerunt a tempore, ex quo non extat memoria, per quos regnum et imperium dividuntur.'[1] And which prescription, the author asked, is more legitimate than a period of hundred years' possession?[2] According to the *Rex Pacificus*, this requirement was amply fulfilled by the kings of France who for more than a hundred years had recognized no superior save God in temporal matters: 'Solum Deum superiorem habent in temporalibus, nullum alium recognoscentes superiorem in istis nec imperatorem nec papam'. The right of supreme power had been completely acquired by the French kings: 'Jus summae superioritatis in regno suo totaliter acquisitum'. It is surely not surprising to find that the modern concept of sovereignty had its birthplace in France, even before Bodin in the sixteenth century. But apart from these—certainly original—definitions of the idea of sovereignty there is still no answer in the *Rex Pacificus* to the abstract question, Why was there no empire, or why was the empire superfluous?

An attempt to give some reasons for France's independence is to be found in the tract *Quaestio in Utramque Partem*, by an anonymous author. Like its predecessor, this tract, probably written in 1302,[3] dealt with the power in temporal matters and therefore also touched upon the position of France within the political framework of the empire. The author based the French claim to independence on the medieval French version of the Trojan legend[4] and declared that the Trojans, filled as they always were with great hatred for the Roman empire, refused tribute and were finally repelled from Sicambria where they had settled. Not bowing to Roman rule, they became known as 'franci'. If there are some, the author argues, who on the

[1] Bulaeus, *op. cit.* p. 923.

[2] 'Per praescriptionem legitimam jus acquiritur praescribenti; nulla autem praescriptio magis est legitima quantum ad cursum temporis quam centenaria.'

[3] Cf. R. Scholz, *Die Publizistik zur Zeit Philipps des Schönen und Bonifaz VIII*, Stuttgart, 1906, p. 224.

[4] Goldast, *Monarchia*, tom. ii, p. 102.

strength of Innocent III's decretal *Per Venerabilem* say, that *de facto* the French kingdom is exempted from imperial and Roman rule, but that *de jure* it is part of the empire, an adequate interpretation of that decretal in conjunction with the study of history will convince them that *de jure* also France is independent of the empire, because the French had never been subjected either to the emperor or anyone else.[1] The historical perspective of the tract emerges from the reference to the chronological precedence of France over the empire ; in the same context the author boldly declared that France had an 'imperium', and in medieval terminology this concept signified wielding of supreme, uncontrollable and independent power : 'Regnum Francorum prius habuit imperium quam regnum Teutonicorum, lxiii, ego Ludovicus'.[2] But apart from these historical considerations the author of the *Quaestio* also adopts a legalistic point of view. A few lines after the above quoted passage he referred to the gloss on Innocent III's decretal and retorted that the independence of the kingdom had been a fact which had been transformed into a customary right, never impugned by the emperor and always acknowledged by the pope.[3] Consequently, this tract considers king and emperor as equal partners within the European commonwealth : 'Igitur videtur, quod imperator et rex Franciae sunt pares'. All the privileges and rights applicable to the emperor by virtue of his position must also be enjoyed by the king of France, 'qui est imperator in regno suo'.[4]

[1] Goldast, *op. cit.* p. 102 : 'Sumamus testimonium summi pontificis ipsius, videlicet Innocentii, "extra, qui fil. sunt leg., c. per venerabilem : rex Francorum superiorem in temporalibus minime recognoscit". Si dicas quia etsi non recognoscit, tamen de jure deberet, respondemus per interemptionem, quod non debet. Quia Franci nulli umquam fuerunt subditi, nec imperatori, nec aliis, sicut probatur ex antiquis historiis, quod post eversionem Trojae xii M. Trojanorum ad partes Pannoniae pervenerunt, ubi civitatem Sicambriam construentes, manserunt ibi usque ad tempora Valentiniani imperatoris, semper infesti Romano imperio. Expulsi vero inde ab imperatore praedicto pro eo, quod tributa Romanis solvere recusarent, juxta morem aliarum nationum, habitaverunt juxta Rhenum in confinio Germaniae et Allemanniae. Quos cum multis proeliis post, idem Valentinianus sibi subjugare tentaret, nec aliquatenus potuisset, appellavit eos Francorum. Et Galliam habitantes denique Franciam appellantes, nec Romanis nec aliis quibuscumque voluerunt esse subditi.'

[2] A similar thought was expressed a few years before this tract was written, by the magister Thomas de Poilliaco (Pouilly) when speaking of the rights of the French king concerning Lyons, see F. Kern, *Acta Imperii Angliae et Franciae ab* A.D. *1267 ad* A.D. *1313*, Tübingen, 1911, p. 198, no. 270, and especially pp. 203, no. 7, 205, no. 17, and 159, no. 271, ll. 9 ff. : 'Rex Franciae omne imperium habet in regno suo, quod imperator habet in imperio . . . nec superiorem habet . . . regem Franciae et alia regna ante fuerunt quam fuerit imperium. . . .'

[3] 'Si dicas, prout dicit glossa "verum est de facto (i.e. Innocent III), sed non de jure, quia de jure debet recognoscere imperatorem, ut patet 4 q. 1, c. in apibus, et extra de elect., cap. venerabilem", respondeo illud factum versum esse in consuetudinem, quae dat jurisdictionem.'

[4] *Loc. cit.* ll. 21 f.

This tract, then, denied the universal overlordship of the emperor and it based this denial partly on historical and partly on legalistic grounds. Instead of adopting this negative standpoint, the tract of John of Paris, *De Potestate Papali et Regia*, went a step further and elicited a positive argument from sociological considerations. John set out from the Aristotelian axiom that human creatures were possessed by an urge to live in a community. According to John, this urge was a natural instinct 'qui ex Deo est', but did not emanate from the divine law itself. In order to live peacefully and in prosperity it was therefore necessary that these communities should elect their own superior who, however, should be different 'secundum diversitates communitatum'.[1] It was a fundamental tenet of John of Paris—as it was one of his fellow countrymen, Jean Bodin, nearly three hundred years later—that the secular power showed far greater complexities and diversities in its structure than its spiritual counterpart. For this reason alone it would not be advisable to have the same idea of universality as there was in spiritual affairs.[2] In the subsequent lines, John of Paris elaborated his thesis and declared, somewhat realistically, that unlike his spiritual partner one supreme ruler could not possibly rule the whole world in temporal matters, since the spiritual power is able to effect its postulates and precepts by words and reaches everyone by the same method: it is, John says, easier to transmit the power of the word than the power of the sword.[3] Thus, John considered the whole problem from the practical point of view of the enforcement of the laws and commands. But he went a step further and emphasized the advisability of different governments for different peoples. There are, he said

[1] Page 111, ll. 42–9: 'Hunc autem ordinem ad unum supremum magis invenimus inter ministros ecclesiae quam inter principes saeculares, quia ministri ecclesiastici divino cultui specialiter deputati sunt domino, tamquam populus peculiaris. Et ideo ex divino statuto est ordo omnium ministrorum ad unum. Non sic autem fideles laici sic habent ex jure divino, quod subsint in temporalibus uni monarchae supremo, sed ex naturali instinctu, qui ex Deo est, habent, quod civiliter et in communitate vivant, et per consequens, ut ad bene vivendum in communi rectores eligant diversos quidem, secundum diversitates communitatum. Quod autem ad unam supremam hierarchiam in temporalibus reducantur, nec ex inclinatione naturali, nec ex jure divino habent; nec eis convenit ita, sicut ministris ecclesiasticis.'

[2] 'Primo quidem, quia sicut in hominibus est diversitas magna ex parte corporum, non autem ex parte animarum, cum omnes sint in eodem gradu essentiali constitutae, propter unitatem speciei humanae: ita saecularis potestas plus habet diversitatis secundum saecularitatem et complexionum diversitatem, quam spiritualis, quae minus in talibus variatur. Unde non oportet esse tantam universitatem in una, sicut in alia.'

[3] 'Potestas spiritualis censuram suam transmutare potest faciliter ad omnes, tam propinquos quam remotos, cum sit verbalis, non potestas saecularis, gladium suum cum effectu transmittere tam faciliter potest ad remotos, cum sit manualis; facilius enim est verbum extendere quam manum.'

different modes of living, according to the differences of climate and geographical situations of the peoples concerned. What may be good for the one nation, may not be so for the other. Let us quote this important passage in full :

> Sic autem non est necesse omnes fideles uniri in aliqua republica communi : sed possunt secundum diversitatem climatum, regionum et conditionum hominum esse diversi modi vivendi et diversae politiae et quod est virtuosum in una gente, non est virtuosum in alia.[1]

Continuing in a sceptical vein, John of Paris denied that there had ever been peace during the reign of emperors, although the periods preceding and succeeding were markedly peaceful, according to John's reading of history ; imperial rules were characterized by patricide, fratricide and matricide—an assertion in striking contrast to those exuberant glorifications of imperial and universal government which appear in the contemporary *Monarchia* of Dante.[2] The conclusion which John of Paris reached on this point is not therefore surprising : it is better, he concludes, to have several kingdoms than one comprising the whole world : 'Melius est plures pluribus regnis dominari quam unum toti mundo .'[3]

John of Paris's tract marked a decided advance in political thinking as compared with contemporary juristic thought. He plainly envisaged regional kingdoms whose rulers embody supreme power. He flatly denied the possibility of a universal empire, because of the difficulties of enforcing a universal overlord's commands in remote places—and also because of the necessity of adjusting the government to the exigencies and peculiarities of various nations, essentially and fundamentally different on account of diversities of climate, geographical position and peculiar social conditions.

V

The idea of a universal overlordship exercised by the emperor as the 'dominus mundi' had indeed received shattering blows. The practical test-case had yet to come : could the emperor actually maintain his overlordship over the kings ? It is, we think, symptomatic of the state of political thinking that ideas, such as those we have examined, should have been so loudly propounded at a time when an emperor was making strenuous efforts to uphold the position which the abstract letter of the law bestowed upon him. The fabric and structure of the political

[1] *Loc. cit.* p. 112, l. 7.
[2] *Monarchia,* I. xvi ; II. ii, &c.
[3] *Loc. cit.* p. 141, l. 23.

edifice, skilfully assailed by these French political and juristic writers, had been undermined just at a time when the emperor would have needed all available forces to translate the idea of overlordship into a practical reality. Yet the final blow to this imperial edifice did not come from the French writers, but from those in the southern half of the Italian peninsula, from the Neapolitan school of law. And it is, moreover, significant that the emperor and the idea of a universal empire suffered a decisive defeat at the hands of the Neapolitan king, Robert of Naples. The assumption that Robert would have challenged the imperial authority without the necessary legal and political advice can certainly be dismissed. On the contrary, the very fact that he staunchly maintained an uncompromising and unbending attitude against a far more resourceful emperor, and that he allowed affairs to drift to a point from which there was no return, suggests that, although he was the less well equipped in material resources, he was the better armed with legal and political arguments furnished as they were by the jurists of the brilliant Neapolitan school. And it was precisely these jurists who carried out the successful theoretical onslaught upon the empire. Naples claimed a position not unlike that of France : the Neapolitan kingdom was a fief of the papal curia and for this reason, if for no other, the kings maintained that they were exempted from imperial rule and overlordship. But legal proof and a test case had not yet been furnished. Now it is interesting to note that at the very same time as the French political writers vociferously impugned the universal overlordship of the emperor and established a case for French independence, the Neapolitan jurists busied themselves with exactly the same problem, seen of course from their own (Neapolitan) point of view. Whether or not the French stimulated the Neapolitans or whether the former were influenced by the latter, cannot now be decided. The one fact that can be safely asserted is that there was a close intercourse between Naples and France, owing to the rule of the house of Anjou. Let us now turn to an examination of the ideas as set forth by the southern jurists.

A considerable time before the French writers challenged the imperial universal authority in the interests of France, the glossator of the *Constitutiones Utriusque Siciliae*, Marinus, elaborated (about 1275) the legal and political position of the Sicilian king and his relationship with the emperor. Marinus wrote lucidly and, unlike later writers, without compendious references to passages of the Old and New Testaments. His exposition was unambiguous and uncompromising as regards any superior authority on the part of the emperor. The state of mind of this glossator is revealed by his opening words on this topic :

'Audacter dicimus'. For him there could be no doubt that the Neapolitan king was emperor in his own domain: he was therefore entitled to legislate on all matters with the same powers as the emperor himself, and even against the universally valid Roman law—all this by his own right: 'Sicut imperatoris, ita regis est proprium condere legem'. Royal authority, according to this glossator, was by no means inferior to imperial authority, the difference between them being only nominal: 'Non minorem authoritatem regiam quam imperatoriam arbitremus, scilicet imperatorem ac liberum regem indistincte dicimus dignitatis . . . licet sit distincte in nomine'.[1] Consequently, the term 'princeps' employed in the law books, was applicable not only to the emperor, but also to the king: 'Principis nomen est commune tam regi quam imperatori'. The powers with which Marinus invested the king, were identical to those of the emperor. Apart from the already mentioned right of legislation, even against enactments of Roman law, the king had also the right to legitimate and the right to have his own fisc. Moreover, Marinus denied an appeal from the royal curia to the emperor, the king being supreme judge with no temporal superior: 'A rege Siciliae appellari non potest . . . rex Siciliae superiorem non habet'.

Just as some French writers were anxious to refute the emperor's legal claims to universal overlordship by historical arguments, so did our glossator attempt to disprove the legality of the alleged universal overlordship by the same method. He asked, To what did the empire of the Romans whose successor the Holy Roman Empire was, owe its existence? Now, he said, anyone reading through the deeds of the Romans must needs come to the conclusion that the Romans acquired their empire through sheer force of arms. This subjugation and oppression of foreign peoples was a factual phenomenon rather than a legal one. Apparently the Neapolitan glossator rejected the idea of right being derived from might. 'Certe', he said, 'quicumque Romanorum gesta evolvat, non inveniat, quod aliter quam per armorum fortitudinem solam, et sic de facto potius quam de jure, Romani cives et imperatores sibi regna et gentes subjugaverunt . . . opprimendo videlicet, qui sua imbecillitate eorum ditioni coeperunt esse subjecti'. Indubitably gratified by the diminution of the authority of the Roman empire, the glossator sarcastically remarked that this decrease in power did not happen 'sine optima ratione'. The Romans had merely lost an illicitly acquired empire and if it was a crime to recede from Roman rule, it was also a crime to establish an empire by force: 'Et sic paria

[1] Cf. with this an incidental utterance of St. Bernard in his epistles, Migne, *Patrologia Latina*, vol. clxxxii, col. 294: 'Omnis, qui in Sicilia regem se facit, contradicit Caesari'.

delicta mutua compensatione tolluntur'. In short, the Sicilian king is the 'princeps in regno'.[1]

This brief exposition leaves little doubt as to the attitude of influential circles in the southern law school. The famous Neapolitan professor, Andreas de Isernia, was, if possible, still more outspoken.[2] He also commented upon the *Constitutiones* and wrote, probably just at the turn of the century, commentaries on the feudal laws. Both these commentaries set forth his ideas on the present topic. A short sketch of his views may shed further light on the thoughts of those scholars by whom the king was influenced. Andreas's exposition does not show the same terseness and conciseness as that of the glossator Marinus. In the true dialectical manner Andreas dealt first with certain views opposed to his political thoughts and dogmas. He singled out the canonists Johannes Teutonicus and Hostiensis (Henricus de Segusia) as the representatives of a school of thought insisting upon the unity and supreme sovereignty of the imperial government. It will be recalled that Teutonicus, the glossator of the *Decretum*, maintained that there was a *prima facie* presumption for every king's being under the emperor's power, unless an exemption from this rule was found. If Johannes's opinion were followed, Andreas argued, imperial laws should therefore be observed. In that case, he asked, was everyone bound by the feudal laws? To this imperialistic-universal view of the canonist the Neapolitan professor and counsellor of the king[3] replied in the following way:

Firstly, as regards the origin of the emperor's dominion, it must plainly be stated that the Roman empire subjugated 'the world' solely by the use of force. This, Andreas said, follows clearly from a perusal of the chronicles. He believed he found support for his view in *Dist.*, xxiii. 1, and in *Decretales*, i. 6. 34. With a reference to St. Augustine's *De Civitate Dei* the Sicilian complained of the injustice of free individuals being subjugated against their own will. For Andreas therefore all 'Romani principes' must be classed as 'improbi'. Secondly, a number of kings had never recognized the emperor as their overlord, and the exemption from imperial rule mentioned by the gloss

[1] Calasso, *loc. cit.*, goes too far in deducing from certain expressions the exclusively Sicilian (Neapolitan) origin of the idea, particularly his interpretation of some utterances of Carolus de Tocco in the *Apparatus ad Lombardam* appear artificial. It is always difficult to ascribe the paternity of certain ideas to one man or to one country. That there was a close connexion between Sicily and France owing to the Angevin rule, cannot be denied, and it is this undeniable fact which largely explains the simultaneous exposition of anti-imperialist views.

[2] About whom see L. Giustiniani, *Memorie Storiche degli Scrittori Legali del Regno di Napoli*, Naples, 1787, ii. 161–8.

[3] See H. Finke, *Acta Aragonensia*, ii, no. 442 note.

can surely be presumed in the case of those kings who for more than a hundred years had paid no homage to the emperor. What presumption could be more effective than one extending over more than a century ? This question reminds us clearly of the almost identical wording of the *Rex Pacificus*. Consequently, 'ex cursu temporis praesumeretur exemptio '.[1] Only one right could not be acquired by prescription, Andreas continued, and that was the papal right of demanding submission from everyone, because that right was derived directly from God, and has also been instituted by Christ Himself. The nationalistic-conservative outlook of the Sicilian professor appears perhaps best in this point. He insisted upon the fixed character of the contemporary political structure of the empire, that is to say, the empire in its 'present' form could not be changed. For although in the past kings acquired the freedom of their kingdoms from imperial rule, this prescriptive acquisition could not take place in future. The reason for this view was that prospective free kings had not protested against imperial rule and therefore 'purgatum fuit vitium ex voluntate sequenti '.[2] Thirdly, Andreas avowed that if Johannes Teutonicus and others based their universal-imperialistic views upon the passage *In apibus*,[3] this interpretation was too narrow and superficial. It was a purely arbitrary explanation of this text to infer from it the universal overlordship of the Holy Roman Empire. For, as Andreas observed, this passage can refer only to 'just' empires ; moreover, each province can have its own monarch : 'Et quaelibet provincia habet suum regem, qui suus monarcha est '. Although the church and the pope 'approve' of the emperor, in so far as he is the defender of the faith, they do not approve of his aggressions merely because he is the emperor.

Thus, according to Andreas, there are free kings who had protested against the forceful subjugation under imperial rule in good time, and one of these free kings was the Neapolitan. 'Illi, qui se non submiserunt Romano imperio, dicebantur liberi.' Since they had no superior, no appeal against sentences of the royal curia was allowable. These free kings were not bound to accept imperial laws, of which the Roman was the outstanding example. If imperial laws were in fact applied, this would merely mean that the free king had recognized them as reasonable

[1] Andreas de Isernia, *In Usus Feudorum Commentaria*, Lugduni, 1579, 'Praeludia', no. 35, fo. 4 vo.

[2] *Op. cit.*: 'Aliis vero, qui de novo vellent se eripere in libertatem, videtur obstare, si imperium diceret, quod praedecessores tui voluntarie se imperio submiserunt, quod probabitur ex diuturnitate temporis . . . nam etsi verum est, quod armorum potentia a principio subjugavit sibi Roma provincias, post voluntarie elegerunt sibi in regem . . . purgatum fuit vitium ex voluntate sequenti.'

[3] *Decretum*, vii. l. 41.

laws; this recognition would not imply that their imperial character was the basis of their acceptance and application by the king.

It is quite in harmony with these foregoing considerations of Andreas de Isernia that he employed the phrase: 'Rex est monarcha in regno suo'. The question, however, arises, why a universal monarch was not to be preferred to a number of kings. Certainly, the political structure of the empire would have been simpler, if, as the law books laid down, there had been one single monarch. This consideration must also have been at the back of Andreas's mind, and the reason he gave for his rejection of the one single emperor, was the practical observation that kingships were hereditary: kings were far more anxious to do their best for their heirs than were emperors who were elected and had therefore no specific reason for having the prosperity of their successors at heart. 'Curant (*sc.* reges) de utilitate regni propter filios, qui sunt reges sicut et ipsi . . . imperatores autem non sic, quia electione, non successione.' In order to make his views quite plain, Andreas elsewhere declared that the elected Teutonic princes did not care for the well-being of Italy, only for that of Germany 'as we see happen in our own days'.[1]

Now, what rights had the kings according to Andreas's conception? This question afforded him an opportunity to cross swords with Hostiensis who denied kings the rights of coining money, changing its value, concessions of tolls and other taxes, and so forth, and declared these rights, the so-called *regalia*, the sole prerogatives of the universal monarch. Andreas contested this opinion: according to him, every king was monarch in his own kingdom, and therefore free kings had the same rights as the Roman emperors: 'Liberi reges habent illud jus, quod Romani principes'.[2] His argumentation was based upon the conception of the emperor as the king of the Romans before his coronation. For prior to the ceremony of coronation the emperors were simply kings of the Romans. And yet even in this capacity they had, according to Andreas, 'majestas', that is to say, supreme political power and the subsequent coronation did not increase their powers.[3] Andreas argued that anyone who had read history, must admit that there were many German and Roman princes who had not been crowned

[1] *Usus Feudorum*, 'Quae sunt regalia', Rubrica, no. 64, fo. 303vo: 'Non curant Theutonici electi ad imperium de jurisdictione Italiae, ut videmus diebus nostris, curaverunt de Alemannia; curare debent non minus de Italia'.

[2] *Usus Feudorum, loc. cit.* no. 77 fo. 307vo; *loc. cit.* 'Monetae', no. 18, fo. 291vo: 'Reges liberi habent illud posse quod imperator in imperio'.

[3] On the various views concerning the idea of coronation, see the present writer's *Medieval Idea of Law*, pp. 175–80.

as emperors and who still exercised all rights appertaining to them without regard to the formal act of coronation.[1] Moreover, the study of the Bible proved conclusively that the ideas of empire and emperor were alien to the Old Testament, where only kings could be found. The idea of an emperor was a relatively new one, and a Christian emperor could not be found before Constantine. Consequently, the historical perspective would lend no support to the claims of a universal monarch. In other words, the position of the emperor was a purely formal one, and the rights usually ascribed to him alone must necessarily be attributed also to the free kings. And these rights embodied the supreme political and legal power.

This sovereign position of a free king entailed, above all, the possibility of committing the *crimen laesae majestatis* against his person. The question whether a king could be the object of this crime, was therefore a test case as to whether the concept of sovereignty was grasped in its full implications. And Andreas speaking of this crime said some ' moderni ' declare 'crimen laesae majestatis non cadere in regem '. He was very emphatic on this point and roundly stated that this view ' nulla ratione defendi potest '.[2] The other rights commonly thought of as the prerogatives of the emperor as the sole bearer of political and legal plenitude, should also be attributed to the free king. We have already mentioned that Andreas would allow no appeal against a sentence of the royal curia. One point in his theory dealt with an aspect of international law, that is, the right of free kings to wage wars : if waged against the emperor, they would not be rebellions, but merely wars between sovereign rulers. The creation of magistrates and other public officials was no longer the sole prerogative of the emperor, but that of the king within the territory of his kingdom. The Neapolitan scholar, in short, restricted the imperial power to those territories over which it could be effectively exercised. The emperor became a mere king over a certain territory which, as Andreas sarcastically remarked, was ' nowadays moderate in its size '. As regards the scope of powers, Andreas recognized no difference between an emperor and a king : each is restricted to his own territory. ' The king can do in his realm what the emperor can do within imperial territory.' That is the implication of the important passage in which the Sicilian professor declared : ' Rex

[1] Andreas de Isernia's *Proemium Super Constitutionibus Regni*, in *Constitutiones Regni Utriusque Siciliae:* ' Sed certe, antequam coronentur Romae imperatores, sunt reges et habent majestatem et fiscum, et multi fuerunt reges Alemanniae et Romanorum, qui non fuerunt incoronati imperatores, sicut patet ex chronicis tempore jurisconsultorum et imperatorum, qui fecerunt leges Codicis. Imperator erat (!) dominus totius mundi. . . .'

[2] *Loc. cit. Proemium* (without pagination or division in sections).

poterit in regno suo, quod imperator in terra imperii, quae hodie modica est in Italia, non habet nisi Lombardiam et illam non totam, et partem Thusciae . . . *liberi reges tantum habent in regnis suis quantum imperator in imperio* '.[1]

VI

The French publicists were on the defensive and merely asserted sovereign rights of the French king. The Neapolitan elaborated the idea of sovereignty theoretically and pushed this idea to its logical conclusion. Hence the emperor ceased to be a 'dominus mundi', and he was refused any pre-eminent powers outside his own (German) dominion, whilst, on the other hand, the free king embodied all those prerogatives which, by virtue of his universal overlordship, used to be attributed to the emperor alone. The Holy Roman Empire as a universal monarchy had not only practically, but also theoretically terminated. The emperor's power was limited to a certain territory only. It is against the background of such views that we must visualize the contest between Henry VII and Robert of Naples. When Henry charged Robert with the *crimen laesae majestatis*, the latter claimed that he too was a sovereign, inferior to nobody and could not thus be cited and tried by an equal. Robert had on his side not only the facts, but also the theory current at his capital's seat of learning. The contest between him and the emperor concerned a purely legal-political point which had been decided long before in favour of the king. The case against Robert rested on the assumption that he was subject to the laws and orders of the emperor as the universal overlord. In substance the charge maintained the perpetration of the *crimen laesae majestatis* against the emperor in that he incited imperial enemies in Lombardy and Tuscia to revolt against the empire, that he had concluded treaties with them and finally that he had occupied imperial territory illegally and expelled imperial officials. Whether or not these charges were true, it is not our task to investigate. What is of interest and importance is the fact that Robert, summoned to appear before the emperor through the imperial edict of 12 September 1312,[2] completely ignored the summons. What is of still greater interest is the law passed by Henry VII on 2 April 1312 in which the universal overlordship of the emperor was solemnly re-affirmed: it was this law upon which the subsequent proceedings and the eventual condemnation of Robert were based.

The very fact that the emperor saw himself compelled to issue

[1] *Usus Feudorum*, 'Quae sunt regalia', Rubrica, no. 2, fo. 286.
[2] See *M.G. Const.*, iv, no. 849, p. 857.

a law in which he declared that 'every soul was subject to the emperor without any exception '[1] sheds a significant light upon imperial claims. After all, were the texts in the law books insufficient to support the charge against Robert ? Did they not plainly express the idea that the emperor was 'dominus mundi' ? It was assuredly superfluous to declare in the second title of this law that those 'who plot against the prosperity of our empire' or attack 'our honour' were to be declared rebels and traitors.[2] Moreover, the reference to imperial officials makes this law appear as an *ad hoc* manifestation of imperial legislation. The reason for the promulgation of this law can be no other than the realistic recognition of the emperor that the functions attributed to him by the law books were no longer validly upheld. To be sure, there was nothing new in this law, except the pomposity with which the imperial overlordship was re-affirmed : this law constituted an attempt to revivify, recapture and resurrect the position of the emperor as the universal overlord. Strictly speaking, the legal basis of the proceedings and of the sentence against Robert could not be impugned, but their unreality deprived them of even a shadow of an enforceable claim. That sentence was the last solemn word of the Holy Roman Empire, and the law upon which it was based, was the last law carrying the flag of imperial and universal legislation. Although expressly declared a rebel by this law, Robert did not appear : in his absence he was found guilty of high treason, his goods were to be confiscated and he himself to be deprived of all dignities.[3]

VII

It was unfortunate for the emperor that the blow he aimed at Robert also hit the papacy. Perhaps events might have taken a different course if his opponent had not been a Neapolitan king. For the kingdom of Naples was a papal fief and the pope claimed supreme jurisdictional powers in this southern kingdom. It is not therefore difficult to perceive that the imperial claim to universal overlordship which might otherwise have found a willing supporter in the papacy, greatly antagonized Clement V : already

[1] See *Extravagantes* (XI Collatio), tit. i, 'Ad Reprimendum'. The resemblance with Boniface VIII's claims in *Unam Sanctam* is too striking to be overlooked. Henry must have found support in the views expressed by King Frederick III of Trinacria, see *M. G. Const.*, iv. no. 1248.

[2] Here again the resemblance with Boniface's diction at the end of *Unam Sanctam* is striking. Cf. also F. Bock in *Römische Quartalschrift*, 1936, pp. 105ff, 169ff.

[3] For an account of these events, see W. Götz, *König Robert von Neapel*, Tübingen, 1910, pp. 16 ff., &c. ; see also *M.G. Const.*, iv. 2, no. 947, pp. 991 f. ; no. 1252, pp. 1362 ff. ; no. 1253, pp. 1369 ff. For anonymous writings against Henry, see especially *M.G. Const.*, *loc. cit.* no. 1249, pp. 1317 ff., no. 1250 questio vii, p. 1335, no. 1251, pp. 1342 ff.

friendly disposed towards the French king—the pope had by this time taken up residence at Avignon—Clement V was considerably perturbed by this law of Henry VII and still more by Robert's condemnation. In other words, Henry also claimed the Neapolitan kingdom as his own territory. Furthermore, the French cannot but have felt the sting directed against them through that law and sentence. With one stroke Henry drove the pope and the French into the same camp: Henry had to face papal antagonism aroused by his claims, as well as the obviously hostile sentiments of the French ever highly sensitive to the possibility of a powerful and really universal empire.[1]

As the papal interests were directly at stake, the pope was bound to act, if he did not wish the imperial treatment of Robert to become a dangerous precedent. The challenge thrown out to Henry by the pope's bull *Pastoralis cura* also worked effectively in the interests of the French monarchy: the pope did the work for the French king who remained cautiously in the background, although his interests were at least as much affected as those of the pope. This bull denied the universal overlordship of the empire, not on grounds of political or legal theory, but simply because the papal interests were threatened by Henry's claim. But by declaring the sentence against Robert null and void, the pope acted in the interests of those who welcomed the disintegration of the empire as a universal monarchy. The coincidence of papal interests with the anti-imperial forces is one of the most fascinating aspects of the political life in the later middle ages: the pope found himself, compelled by circumstances, driven into the ideological company of precisely those who only a few years before had assailed his predecessor, Boniface VIII, in the most vituperative manner.

Pastoralis cura, incorporated in the Clementine collection of papal decrees,[2] briefly recalled the circumstances which had led to Robert's condemnation as rebel, traitor and enemy of the empire. This sentence, Clement V stated, was not based upon justice, but 'upon the step-mother of justice'; it was an arbitrary decision and proceeded from the overhastiness of the judge himself. After some purely legalistic arguments purporting to show that the citation of Robert was legally invalid—we will

[1] On contemporary papal policy see F. Baethgen, 'Der Anspruch des Papsttums auf das Reichsvikariat', in *Zeitschrift der Savigny Stiftung, kanon. Abt.* x (1920), 168–268, at pp. 241–2, and H. Kämpf, *Pierre Dubois und die geistigen Grundlagen des französischen Nationalbewusstseins um 1300*, 1935, pp. 87–8, and *passim*. On the character of Clement V as a politician see G. Lizerand, *Clément V et Philippe le Bel*, 1907, pp. 375 f., 385 ff. and F. Bock, *Reichsidee und Nationalstaaten*, 1943, p. 140.

[2] *Clem.* ii. 11. 2. In a public disputation Cynus called this bull one more error of the canonists, see Bartolus in his gloss on *Qui sint Rebelles*, versus 'Per Edictum'. Cf. also *M.G. Const.*, iv, no. 1166.

return to this point shortly—the pope, in somewhat heated and emotional tones, exclaimed that the procedure adopted by the emperor must be classed as despicable and detestable. The political reasons which Clement V set forth to demonstrate the invalidity of the sentence because of the invalidity of the citation, are of greater interest to us than the legalistic arguments. According to the bull, the emperor could not summon the king 'extra districtum imperii'; nor could an emperor use force to bring a king to book 'extra imperium'. Although this line of argument was familiar since Andreas de Isernia's lucid exposition of the theory of distinct domains, and although this conception was identical with the French ideas of kingship, it is nevertheless remarkable that Clement V adopted it as though it had been an unquestionable and uncontroversial point. Yet the motive for Clement's declaration appears to us less political than personal.[1] Indignantly he declared in the bull that he himself was the natural judge of the Neapolitan king—'nos quoque regis ordinarius judex'—and that a valid citation would have presupposed his own consent, but he was never even requested to consent to the procedure. No earthly reason could be adduced to prove that the king owed allegiance to Henry VII or that the latter was his superior: 'Nulla ratione terrarum debitam superioritatem habebat'. It would be idle to deny an emperor the right to punish crimes committed 'intra districtum imperialem', provided that the criminal stayed within imperial territory. Jurisdictional powers were denied to an emperor for crimes perpetrated 'extra districtum imperii'. In short, since the emperor had no powers whatever over the king—'cum nullam potestatem haberet imperator in regem'—the pope felt himself compelled, thereby maintaining his own superiority over the emperor, to declare the sentence pronounced at Pisa to be null and void and to deprive it of all consequences; as far as Clement V was concerned, Robert emerged unscathed from his quarrel with Henry VII.

VIII

The position adopted by Clement V was a concrete application of the theoretical views set forth by Andreas de Isernia. It

[1] This is also borne out by some statements quite independent of each other, see, e.g., S. Schard, 'Hypomnema', in Petrus de Vineis, *Epistolae*, tom. ii, p. 303: 'Clemens odio Henrici incensus . . . Rupertum regem Apuliae, quem is juridico ritu laesae majestatis condemnarat, hostemque imperii judicarat, defecit, atque sententiam in eum latam non tam jurisprudentia quam odio imperatoris improbavit atque rescidit'. The curialist partisan, Johannes Andreae, in his gloss on *Clementinae*, ii. 11. 2, also speaks of 'odium capitale' and 'inimicitia mortalis' between Pope and Emperor. Cf. also Clement's own words in *Clem.* ii. 9, cap. un.

was he, it will be recalled, who first spoke unambiguously and plainly of territorial limitations. Therefore, the term ever recurring in the bull—'extra districtum imperialem'—meant the solemn declaration by Clement V as Pope that Emperor Henry VII was no more 'dominus mundi' and that there was neither theoretically nor practically a world-embracing empire. But it certainly would be rash to assume that Clement himself had direct knowledge of Andreas's views. It may even be doubted whether Clement himself had drafted this decree. But it is a certainty that, before the bull was issued, Clement V consulted a jurist of great fame, Oldradus de Ponte. This we gather from the *Consilium* 43 of Oldradus which expressly dealt with the validity of Robert's summons by Henry VII. This *Consilium* was given specifically for the case in question, and was in many parts identical to the tenor, diction and wording of the bull.[1] Oldradus concluded that the citation of Robert was invalid, because he had not had the 'facultas defendendi': furthermore, he was outside the jurisdictional district of Emperor Henry VII. Above all, Oldradus denied that an emperor had *plenitudo potestatis*, and his powers were restricted to a smaller district. As to the charge itself, Oldradus logically enough declared that the *crimen laesae majestatis* could not be committed by Robert, since Henry VII had no 'major potestas'. Consequently Robert should have been acquitted of high treason.

The case of Robert against Henry apparently stimulated Oldradus de Ponte to examine the whole idea of a world empire afresh, on a purely theoretical plane and without any reference to the actuality. It may have been argued against him that his *Consilium* 43 was drawn up at the special request of Pope Clement V and his cardinals and that it had therefore only an application limited to the case in question. It is true that this *Consilium* was negative in so far as it denied the validity of citation and of judgement. Scholar and thinker as he was, Oldradus felt bound to investigate the whole imperial idea of the state, its theoretical foundation and legal basis. His views are contained in his *Consilium* 69.[2] It has been suggested that Oldradus was the originator of the idea of sovereignty,[3] but this claim cannot be supported by the evidence available. Nevertheless, there are certain features in his treatment of the

[1] See also E. Will, *Die Gutachten des Oldradus de Ponte*, Berlin and Leipzig, 1917 (in *Abhandlungen zur mittleren und neueren Geschichte*), p. 49.

[2] It is also printed by the author of the *Somnium Viridarii* which is in Goldast, *Monarchia*, tom. i, pp. 58 ff. About its probable author see Scholz, *Publizistik*, p. 138, and F. Schulte, *Quellen*, ii. 372, n. 6. The contents of the *Consilium* were noted by Scholz, *Unbekannte kirchenpolitische Streitschriften*, Rome, 1911, p. 214, and by F. Aistermann, *Beiträge zum Konflikt Johanns XXII mit dem deutschen Königtum*, Bonn, 1909, p. 27, and by Stengel, *loc. cit.*

[3] See Bodin, *De Republica*, i. 4, and Woolf, *op. cit.* pp. 380–1.

problem which are somewhat novel and warrant a closer examination. His views were an amalgamation of the current French and Neapolitan ideas, though strangely enough he never referred to either of them. And this lack of reference on the part of Oldradus may have given rise to the assumption that the idea of sovereignty was born with him. In fact, however, he stood not at the beginning of an ideological movement, but at its end. No doubt Oldradus tackled the problem independently and with some justifiable claim to originality, but the cardinal tenets as well as the phrase 'rex in regno suo est imperator' were by no means Oldradus's own. It should be mentioned that his *Consilium* was made the target of many abusive utterances as late as the middle of the sixteenth century.[1]

He chose as the heading of his *Consilium*[2] the title 'De Majoritate et Obedientia', and the very first words of his essay put the whole problem into a neat question: 'Consuevit dubitari, an omnes reges et principes debeant de jure subesse imperatori?' This beginning reflects the state of mind of political thinkers at the time of the contest between Henry VII and Robert of Naples better than any lengthy tracts. Was the emperor *de jure* overlord? This *Consilium* may conveniently be divided into three parts. In the first part the author, in typical medieval fashion, answered his question in the affirmative—'et videtur, quod sic, mundi enim dominus est',[3] and marshalled all those arguments which may be adduced to support this answer. The second part contained his own constructive exposition and theoretical explanation as to why an emperor was not universal overlord and why kings had the powers usually attributed to an emperor alone. In the third and last part Oldradus set forth arguments purporting to destroy those of the first part. It will be convenient to select the more important points of the first part and, in order to avoid repetition, to set against them the counter-arguments of the third part, before we attempt to reconstruct the second part. Now the very first argument adduced by Oldradus to prove that the emperor was overlord, was brushed aside: the emperor could not claim to be overlord, since a number of passages in the law books know of princes who were not 'subditi', and these were called 'friends', 'confederates', 'kings' and the like.[4] An argument popular with

[1] See, for instance, Michael Ulcurrunus in his *Tractatus Regiminis Mundi*, contained in *Tractatus Illustrium Jurisconsultorum*, tom. xvi, fos. 103vo–130vo, particularly at no. 9, fo. 117, and no. 1, fo. 121vo *seqq.*; this author devoted 9 folio columns, mainly consisting of abusive remarks about Oldradus de Ponte. See also Franciscus Zoanettus, *De Romano Imperio*, also in *Tractatus*, *loc. cit.* fos. 21–30, especially no. 229 at fo. 28vo. Ulcurrunus was imperial counsellor at the court of Charles V.

[2] Fos. 23vo–25 of the edition Lugduni, 1550.

[3] With a reference to the well-known passages in Roman law.

[4] No. 9 with a reference to D. 49. 15. 19 and C. I. l. 1.

the imperialists was that deduced from the *Decretum*, vii. i. 41, and Oldradus himself declared that a plurality of rulers would be a monstrosity—' si sunt multi, erunt multa capita quasi monstrum '—and they would easily be given to factions and quarrels ; therefore, so runs his arguments, it was found necessary to confer the government on one individual, and not on a plurality of individuals, as this canon was usually interpreted. But Oldradus challenged the validity of this argument : he would not say that there were to be two kings within one and the same kingdom ; what he would say, however, was that this legal text did not declare one ruler to be overlord. ' Nec ego dico ', Oldradus stated, ' quod in uno regno sunt duo reges, sed in quolibet regno unus rex . . . unus apes non est rex omnium apum de mundo '. Herds of animals, too, did not follow one leader only, but ' una congregatio sequitur unam, et alia aliam '. Consequently, the imperial overlordship could not be based upon this canon law text, and, therefore, ' in quolibet regno erit unus rex '.

The imperialist jurists furthermore could refer to the prevailing ideas of the origin of the empire, as laid down in *Collatio* VI : God has sent the emperor into the world as a ' lex animata ' ; therefore God Himself could be said to be the founder of the universal empire—' quia nec potestas nisi a Deo '.[1] Thus disobedience to the emperor's commands meant disobedience to a divine ordination and could be classed as an insult to God.[2] But these arguments could not perturb Oldradus. As to the ' divine ' origin of the empire Oldradus stoutly maintained that if this were true, at least one reference should be found in the Old and New Testaments, but he was unable to find even a trace of this idea in the Bible. ' Ego non invenio per legem novam neque veterem.' On the contrary, the idea of an empire was quite alien to the Old Testament, where kings only are mentioned, such as David, Saul, and so forth. One might adduce Christ's famous dictum ' Render unto Caesar . . .' but this utterance of the Lord did not, in Oldradus's opinion, amount to an approval of the idea of the empire : what Christ meant to convey with this utterance was that Christians should pay taxes to the emperor so as to avoid giving public scandal. Christ Himself had paid tribute [3] so as not to give offence.[4] And the assertion that disobedience to temporal commands constituted sinful behaviour, can be applied to every legitimate ruler, whether

[1] With a reference to Innocent III's dictum in *Liber Sextus*, v. 4. 1.

[2] Oldradus deduced this from the *Decretum*, xi. 3. 98.

[3] He refers to Matt. xvii. 24.

[4] He mentioned Matt. xviii. 7 and *Decretum*, xviii. 1. 8, in which canon St. Augustine said, though in a totally different context, that Christ paid tribute ' ne scandalizaret '. This was the usual canonistic interpretation of the preceding century.

emperor or king: 'Non loquitur tantum in imperatore, sed in alio quolibet principe veritatem jubente'.

It is, furthermore, true, Oldradus continued, that canon law expressly lays down the universal overlordship of the emperor,[1] but the passage in canon law does not say that the emperors held their empire on the grounds of justice: and Oldradus flatly denied that they had justice on their side when claiming to be universal overlords.[2] Secondly the Persians, Syrians and Greeks had their empires at their times, and yet nobody would consider them as 'domini mundi'.

Lastly, some support for the undivided sovereignty of the emperor might be found in Innocent III's utterance in which he referred to the king of France who did not recognize a superior. True, glossators had interpreted this dictum of Innocent III in a sense which meant that the emperor was *de jure* superior to the French king, but Oldradus would not bow before the authority of glossators. Their dicta may be reasonable, though not authoritative: 'Eorum dicta licet sunt rationabilia, non sunt authorizabilia'.[3] Moreover, Johannes Teutonicus was a German and therefore biased in the question. As to the position of the Spanish king, Oldradus mentioned that this monarch recognized the emperor so little 'de jure' that the mere citation of an imperial law in a Spanish court was threatened with death penalty.[4]

In his constructive part of the *Consilium* 69 Oldradus went little beyond the standpoint of Andreas de Isernia. The fundamental problem as seen by Oldradus concerned the legality of the emperor's position. Where and how did he acquire his alleged universal overlordship? Oldradus strongly emphasized the necessity for enquiring into the legal basis of the emperor's rulership. The argument of Andreas that the empire was founded by force and violence appeared with Oldradus in a far more generalized manner. All empires, he said, started by violence and usurpation, and that was precisely the reason why Christ had 'specialiter' reproved the Roman Empire, since He had destroyed all empires.[5] More than that: divine and natural law forbid, Oldradus averred with a reference to *Prov.* xxii. 28, that rulers should enlarge their dominions by violent means. The Decalogue, too, declared that 'thou shalt not covet any thing that is thy neighbour's'. Oldradus applied this injunction to the present problem saying that 'in quo (scil. praecepto) omnis rapina et violentia prohibetur'. Therefore, the right of

[1] *Decretum*, xii. l. 15.

[2] Canon law said: 'Romani principes, qui pene totius orbis monarchiam tenebant'. Oldradus said: 'Hoc non negatur, quin tenuerint, sed negatur, quod juste tenuerint'.

[3] In *Decretales*, iv. 17. 13.

[4] 'Scio, quod inter alias Hispani fecerunt unam (scil. legem), quod quicumque allegaret legem imperatoris in judiciis, capite puniatur.'

[5] 'Imo per Christum omnes monarchiae fuerunt destructae et etiam reprobatae.'

the emperor to transfer property [1] or to confiscate it for the sake of the public good, was devoid of any basis in divine or natural law. But if the followers of the idea of universal monarchy should assert that this and similar rights were contained in the law books, they were referred by Oldradus to the old legal maxim that nobody can be witness in his own affairs.[2]

From a purely legalistic point of view it may be asserted, Oldradus argued, that the emperor received his powers from the Roman people through the *Lex Regia*, whereby they had transferred to him all the powers previously vested in them. Although this was a very favourite argument amongst medieval jurists to justify the legality of the emperor's position,[3] Oldradus did not adhere to the current fashion. For if the Roman people should have validly transferred powers to the emperor, they must have had the power to do so, otherwise the transfer would be invalid. But Oldradus denied the Roman people the legal right to effectuate this transfer. They could not transfer more rights than they themselves had, since the Romans lacked all right to rule other peoples : 'Sed populus Romanus non habuit de jure dominium super alias nationes, ergo nec ipse'. It was a notorious fact that the Roman people had kept up their rulership 'injuste et violenter'. The rightful and lawful rulers of Rome were Romulus and Remus, because the 'civitas Romana' had been built by them : they and their successors were indeed kings, but they were expelled by the people in an illicit and revolutionary manner, and all further actions of the Romans, especially the enlargement of their dominions, must be classed as illegal. Their actions were based upon an illegal expulsion of rightful rulers. Therefore, the establishment of emperors after the republican period could not be supported by law or the idea of justice. The only consequence from the legal point of view was, Oldradus said, that the Romans had no power to transfer any lordship, let alone universal overlordship, to the emperor. Nor could it be said that the Romans might have acquired their powers by prescription, for they all were in bad faith which excluded prescriptive acquisition. Oldradus concluded : 'Imo omnes videntur esse successores vitiorum et culpae', and therefore no valid transfer of powers could have taken place.

However, canon law might lend some support to the claims of a universal overlordship of the emperor. The *Translatio Imperii* from the Greeks to the Germans was carried out by the

[1] Hitherto reckoned as one of his foremost privileges, see *Medieval Idea of Law*, pp. 100, 179, 181.

[2] 'Si hoc dicerunt, non crederetur, quia in facto proprio, in quo nullus idoneus testis invenitur'; reference is made to D. 22. 5. 10.

[3] See Gierke-Maitland, *Political Theories of the Middle Age*, Cambridge, 1938 (reprint), p. 43.

Church herself.[1] But the Church had, in the opinion of Oldradus, arrogated rights in this translation of the empire which she had not had before : 'Ecclesia plus juris sibi concesserit ex ista concessione quam antea habuerit'. This translation had not a constitutive effect, but was only declarative, that is to say, had only confirmatory character : but a confirmatory act could not bestow more rights than were possessed before : 'Per confirmationem non tribuitur jus'.[2]

From a positive point of view it might lastly be maintained that Roman law was a universal, civil law, but this argument is set aside by Oldradus whose definition, allegedly derived from D. 41. l. 1, had little in common with the definition of Gaius as given in that passage. For Oldradus civil law was all that law which was peculiar to a certain state : 'Jus civile dicitur jus proprium cuiuslibet civitatis'. In fact Oldradus had substituted 'cuiuslibet civitatis' for Gaius's 'civitatis nostrae'. Hence, he shaped a definition which was suitable to his own conceptions of a divided sovereignty. As an example he quoted the civil law of Spain and France, to demonstrate that each particular state had its own particular law which was the civil law of that state. This conception, if nothing else, justifies our assumption that Oldradus truly understood the nature of the sovereign state—and not only of the sovereign prince. With Oldradus de Ponte, the juristic counsellor of the papal curia, the ideological movement embodying the conception of sovereignty had found its conclusion.

Emperor in name, though in reality a cipher without the power his apparent position would have warranted, Henry VII failed to sense the temper of the time and its prevailing political ideas : by forcing the issue he antagonized the papacy without whose help he could hardly have hoped to realize his lofty aim ; moreover, he drove the papacy into the hands of its fiercest adversaries, thus not ineffectively contributing to the eventful seven decades which left their mark on the history of the Church. But to Dante Henry VII remained the universal pilot [3] and a true Caesar.[4] The empire of the *Monarchia* is the vision of an idealist.

[1] See Innocent III in *Decretales*, i. 6. 34. Innocent III must be credited with the invention of the *Translatio Imperii*, see the now famous, but then secret *Deliberatio Domini papae Innocentii super facto imperii de tribus electis*, in Migne, *Patr. Lat.*, vol. ccxvi, cap. xxix, col. 1025 ; cf. also the letter to the archbishop of Cologne, cap. xxx, col. 1032, the communication to the archbishop of Mainz, in Raynaldus, *Annales Ecclesiastici*, ad annum 1200, § 27, and the letter to the German princes of 3 May 1199, *Registrum de negotio Romani imperii*, Migne, *loc. cit.* cap. ii, col. 998.

[2] With a reference to *Decretales*, ii. 30. 1 and 2.

[3] *Convivio*, iv. 4 : '. . . conviene essere uno quasi nocchiere . . .'.

[4] *Epist.*, vii. 1, written to Henry VII : 'Cumque tu, Caesaris et Augusti successor, Apennini juga transiliens, veneranda signa Tarpeja retulisti, protinus longa substiterunt suspiria, lacrimarumque diluvia desierunt'.

VIII

A Medieval Document on Papal Theories of Government

THE treatise of John of Paris, *Tractatus de Potestate Regia et Papali*, and the *Defensor Pacis* of Marsiglio of Padua mark a definite stage in the development of medieval political thought. Whilst opposing the extreme claims of papacy, theologians and canonists, they attempted to define the respective spheres of authority of ecclesiastical and secular powers. The problem originally arising out of the disputed clerical taxation by the king became eventually the vast and complicated one of Church and State. It is not, however, generally recognized that the main theses propounded in these two writings were foreshadowed in the earlier tract *Quaestio de Potestate Papae*. This tract, too, dealt with the question of which were the interests in which the ecclesiastical power exercised exclusive authority, and which were those in which the secular power was called upon to reign supreme. Although smouldering for many a decade underneath the surface, the problem only fully emerged when Boniface VIII powerfully and insistently put forward, in the bulls *Clericis laicos*, *Ausculta fili*, and, lastly, in *Unam sanctam*, claims which met with the fiercest opposition from his adversary, Philip the Fair of France. It is true that the crisis caused by the claims of the pope still appeared in the typically medieval garb of a conflict between ecclesiastical (or spiritual) and secular (or temporal) jurisdiction, but the issues and implications went far deeper than this external cloak would suggest. Throughout his quarrel with the king, the pope, encouraged by extreme theologians and canonists, claimed the supremacy of the ecclesiastical power over all other powers, and consequently that even in temporal matters the king and his kingdom were subjected to ecclesiastical authority.[1] The real issue, therefore, concerned the exercise of political authority, that is, of an authority which

[1] As late as the middle of the fourteenth century the bull *Unam sanctam* was held to be an official declaration of the dependence of the Emperor on the Church. See, e.g., Bartolus, *Commentaria in Authenticum*, Lyons, 1523, collatio I, no. 12, fo. 10^v: although Innocent IV declared that 'jurisdictio papae et Imperatoris sunt distinctae', it seems now that after Boniface's bull 'papa utramque gladii habeat potestatem et ab ecclesia imperium dependeat, ut habetur in extravaganti Bonifacii, quae incipit "unam sanctam"'.

is vested with coercive power. In the extremists' opinion, the king became a mere deputy of the pope.[1] His claim to supremacy was emphatically contested by the French king. Nothing reflects the mood of the time and the French attitude better than the answer which Petrus de Flotte, the king's emissary, gave to the pope at the occasion of the delivery of a personal message ; the pope declared ' nos habemus utramque potestatem ', whereupon Petrus laconically replied : ' Utique domine, sed vestra est verbalis, nostra autem realis '.[2] The king was energetically supported by a considerable political literature of which the *Quaestio de Potestate Papae*, or as it is also called according to its incipit, the *Rex Pacificus*, is one of the most striking and illuminating documents of the time.

Professor Scholz drew attention to this document,[3] yet his treatment of it is neither accurate nor complete. Both defects result from his using a source which omitted long and important passages, in one case even more than a folio. The treatment of the document by Professor Rivière,[4] though very valuable in many respects, is a critical and polemical examination rather than an exposition, reconstruction and representation of the thoughts expressed in the tract. As the subtitle of Rivière's book already suggests,[5] he is more concerned with the religious and theological aspects involved in the controversy, than with its practical and political implications.[6] The contents of the tract as well as the advanced state of political thought reached by its author, warrant a more careful treatment than it has hitherto received. Both these modern authorities fail to see that, by his penetrating analyses and by his employment of the very same concept upon which the famous and brilliantly conceived system of Egidius Romanus rested,[7] the author of the *Rex Pacificus* plays havoc with the ideas of this papal extremist. Nor do these two modern writers seem to have noticed that, by

[1] See, e.g., Augustinus Triumphus, writing about 1308, and maintaining that princes and kings ' ought to be his (the pope's) organs and instruments ', see McIlwain, *Growth of Political Thought in the West*, p. 262.

[2] *Acta inter Bonifacium VIII, Benedictum XI, Clementem V et Philippum Pulchrum Regem Christianum*, Troyes (?), 1614, fo. 164v. On Petrus see Powicke in Rashdall's *Universities of Europe in the Middle Ages*, ii, 168.

[3] *Die Publizistik zur Zeit Philipps des Schoenen und Bonifaz VIII*, Stuttgart, 1903.

[4] *Le problème de l'église et de l'état au temps de Philippe le Bel*, Louvain, 1926, in the series *Spicilegium Sacrum Lovaniense*.

[5] ' Étude de theologie positive.'

[6] There are very brief references to the tract by Riezler, *Die Literarischen Widersacher der Paepste zur Zeit Ludwig des Baier*, Leipzig, 1874, p. 141 ; Finke, *Aus den Tagen Bonifaz' VIII*, Muenster, 1902, p. 159 ; A. J. Carlyle, *History of Political Thought*, vol. v, 1928, p. 421 ; McIlwain, 263 ; C. N. S. Woolf, *Bartolus of Sassoferrato*, 1913, pp. 347 f., 353 and 360 f.

[7] *De Ecclesiastica Potestate*, ed. R. Scholz, Weimar, 1929. This treatise was written about 1301, and was the basis of *Unam sanctam*, see Scholz, p. x.

sagacious reasoning, the document destroys one by one the arguments of James of Viterbo who, next to Egidius, exercised greatest influence upon political reality and scholarship in the beginning of the century with his *De Regimine Christiano.* It will be recalled that the two tracts of Egidius and James plausibly advance the extreme views of the pope's universal monarchy, that is, of his supremacy in temporal as well as in spiritual matters, the former by asserting a universal dominion (' dominium universale ') of the pope over all things and persons, including kings and emperors, the latter by constructing the idea of one realm (' unum regnum ') which is identified with the Church, ruled by her alone and whose temporal government is entrusted to the prince. Several arguments contained in the document *Rex Pacificus* foreshadow those of the more famous tracts of John of Paris and Marsiglio.

The authorship of the tract is not known, and we have to rely on the testimony of the historian of the university of Paris, Bulaeus,[1] who says that it represented the well-considered opinion of the Masters of the university who had been consulted on the bearing of the bull *Unam sanctam* upon French rights and liberties. They wrote this tract as the reply to the pope's claims, suppressing their names ' ad tuitionem jurium libertatumque regis et regni '.[2] The historian himself, although writing two centuries after the events, still feels indignant at the pope's treatment of Philip. The tract was written, he says,[3] in the days when Boniface VIII dared to prescribe laws to the king, in the manner in which a master orders his servants, which treatment was rejected by the king, who pointed out the only domain wherein the pope enjoyed absolute authority.[4] The university being consulted on the justification of the pope's claims, replied, in its usual manner, as Bulaeus reports, ' vigorously ' (' fortiter ') that the king had no superior in temporal matters except God. Considering Bulaeus' detailed knowledge of all matters concerning the university and the reliability of his reports as well as the attitude of the university towards papal questions,[5] no reason can be adduced to support the contention made by Scholz and, following him, Rivière, that this tract was not written by the university. They themselves do not suggest any reason for rejecting Bulaeus' positive statement, but merely assert that

[1] *Historia Universitatis Parisiensis*, Paris, tom. iv, 1668.

[2] *Loc. cit.* p. 37.

[3] *Loc. cit.* p. 935.

[4] ' Bonifacius ausus est Philippo Pulchro leges dicere tamquam dominus subdito ', p. 935.

[5] For an account of the university's attitude during the struggle, see E. Friedberg, *Die mittelalterlichen Lehren ueber das Verhaeltnis von Staat und Kirche*, Leipzig, 1874, p. 22; *Preuves des libertés de l'église gallicane*, Paris, 1651, ii. 34; and especially P. Féret, *La faculté de theologie de Paris*, Moyen Age, tom. iii, Paris, 1896.

he did not prove it.[1] This document was also published by Dupuy [2] and is, furthermore, contained in the anonymous collection of documents relating to the struggle between Boniface and Philip,[3] though in both cases with serious omissions.[4] The date of the tract is uncertain. Bulaeus maintains that it was written as the university's answer to *Unam sanctam*, thus at the earliest in November 1302 ; whereas the *Acta* give the improbable date of 1300.[5] There is no direct evidence in the tract itself as to when it was composed : neither events nor persons are mentioned, although some phrases suggest that it was written after the issue of the forged bull *Deum time* and after the king's letter *Antequam essent*.

The importance of this document lies not only in the bold, clear, and uncompromising rejection of papal claims to temporal supremacy, but also in the realistic and original approach to the problem, in the pungency of the arguments employed, in the new ideas it brings to bear upon the dispute, and in the shrewdness of its argumentation. Moreover, the author of the document employs the very same basis which the papal theorists were wont to employ, and he gives well-worn concepts an interpretation which was, at the time of its writing, entirely new. The author was bent on defeating his opponents by their own weapons. This novel approach renders the tract a highly significant and interesting document of the time. The refutation of the well-tried papal arguments is carried out with a naturalness and simplicity which reveal the author's skill in political thinking.

[1] Scholz, *Publizistik*, p. 254, and Rivière, p. 135.

[2] Dupuy, *Histoire du differend d'entre le pape Boniface VIII et Philippe le Bel*, Paris, 1655 (Preuves du differend, pp. 663–83).

[3] *Acta*, &c., see *supra*, p. 181, n. 2.

[4] On the nonsensical composition by Dupuy, see Rivière, appendix v, p. 431. The editio princeps suffers from the same serious omissions, unobserved by Scholz, who seems to have collated Dupuy with editio princeps. It is very likely that both *Acta* and Dupuy reprinted from the editio princeps ; in this way the lacunae may be explained, whilst Bulaeus consulted the manuscript which was at his time in the library of St. Victor Abbey, see Bulaeus, p. 935. This manuscript is now in the Bibliothèque Nationale, Cod. lat. 15004. The editio princeps is printed by Jean Barbier for Jean Petit, Paris, 1506, 4to, 10 leaves, sig. A1-4, B1-6. It is contained in the collection of tracts by Durandus episcopus Meldensis ordinis predicatorum, *De origine jurisdictionum*, and is printed after the treatise of John of Paris. The title page says : ' Quidam tractatus de eodem, qui incipit rex pacificus, cuius autor ignoratur ', whilst the tract itself is headed : ' Incipit questio de potestate pape '. It is interesting to note that these two tracts were first edited by the Dominicans, a fact which may throw some light on the somewhat obscure position of John of Paris. There are two copies of this rare edition in the University Library, Cambridge, both of which I have seen ; there is also one copy in the Bodleian Library and another in the University Library, Edinburgh, according to the catalogues of these two libraries. The following manuscript versions, apart from the already mentioned one in the Bibliotheque Nationale, are extant : (1) MS. Lat. 12467 (St. Germain), saec. 14, fos. 127–30v ; (2) Lat. 15690 (Sorbonne 372), saec. 14, fos. 128–36 ; see Scholz, *loc. cit.* pp. 252 f.

[5] Fo. 58r : ' Scriptum circa annum 1300 '. The editio princeps does not give any date.

Though on the whole not favourably disposed to the theses set out in the tract, Professor Rivière is bound to admit that it developed the theme 'avec une ampleur dont le moyen âge fournirait sans doute peu d'exemples et donne l'impression d'une vigueur au-dessus du commun'.[1] And Professor Scholz stresses that the *Rex Pacificus* prepared the ground for Marsiglio's *Defensor Pacis*.[2] Indeed, Marsiglio is hailed as a prophet anticipating the modern distinction between morals and politics,[3] but the germ for this distinction is clearly perceptible in the *Rex Pacificus*. More than that: the document quite unmistakeably conceives the State as the only source and the sole foundation of all real, that is, coercive power; whoever exercises power 'in the kingdom', does it by permission of the king who is the embodiment of all earthly authority. In the tract the State is represented as the foundation of all political and ecclesiastical life. The Church, in its temporal existence, is subordinated to the State. Church and State are not two co-ordinated powers: as a concrete and organized body the former is inferior to the latter. Thus, also in the conception of Church and State, the author of the *Quaestio de Potestate Papae* takes a step towards the theory of the *Defensor Pacis*.

The tract consists of four parts. In the first the author deals, in typical medieval fashion, with the arguments which can be advanced to demonstrate papal supremacy, even in temporal matters, so that the emperor or king becomes merely an executive organ for the pope's orders.[4] In the second part the author presents those arguments which can be adduced to prove the supremacy of the temporal power. The third part, which forms the main body of the tract, is based upon biblical texts and authoritative utterances of the Fathers, philosophers of the Church and theologians, and this part elaborates the idea that, in the domain of the temporal, the secular ruler is supreme lord, independent of the pope and responsible to God alone: in the temporal domain, the pope and all ecclesiastical authorities are subordinated to the secular power. In this constructive part of his thesis the author restricts the Church's authority to purely moral issues, whilst true political power is reserved for the king. The fourth and last part of the tract refutes, one by one, the arguments contained in the first part. From the point of view of

[1] *Loc. cit.* p. 137. [2] *Loc. cit.* p. 272.

[3] D'Entrèves, *The Medieval Contribution to Political Thought*, 1939, p. 76; see also p. 64.

[4] One of the most extreme writers on the papal side, Hostiensis (Henricus de Segusia), asserts that the emperor is the vicar of the pope or his official: 'Imperator ab ecclesia Romana imperium tenet, et potest dici officialis eius, seu vicarius', *Summa Decretalium*, Lyons, 1588, iv. 17, 13, 9. There is a long review of Hostiensis's theories in Carlyle, *op. cit.* v., 324 ff.

reconstructing the ideology of the *Rex Pacificus* it appears advisable to group the first and fourth parts together.

We may now profitably turn to a brief consideration of the arguments in favour of the pope's spiritual and temporal overlordship, and their refutation by the Frenchman.[1] The papal partisans found the main support for their view of the pope's plenitude of power in the idea of his being the vicar of Christ. This argument appealed strongly to the medieval mind, mainly on account of several allegorical biblical passages adduced to support this viewpoint. Thus the saying of Christ that 'all power is given unto me in heaven and in earth '[2] was interpreted as meaning that the pope as Christ's vicar necessarily wielded the same plenitude of power which characterized Christ; accordingly, they asserted, the plenitude of power embraced also the power to judge temporal matters. This argument is brushed aside by our author: if Christ's dictum were taken literally, the pope would have the power to work miracles, a power which Christ undeniably had and which the pope unquestionably never had. Furthermore, the pope is certainly not allowed to institute new sacraments or to alter the sacramental character of existing institutions, a power which Christ certainly had. This conception of the pope as vicar of Christ underlies yet another argument, lavishly employed by the papal theorists, namely that of St. Augustine that no commonwealth can live without justice, but justice cannot be attained, unless Christ is made the head of the community; the pope being Christ's vicar, becomes therefore automatically the temporal overlord in order to ensure the reign of justice on earth.[3] Our author is not perturbed by this argument either: the truth of St. Augustine's dictum cannot be denied, since the Supreme Ruler is 'verax Deus', but, he argues, there are two vicars, one in the spiritual, and the other in the temporal sphere. The former is the pope, the latter the secular prince, the author says referring to St. Paul,[4] who receives his power directly from God and not through an intermediary.[5] The secular

[1] This short consideration is all the more necessary and justifiable as Scholz and Rivière, the only authorities who pay attention to the tract, treated this part in an especially cursory way.

[2] Matt. xxviii. 18.

[3] This argument was elaborated at great length by Egidius, *loc. cit.* pp. 73 f. Dr. Carlyle says that Egidius's reference to St. Augustine 'is indeed not very happy or well considered', *op. cit.* v., 405.

[4] Rom. xiii. 1.

[5] 'Quando dicitur, quod papa est Christi vicarius, dico, quod verum est in spiritualibus, sed bene habet alium vicarium in temporalibus, videlicet potestatem temporalem, quae cum sit a Deo, sicut dicitur Rom. 13, potest dici vices Dei gerere in regimine temporali.'

That this was also the view of eminent, contemporary lawyers, follows from the statement of Cynus, writing at the end of the first decade of the century. In his commentary on the *Digestum vetus* (Francfort, 1578), fo. 8, no. 1, he says: 'Imperium est a Deo . . . et ab ipso Deo immediate processit, unde inter Imperatorem et Deum non est ponere medium'. A few lines later the same jurist says: 'Dico, quod

ruler is the real vicegerent of God on earth—a conception of the ruler which anticipates the political thought current in the sixteenth century.[1] It is in the same line of thought that the author dismisses the other favourite argument of the papal extremists that the emperor derives his power from his coronation by the pope, and thus becomes dependent on him.[2] If the full implications of this argument were followed up, the counter argument runs, the bishop of Ostia would then have jurisdiction over the pope, since it is he who performs the coronation, but nobody would seriously endeavour to uphold this point of view. Whatever the case may be with the emperor, he continues with a touch of derision, the kings of France, Spain, and England are not crowned by the pope, and therefore this argument is of no avail.[3]

The papal extremists found further support for their thesis of the king's dependence on the pope in the allegory of the two lights.[4] According to their interpretation, the pope assumed the role of the sun, whilst the prince had to be contented with the position of the moon ; and, since the moon depended for its light on the sun, the conclusion was quickly reached that the prince is dependent on the pope.[5] The author disposes of this

Imperator a populo est, sed imperium, cuius presidatu Imperator dicitur, dicimus a Deo '.

It must not be assumed, however, that this was the general opinion amongst the lawyers. A contemporary and colleague of Cynus, Oldradus de Ponte, held theories which are not distinguishable from the extreme papal writers. Oldradus said : ' Constat etiam jurisdictionem et administrationem imperii esse penes papam ; quicumque eam sibi sine superioris authoritate usurpat, praedo est ', *Consilia* (Lyons, 1550), consilium 191, fo. 73r.

[1] A similar phrase denoting the emperor's role as God's vicegerent appears also with other fourteenth-century legists. See, e.g., Lucas de Penna, *Commentaria in Tres Libros*, Lyons, 1597, in his commentary on C. xi. 71, 1, no. 11, fo. 638r : ' Sibi (imperatori) Deus res humanas regere deputavit . . . nec eius potestas dependet a papa '.

The idea of the people's sovereignty is already clearly recognizable in Petrus de Bellapertica, a fellow-countryman and contemporary of our author. Petrus maintains that the emperor derives all powers from the people through election, but ' populus non habet superiorem ; verum est, quod Imperator est superior quolibet de populo, sed non est superior populo ', see his commentaries on the *Codex*, Paris, 1519, fo. 36v.

[2] See again Hostiensis, and Carlyle, *loc. cit.* p. 329.

[3] It may be interesting to compare with this view the ideas of a contemporary jurist. Cynus attributes to the coronation of the emperor purely ' spiritual effects .' He says (lecture on C. vii. 37, 3, no. 5, fo. 446v) : coronation pursues the aim ' ut spiritualia bona sive dona et spiritus sancti gratiam consequitur, ut augeatur interius, quod exterius unctio praefigurat '. Coronation, then, means nothing but a change of title. It was already Jacobus de Arena who, according to Cynus's report, held this view as early as the second half of the thirteenth century.

[4] Gen. i. 10.

[5] See Hostiensis, *loc. cit.* : ' Dico, quod sicut luna recipit claritatem a sole, non sol a luna, sic regalis potestas recipit auctoritatem a sacerdotali, non econtra . . . sacerdotalis clarificat dignitas mundum per regalem '. This extreme canonist went even so far as to calculate, in mathematical terms, the relative strength of papal and secular power : ' Per hoc etiam innuitur, quod septies millies et sexcenties et quadragies quater, et insuper eius medietatem est major sacerdotalis dignitas quam regalis '.

argument, so dear to the medieval mind, by the acute observation that the moon is, in many respects, quite independent of the sun and works as an agency which proves its own inner force. He quotes as examples the effects of the moon on the tides, on the mood and temper of man, on the rise and increase of the nightly dew ; and, lastly, the actual phases of the moon demonstrate its independence. Moreover, he continues, this argument can no longer be upheld when due place is given to the consideration that there was a secular authority long before there was ever an ecclesiastical authority. It would therefore be absurd to make the chronologically preceding secular power dependent on the chronologically succeeding spiritual power, as both Egidius and James of Viterbo emphatically desired.[1]

Closely allied to the foregoing considerations of the papal supporters was another argument by which they tried to prove that God had bestowed the plenitude of power upon a priest, that is, Jeremiah, who by explicit divine ordinance became the spiritual as well as the temporal overlord.[2] That the same plenitude of power must be conceded to the pope, was a foregone conclusion, since he is 'summus sacerdos'. This argument is refuted by means of the interpretation given by the gloss and by St. Bernard of Clairvaux to that passage of the Old Testament. Both interpreted it in such a way as to leave no doubt that the temporal government was not included in the mandate of God.[3] St. Bernard even went so far as to declare that the supremacy of Jeremiah solely concerned his task to pronounce publicly and authoritatively the moral injunctions of God and to insist on the improvement of morals ; Jeremiah's task, as set him by God, was not concerned with a judgement in temporal matters. Consequently, the only legitimate sphere of the pope's authority is the spiritual.

Another common argument of the pope's advocates was found in the allegory of the keys.[4] Since he is the successor of St. Peter, the pope must have the power of the keys. The reply which we find in the document, points out that that sentence of Christ must not be torn out of its context. True and faithful interpretation has to take into account the whole passage, which gives a different meaning to Christ's utterance. What Christ meant to say was that St. Peter should exercise supreme authority in spiritual matters, because temporal matters can neither be bound nor loosed in heaven : 'Nam in coelis nullum locum habere potest ligatio vel solutio temporalis'. In this way the author of the

[1] This retort is reminiscent of Philip's letter to the pope : 'Antequam essent clerici, rex Franciae habebat custodiam regni et poterat facere statuta', see *Acta*, fo. 3^r.

[2] Jer. i. 10.

[3] The gloss said : 'Ecce constitui te super gentes et super regna, ut evellas mala et destruas et dissipes regna diaboli et aedifices ecclesiam et plantes bonum'.

[4] Matt. xvi. 19.

Rex Pacificus disposes of one of the chief arguments of James of Viterbo. According to the latter, the divine kingship of the pope 'includes a priestly power, but it is also a truly royal and judicial power, for it contains the power of binding and loosing'.[1]

The argument of the canonists that the pope is 'dignior' than the emperor and that therefore the former is superior to the latter is, according to our author, valid only in its premiss, because 'spiritus dignior est corpore',[2] but not in its conclusion, for the emperor shows reverence to, and bows and genuflects before, the lowest priest to whom he expresses his submission in spiritual matters, such as in hearing mass, in confessions and in asking absolution, and the like, but this submission leaves his superiority in temporal matters untouched.

Finally, it is alleged by the papalists that the monistic principle characterizing celestial government, should be copied for the benefit of terrestrial government of Christians; just as there is only one superior at the head of the former, so there should be only one presiding over the latter, and this one can be no other than the pope.[3] This monistic idea of the government on earth constituted one of the most persuasive and formidable arguments for his supremacy. Whilst disputing not the premiss of the argument, but its conclusion, the author says that the identity of celestial and terrestrial government would presuppose an identity of the conditions, qualities and properties of the beings to be governed. The celestial body consists of angels, the terrestrial is composed of man. And there are no features common to angels and men except their spiritual natures. For angels, unlike men, are 'incorporales'; measurements of time are inapplicable to angelic beings, because they live in eternity; nor are they in need of temporal necessities. But angels and men have in common the spirituality of their natures—'conveniunt quantum ad spiritum'.[4] Therefore, the adaptation of

[1] McIlwain, reviewing James's views, p. 262.

[2] That was the general opinion amongst the author's contemporaries. See, e.g., Richardus Malumbra: 'Sacerdotium est majus imperio, patet, quia sacerdotium immediate est a Christo, imperium a populo. Item alio respectu est major, scil. quia praeest divinis rebus, quae perfectissimae sunt; item praeest animae, quae est immortalis, imperator corpori, quod est mortale et corruptibile', quoted after Salycetus, *Commentaria in Codicem*, Venice, 1574, C. i, *Rubrica*, fo. 3r.

[3] Mostly referring to Hostiensis, the papal supporters were never weary of pointing out that two heads governing the world would be a unique monstrosity. This was put forward as late as the middle of the century. See, e.g., Albericus de Rosciate, *Commentaria in Codicem*, Lyons, 1517, C. vii. 37, 3, no. 21, fo. 109r: 'Unde papa non puri hominis, sed veri Dei vicem gerit in terris . . . absurdum itaque videtur dicere, quod Christus alium in terris vicarium dimiserit nisi Petrum, quia cum omnes sumus unum corpus in Christo, monstruosum foret, quod unum corpus duo capita haberet'.

[4] 'Conveniunt autem homines cum angelis, non ratione corporis, quia angeli sunt incorporales (Damascenus), nec ratione temporis, quia angeli non mesurantur tempore, sed aevo (Augustinus, De civ. Dei, 12), nec ratione alicuius rei temporalis, quia talibus non indigent nec utuntur . . . sed bene conveniunt. . . .'

the terrestrial government to the celestial pattern can apply to spiritual matters only, and thus the terrestrial government must needs be characterized by dualism.

After the refutation of the arguments commonly advanced by the pope's advocates for his supremacy, the author marshals those arguments which positively disprove the alleged papal supremacy in temporal matters. Not all of these arguments can be classified as new. Some of them can be found in the *Quaestio in Utramque Partem* by an unknown author,[1] in the *Disputatio inter Clericum et Militem*,[2] and also in the juristic writers of the late thirteenth century, especially Odofredus, Andreas de Isernia [3] and Petrus de Bellapertica, who, as a rule, merely maintained the temporal superiority of the emperor without attempting to justify their statements. But it is not so much the originality of certain arguments which provokes interest as the methodical, concise, and constructive manner of their presentation.

There are, above all, those arguments postulating that the true criterion of temporal overlordship is the power to decide feudal litigation and litigation concerning inheritance and possessions. A glance at the actual conditions shows that those litigations are not decided by the Church, and the author is not slow to remind his opponents of the injunctions issued by Alexander III and Innocent III to the clergy forbidding them to interfere in these litigations, because they are matters to be decided by kings.[4] Nor does he fail to point to St. Paul's words that nobody fighting for God shall meddle in temporal matters ; nobody fights for God more than the pope and, consequently, St. Paul's words should be particularly heeded by the vicar of Christ. Furthermore, if it were true that the pope were supreme in the temporal matters of Christendom, the bishop then would have jurisdictional powers in his diocese as regards temporal matters—which is palpably wrong. The supremacy of the pope in temporal matters would mean that he is the highest judge and that a final appeal in temporal affairs against decisions of inferior judges can always be made to him—which again fails to correspond with the reality. The restriction of the pope's dominion to spiritual matters was already deduced from several passages in the gospels by his earlier opponents, especially Odofredus and Andreas de Isernia. These writers were certain that Christ entrusted the pope with the spiritual jurisdiction only. That he is only the spiritual head of Christendom, and that he cannot be its temporal one at the same time, follows from

[1] On this treatise see Scholz, p. 224 ; Rivière, p. 274, also Carlyle, p. 420.
[2] See Rivière, p. 253, and McIlwain, p. 242.
[3] On these authors see Carlyle, pp. 355, 359. [4] See *Decret. Greg.*, iv. 17, 5 ; ii. 1, 13.

the idea of his vicariate, for Christ Himself did not claim to be the temporal overlord of the world as is clearly shown in the gospel of St. John,[1] where Christ is reported as saying that He came to save, not to condemn, the world. This statement makes it abundantly clear, according to the author of the document, that Christ did not ascribe to Himself any temporal power, since salvation is possible in spiritual matters alone. Further support is drawn from another passage in St. John's gospel,[2] where Christ bluntly rejected the idea of an earthly kingdom at whose head He should be. And did not Christ, the argument continues, when appearing before Pilate, assert that 'My kingdom is not of this world'? This reminder seems to be especially directed against James of Viterbo's main thesis that the Church is a *regnum*: by the declaration that '*regnum meum* non est de hoc mundo' James's conception seems implicitly rejected by Christ Himself. That St. Peter, too, wielded purely spiritual powers and expressly repudiated any temporal authority, is deduced from the Acts.[3] Thus neither Christ nor Peter claimed for themselves any temporal power, let alone supremacy in temporal matters. With good reasons, the pope's antagonist points out, Christ enjoined His apostles to be His 'imitatores'.[4] Nor should the vicar be so presumptuous as to claim more power than his 'dominus' wanted him to have.[5]

The strongest weapon in the armoury of the anti-papalists was the distinction drawn between Caesar and God by Christ Himself, an argument which is eagerly snatched at by the author. The idea of payment of tribute, he says, excludes the supreme temporal authority as a subject of payment; on the contrary, he can only be the object of payment.[6] Not only was this made clear by Christ's famous saying 'render unto Caesar . . .', but also by the incident recorded in another passage.[7] Lastly, the author resorts to giving advice. In his opinion, the exercise of temporal power is incompatible with Christian dignity which, by meddling in temporal matters, is bound to suffer serious loss.[8]

The third part of the document[9] opens with the significant remark that in this question 'multi multa et diversi diversa senserunt'. Two schools of canonistic thought are singled out

[1] John iii. 17.
[2] vi. 15.
[3] Acts, iii. 6.
[4] 1 Cor. xi. 1.
[5] Matt. x. 24. This argument recurs in the main part of the thesis, see *infra*, p. 199.
[6] 'Solvere tributum numquam pertinet ad superiorem dominum temporalem, ergo magis tributum sibi debet solvi.'
[7] Matt. xvii. 24–7.
[8] With a reference to St. Bede who is reported by the author as saying that 'non est Christianae dignitatis in temporalibus exaltari, sed potius deprimi' (Bulaeus, p. 938).
[9] Headed 'Determinatio Quaestionis' in Bulaeus, p. 938, but as 'Decisio' in *Acta*, fo. 69r, and Dupuy, p. 669.

by the author as an object of stern rebuke. The one, the extreme point of view, represented by Hostiensis, is accused of employing ideas which do not at all bear upon the problem, such as that of the virgin birth of Christ, and which are also 'multum frivolae'. Whilst Hostiensis maintained the complete dependence of king and emperor on the pope's mercy, so that the ruler became a mere instrument in the hands of the pope, other canonists, such as Alanus and Tancredus, belonging to the more moderate school of thought, held that the Church, although possessing both swords, handed the temporal one over to the ruler so that he might wield temporal power at his own discretion. The author, once again stressing the historical fact that the French king had never received any sword from the pope, because he succeeds to the throne by hereditary right and not by election, declares that the pope has temporal power neither in the sense of a direct control over princes (*potestative*) [1] nor in the sense of an indirect control as the result of the handing over of the temporal sword (*executive*).[2] The pope has no political (temporal) authority whatsoever. This dictum of the author is based upon the following considerations.

He sets out from the axiom that man is an epitome of the universe, that in other words, man represents the universe in miniature. Rightly, therefore, have the Greeks called man a microcosm. Now the universe is composed of two distinct substances, or elements, namely, a spiritual one which is the so-called angelic substance, because it appertains to the angels, and a corporeal one, which is the terrestrial substance. These two elements constituting the universe are also the constituent elements of man or, in other words, the dualistic conception of the universe is also applicable to man. And man is an image of God, precisely because of his endowment with spiritual properties which, constituting his angelic nature, he has in common with the angels. For no other earthly creature possesses these properties which are will, intelligence, and memory. Thus man is God's image. Man's physical substance is his body, whilst his spiritual substance is his mind. In particular, two organs represent the two substances in an easily recognizable manner: the heart and the head. Both these organs are quite distinct in their functions, tasks and operations, but their harmonious

[1] On this idea of Hostiensis and Egidius, see McIlwain, p. 254.

[2] This moderate view influenced the legists to a considerable degree. Albericus de Rosciate, after a long discussion of some 6 folio columns, came to the conclusion: 'Satis igitur liquet ex praedictis unicum esse Christi vicarium et eum debere confirmare et ordinare imperatorem et dare ipsi imperatori gladii potestatem et eius exercitium' (*loc. cit.*). The same view was entertained by earlier jurists, such as Jacobus Butrigarius (*ob.* 1335) who said, according to the report of Salycetus, *loc. cit.*, fo. 3^r: 'Omnis jurisdictio originaliter est in papa, solum autem exercitium temporalis jurisdictionis est in imperatore'.

co-operation and interplay is an indispensable prerequisite for man's well-being: should either fail to work, disease or death is the inescapable consequence. With one bold stroke our author projects this dualistic view of man on to human society. The function of the heart is symbolized by the secular authority, in modern terminology, by the body politic, whilst the function of the head is represented by the ecclesiastical authority, that is, by the body mystical. Just as with man, the respective functions, tasks and operations of the two powers are completely different from each other 'in mundano regimine'. The proper equivalent for function, in this respect, is 'jurisdictio'.

Now at this stage of the argument there follows a very significant consideration. After declaring that man needs the co-operation and interplay of heart (body) and head (mind), the author does not declare that the same co-operation is necessary for the integration of human society. If either 'jurisdictio' ceased to work, the inescapable consequence would be the destruction of the Church throughout the world, but, on the other hand, the cessation of ecclesiastical jurisdiction alone would not entail the destruction of the State. In other words, the State is recognized as the foundation of the Church's existence: the Church is dependent on the State, but the State is independent of the Church. It is worth while quoting this interesting passage: 'Sicut in humano corpore carentia capitis vel cordis esset causa dissolutionis et mortis, sic cessatio alterutrius istarum jurisdictionum esset causa destructionis ecclesiae per universum mundum'. A further correspondence is not envisaged by the author. This is a political standpoint which has more in common with French political thought of later centuries than with the views current at the beginning of the fourteenth century.[1] This statement allows of the conclusion that the author already vaguely envisages a moral self-sufficiency on the part of the State, that is to say, that the State itself produces its own spiritual law.

After these introductory statements the author tries to justify his choice of symbols. The head as the seat of the mind directs all bodily movements, through the faculties of perception, discernment, and judgement; and the channels through which the mind works as a directing force, are the nerves radiating from the head as the nerve centre. The head guides man in his choice between morally good and bad actions, which choice is transmitted to the various parts of the body by the nerves. The function of the pope is therefore quite analogous to that of the head. Being the recognized spiritual father of all Christians, he should possess that degree of discernment, wisdom, and judgement

[1] The significance of this passage escaped both Scholz and Rivière.

which is necessary to guide man to works of salvation.[1] In particular, the pope should be distinguished by great learning which proves beneficial (' gratiosa eruditio '), as well as by the soundness of his conceptions (' sana doctrina '). His own life and work should constitute an example, worthy of imitation. The virtuous discharge of his functions should impel Christians to desire to perform good works also.[2] The nerves radiating from this head are represented by the inferior ecclesiastical offices, degrees, and ranks. They convey the intentions of the pope to Christians, and it is through their integrating and co-ordinating activities that the unity of the faith is ensured and that, consequently, Christ's followers are moulded into one consistent whole, that is, into one body.[3] As the visible head of this mystical body stands the pope.

The choice of the heart as the symbol for the secular ruler is justified by the close resemblance of their respective functions and properties. St. Isidore of Seville declared, the author reminds his opponents, that the heart is ' totius corporis fundamentum ' which is also, according to Aristotle, the fountainhead of the arteries which carry life-giving blood to the various parts of the body. Moreover, and this point is very important to the Frenchman, Aristotle taught [4] that the heart is created before the head. And just as the heart is the foundation of human life, so also is the ruler the ' fundamentum rei publicae ', on account both of the stability of his reign and the firmness of his justice. Without him no commonwealth can become stable or durable, just as no building can exist without a base. The author claims to find support for his views in the somewhat hasty philological statement of St. Isidore that the Greek *βασιλεύς* is derived from *βάσις*, ' quod tamquam bases populum sustinebant '. Furthermore—the following statement can cause little surprise in view of the foregoing considerations—secular rulers are the pillars (' fundatores ') of the Church, or, in other words, the existence of the Church depends on the State. Now just as the human heart is the source of the blood, so is the ruler the source of that substance which infuses life into the commonwealth, that is, his laws. Without this ' substantia temporalis ',

[1] ' In papa, qui omnibus praeesse noscitur spiritualiter, vigere debet discretio et sapientia, qua Christi fideles, qui sunt membra ecclesiae, dirigantur ad opera salutis.' The author refers to St. Gregory's *Registrum*.

[2] ' Spectat etiam ad ipsum dare fidelibus motum bonae operationis per virtuosam operationem et bonam vitam, seipsum praebendo bonum exemplum fidelibus ' (Bulaeus, p. 940).

[3] ' Nervi autem ab isto capite derivati sunt diversi gradus et ordines ecclesiastici, quibus secundum eorum diversa et distincta officia membra ecclesiae suo vero corpori, scilicet Christo, et sibi invicem quasi quibusdam connexivis compagibus colligantur, unde in unitate fidei faciant unum corpus ' (Bulaeus, p. 940).

[4] The author's erroneous reference to *De Animalibus* is accepted by Scholz. The correct reference should be : *De Partibus Animalium*, lib. iii, cap. 4.

that is the substance vivifying the body politic, there can no more be political life than there can be human life without blood. And the purpose manifested in this 'substantia temporalis' is the rendering of justice and the liberation of the oppressed. The author concludes with these words: 'Patet ergo ex praedictis, quod sicut in humano corpore sunt duae principales, officia distincta et diversa habentes, scilicet caput et cor, ita quod una de officio alterius se non intromittit: sic in orbe duae sunt jurisdictiones distinctae, scilicet spiritualis et temporalis, habentes officia distincta'. That is the core of the doctrine set out in the document, which contains the germ for Gallicanism as well as for the later distinction between the moral and the political. For it appears plain that what the author struggles to express is the idea of the spiritual without coercive power behind it, working, so to speak, in a persuasive manner, whilst on the other hand the temporal, for which we may legitimately substitute political, enjoys the power of the State for its enforcement. This idea, not yet recognizable in its far-reaching consequences, depriving the pope, as it does, of any power worthy of the name, is but the natural reaction of a secular writer towards the pretentious aspirations of papal extremists, so ably and brilliantly represented by Egidius Romanus and James of Viterbo. Their claim to papal absolutism in the temporal sphere was bound to excite the growing national sentiment in France to energetic protest which went farther than it may have been intended. For the author, though professing that a dualism of government is indispensable to the community, throws this dualistic conception overboard, when it comes to the actual application of his theory. If we interpret the author correctly, co-operation and interplay between Church and State do no longer appear essential to the integration of human society. On the contrary, in his system, Church and State become two entities, which do not merely not interfere with each other, but are wholly self-sufficing and self-dependent. The independence of the State, as conceived by the author of the document, has not merely negative character, but definitely assumes positive aspects. Little wonder then that this thesis developed later into a conception of the State which tolerates the Church and is, as it were, self-supporting, even in 'spiritual' matters which become a concern of the State itself. This increase and expansion of the State's power was all the easier as it was the State alone which was capable of enforcing its commands.

The idea of strict separation of the two authorities, the author assures us, is fully borne out by an unprejudiced interpretation of the Old and New Testaments. In the Old Testament the two institutions of Church and State are conceived as two separate entities, and these by explicit divine ordinance. The author's constructive argumentation is at once proof of his dialectical versatility and a testimony of his abilities as an interpreter of biblical texts. In his opinion, God decreed that the Jewish people should be guided by political as well as by spiritual leaders. The first to assume political leadership over the Jews was Moses, for he became by God's declaration 'dux populi'. To him alone and to no one else God said: 'Now go and *lead the people* into the place . . .'.[1] On the other hand, the first to be entrusted with spiritual leadership was Aaron: he became the first priest and 'pontifex maximus', because God ordered Moses to take Aaron with him that 'he may minister in the *priest's office*'.[2] By divine will, the two authorities were clearly kept apart. The author is bound to admit that it is true that a few passages may be found in which Moses is also spoken of as a priest, but this designation merely means that he combined the temporal with the spiritual power.[3] This designation must not lead to the assumption that Moses was ever a priest. Priesthood, in the strict meaning of the term, was the sole prerogative of Aaron, just as political leadership was the sole prerogative of Moses. For it was Aaron who constantly offered the sacrifice to God, and not Moses. The description of Moses' office as dukedom, on etymological grounds, clearly implies the political character of his functions. His office was then transferred to Joshua, then to the judges, and, lastly, to the kings, about whom not the slightest doubt can exist that they were purely political leaders of the Jews. Moreover, as we can read in Numbers, God commissioned Moses with the adjudication of possessions and of inheritances amongst the sons of Israel.[4] Any remaining possible doubt about the God-willed temporal character of Moses' function would be dispelled by the authoritative opinion of St. Augustine who declared in unequivocal terms that the apportionment and protection of private property is the exclusive concern of human law, which is the law of the emperors, and it is God Himself who, through the medium of earthly kings and emperors,[5] dispenses His law to mankind. Without human law there can be no property: 'Per jura regum possidentur possessiones', said St. Augustine.[6] On the strength of this positivist idea expressed by St. Augustine, the author finds one of his principal arguments proved, the argument namely that secular law and

[1] Exod. xxxii. 34.

[2] *Ibid.* xxviii. 1.

[3] Bulaeus, p. 942.

[4] Num. xxxv. 1–8.

[5] This dictum of St. Augustine is laid down in the *Decretum*, dist. viii, can. 1: 'Jura autem humana, jura imperatoris sunt, quare? Quia ipsa humana jura per imperatores et reges saeculi Deus distribuit humano generi'.

[6] St. Augustine very significantly added: 'Tolle jura imperatorum, et quis audet dicere: mea est illa villa . . . ?'

jurisdiction are the bases upon which private property rests.[1] It is through this kind of judicious argumentation that the author destroys the basic tenet of Egidius' extreme theory of the pope's *dominium universale* over all earthly things and persons. According to Egidius, it will be recalled, everything on earth is in the property of the pope who therefore becomes the temporal lord over kings also.[2] Diametrically opposed to this view is the author's thesis. According to him, there is no property, unless a temporal ruler safeguards it through his law. And the author seems to enjoy the corroboration which he receives from the authority of St. Augustine.[3] We shall presently see that this fundamental idea of property is as indispensable to the author of the *Rex Pacificus* for his justification of the inferiority of the pope in temporal matters, as it is indispensable to Egidius for his justification of the pope's temporal superiority.

Nowhere can any passage be discovered, the author continues, in which Aaron interfered in matters solely entrusted to Moses. More than that: Aaron himself spoke of Moses as 'my lord'.[4] The symbol for government and jurisdiction in the Old Testament is the rod. Consequently, there are two rods. The one symbolizing temporal government and jurisdiction—the 'virga ferrea'—was in the hands of Moses [5] who returned to Egypt with it and used it to bring the plague into the country. The other rod representing the spiritual or priestly government and jurisdiction, was preserved in the tabernacle [6] and in the ark of the covenant.[7] The iron rod of Moses is therefore the 'inflexibilis justitia', whilst Aaron's rod stands for the 'potestas sacerdotalis'. The interpretative skill of the author shows itself in his explanation of the passage in Jeremiah,[8] where the prophet, in his vision, sees one rod only: this passage can have only one meaning, namely, that the priest Jeremiah neither sees the temporal rod nor wants to aspire after it. Therefore, every priest should be mindful only of the spiritual government of his flock.[9]

Thus the strict separation of the two powers is a fundamental tenet of the Old Testament, where neither meddles in the affairs of the other. It is true that Aaron sometimes wielded Moses' rod, but then the priest Aaron exercised temporal power in these

[1] 'Ex quibus patet, quod divisio haereditatum et possessionum pertinet ad jurisdictionem temporalem, cuiusmodi est jurisdictio imperatorum et regum' (Bulaeus, p. 942).

[2] See Carlyle, p. 407, and especially McIlwain, pp. 250–4.

[3] This aspect, too, escaped the attention of Scholz and Rivière.

[4] Exod. xxxii. 22: 'Ne indignetur dominus meus . . .'.

[5] *Ibid.* iv. 4.

[6] Num. xvii. 10.

[7] Heb. ix. 4

[8] Jer. i. 10.

[9] 'Respondit (*scil.* Jeremiah) per hoc tam discrete quam sancte significans, quod quicumque sacerdos domini, hoc est sacris praesidens in domo domini, non ad duas virgas, i.e. duas jurisdictiones ubique habendas, sed ad virgam vigilantem, i.e. ad jurisdictionem spiritualem debet respicere.'

specified instances only by the special permission and authorization of Moses: 'Semper tamen de expressa auctoritate Moysi'. Consequently, whenever the pope should exercise temporal jurisdiction, he would do it only within the ambit of the prince's authorization: 'Non nisi quantum sibi datum vel permissum est ab illis, qui habent in hoc mundo temporalium potestatem, videlicet ab imperatoribus, regibus et aliis principibus'.[1] That the pope is inferior to the secular ruler, as far as temporal government goes, is explicitly stated by a divine of highest rank, St. Isidore. His dictum as recorded in the *Decretum* is that the princes are commissioned with the protection of the Church and that they have to render an account for their policy towards her. The protection of His Church was handed over to the princes by God Himself, declared St. Isidore.[2] According to the document, this is a plain statement of the fact that in the temporal sphere the Church is in the hands of, and subjected to, the secular ruler: 'Ex quibus (*scil. verbis* Isidoris) habetur, quod ecclesia quantum ad temporalia potestati regum et principum est tradita et subjecta'.

The further history of the Jews entirely bears out the view of strict separation of Church and State. The kings had the temporal government, whilst priests and prophets possessed the spiritual leadership. Nowhere is a passage discoverable in which a priest or a prophet gives orders to a king. What, at first sight, may seem to be a priest's command to a king, was nothing else but the public pronouncement of God's commands, but, on the other hand, it was the kings as 'veri domini' who gave orders to priests: 'Licet bene legantur anuntiasse regibus praecepta Domini . . . sed reges sicut veri domini praecipiebant sacerdotibus et prophetis'.[3] Three of the best kings the Jews ever had, David, Hezekiah, and Josiah, are reported to have given orders to priests, as is amply testified by the respective passages.[4] The kings regarded themselves as true masters, and priests never acted in any way which might have tended to restrict the king's freedom of action; on the contrary, the kings were directly under the authority of God. The argumentation from the Old Testament is concluded with these words: 'Ecce isti tres reges et super omnes, qui unquam rexerunt populum Domini meliores imperando, praecipiendo et mittendo se ostenderunt, sicut et vere erant, post Deum esse dominos principales, super quos nec prophetae nec sacerdotes unquam alias attentaverunt aliquid, quod esset eis in diminutionem sui dominii temporalis'.[5]

[1] Cf., for instance, the opposite view of Oldradus, *supra*, p. 186 (note).

[2] 'Cognoscant principes saeculares Deo se debere rationem reddituros esse propter ecclesiam, quam a Christo tuendam suscipiunt' (Bulaeus, p. 943).

[3] Reference is made to 1 Sam. xiii. 13 and xv. 16–17.

[4] 1 Kings i. 33; 2 Kings xix. 1–2; xxii. 13. [5] Bulaeus, p. 943.

The author maintains that the idea of separation of Church and State and the former's subordination, in temporal matters, to the latter, is also a basic idea of the New Testament, because it is expressed in numerous utterances of Christ Himself. When asked to divide an inheritance, Christ flatly refused this request with the remark that He had not been made a judge or a divider.[1] Thus Christ declined to interfere with apportionments and divisions of property, which is the sole prerogative of the civil power. That, the author continues, is not only his view, but also that of high theological authorities, such as St. Ambrose who, in his commentaries upon this passage of the gospel, declared that Christ descended from heaven ' propter divina ' and did not express the wish to become entangled in the ' terrena '. Christ judges man's intrinsic moral worth and his merits in the purely ethical sense, but intentionally abstains from passing judgement on petty quarrels and from distributing possessions and inheritances. That there was intention behind Christ's refusal, follows from the counsel He gave to the apostles immediately after the incident recorded. He warned them against the greedy desire for temporal possessions, because this ambition—the author infers this from the text—gives birth to the further ambition to be a judge amongst parties contesting property rights.[2] As if prompted by the wish to be quite certain of defeating Egidius' fundamental thesis of the pope's universal dominion, the author enlists the support of no less a theological authority than St. Bernard for his bold interpretation of the gospel. St. Bernard wrote, the author reminds his opponents by referring to the *De Consideratione ad Eugenium Papam*, that never had any of the apostles sat as a judge apportioning land and delineating its bounds.[3] What is worthier, asked St. Bernard, Christ's power to absolve from sin or the power to divide spoils ? The following question was put to Pope Eugenius by St. Bernard : ' Quidnam tibi major videtur, et dignitas et potestas dimittendi peccata, an praedia dividendi ? ' And the saint himself answered and avowed that ' this frail and earthly matter ' is purely a concern of the secular authority : interference amounts to an ' invasion of foreign territory ' (' fines alienos invadere '). The possible objection that St. Bernard did not deny the right of the Church to deal with these frail matters, but merely suggested that this temporal jurisdiction is unworthy of the Church, is repudiated by the author with a reference to the saint's justification of his statement on ' the invasion of foreign territory ' ; he said that dealing with temporal matters is an encroachment ' non quia nos indigni, sed quia indignum vobis talibus insistere *quippe potioribus occupatis* '.[4] There is only

[1] Luke xii. 14. [2] *Ibid.* xii. 15. [3] See *Patrologia Latina*, clxxxii. 736.

[4] On the influence of St. Bernard upon papal opponents, see Rivière, appendix iii, p. 405.

one conclusion admissible, the author says, namely, that temporal jurisdiction on the part of the Church is an ' impertinentia ', because she is not competent to deal with temporal affairs.

' My kingdom is not of this world ' furnishes the author with yet another argument intended to support his thesis, and at the same time to destroy the very basis of James of Viterbo's theory. St. Chrysostom rightly interpreted this significant utterance as an authoritative refusal of Christ to possess any temporal dominion : He has dominion, it is true, but this dominion has no human character (' habet principatum, qui non est humanus '). Since Christ Himself had no ' temporale et humanum regnum ', He could not transfer any such to successors, according to the old legal maxim that nobody can transfer more rights than he himself possesses. But quite apart from this purely legalistic consideration, Christ exhorted the apostles and successors that they as His disciples should not be above their master,[1] since apostleship is distinguished by strict adherence to the master's words and intentions. And this applies to everyone—' quicumque Christi servus, quicumque discipulus, quicumque apostolicus '.

One more idea based upon the interpretation of the gospel is advanced as an argument for the author's thesis. The sublime character of the pope's position and function is utterly incompatible with a temporal government and jurisdiction. All theologians agree that the rank and status of an ecclesiastical dignitary, such as that of a bishop, is one of perfection. The pope is the highest dignitary, and therefore ' maximae perfectionis '. But possession and use of temporal powers injures the dignity of an ecclesiastical leader and that is the very reason why Christ counselled those aspiring to perfection to rid themselves of all temporal possessions and to give them to the poor.[2] Accordingly, the pope should give up all ambitions as to temporal dominion : he should ' suum affectum retrahere a temporalibus '. From this discussion of ownership the author proceeds to consider the legal relations existing between the bishop and ecclesiastical possessions. It is undeniable, he says, obviously alluding to Egidius' thesis of the pope's universal property, that bishops are not the owners of ecclesiastical goods and estates, but only administrators (' dispensatores tantum '). How then, he asks, can any bishop, including the pope, claim dominion over non-ecclesiastical goods, such as the kingdoms and the lands held by secular princes ? As regards ecclesiastical goods they have at least the right of administration, but as regards non-ecclesiastical goods they have no right whatsoever.[3] The weapon ingeniously forged by Egidius for the attack on the prince's temporal superiority

[1] Matt. x. 24. [2] Matt. xix. 21.

[3] ' Quomodo ergo praelatus aliquis quaerit dominium super res non ecclesiasticas videlicet super regna et terras regum et principum ? Plus enim super res ecclesiasticas habent quam super saeculares ' (Bulaeus, p. 944).

becomes, in the hands of his opponent, a powerful weapon for the defence of the prince's position. The adroit design of Egidius appears to be deprived of its own basis : instead of being a universal monarch with a dominion over all things and persons, the pope is reduced from his exalted position to the rank of the spiritual head of the Church which is held to be dependent on the State for its existence. One of the most brilliantly executed systems upholding the temporal overlordship of the pope was shaken in its foundations by the employment of the very concept upon which the system was erected.

But one more argument may be adduced in favour of the pope's temporal jurisdiction, the author says. True that the pope's vicariate excludes any temporal government, because, as an unbiased study of the Bible shows, his vicariate makes him ' pater spiritualis '. But it may be asserted that he has temporal jurisdiction on the ground of the donation of Constantine to Pope Silvester. Whatever one may think of this, the author says, not doubting the authenticity or legal validity of the donation,[1] it is at any rate certain that the Eastern Empire was not included in it. For that reason alone the pope cannot be held to be the temporal overlord of all Christians. Now as regards France itself, popes in earlier days never considered themselves as temporal overlords in their dealings with French affairs. It will be recalled, he continues, that Pope Stephen anointed Pepin as king of France in the Church of St. Denis, without behaving like a ' dominus temporalis '. On the contrary, Stephen blessed the king and all hereditary successors to the throne, and laid down the ruling that every foreigner was forbidden, under pain of apostolic excommunication, to encroach upon the rights of the kingdom ' sicut apparet historias illius temporis diligentius intuenti '. But history proves even more. The French, though not recognizing any superior in temporal matters, be he pope or emperor, were always staunch defenders of the Church, as is amply demonstrated by the efforts which the present king's predecessors made for the preservation and also for the propagation of the true faith. To mention but one obvious instance, Louis's canonization by the Church and Christ's approbation of that king's sanctity by means of many and conspicuous miracles, are sufficient evidence for the esteem in which that king was held

[1] John of Paris denied the legal validity of the donation ; before him, however, Accursius and Azo in the thirteenth century held the same view. The attitude of Bartolus in this question was very interesting. Great jurist as he was, he could not but arrive at the conclusion that the donation was invalid. But for reasons which had nothing to do with law, he suggested to his hearers in his lecture on the *Digestum vetus* that they should consider the donation as valid : ' Videte, nos sumus in terris amicis ecclesiae, et ideo dico, quod, ista donatio valeat . . . sequitur, quod papa non habet jurisdictionem aliquam '—and the following sentence is most revealing—' sed volens favere ecclesiae, dico, quod illa donatio valuit ' (*Commentaria in Digestum vetus*, Lyons, 1523, *Rubrica*, fo. 4r).

by the 'author fidei, Jesus Christus '.[1] But this appreciation and the practical efforts made by all French kings for the cause of the Church only prompts the author to put forward the justification of the king's claim to the right of taxing the clergy. Their financial contributions to the king were the price they had to pay for their protection. The document concludes with these words: 'Ex praemissis ergo omnibus colligitur evidenter, quod papa non est super omnes Christianos superior dominus in temporalibus '.

Whether the collegiate effort of the university of Paris or the tract of an unknown political writer, the *Rex Pacificus* is a thesis which impugns the massive and formidable systems of Egidius Romanus and James of Viterbo. Rather by implication than by explicit objections, it tries to sap the foundations of the papacy's extravagant claims to universal monarchy. The document constitutes one of the first systematic attempts to free the secular power from tutelage and bondage, to deny, by methodical reasoning, the supremacy of the Church in matters not belonging to it, thereby raising the secular authority to the fountainhead of all political and social life, even that of the Church herself. No wonder that the idea of the superiority of the prince was bound to develop into the idea of the omnipotent State which found its clearest expression in the concept of sovereignty. The crispness of its style and freshness of its language, the fascination of its far-flung argumentation, the bold interpretation of texts and the utilization of authoritative commentaries to support these interpretations, and the unmistakeable youthful impetuosity in arriving at conclusions—all go to make the *Rex Pacificus* a document extremely illuminative of early French political thought as well as of the newly roused French nationalism. Though later degenerating into a deplorably aggressive form, in those days the sentiment of nationalism proved a healthy stimulus to vigorous political thought. The *Rex Pacificus* paved the way for John of Paris and Marsiglio, and may well be classified as an early methodical orientation toward the conception of the modern all-powerful State, self-sufficing and self-dependent, even in 'spiritual' matters, that is, moral matters. Little imagination is needed to perceive that, in modern times, the relations of Church and State are reversed. Whilst in medieval days the State was on its guard against the 'temporal' aspirations of the Church, it is now the Church which is on the defensive against the policy of encroachment and expansion on the part of the State.

[1] This reference no doubt is a subtle reminder to the pope who, in his bull *Ineffabilis*, of 25 September, 1296, had himself used this canonization as an illustration of Philip's unkindness and ingratitude towards himself at a time 'when we are concerned with the canonization of your grandfather Louis'. This bull is printed in Raynaldus, *Annales Ecclesiastici*, ad annum 1296, sect. 25 ff.

IX

PERSONALITY AND TERRITORIALITY IN THE «DEFENSOR PACIS»: THE PROBLEM OF POLITICAL HUMANISM

The occasion provides a good opportunity for some observations in the form of a few marginal glosses and questions on Marsilius' *Defensor Pacis.* A presupposition for the understanding of his thought is the rebirth of the individual in his political function as a citizen, in which he is the autonomous bearer of rights and duties and as such entitled to take part in government and in the creation of the law. The individual is no longer a sub/ject, a *sub/ditus*, an *Unter/tan.* Here is the humanist standpoint correctly understood, embedded as it was in a historical setting. The advance of Marsilian thought can adequately be explained only on this basis. To him the State is the citizen writ large, that is, the *universitas civium.* To the individual citizen as a political entity corresponds the State as the collective unit.

Marsilius' thesis is perhaps the most mature manifestation of *humanitas* within what can now properly be called a political frame. Quite in conformity with antecedent doctrine the primary function of the *universitas civium* is legislation. The Marsilian terminology of the *legislator humanus* is indicative: it personifies the State. This *universitas* is certainly a sovereign corporation consisting exclusively of citizens (and not of subjects), but it still is essentially an association or a community of persons – it is a *Personenverband* – and the very terminology of *universitas* leaves no room for doubt on this score. It demonstrates beyond question how firmly rooted Marsilius' thought-pattern was in ancient as well as in old-Germanic ideas of corporate bodies.[1] The personalized conception of the State is re-

1. Th. Mayer, *Die Ausbildung der Grundlagen des modernen Staates im hohen Mittelalter,* in *Herrschaft und Staat im Mittelalter*, ed. H. Kämpf, Wissenschaftliche Buchgesellschaft,

flected in the personalized designation of the *legislator humanus.* As the law-creative organ "he" is compellingly reminiscent of the former monocratic *gubernator* whose prime function indeed was identical with that allocated by Marsilius to his *legislator humanus.* For Marsilius however the law is enforceable – a *praeceptum coactivum* – precisely because it was of human provenance to deal whith mundane matters and was not of divine origin and did not deal with divine matters: its material ingredient was consent.

The *universitas civium* is a collective unit, though we are told virtually nothing about its location, its earthy or terrestrial connexion, its link with anything concrete, let alone with anything approaching a territory. Considered from the purely conceptual standpoint, the *universitas civium* is functionally the *legislator humanus* and is identical with the former *rex* or *princeps* who ruled over a mere *gens*, for instance, the *rex Francorum*, the *rex Anglorum* or the *rex Burgundionum*, and so on. These intitulations clearly express personal sovereignty. But with Marsilius the personal sovereignty has undergone a transformation in regard to the bearer of sovereignty which is now the totality of the citizens – hence the operation of the ascending theme of government and law. No longer does the single *gubernator* act within the framework of the descending theme of government. In both instances sovereignty relates essentially and substantially to persons.[2]

Darmstadt 1960, 284 ff., especially 289ff., was the first modern authority to have realized the fundamental difference between the old-Germanic units and the medieval and early modern concept of the State as a unit comprising a definite territory (« institutioneller Flächenstaat », 294). But he did not take into account scholarship, such as Marsilius. For the latter and his *legislator humanus*, see A. Gewirth, *Marsilius of Padua: The Defender of Peace*, I, Columbia Univ. Press, New York 1951, 167ff.; W. Ullmann, *Principles of Government and Politics in the Middle Ages*, Methuen, London 1978[4], 271; 273ff.; J. Quillet, *La philosophie politique de Marsile de Padoue*, Vrin, Paris 1970, 83ff. For the juristic background of the corporation and its influence on some of the problems touched in this communication, see the excellent study by J. P. Canning, *The corporation in the political thought of the Italian jurists of the 13th and 14th centuries*, « History of Political Thought », 1 (1980), 9-32. For the preceding period see the analyses by P. Michaud-Quantin, *Universitas: expressions du mouvement communautaire dans le moyen-âge latin*, Vrin, Paris 1970.

2. For some details on this point see W. Ullmann, *Zur Entwicklung des Souveränitätsbegriffs im Spätmittelalter*, Variorum Reprints, London 1978 (Collected Studies 3), Ch. 9 at 10ff.; 21ff.

The very concept of the law as a *praeceptum coactivum* prompts a few questions. To begin with, what is the spatial extent of the enforceability of the law? Is enforceability in fact restricted in space? There is no indication in the tract itself. On the contrary, there is some considerable vagueness surrounding the extent and scope of enforceability, and this vagueness is heightened by the indeterminate nomenclature which Marsilius employs, for instance, *civitas* or *regnum* or *provincia*. The difference between a *regnum* and a *civitas* lies for him in quantity.[3] There are a number of passages in which *regnum, civitas* and *provincia* are interchangeable.[4] The concept of *universitas* itself was a technical and juristic term which had a very pronunced legal complexion and sharp contours, and that Marsilius used this well-defined and profiled notion in so vague a manner is significant enough to be pointed out. Indeed, in his *De translatione imperii* he refers to the *universitas inhabitantium regionem civium et nobilium* and sends the reader back to the *Defensor Pacis*.[5] But he certainly does not advocate universal applicability of the law, and hence no universal enforceability. What one is left with is the surmise which many interpreters of Marsilius have stated, and that is, that he had the Italian city states in mind.[6] That may

3. Cf., e.g., *DP* (Scholz), I, II, 1-2; I, III, 2-5. See especially I, XII, 3, 63-65, which is particularly enlightening. Here he says that the *universitas civium* or its *valencior pars* is the legislative organ « in communitate illa super quam lex fertur, sive id fecerit universitas predicta civium aut eius valencior pars per seipsam immediate sive id alicui vel aliquibus commiserit faciendum... ». See in this context also the observations by C. Pincin, *Marsilio*, Giappichelli, Torino 1967, 64ff.

4. Cf. *DP*, I, II, 3; I, XVII, 3; 7; 11; 13; II, XXVIII, 14; also I, XV, 2; I, XVI, 17; and so on. The point is rightly stressed by *DP* (Quillet), 37 n. 124. The same vagueness can be observed in regard to the faithful « in communitate illa, in qua debet aliquis tali iudicio iudiciari » (*DP* Scholz, II, VI, 12, 210 10-12) or « in certa provincia vel communitate » (*DP* Scholz, II, XV, 9, 335 12-13) or « universitas fidelium in loco sive provincia » (*DP* Scholz, II, XVII, 5, 359 12). There are many more examples of the same kind.

5. See Marsile de Padoue, *Oeuvres Mineures*, Texte établi, traduit et annoté par C. Jeudy et J. Quillet, Éditions du C.N.R.S., Paris 1979, 402.

6. Among the more recent expositors H. Segall, *Der Defensor Pacis des Marsilius von Padua*, F. Steiner, Wiesbaden 1959, 51-57, tries hard to prove that the North Italian communes served as models for Marsilius, but I cannot find his argumentation convincing. However, his is certainly the most thorough attempt to establish a link between Marsilius and the city-states. For Marsilius' view on the universal empire see *DP* (Quillet), 31ff. and *Oeuvres Mineures*, 345ff., especially 363ff.; edition and translation of the tract itself: 369-433.

or may not be correct, but the one thing that is certain is that this very long tract contains no explicit declaration to what physical extent and how far the law consented to by the citizens, is binding, valid and enforceable. What is the actual territorial reach, that is, the spatial scope of the law?

This is a question which should long ago have been asked and considered. Can the judiciary demand enforcement of the law in communities other than its own? Does the law also bind those in a given place who have not consented to it, because they were only temporarily dwelling there? Does, in other words, the sovereign body of citizens float along without any terrestrial foothold? Were the citizens bound by their own law arrived at by the majority principle, in whatever form one interprets it,[7] wherever they may be? One is at once reminded of the old *Stammesrechte*, according to which the Burgundians, Lombards, Bavarians, etc. lived according to their own personal law. To go still one step further: could the citizens be made responsible for actions, wrongs, measures wherever they might be committed or enacted? What law is enforceable against them? Is it their own law or the locality's law? These were indeed all questions which, for instance, Bartolus, the exact contemporary of Marsilius, asked.[8] Has the *legislator humanus* the right to enforce his law within another *Universitas civium*? These questions could easily be multiplied and show, I think, clearly what difficulties the Marsilian concept of personal sovereignty encounters. One is almost tempted to ask: in what respect does

7. E. Lewis, *The Positivism of Marsiglio*, «Speculum», 38 (1963), 541-582, at n. 98, remarked that «one really does not know what Marsiglio meant to imply by his statement 'with due consideration of quantity and quality of persons' ». For a penetrating analysis see A. Gewirth, *Marsilius of Padua*, 182ff.; and G. de Lagarde, *La naissance de l'esprit laïque au déclin du moyen âge*, III: *Le Defensor Pacis*, Nauwelaerts, Louvain-Paris 1970, 141ff. Segall, *Der Defensor Pacis*, 65ff., despairs of a reasonable explanation of the *valentior pars*, but concludes (67) that his *Staatstheorie* «ist fragmentarisch, wissenschaftlich unzuverlässig». See also *DP* (Quillet), 93ff.

8. See Bartolus, *Tractatus repraesaliarum*, Augustae Taurinorum 1577, fol. 122ff., at n. 11, fol. 122vb. He himself has here also a *Consilium* (n. 29) on the question of citizenship, fol. 62vb-63ra. These were indeed problems with which earlier jurists, such as Gandinus and Odofredus, long before Marsilius, had dealt, see Baldus de Ubaldis, *Commentaria in Codicem*, Venetiis 1616, ad C, 1, 1, 1 («Cunctos populos»), ns. 96-97, fol. 8vb-9ra. De Lagarde, *Le Defensor pacis*, 161ff., did not notice the kind of problems mentioned in the text, although the section is headed «Portée de la loi».

the *universitas civium* differ a from a guild, from an association of journeymen, from a *universitas scholarium*, and the numerous other *corpora* or communities which existed in abundance at his time.

If one point is indisputable, it is that sovereignty contains *per definitionem* jurisdiction. But when one examines the numerous passages in which Marsilius deals with jurisdiction, one will again miss the same spatial element which has just engaged our attention. All the passages are personality-orientated, that is jurisdiction of the clergy over the laity, and vice-versa, the extent of jurisdiction in regard to things and persons, *ratione rerum, ratione personarum*, etc. It is a subjectivized conception of jurisdiction with which one is here confronted, that is, *who* has jurisdiction over *whom* in what matter? But to be meaningful jurisdiction as a structural element of sovereignty has to be territorially orientated. Applied to the present problem this means that personal sovereignty would have to become reified, that is, *verdinglicht* or *versachlicht*, if it were to serve as an operational element in the public field. Differently expressed, the subjectivized sovereignty must be supplemented by its objectivized component part, and that means that sovereignty, or what is the same, jurisdiction must be territorially anchored, must have a territorial connexion. The absence of any mentioning of a territory or of a consideration of space in the exercise of jurisdiction or of any contemplation of a locality in Marsilius' tract, makes abundantly clear that this postulate of a reification of sovereignty did not form part of his thought-processes.

This absence of a territorially conceived sovereignty is all the more striking as precisely in Marsilius' time the very concept had formed the subject of juristic discussion, according to which territorial boundaries had become boundaries of the law, jurisdiction and hence of sovereignty. The territory had acquired juristic personality. Both governmental practice and juristic doctrine had postulated that the personal kind of sovereignty must be complemented by its territorial counterpart. Further, practice and doctrine made the residence of the citizens an integral part of justiciability: domicile provided the link between the *res* – the territory – and the *persona*, no matter whether he was a citizen or a subject. In contemporary practice and doctrine domicile had assumed an essential legal element serving as a nexus between the animate persons and the inanimate soil.[9]

In order to be effective in the public field, the sovereignty of the *universitas civium* needs a more or less well defined space, with the consequence that no other government had any legitimate jurisdiction within its territory. Thus a citizen who had his domicile in a particular territory could not be cited or summoned to a court outside the territory. This was precisely the bone of contention in the *cause célèbre* of Henry VII and Robert of Sicily. Here the concept of territorial sovereignty was plainly operational in so far as someone who had residence, that is, domicile within a particular territory «non potest trahi extra territorium». It is particularly interesting to point out that this principle was adopted and enacted by Clement V in the decree *Pastoralis Cura* (1313) which Marsilius attacked several times on grounds of unwarranted papal interference resulting from the exercise of papal plenitude of power in regard to Henry VII.[10] Clearly, Marsilius had not seen the juristically relevant issue of this decree, which in many respects merely summed up antecedent juristic theory. It would certainly be too much to claim that the concept of territorial sovereignty was born with this decree, but what can with confidence be asserted is that the pope simply applied old-Roman and ecclesiastical practice and

9. The roots go back to Roman law and ecclesiastical practice. For some details cf. Ullmann, *Zur Entwicklung*, 23. See here again the discussion of Baldus (preceding note), and the perceptive points made by Canning, *Corporation*, 22-24. Cf. also Bartolus below n. 18. In this context one should bear in mind that for large kingdoms the need to define the territorial extent of the king's jurisdiction was clearly perceived and hence recourse was to be made to a detailed enumeration of all the relevant localities under the king's jurisdiction. An example of the 14th century in R. Fawtier, *Comment le roi de France, au début du XIVe siècle, pouvait-il se représenter son royaume?* in *Mélanges offerts à M. Paul-R. Martin*, Fonds Rapin, Genève 1961, 65-77, at 71ff. Part of the explanation was the absence of adequate maps: « il n'existe pas de carte de la France » (66), hence « le roi de France était hors d'état de se représenter son royaume » (71). On this problem see also H. Quaritsch, *Staat und Souveränität*, Athenäum Verlag, Frankfurt 1970, 115.

10. Cf. *DP* (Scholz), I, XIX, 10, 133; II, XXII, 20, 438f.; II, XXIII, 12, 450; II, XXV, 17, 484f.

current juristic doctrine, just as his counsellor and author of the decree, Oldradus de Ponte, did.[11]

But this enactment is only a specific instance of contemporary practice and doctrine. Other instances are the reified intitulations of kings, so that the *Rex Francorum* was giving way to the *Rex Franciae*, or the *Rex Anglorum* to the *Rex Angliae*, and so on, not to mention the age-old *lex terrae* exactly a century earlier used in Magna Carta (art. 39),[12] all instances which go to show that the territorialized conception of law and jurisdiction was quite common at the time. In order to be effective, and this means enforceable, the law had to be spatially restricted which is the same as saying that sovereignty correctly understood must embody both the personal and territorial component parts. Here the difficulties of the allegedly universal Roman empire of medieval complexion are strikingly illustrated. These difficulties are clearly avoided in the contemporary «Golden Bull» of Charles IV: in it the territorial sovereignty of the kingdom was made a specific feature. Moreover, this law used exactly the same terminology as *Pastoralis cura* did – by which I do not imply that there was any connexion or borrowing – when it declared that no citizen, nay «nulla denique persona eiusdem regni... *extra regnum* ipsum (i. e. Bohemiae) ad quodcumque tribunal... citari potuerit sive *trahi* nec *vocari* debeat».[13] That the antecedent historical development in some European regions had prepared the ground for the territorialization of law and

11. Cf. Oldradus de Ponte's *Consilia* 43, 69, about which see Ed. Will, *Die Gutachten des Oldradus de Ponte zum Prozess Heinrichs VII. gegen Robert von Neapel*, «Abhandlungen zur mittleren und neueren Geschichte, 65», Leipzig-Berlin 1917; W. Ullmann, *The development of the medieval idea of sovereignty*, «English Historical Review», 64 (1949), 1-29, at 27ff. (here also the views of Andreas de Isernia, the famous contemporary Sicilian jurist, at 21ff.); cf. further F. A. von der Heydte, *Die Geburtsstunde des souveränen Staates*, J. Habbel, Regensburg 1952, 90, 416.

12. On this see Ullmann, *Principles of Government*, 163ff.; Id., *Individuo e Società nel medio evo*, Laterza, Bari-Roma 1974, 60ff.*

13. W.D. Fritz (ed.), *Die Goldene Bulle Kaiser Karls IV. vom Jahre 1356*, «Monumenta Germaniae Historica: Fontes iuris Germanici antiqui, 11», Weimar 1972, cap. 8, 63[4ss]. The whole chapter is a constitutional exposition of territorial sovereignty. On this see also A. Wolf, *Die Gesetzgebung der entstehenden Territorialstaaten in Europa*, in *Handbuch der Quellen und Literatur der neueren europäischen Privatrechtsgeschichte*, ed. H. Coing, I, C.H. Beck, München 1973, 517ff., at 593; 735. The document clearly distinguishes between citizens and subjects (*sub/diti; Unter/tanen*).

* See *The Individual and Society in the Middle Ages*, London 1967, 71ff.

hence reflected State sovereignty in territorial respects, can convincingly be shown by the kingdom of Sicily from the twelfth century onwards, where indeed the claims of ecclesiastical jurisdiction were quite effectively challenged by royal jurisdiction on grounds of territorial dominion.[14]

In this context some contingent questions obtrude themselves and are of some direct concern. Assuredly, the hallmark of the *Defensor Pacis* is the concept of the status of the citizen, yet there is no indication about what might well be called the process of becoming a citizen. Of course, Marsilius is very expansive, detailed and comprehensive about what persons are, and what persons are not, citizens. This is not only the strongest possible proof of the all-pervading personality viewpoint, but also a purely static conception, since, evidently, any association does and can change its membership. In any case, there is nothing in the tract on the kinds of citizenship and the diversity of fortunes which may affect it. How far in fact any earthy, that is, territorial conceptions were removed from Marsilius' thought-pattern, can perhaps most clearly be seen from the total absence of any consideration of the birth place as one of the basic elements that constitutes citizenship. Certainly, he excludes foreigners from citizenship, but here at once the question arises: Who is a foreigner? As has rightly been remarked, Marsilius' definition of the citizen is simply Aristotelian, as he himself avows at the very beginning of the relevant chapter.[15] But to the question of who is a foreigner there is no answer: he seems to adhere to the view that « once a foreigner always a foreigner ». Here again practical contingencies in his own native Italy gave rise to considerable discussions concerning the substance of citizenship. Fortunately, a great deal of work has been done in this respect by modern scholarship. It is plain that citizenship provoked a great amount of contemporary literature, both in doctrine and in the

14. For some details cf. W. Ullmann, *Roman public law and medieval monarchy: Norman rulership in Sicily*, in *Jurisprudence in the Middle Ages*, Variorum Reprints, London 1980, (Collected Studies, 4), Ch. 5, 170ff.

15. *DP*, I, xii, 4. On this see Gewirth, *Marsilius*, 175ff.

numerous *Consilia* written by Marsilius' exact contemporaries.

The rights and duties of citizenship obviously necessitated sharp definitions, and these had perforce to invoke territorial considerations. The basic distinction is that of *civilitas originaria* (that is, the citizen who had the *ius soli*, a terminology in itself very revealing, or the *ius sanguinis*)[16] and *civilitas acquisita.*[17] That problems concerned with citizenship did in fact frequently arise, was due to the special position which citizens had within the (Marsilian) *universitas civium* that was situated within a definite territory and which necessarily involved residence or domicile. Otherwise one could hardly explain the multitude of problems relating to citizenship of which the juristic literature of the time is replete. These problems concerned performance of military duties or the exemption from them, taxation of property or of mobile goods, imposts on goods traded, trading rights, marketing rights, municipal obligations, and many other items, including testamentary dispositions, inheritance and contingent duties, marriage, and so on.[18] Citizenship could be acquired *per privilegium* or *de gratia*,[19] and again the terminology is significant: *de intus, de extra* which can make sense only in a

16. Later King Alfonso IX of Castille was to refer to the *ius naturalitatis* in his « Siete partidas », thereby neatly denoting personal and territorial sovereignty. See *Las Siete Partidas del Salbio rey Don Alonso el Nono*, Madrid 1611, Liber IV tit. 24, lex 5, fol. 61ra: « ... ome de la naturaleza que ha con su senor a con la tierra en qua vive ».

17. Cf. Ullmann, *Principles*, 286; 294; 296.

18. Cf., e.g., W.M. Bowsky, *A new Consilium of Cino da Pistoia (1324): Citizenship, residence and taxation*, « Speculum », 42 (1967), 431ff.; J. Kirshner, *Paolo di Castro on cives ex privilegio*, in *Renaissance Studies Hans Baron*, Chicago Univ. Press, Chicago 1971, 227; and especially Id., *Between nature and culture: an opinion of Baldus de Perugia on Venetian citizenship as second nature*, « J. Med. Renaiss. St. », 9 (1979), 179-208, with rich material, and the same author's earlier studies on the same topic. It is perhaps advisable to point out that Marsilius' exact contemporary Bartolus (as Cynus, his teacher, before him) had attached great importance to territory in questions of jurisdiction, and he constructed his thesis in the context of his fruitful distinction between the *statuta realia* and the *statuta personalia*. Having dealt with the *litis contestatio* he went on to ask « utrum iurisdictio cohaeret territorio ... sicut ergo dominium cohaeret *personae* domini, tamen est in *re*, ita iurisdictio cohaeret officio et *personae* eius qui habet officium, tamen est in *territorio*, set sic non est qualitas territorii, sed magis personae » (Bartolus, *Commentaria in Digestum vetus*, ed. cit., *Dig.* De iurisdictione omnium iudicum, l. Ius dicentis (2, 1, 1), no. 14f., fol. 47ra. P. Vaccari, *« Utrum iurisdictio cohaeret territorio ». La dottrina di Bartolo*, in *Bartolo da Sassoferrato: Studi e documenti per il VI Centenario*, Giuffrè, Milano 1962, 735-753, barely touches on the really vital problem. Bartolus' kind of statement was exactly what Marsilius lacked.

19. A good example in J. Kirshner, *Between nature and culture*, 207f.

territorial context.[20] It is not difficult to understand that these citizen-related contingencies were to give birth to what came to be called the *superioritas territorialis* – in a word, territorial sovereignty.[21]

The topic of citizenship very ostensibly involved the reification of the concept itself, and that means in this context domicile. It was perhaps the most frequently debated question within the precincts of public law. Yet there is no hint or reflexion of all this in the Marsilian tract. A close study of the relevant sections in his work demonstrates beyond a shadow of doubt that here too he moved entirely within the confines of the personality principle by wholly ignoring the territorial origins, consequences and implications of citizenship. Yet, the concept of citizen is assuredly the crucial and basic foundation of his whole system. To his juristic contemporaries these territorial considerations were as important as the personal side.[22] But he himself was solely attracted by the personality of the plaintiff or defendant, the personal aspects of litigious issues, the kind of tribunal in the case of a criminal prosecution, and the like – all items which provided him with ample opportunity of playing havoc with allegedly spiritual and/or ecclesiastical *causae.* But nowhere does he approach litigation or criminal prosecution from the angle of a territorially anchored citizenship. How can one explain this glaring lacuna in the writings of so talented, perceptive and learned man as Marsilius was?

20. For Venice in particular see J. Kirshner, *Between nature,* 184f.

21. Cf. in this context D. Willoweit, *Rechtsgrundlagen der Territorialgewalt: Landesobrigkeit, Herrschaftsrechte und Territorien in der Rechtswissenschaft der Neuzeit,* Böhlau, Köln-Wien 1975, 124; 274f.; especially 295ff.

22. See the literature cited in n. 18, and W. Ullmann, *De Bartoli sententia: Concilium repraesentat mentem populi,* Variorum Reprints, London 1976 (Collected Studies, 2), Ch. 10. That Jacobus de Arena, Cynus, Guilielmus de Cuneo as well as Oldradus de Ponte had been engaged on this kind of problem, was made clear by Bartolus (above n. 18) and his pupil Baldus, *Commentaria in Digestum vetus,* Venetiis 1616, De officio praefecti urbi, l. Omnia (D, 1, 12, 1), n. 35, fol. 14ra. Juristic opinion was perfectly familiar with the problem of the validity and enforceability of law « *extra fines territorii* sive domicilii vel originis ». It is most interesting to note that Baldus in his comments on *Cunctos populos* operated with the tutorial principle in regard to the legislator and the territory. After referring to Odofredus he answers the question « Utrum civis extra territorium delinquens veniat puniendus » by declaring that justiciability concerning crimes « in suo territorio, cuius *tutela pertinet ad statuentes, non autem* de commissis *extra territorium* » (C, 1, 1, 1, n. 98, fol. 9rb).

A possible answer may lie in the purpose of his writing the tract. Peace was disturbed by the claims of jurisdiction made and largely exercised by the papacy and the law which it administered, based as it was on an interpretation of the Bible which he rejected. In other words, the target of his attack was the ecclesiological system as it presented itself to him. It was the vastly extended claims arising out of the papal plenitude of power which he vigorously assailed. The other line of his attack was on the ecclesiological level which involved the application of the corpus-idea in conjunction with the allegory of *caput et membra* and consequently the employment of the descending theme of government and law in all its rigidity. The evils besetting contemporary society were (for Marsilius) due to a papal governmental scheme which was wholly unjustifiable, but which could be rendered harmless by destroying its bases and thus by completely reshaping its structure. The existent ecclesiological framework and its presuppositions dictated Marsilian strategy and tactics. The employment of the very same concepts and thought-patterns which were specific and articulate within the ecclesiological system forced itself upon him. In other words, the object and target of his attack determined the means of the attack which is the same as saying that in his attack he adopted arguments which were akin and appropriate to the ecclesiological premisses.

It is therefore understandable that one of the aims by which the system could be made inoperative was what for want of better term may be called the de-mundanization (*Entweltlichung*) of the Church. On the basis of its own loudly proclaimed axioms the Church (and with it, the papacy) was a divine, that is, supranatural foundation. As a society that did not evolve on natural premises and had not come into being by virtue of any natural impulse, it was demonstrably not supposed to pursue any natural aims, but solely transcendental, supranatural ends. For the attainment of this aim there was (for Marsilius) no need for any mundane, earthy, purely terrestrial jurisdiction, law, enforcement of commands, and still less need for property and all the paraphernalia of a mundane society and its corresponding government.

With this de-mundanization of the Church went hand in hand the complementary feature: the rehabilitation or resuscitation or revival or, if you like, the rebirth of the citizen who took the place of the sub/ject. He was a member of a natural society, of one that followed all the laws of nature and had little to do with divinity.[23] As a supranatural society the Church had *per se*, in the view of Marsilius, neither the right nor the means of creating laws enforceable on the natural plane within natural society, that is to say, the State (in whatever sense he may have taken the term). On its part the *universitas civium* alone had the power to create enforceable law when functioning as the *legislator humanus*, where the accent lies on the *humanus*. What is therefore characteristic of his system of thought is the conceptual dichotomy of the *universitas civium* and the *universitas fidelium*. Each acts in different capacities and each pursues different aims and has different functions. In a word, they are two corporations of entirely different substances.

These considerations will have made clear that in the one society – the *universitas fidelium* – the descending theme of government was operative, whereas in the other it was the ascending theme. Within the latter the material ingredient of the law was consent of the citizen, while in the other it was faith. What was common to both *universitates* was that they exhibited the character of corporations in the purest sense and therefore possessed all the organological appurtenances.[24] The ecclesiological society, the Church, had (and has) by its very origin, provenance and history no terrestrial boundaries – it was (and is) a universal body: indeed, physical, ethnic, linguistic,

23. Evidently, the Marsilian standpoint did not preclude the pursuit of a double end – a civic as well as a transcendental end – the hallmark of the principle of bipolarity that replaced the former unipolarity. Cf. on this also *DP* (Quillet), 36, and W. Ullmann, *Medieval Foundations of Renaissance Humanism*, Elek, London 1977, 123; 134; 153. Further observations in F. Prinz, *Marsilius von Padua*, «Zeitschrift für Bayerische Landesgeschichte», 39 (1976), 41ff., especially 62; 73.

24. For the history of the concept see now T. Struve, *Die Entwicklung der organologischen Staatsauffassung im Mittelalter*, Hiersemann, Stuttgat 1978 (Monographien zur Geschichte des Mittelalters, 16); on Marsilius 257ff., especially 276ff.

biological, natural frontiers could never be of any concern to it. It focused attention solely on the person. The very concept of territory was meaningless within ecclesiological considerations. Here seems to lie at least a large part of the explanation of why Marsilius never came to consider the reification – the *Verdinglichung* – of the citizen and to make the *universitas civium* a territorially anchored body. Marsilius de-mundanized the Church, but he did not take the necessary subsequent step: he did not mundanize, that is, territorialize the citizens' body. His system perfectly and uniquely mirrored the ecclesiological corporation, only of course in an obverse sense.[25] His attack was monothematic, concentrating as it did on showing the ecclesiological system in reverse. It does seem clear to me that the absence of the territorial component part of sovereignty can be explained by his all too closely following ecclesiological footsteps. He was obviously unable to emancipate himself from the very thought-patterns which he so vigorously attacked. He still moved within the traditional framework.

To Marsilius it must have seemed that the only way to demolish the extravagant claims of the papacy lay in adopting the humanist ideology rigidly and consistently, so consistently that he neglected some of its vital parts. By exclusively focusing on the *homo* and the *humanitas* and its contingent features he literally left no room for space, that is, for the impersonal and a-human territory. His was the purest kind of political humanism. His system was an unadulterated humanist philosophy of society. It was not a theory of the State. The paradox is there for all to see: political humanism neglected the very soil upon which ordinary *humanitas* lived, moved and thrived. The most one can say is that his tract pointed to « une préfiguration de la doctrine moderne de l'état ».[26] His thesis was not only monothe-

25. *DP* (Quillet), 46: « Toute l'entreprise marsilienne consiste dans une sécularisation poussée à l'extrême des conceptions ». See on this also Ullmann, *Principles*, 274f., and especially *Medieval Foundations*, 124ff.

26. Cf. also the remarks by *DP* (Quillet), 34. Although not dealing with the subject of this paper, Segall, *Der Defensor*, 64, suggests that the term « State » in Marsilius should be rendered by « Gesamtheit der Bürger » or « Gemeinschaft ».

matic, but also, like its counterpart, purely ideographic. For practical purposes it did not readily lend itself as a model, and this may well explain the paucity of references to it in writings and enactments where one might have expected them.[27] Its influence is marked in the fields of philosophy and ideology rather than in that of politics and the State: he was no jurist, though he tackled a highly juristic problem.

Was there a solution of the problem of political humanism? I believe there is and it lies in conjoining the political humanism of Marsilius with his contempory jurisprudence. In setting forth a philosophy of politics, Marsilius did not intend to propound a theory of the State or of its sovereignty, though this is exactly what many modern authors have foisted upon him. The jurists – and governments – on the other hand, standing so to speak with both feet firmly on the ground, on the *solum*, offered a State sovereignty and an adequate theory of citizenship, but without a corresponding philosophy of politics, the very philosophy which Marsilius had set forth. What was required was the combination of practical jurisprudence with political philosophy, but for this integration scholarship was not yet prepared and the time not yet ready.

27. See de Lagarde, *Le Defensor pacis*, 59: « Nous avons cherché en vain la trace d'une connaissance de *Defensor* soit chez un juriste comme Bartole ... soit dans les commentaires de la *Politique* de Buridan ou d'Oresme, soit dans les proclamations des incitateurs démocratiques fomentés à Florence (1343), Rome (1347), Paris (1357) ou dans les Pays-Bas (1340-1360) ». In fact, it was only in the following generation that author of the *Somnium Viridarii* made reference to the *DP*; see J. Quillet, *La philosophie politique du Songe du Vergier: sources doctrinales*, Vrin, Paris 1977, 126ff.; 134ff.; 156f. The influence of the *DP* made itself felt in theological disputes during the Reformation period rather than in the field of politics proper.

X

BALDUS'S CONCEPTION OF LAW.

INVESTIGATIONS into the history and past conceptions of the social phenomenon, Law, are justified by their contributions to the understanding and cognition of the idea of Law. They are part of legal history no less than of social and cultural history.

Civilization progresses in accordance with the rules of evolution, and no other social feature reflects the interests, problems, spiritual conflicts and influences of ideas more accurately than Law as the very function of civilization. It was John Austin and his school who made the abortive attempt to deny this function of Law, to detach it from its proper environment and to conceive it as a separate entity in itself. Austin's jurisprudence tried to force Law into an esoteric isolationism chiefly by deriving its axioms, premises and criteria from within itself alone regardless of the forces from which Law takes its origin and its inner significance. That rigid and extreme conception of Law as a body of static concepts is bound to lead to stagnation and ossification of the ideas and notions forming the bases upon which all legal systems are built.

Study of legal history will prove that ever since its nature and origin were made the object of scientific investigation, Law has been envisaged as a function of the civilization in which it is articulated and a product of the factors determining the social life in an advanced and organized community. Moreover, that study will ascertain that Law has been conceived as the ideological resultant of the ideological component parts. As far as Western civilization is concerned jurisprudence proper as a system of the sources, nature, meaning and scope of Law, was created by the scholar jurists of the North Italian Universities in the Middle Ages. That achievement is the more remarkable and praiseworthy since those Professors of Law were in the first place commentators of Justinian's *Corpus iuris civilis*, and commenting upon individual passages of a given body of legal rules does not usually make for systematic and methodical investigation. The attempt at a systematic inquiry into the problems connected with Law and at a clear methodic treatment of its underlying principles was the result of their training in philosophical thinking. Christian moral philosophy at that time dominated all spheres of intellectual activity and fertilized all intellectual exercises. The Christian interpretation of the Universe influenced the workaday world no less than the intellect of the jurists; it was one of the main ideological forces of that age influencing all functions of civilization.

Like all other schools of thought the Italian theory of Law is not the work of a single scholar, nor was it created *ex nihilo*. Many thinkers contributed connecting ideas and helped to form that conception of Law which gradually emerged at the time of the classical legal school at the end of the fourteenth century. No excuse is necessary for singling out from among the medieval Italian jurists Baldus de Ubaldis (1327—1400): an extraordinary genius with a profound and erudite knowledge of the theory and history of Law; unlike so many of his contemporaries he no longer clung to the outworn scholastic patterns but critically investigated the work of the great jurists, particularly that of Azo, Cynus and Bartolus (whose pupil he was). He may be termed the last representative of the classical Italian school. His fifty-six years as Professor of Law and his participation in many important political and ecclesiastical affairs enabled him to enjoy unusually great authority and to exercise exceptional influence upon the Courts and the countless scholars who attended the Italian Universities. The study of Plato and Aristotle as well as of the great Roman thinkers enabled him to approach the theoretical problems of Law from the wider philosophical viewpoint: he based legal concepts and all that they imply upon the firmer and broader ground of philosophy.

I.

'Philosophia moralis est legum mater et ianua'[1] . . . 'Ius nostrum applicat sibi totam moralem philosophiam'.[2] The gist of Baldus's theory of Law is contained in these two sentences, which recognize the crucial part played by moral philosophy in the understanding of the origin and aim of Law. More precisely, these utterances reveal his conviction that the principles, axioms and criteria upon which the concept of Law is built, above all the principles of good and equity, are identical with those evinced by moral philosophy.[3] It was the sublime and austere task of the Professors of Law to elaborate the philo-

---

[1] Baldus de Ubaldis, *Commentarius ad Digestum vetus*, Venetiis, 1616, titulus *De Iustitia et iure*, lex *Huius studii* (D. 1, 1, 2), no. 6.

[2] *L.c.*, *De Iustitia et iure*, *Rubrica ad legem primam*, no. 21.

[3] See *infra*, section II.

sophical principles underlying juristic conceptions, particularly that of the origin and nature of Law. Owing to the species of philosophy which evoked, as it were, metaphysical speculations, and because of the duties allotted to the Doctors, Baldus claimed that 'legum professores dicuntur sacerdotes'.[4]

The scrutiny of the philosophical ideas underlying the concept of Law was undertaken not for its own sake, but as a means to an end. For the knowledge thus acquired was envisaged by Baldus, following Aristotle, as the presupposition for the scientific treatment of good and equitable conduct forming the foundation of Law. Teleological aspects, obviously suggested by moral philosophy, entered the field of jurisprudence. He continued the above passage: 'Nota verbum Aristotelis quod non, ut sciamus quid est bonum, scrutamur, sed ut boni efficiamur . . . scientia non requiritur ut finis, sed ut ducens ad finem, quia sine scientia nulla procedit recta operatio intellectus. Concluditur igitur ex praedictis quod bonum et malum et voluntates hominum sunt materia huius scientiae.' It can be clearly seen from this quotation that Baldus adhered to the opinion generally held at his time that jurisprudence is part of ethics.[5]

II.

Baldus was primarily concerned with a theoretical clarification of the origin of Law, for 'qui vult scire consequentes, debet primo scire antecedentes; qui vult scire principiata, debet noscere principia'.[6] In full accord with his precursors he affirmed as an axiomatic truth that Justice, in the abstract sense of the word, is the source of Law—'Ius descendit, id est, nascitur a iustitia[7] . . . ius noscitur ex sua causa praesertim essentiali et intrinseca: Iustitia est causa intrinseca iuris . . . ius sine causa nasci non potest'.[8]

Pursuing this axiomatic idea Baldus proceeded to formulate the concept and import of Justice. His basic views on man and his teleological explanation of human conduct enable us to understand his conception of Justice. Although he was committed to the belief in a fixed moral code he did not interpret the idea of Justice in transcendental terms; instead, conceiving

---

4 *L.c.*, *De Iustitia et iure*, lex *Iuri operam daturum*, no. 5.

5 See, *e.g.* Cynus de Pistorio (d. 1336), in his *Proemium ad lecturam super Digesto veteri*, Francoforti, 1578, no. 9: 'Videndum est, cui parti philosophiae subalternatur nostra scientia. Multa possent dici, tamen Doctores communiter dicunt quod subalternatur ethicae.'

6 *L.c.*, no. 2.

7 *L.c.*, no. 3.

8 *L.c.*, no. 7.

it to be derived from the Absolute, to be a reflection of the Absolute in the human conscience. By Justice Baldus meant human justice. That belief in a fixed stated moral code was the basis of his legal philosophy, which is in reality a mere application of Christian moral philosophy. 'Iustitia creatoris fuit ab aeterno antequam orbis crearetur et formaretur. Sed iurisconsultus non intellexit de illa iustitia nec posuit os in coelum, sed sicut naturalis philosophus locutus est de natura in coelo constituta, id est, de ordine et dispositione rerum animatarum.'[9]

This fundamental conception of necessity involved a consideration of the essential nature of Justice. In accordance with Christian moral philosophy he maintained that Justice is a habit[10] of the will which prompts man to render everyone his own according to his merits. This habit takes the form of a guiding force leading man to do what is good and equitable in conformity with the fixed moral code, and is born of man's faculty for good in the moral sense and is intrinsic in him. Justice is an appurtenance of the will which has to be led in the morally proper direction. Following Aristotle's dictum that man is a social animal,[11] Baldus held that man must live in society, which, being of God, directs man's volitive actions and inclines him to morally good and equitable conduct. Though essentially free, man's will is directed by society, *i.e.* by the laws of society, to good and equitable actions. Free choice (*liberum arbitrium*) is thus limited. Human society moulds the individual's will by the promulgation and application of the laws, gradually promoting a habit which implies a real modification of man's character. This habit of acting justly is a moral quality[12] which is a virtue of the highest order. His whole doctrine was based on the acceptance of the fundamental idea of Christian moral philosophy that man is God's creature and is born for a destined end. 'Voluntas libera est, tamen lex temperat eam, ut non declinet ad pravum, et sic liberum arbitrium limitatur ad aequum et bonum, cum enim omnia

---

[9] *L.c.*, no. 3. It may be of some interest to quote some of the earlier jurists on this important point. See, *e.g.* the gloss to *Dig. vet.*, *De Iust. et iure*, lex *op. dat.*: 'Est ius a iustitia sicut a matre sua.' Placentinus (d. 1226), *Instit. De Iustitia et iure*: 'Ex iustitia omnia iura emanant tamquam ex fonte rivuli.' Azo (d. 1230), *ibid.*: 'A iustitia velut a materia et quasi fonte quodam omnia iura emanant; quod enim iustitia vult, idem ius prosequitur.' Cynus, *l.c.*, no. 6: "Iustitia et ius habent se ut producens et productum.'

[10] 'Iustitia dicitur habitus et ponitur sub praedicamento qualitatis '—*additio ad legem* '*Iustitia* ', *Dig. vet.*, *De Iust. et iure*, no. 1.

[11] 'Homo est animal sociale, ut in primo libro Politicae '—*additio ad legem* '*Iuri operam* ', no. 4.

[12] See *supra*, note 10.

fecerit Deus ad bonum finem, et liberum arbitrium ad optimum finem dederit.'[13] The inevitable conclusion of that argument was that Baldus avowed 'totus enim orbis regitur ratione et operatione boni et aequitatis; hominum genus arte et rationibus boni et aequi vivit et mercatur'.[14]

The concept of Justice is composed of two elements, *i.e.*, moral goodness and equity, the implication of which is evidently identical with that evinced from the realm of moral philosophy. The just, the righteous individual is the one whose will is constantly directed towards good and equity. Justice is fair and reasonable dealing with fellow human beings; it is equivalent with righteousness. Justice is perfection of the soul and, like the soul, 'immortal'; it is an ethical value and a social phenomenon. Said Baldus: 'Iustitia est perpetua et immortalis . . . et hoc prout est lex in divino subjecto, id est, in animo virorum constantium et perfectorum. Talis enim habitus non moritur, sicut anima est immortalis et perpetua . . . nam anima est quid divinum et immortale . . . (iustitia) est enim constans, quia inexorabilis et perpetua, quia semper est in viridi et numquam in sicco . . . est quaedam perfectio animae.'[15]

Continuing his analysis of the concept of Justice, Baldus stated that the term may be taken in two ways. It may be considered either in its abstract or in its concrete meaning. Abstractly conceived Justice is an impersonal detached idea containing its two elements. In the realm of legislation, Justice in this abstract sense functions as a norm and as a criterion from which positive laws are derived; it is the origin of Law. In its concrete meaning the term refers to the field of practical application, Justice and Law then becoming tautological expressions. 'Dic quod iustitia potest considerari dupliciter, scil. in abstracto, prout habet in se sua essentialia, circumscripto omni legislatore, et in concreto, prout est applicativa per legislatorem ad certos casus. Primo casu est mater et causa iuris . . . secundo vero casu iustitia et ius sunt unum et idem.'[16]

As a cardinal virtue Justice is comprised of other ethical values which form its most notable parts. Baldus enumerated them in his additional lecture on *Dig. vet.*, *De Iustitia et iure*, lex *Iustitia*, no. 2: 'Iustitia in subiecto infusa vel aquisita

---

[13] *L.c.*, *Rubrica ad legem primam*, no. 13.
[14] *Additio ad legem 'Iuri operam'*, no. 4.
[15] *De Iustitia et iure*, lex *Iustitia*, no. 1.
[16] *L.c.*, lex *Iuri operam*, no. 9.

informat ad religionem, pietatem, severitatem, vindictam, misericordiam, gratiam Dei, laetitiam, charitatem et innocentiam.'[17]

Coherent and consistent with the conception of Justice as an ethical axiom was Baldus's recognition that Law itself, being derived from Justice, is merely the translation of the abstract idea into actual rules of action. Law is the instrument, taking the form of a precept, by which the principles of good and equity are carried into effect. In other words, Law is the practical execution and the concrete expression of the abstract idea of Justice. Baldus professed that Justice is 'materia disponens, de cuius virtute intrinseca et forma latenti egreditur forma patens in formale iuris nostri praeceptum'.[18] Law is 'essentia legis in se ipsa'.[19] In his description of Law as an art Baldus was following Celsus and was in full agreement with the doctrine already expounded by the glossators. 'Iustitia non est aliud quam bonitas et equitas. Et ius non est aliud quam ars boni et aequi.'[20] Law is a sanction which renders effective the principles of good and equity[21]; in this capacity it functions as a guide of man to his destined end—'ius est ars boni et aequi, id est, vim ac potestatem habet ad bonum et aequum'.[22]

Since Law emerged from Justice it was considered to be just—'nam cum iustitia sit praeclarissima[23] . . . sequitur quod ius erit bonum et aequum . . . ius efficit bonos et aequos . . . creat ius in nobis effectum ut omnes fiant boni'.[24] Any conception of Law being unjust would be a contradiction in itself, since unjust Law would not constitute the rules of action for the attainment of man's destined end. Man's actions, being the pattern of social life, are the object of Law and, therefore, the object of the study by jurists. He taught that 'omnis ars assumit sibi naturam pro materia, sicut statuificus assumit sibi aes pro materia, et lanificus lanam. Sic legista pro materia assumit sibi facta hominum . . . ius nostrum est fundatum super accidentibus, id est, super casibus emergentibus ex quibus oritur bonum'.[25]

---

17 This lecture dealt mainly with those ethical values and with exemplifications.

18 *L.c.*, *Rubrica ad primam legem*, no. 5. Cynus formulated thus: 'Iustitia est virtus, ius est executio eius'—*Dig. vet.*, *De Iust, et iure*, lex *Iustitia*, § *iurisprudentia*, no. 2; or 'iustitia est anima non formata in ius, sed ius est aequitas in praeceptis iuris redacta'—*l.c.*, lex *iuri op. dat.*, no. 4.

19 *L.c.*, no. 9.

20 *L.c.*, lex *iuri op. dat.*, no. 7.

21 '. . . est de praedictis (scil. de bono et aequo) manifesta sanctio'—*l.c.*, *Rubrica ad primam legem*, no. 9.

22 *L.c.*, lex *iuri op. dat.*, no. 11.

23 Referring to Aristotle's *Ethics*, lib. 6, and Cicero's *De officiis*, lib. 1.

24 *L.c.*, *additio ad legem 'Iuri op. dat.'*, no. 3.

25 *L.c.*, *Rubrica ad primam legem*, no. 15. The question of the actual law giving authority does not directly come into the scope of this paper; its treatment would lead us too far away from our main concern.

Analysing the conception and functions of Law Baldus distinguished between its formal and final cause. The formal cause of Law is its outer form appearing in the shape of the individual law: 'Causa formalis est ipsa legum forma; nam lex appellatur forma, a qua non licet recedere.'[26] The final cause of Law has a threefold aim. Firstly, Law is a moral agent which aims at man's moral improvement by appealing to, and working upon, his spiritual and mental personality. Secondly, Law's economic aim is sound administration of man's household and of his domestic affairs as far as they lie within the scope of Law.[27] Lastly, Law politically conceived tries to provide a basis for the salutary government of the State. He declared: 'Causa finalis iuris est triplex, scil. in homine, ad hominem et ad Rempublicam. In homine, ut bonus sit, et hoc pertinet ad ethicam; ad hominem, ut quis bene regat familiam, et hoc pertinet ad aeconomicam; ad Rempublicam, ut Respublica salubriter regatur, et hoc pertinet ad politicam.'[28]

In general the aim of Law is to guide man's development towards perfection. This is why Baldus emphasized that Law delimits the path that man follows in his social life, and stressed the limitations Law imposes on man's free will. Law is merely a means to the attainment of man's destined end; this recognition necessarily entailed the employment of the teleological method.

III.

The fundamental ideas of Baldus's theory of Law are now before us. We may now, therefore, turn to an examination of the special departments of Law as he conceived them. The complex phenomenon Law is divided by him into Natural Law, Civil Law with the subdivisions public and private Law, and the Law of Nations. The common feature of all those species of Law is the conception that they constitute rules for good and equitable actions. Their distinctive feature lies in the respective spheres of their application.

Justinian's *Corpus iuris* did not contain an elaborate theory of those branches of Law, though their scientific treatment was

---

[26] *L.c.*, no. 19.

[27] The family was conceived as the economic unit of society. Baldus obviously had in mind the idea of a 'bonus pater familias'.

[28] *L.c.*, no. 20. It may be noticed that Baldus did not extensively treat of the three basic legal precepts as enumerated in Justinian's Law-books. That, of course, is no omission on the part of Baldus. On the contrary, he elaborated his doctrine on broader principles than the Roman jurists by basing his theories on general moral-philosophical conceptions. Those three basic precepts could assume merely an illustrative character in Baldus's theory—see *l.c.*, *De Iust. et iure*, lex *Huius studii*, no. 2.

intimated by many references and practical applications. Nor did the glossators treat of them at any length but merely mentioned them without further discussing their implications. Only the post-glossators and above all Baldus dealt with them separately and elaborated a theory about those departments of Law.

(1) *Natural Law.*—Before Baldus proceeded to examine the concept of Natural Law itself he felt it necessary to clarify the general concept of Nature. He realized that Nature is a quality with which all animate objects are endowed by divine means; Nature is a divinely arranged order of animate objects. 'Natura enim dicitur quaedam proprietas inserta rebus ab intellectu divino in rebus animatis; natura est divina quaedam dispositio et ordo, rerumque status.' [29] In his additional lecture on *Dig. vet.*, *De Iustitia et iure*, lex *Huius studii*, § *Ius naturale*, no. 1, he once more analysed the notion of Nature and modified his earlier opinion stating that Nature is no static quality but a dynamic force with a definite end in view. His new definition substituted 'vis' for 'proprietas' and added the idea of procreation: 'Est natura vis insita rebus naturalibus ex similibus similia procreans et quale unumquodque est in generatione perfecta—hanc dicimus esse naturam.' In his final analysis he recognized that it is possible for the term 'Nature' to bear three interpretations. First, it may be considered from the point of view of its purpose—but this is not the province of the jurists.[30] Secondly, it may be conceived as a natural power springing from man's sensual being, and thirdly, as a natural power which emanates from his mental being—human actions being instigated in both these ways. These two last named conceptions of Nature, by which Baldus indicated two specified elements in the human character, *i.e.*, man's sensual and rational nature, are the subject of study by the jurists.[31]

According to Baldus Natural Law (*ius naturale*) is that rule of conduct which is based on the innate instinctive sense of animate objects as organized beings, and it takes its origin in the natural power emanating from man's mental and sensual being. As by divine foresight all animate objects are endowed with nature in the above-mentioned sense of the term, natural law is also applicable to animals. 'Quod a divina procedit

---

[29] *L.c.*, lex *iuri op. dat.*, no. 16.

[30] 'De intentione naturae . . . non est sermo legistis, sed naturalibus philosophis', *l.c.*, no. 1.

[31] 'De natura, id est, de naturalibus motibus animae sensitivae est tractandum nobis, prout est applicabilis humanae societati; de natura, id est, de naturalibus motibus animae intellectivae principaliter per se oportet nos considerare, quia subiectum in legibus est homo'—*l.c.*

seu descendit providentia est commune omnibus animalibus naturatis naturatione perfecta[32] . . . illud est ius naturale in quo conveniunt omnia animalia '.[33] Natural Law, according to Baldus, was nothing else but the application to human conduct of the principles in the working of Nature and their transformation into rules for actions which were envisaged by him as 'natural' and 'instinctive' functions.

Since the operations of Nature are invariable and decreed by necessity, Natural Law itself is equally invariable: 'Natura est illa quae non asuescit in contrarium: sicut ignis ubicumque ascendit et grave semper descendit . . . ius naturale non mutatur.'[34] It is evident that a case which is not covered by Natural Law could not be included in it by extensive interpretation.[35]

In accordance with Roman Law Baldus applied the idea of Natural Law to the case of copulation. He reasoned with due reference to Aristotle that among all animals, man included, there is a general recognized tendency towards the preservation of the species.[36] In pursuance of this idea he concluded that the first impulse to sexual union is 'natural' and cannot, therefore, constitute sin.[37] Consequently, provided that it aims at procreation, sexual union itself must fall within the province of Natural Law: 'Si primus motus est de iure naturali, ergo et finis, cum natura agit propter finem, et sic est causa causae et causa causati.'[38]

When treating Natural Law Baldus took the opportunity to deal with the institution of matrimony. It may be considered, he held, from three aspects. From that of procreation, it is a subject for Natural Law: 'Conjunctio matrimonialis potest considerari tripliciter; uno modo respectu finis, id est, procreationis, et est de iure naturali, quia naturalissimum est

[32] *L.c.*, § *ius naturale*, *pr.*

[33] *L.c.*, *additio ad* § *ius naturale*, no. 2. The term 'animal' was used in its widest sense. Though Baldus understood Natural Law as a phenomenon which comprises the actions both of man and animal (man being conceived as a species of animal), the idea of Natural Law proper was applicable to human society only, see *supra*, note 31.

[34] *L.c.*, § *ius naturale*, no. 5.

[35] 'Casus ommissus a natura non potest suppleri, ut sit de iure naturali, quia ius naturale non recipit interpretationem extensivam '—*l.c.*, no. 23.

[36] 'Nota quod omnia animalia sunt docta in quibusdam instinctibus per quem tendunt ad conservationem propriae speciei . . . et ad conservationem sui esse '—*l.c.*, lex *Huius studii*, no. 4.

[37] 'Consideramus primos motus, qui non sunt in potestate nostra, nec in voluntate, et tales motus sunt de iure naturali . . . in eis non est peccatum '—*l.c.*, § *ius naturale*, no. 4.

[38] *L.c.*, no. 5. Azo, however, contested that juristic conception of the copulation, but was not referred to by his successors: 'Corporalis enim coniunctio non potest dici ius, cum ipsum sit corporale, iura autem omnia sunt incorporalia '—Azo, *Summa in primum librum Institutionum*, no. 4.

producere sibi simile—sic enim conservatur species tota in natura.' [39] From that of matrimonial consent, it comes under the Law of Nations,[40] while in so far as it is a matter of legally prescribed rites it is the concern of Civil Law.[41] He added in no. 9 of the same lecture that when viewed as a sacrament matrimony might also come within the province of Divine Law.[42] Matrimony involved the 'natural' duty of educating the children.

A problematical case of theoretical interest within the scope of Natural Law was alimentation of the father by the son. Is there any natural obligation [43] for a son to support a destitute father? Baldus argued that there were grounds which suggested the existence of a natural obligation: 'Quaeritur circa alimenta, utrum alimentatio patris sit de iure naturali? Et videtur quod sic, nam natura, quae nihil intentatum relinquit, docuit quoddam animal nutrire parentes aetatis gravedine destitutos.'[44] In his 'Solutio' of the problem he declared that the answer depended upon whether man is classified as a species of animal (in which case alimentation fails to constitute a natural obligation) or whether man is conceived as a rational being: 'Solutio: homo potest considerari ut animal, tunc non esset (scil. alimentatio) de iure naturali. Item potest considerari ut ratio, quia homo formaliter est ratio et intellectus, et hoc modo est de iure naturali, nam sine iuris civilis praecepto hoc dictat ratio naturalis, quod genitus suum non destituit genitorem, a quo habet esse.' [45]

(2) *Civil Law.*—Civil Law was a term employed to denote

---

[39] *L.c.*, no. 5.

[40] *L.c.*: 'Secundo modo potest considerari coniunctio matrimonialis quantum ad consensum, et tunc est de iure gentium, quia consensus proprie non est in brutis, cum consensus sit actus electivus, qui habet fieri per intellectum et rationem'.

[41] He continued: 'Tertio modo potest considerari forma matrimonii contrahendi, id est, verborum expressio . . . vel id quod habeatur pro expressione verborum . . hoc modo est de iure civili'.

[42] 'Quarto modo prout est sacramentum, et tunc est de iure divino, unde scriptum est, quos Deus coniunxit, homo non separet'. The problem as to whether marriages could be prohibited by law under the threat of punishment was of some practical importance at the time of Baldus: 'Quaeritur, numquid per statutum civitatis possit matrimonium prohiberi sub poena, puta quod nemo accipiat Gabellinam in uxorem sub poena mille librarum?'—*l.c.* Though matrimony was 'res spiritualis, ergo non potest directe prohiberi per statutum laicorum, sicut nec per pactum' (*l.c.*), he decided for practical reasons that a marriage prohibiting law is valid with respect to its sanction, but does not affect the validity of the marriage: 'Ego credo quod si tale statutum fit propter aliquam publicam utilitatem vel aequitatem, quod teneat statutum respectu poenae', *l.c.*, no. 11.

[43] That is to say, an obligation which is not based on Civil Law.

[44] *L.c.*, *ius naturale*, no. 15.

[45] *L.c.*

those rules of action which neither come within the province of Natural Law nor that of the Law of Nations. Civil Law is that department of Law which applied to the citizens of the Roman State only. In conformity with the contemporary doctrine Baldus divided it into public and private Law: 'Nota quod ius civile, prout est genus, dividitur in duas partes principales, scil. publicum et privatum.' [46]

According to Baldus this division of Civil Law into public and private Law may only be justified by the consideration of the public or private character of the persons with whom the Right is connected. For, Baldus argued, if the Right which emerges from the individual law is considered abstractly, all Law would be public Law: 'Aut consideramus ius legis, et omne ius est publicum; aut ius personarum, et tunc aliud est publicum, aliud privatum.' [47]

Setting out from this conception of Law, Baldus defined public Law as that department of Civil Law which deals with actions which are for the public, *i.e.* common good, whereas private Law concerns actions which are for the private, *i.e.* individual good. He said: 'Nota quod illud est publicum (ius), quod continet publicum bonum principaliter; illud vero est privatum, quod continet privatum bonum principaliter.' [48] The ultimate criterion of the distinction was the utility of the action concerned [49]—whether it was for the welfare of all or merely that of the private individual: 'Ius (civile) principaliter disponit et ordinat circa ista duo, scil. publicam et privatam utilitatem.' [50]

There was some doubt as to whether this distinction is legitimate, since actions which promote public welfare also tend to promote welfare of the individual, the State being composed of the very individuals who benefit by the action. Is not every action for the good of the individual at the same time for the common good? Baldus considered this objection and realized that public and private good complement, and are correlative to, each other; but this view would invalidate the distinction. In this context he said: 'Omne publicum bonum includit in se non solum publicum commodum, sed etiam privatum, cum Respublica non sit aliud nisi ipsi homines. Item omne privatum commodum includit in se publicum bonum, quia interest Reipublicae subditos habere locupletes . . . cum ergo bonum publicum non sit

---

[46] *L.c.*, lex *Huius studii, pr.*
[47] *L.c.*, no. 10.
[48] *L.c.*, *pr.*
[49] Obviously on the basis of Ulpian's dictum (D. 1, 1, 4).
[50] *L.c.*, no. 6.

sine privato nec privatum sine publico, ergo non distinguitur unum ab altero.' [51]

Baldus refused to accept that conclusion and preferred to adhere to the traditional distinction. He thought that the division could be justified by the consideration that public Law deals with the actions which are *primarily* and *directly* useful to the community, and only secondarily and indirectly to the individual citizen, whereas private Law deals with actions which are primarily and directly useful to the individual citizen, and only in their indirect effects useful to the State: 'Solutio: quando bonum publicum includit privatum, vel econtra, istud est secundario, unde principaliter loquendo distinctio remanet vera, et verba simpliciter prolata debent intelligi principaliter, non secundario.' [52]

Following Ulpian Baldus declared that the subject-matter of public Law consists of things or human actions or persons, each of which are characterized by special qualifications. Said Baldus: 'Nota quod ius publicum consistit in rebus, id est, in sacris rebus, consistit etiam in actibus hominum, id est, sacrificiis, consistit etiam immediate in personis, id est, sacerdotibus propter sacerdotium quod est publicum ministerium, et in magistratibus propter publicum officium.' [53] The public character of a priest's or magistrate's position was not derived from their priestly or magisterial function as such, but from their being appointed for the public benefit—for the benefit of all without distinction. In other words, priesthood and magistracy are institutions which are created not for the sake of certain persons or cases, but as organs of public administration. This is the reason for their protection by public Law. Treating of the notion of 'public' Baldus declared that 'quod enim differenter et proprie non potest alicui appropriari sive applicari, sed convenit omnibus sine differentia, id publicum est'. Continuing he said: 'Sacerdos qui est praeses animarum, et magistratus qui est praeses iudiciorum, non sunt instituti propter Titium et Seium, sed propter incertum de incertis; unde quicumque sit ille, qui agit sacerdotium vel magistratum, non curatur, sed Respublica attenditur, ut recte regatur.' [54]

In the final chapter of his lecture on this topic Baldus dwelt on the problem of the so-called 'publica iniuria'. He characterized it as the seamy side of 'publicum ius': An action which proves harmful not only to individual members but to the whole

---

[51] *L.c.*, nos. 7 and 8.
[52] *L.c.*, no. 9.
[53] *L.c.*, no. 15.
[54] *L.c.*, no. 16.

community is ‘ publica iniuria ’. Baldus gave examples of some of these actions: ‘ Quaero econtra de iniuria, id est, quae dicitur publica. Respondeo—quae omnibus fit sub ratione pari, ut haeresis et blasphemia, etc.’; an act may be called a public wrong ‘ propter atrocitatem facti, item propter personae dignitatem, ut qui infertur magistratui vel sacerdoti, qui representant Rempublicam ’.

(3) *The Law of Nations*.—Baldus's investigation into this branch of Law is remarkable for its brevity. It may seem that his conception of the Law of Nations has, at first sight, little resemblance with what is nowadays conceived as Law of Nations. But closer scrutiny would prove that his conception contained the germs of the doctrine which was developed by Hugo Grotius centuries later.

The Law of Nations is constituted of that essentially good and equitable mode of conduct which is practised and pursued by different national units between which it forms the basis of a peaceful intercourse.[55] The Law of Nations arose, in his opinion, from customs exercised by different peoples. These customary rules of life are rooted in reason as distinct from Natural Law which originates in mere instinct. The former rules developed gradually and were acknowledged by the peoples on account of their convenience, whereas rules in the province of Natural Law were intrinsic in man and worked, so to speak, through necessity.[56] From a more general view-point the Law of Nations is that conduct which is exercised by man as member of a world community. ‘ Ius gentium est quod procedit a ratione et intellectu gentium, quo omnes gentes quasi pleraeque utuntur, quod semper est bonum et aequum, et sine quo homines non possunt vivere ’.[57] His idea of a Law of Nations apparently contains the germ of the axiom that Law is universal and that a common mode of good and equitable conduct exists among all men as world citizens, irrespective of their different nationalities; his Law of Nations may be understood as World Law.

The term ‘ gens ’ was considered by Baldus under two main headings: ‘ Dicitur “ gens ” quandoque omnes homines totius

---

[55] Such actions were, for example, possession of property and its bequest, travelling without hindrance, inviolability of heralds, etc.

[56] See *supra* section III (1), and note (40).

[57] *L.c.*, § *ius gentium*, no. 1. He continued: ‘ Et distat a naturali sicut distat cerebrum hominis a cerebro animalium. Nam posuit Deus in homine cerebrum membrum divinum, ubi sensus et intellectus. Sed animalia intellectum non habent, sed quendam instinctum secundum datas animalibus proprietates et complexiones naturales a stellis et elementis, sed anima hominis est immediate a Deo ’.

mundi [58] . . . secundo modo dicitur "gens" provincia, puta Gallia, et sic gens est ab uno principio orta . . . secundum propriam collectionis distinctionem.' [59]

The exposition of Baldus's theory of Law discloses an attempted systematic and analytical elucidation of the complex problems of the origin, nature, sources and functions of Law. The treatment of these problems is characterized by the conceptual framework within which he worked. Fundamental to this framework is the idea that human conduct is purposive and destined to a definite end. Law guides human actions towards that goal. Law, therefore, is conceived as a means which is adapted to the attainment of the recognized end. The idea of Law is based on moral considerations—it is the strongest moral factor in the individual's social life. Particularly significant and important is the employment of the teleological principle throughout all his analyses. Imbued with the spirit of Christian moral philosophy which formed the background of his teachings, he envisaged Law as a cultural phenomenon, and as a function of civilization which derived its meaning and sustenance from the application of the ideas inherent in that philosophy. In respect to method his analyses in most ways reveal a departure from the stereotyped scholastic pattern of research. His own original approach to the problems can everywhere be seen; his disquisitions resolve themselves into a system of legal concepts. He integrated and developed systematically the foundations laid down in Justinian's *Corpus iuris civilis*. But we are bound to admit shortcomings, fallacies and defects in his doctrine. Are not these imperfections pardonable, however, when we bear in mind that Baldus was hampered by the limitations and ideologies imposed upon him by his age? Whatever his shortcomings may be, it is undeniable that Baldus invigorated legal theory, giving it fresh impulses, revealing unseen perspectives and opening up new horizons, and that his theory was referred to by scholars centuries later contributing effectively to the formation of the theory and philosophy of Law in the eighteenth and nineteenth centuries.

---

58 The wording in Justinian's *Corpus* presented no difficulties for Baldus: 'Tamen textus non dicit "gens", sed gentes in plurali, sed certe idem si dixisset in singulari, quia nomen collectivum singularis numeri universalem habet significationem'.

59 *L.c.*, no. 2.

XI

THE MEDIAEVAL THEORY OF LEGAL AND ILLEGAL ORGANIZATIONS.

SEVERAL texts in Justinian's law books distinguished between legal and illegal associations of men. Although some passages specifically mentioned certain associations as legal (licit),[1] it was by no means clear whether other associations not specifically named or not specifically sanctioned by a superior authority, were consequently illegal. Theoretical speculation was certainly not the Romans' strong point: as a modern authority recently put it, their ideas must be deduced partly from their language, and more frequently from the rules laid down in the law books.[2] It was the office of those engaged in interpreting Roman law to discover the idea underlying the various pronouncements of the texts. The discovery of the criterion enabling them to distinguish between legal and illegal organizations necessarily brought to the fore the problem of whether individuals were at liberty to organize and associate themselves in corporate bodies or whether the legality of an organization depended upon an act of a superior authority. Neither of these problems was sufficiently clarified in the Roman texts.

Here, as in so many other controversial topics, the mediaeval commentators of the Roman law first attempted to establish fundamental principles and to find out the criterion which distinguished the legal organization from its illegal counterpart. It was not only their scientific zeal and their urge to clarify concepts in need of clarification that prompted them to investigate this subject, but also the actual political and social state of affairs, which called for an exposition and examination of underlying principles. Members of the same profession, occupation or trade, had associated themselves in vocational groups; men of an identical political aim had joined communities for the enforcement of their objects; whilst charitable and other philanthropic ideals had moved men to found associations aiming at the realization of their ideals. Judging by contemporary writings these manifold organizations greatly increased as time went on, and it became the self-imposed task of the jurists to elicit principles by which the legal organization could be recognized.

Otto von Gierke undertook the arduous and laborious task of reconstructing the mediaeval doctrine of corporations. His masterly analysis revealed to the modern mind the mediaeval ways of thinking about the juristic structure of corporations—their rights, their legal personality, their delictal responsibility, their dissolution, the relations between members and the corporate body, and so forth. But recent researches into mediaeval literature have shown that Gierke somewhat neglected that mediaeval classification of organizations into the categories of legal and illegal corporations which actually formed the backbone of the mediaeval theory. It may not be without interest to sketch briefly the leading ideas of the mediaeval jurists, and to view the basis of their doctrines from the mediaeval perspective.

---

[1] See *e.g.*, D. 3, 4, 1; 47, 22: C. iv, 59.

[2] Mr. P. W. Duff, *Personality in Roman Private Law*, p. ix.

The main problem that interested the mediaeval doctors of law was whether those associations enumerated in the various Roman texts merely represented concrete applications and typical instances of a general principle, or whether they were the only permitted and permissible human associations. The first alternative meant that—besides those cases specified in the texts—there were also associations which derived their legal character directly from the law in that they constituted the application of a general principle : the law itself thus formed the basis for their legal character. The second alternative excluded the law as a basis and made the legality of an organization in each case dependent on the explicit approbation of a superior authority. Setting out from a metajuristic tenet, namely, that all law is the true manifestation, the concrete embodiment and the external expression of the ethical virtue of justice; and that, furthermore, all law has as its aim the realization of this virtue, they were driven to consider all human associations as legal, once the promotion of justice was shown to be the bond holding the members together. All human conduct bore the mark of legality, if it satisfied the demands made by the virtue of justice. For the jurists held axiomatically that legal science was but a department of ethics, and law the vehicle through which the principles of ethics were to be enforced.[3] Any conduct designed to contribute to the realization of the idea of justice was considered to lie within the province of legality. Consequently, the avowed aim of an organization to pursue a just or righteous cause provided the jurists with the argument that such organizations should be declared legal. According to the conception of its members, such an organization was to translate the abstract idea of justice into a living reality : it was thought of as an instrument whereby justice found adequate expression. Since it tried to fulfil the aim of all law, an association of this kind was conceived to be indisputably legal. Thus the purpose alone provided the criterion for the legality or illegality of an organization. Accordingly, associations aiming at the realization of some just cause derived their licit character directly from the law, irrespective of any approbation by a superior authority. Owing to the broadness of the idea of justice and its ethical, political and social implications, the concept of a just cause received an ever widening interpretation, so that even associations whose aim was to provide recreation and entertainment, came to be considered as promoting a just cause.

These ideas were already vaguely conceived by Odofredus.[4] True, he still showed a marked hostility towards any new associations, because, as he argued, the individual in an organized group is far more dangerous to the existing social and political order than in an isolated position : 'that which an individual dare not think by himself, is cried out aloud by a group of individuals'. In this tendency of the group, he recognized the 'motus destruendi civitates'.[5] It is furthermore true that he still clung to the letter of the Roman law far more than his great contemporary Innocent IV. Yet at the end of his lengthy discussion of this topic there emerges quite clearly the idea that certain associations

---

3 See my paper 'Baldus's Conception of Law', in *L. Q. R.*, 1942, pp. 389 f.
4 Odofredus died 1265.
5 Lecture on D. 3, 4, 1, No. 2.

must be judged legal, even though they were not sanctioned by a superior authority, and could not be classified amongst those specified cases in Roman law : ' Regulariter omne corpus factum causae justitiae, valet ', was his verdict, but he failed to elaborate it or to give examples of its application.

The conception that every organization which was founded ' pro causa justitiae ' was licit, was the core of Innocent IV's teaching. Therefore he applied the term ' collegia a lege approbata ' to all associations which had as their aim the realization of an ethical ideal. In his opinion, these ' collegia ' derived their legal character directly from the law.[6] Following him, the jurists—canonists and civilians alike—maintained that even if an association were established for the furtherance of a good cause, it became illegal as soon as its members engaged themselves in activities which did not conform to their professed aim.[7]

An interesting distinction was drawn by Bartolus, which, as his pupil Baldus testified, later became generally accepted. Bartolus distinguished between associations which were permitted by the *jus civile* and those permitted by the *jus gentium*. Both civil law and the law of nations, he held, permit, regardless of a superior sanction or an explicit legal declaration, any association ' pro justitia conservanda ',[8] that is in order to repel some injustice or to ward off some aggression. Bartolus and common opinion after him, reckoned amongst the associations permitted by the *jus civile* not only gold mining and salt mining organizations and tax farming partnerships, but also trade guilds, banking associations and, in unanimous opposition to the glossators, the corporations of university students and doctors. An association formed by poor persons in order to pool their resources was a further instance of such ' civil ' organizations. Moreover, provided that they were composed exclusively by lay people, associations with a predominantly religious aim, such as the third orders and the like, were considered legal, regardless of any intervention by a superior authority; if membership were open to clerical and lay persons alike, papal consent would have to be sought. Baldus subdivided the associations permitted by civil law. The one subdivision comprised those which served the public interest, such as trade guilds and other unions of artizans, communal life being impossible without them; this category also embraced the university corporations.[9] The other subdivision concerned pious organizations, that is those which were founded ' ad honorem Dei '. In his lecture on C. iv, 37, three further categories appeared. Here he repeated the general statement that every association must aim at some final good (' debet esse ad bonum finem '). Now this final good, he said, may be considered under a threefold aspect : either under that of ' common decency ' : this category included all charitable organizations, such as associations for the support and relief of the oppressed, of orphans, widows, the destitute; or under the heading of ' leisure ', such as societies for popular

---

[6] *Commentaria Super Libros Quinque Decretalium*, c. 14, x, 5, 31, No. 2, fol. 526: ' Collegia, quae fiunt pro bono, et ad malum non procedunt, dicimus esse concessa auctoritate senatusconsulti.'

[7] *Loc cit.* No. 3: ' Collegia, licet bonum nomen habeant, tamen quia male operantur, fiunt illicita collegia.'

[8] Lecture on D. 3, 4, 1, No. 1, fol. 113.

[9] Baldus on D. 3, 4, 1, No. 2, fol. 204.

recreation and entertainment on certain feast days; or, lastly, under the title of the 'public good', such as tax farming associations or corporations for the exploitation of the proceeds from Lake Trasimeno near Perugia.[10] These three categories seem to have strongly appealed to later jurists, as can be easily ascertained by reading Bartholomaeus Salycetus's lectures.[11]

The associations, or more correctly speaking, the communities permitted by the *jus gentium* were the towns, boroughs and villages and their councils: they derived their licit character directly from the *jus gentium*, as all jurists after Bartolus affirmed. Baldus added the significant remark that townships, etc., were necessary for good and healthy government, and it was for this reason that the *jus gentium* allowed the establishment of town councils and the like. As far as new settlements came into question—this was not infrequently the case, owing to the expulsion of whole sections of a town by the rival political party—the jurists were unanimous in their opinion that the *jus gentium* allowed the free association of the settlers. It is worth quoting the relevant passage of Bartolus, not only because of its importance, but also because of the somewhat inaccurate quotation by Gierke[12]: 'Debes scire, quod quaedam collegia sunt permissa de jure gentium, quaedam de jure civili. De jure gentium collegium, quod appellatur populus unius civitatis, castri vel villae'.[13] The only restriction which Bartolus and later generations placed upon the free association was that new settlements must not be erected with a view to rivalry with other towns.[14] Baldus was equally outspoken on this point when he said that no legal objection could be raised against the free association of settlers and inhabitants of localities, since 'populi et urbes vel villae . . . sunt de jure gentium et possunt fieri absque auctoritate principis'.[15] Paulus Castrensis, a representative of the fifteenth century, confirmed the general acceptance of Bartolus's teachings and stated in unequivocal terms: 'Si plures homines se invicem congregarent in aliquo loco et construerent ibi aliquod oppidum, *eo ipso censetur approbatum*'.[16] Only in a very formal respect was the approbation of a superior authority to be called for: a town could not have the name of a 'civitas', a city in the proper

---

10 *Loc cit.* No. 6, fol. 104, *verso*: 'Adverte, quod istud nomen debet esse ad bonum finem, quod potest tripliciter considerari. Primo respectu boni honesti, ut societas juvantium oppressos, pupillos, viduas et miserabiles personas. Item boni delectabilis, ut societates, quae fiunt Perusii ad tripudiandum in festo S. Herculani, quae continent delectationem recreativam civium. Item respectu boni utilis, ut societas vectigalium et societas emptorum fructuum aquae lacus Perusii et similes.'

11 See C. iv, 37, 1, No. 1, fol. 98 *verso*. Salycetus was professor at Bologna, Padua and Ferrara, and died 1412.

12 Otto von Gierke, *Das Deutsche Genossenschaftsrecht*, vol. iii, p. 370. In his penetrating analysis 'Organic Tendencies in Mediaeval Political Thought' in *American Political Science Review*, vol. xxxii (1938), E. Lewis strongly criticizes Gierke's doctrine as being 'founded on very doubtful evidence' (p. 853). He says that Gierke's theory is 'inaccurate' (p. 849), 'erroneous' (p. 871), and 'obscures, if it does not misinterpret' (p. 858). Mr. Duff's remarks, *loc cit.*, pp. 209, 222, that Gierke was 'a most persuasive writer', a preacher and historian who sometimes exaggerates, may well be true.

13 D. 47, 22, 4, No. 5, fol. 148.

14 Those communities were permitted 'nisi quando illa aedificiorum collectio tenderet ad aemulationem alicuius civitatis', *loc cit.*

15 D. 1, 1, 5, No. 4.

16 D. 3, 4, 1, No. 2. Castrensis died 1441. This view was also held by the canonists, see, *e.g.*, Antonius de Butrio, c. 13, x, 5, 31, No. 6, and Cardinal Zabarellis, c. 3, x, 1, 31, No. 4. Both canonists belong to the 15th century.

meaning of the term, unless it became the seat of a bishop. But this requirement presupposed intervention and approbation by a superior authority. Unless and until the town had the privilege of being the seat of a bishop, it was, Bartolus taught, 'castrum, terra vel communantia'.[17]

In contrast to these legal organizations were those which did not purport to aim at the realization of some just cause, but which were founded for the promotion of an ethically reprehensible purpose. The idea of injustice, quite as broad as its counterpart, made those associations illegal, both in the realm of the *jus civile* and in that of the *jus gentium.* Monopolies were illegal associations within the province of the former. The jurists, especially those who taught at Bologna, complained bitterly of the pressure exercised by monopolizing organizations, and at the same time they spoke of the weakness of the State power to suppress and dissolve them. Monopolizing agreements entered into by the scribes, and those organized by the butchers, merchants and fishermen were shown as the most glaring examples of illicit organizations.[18] What particularly hampered the display of free economic development seems to have been the effective agreement amongst the Bolognese masons not to continue any work if the employer had dismissed a mason on account of unsatisfactory service. In his typically theatrical manner Odofredus introduced his lecture on the monopolies with this remark: 'O Signori, licet homines mali sunt, tamen retro non fuerunt omnes sancti. Olim fiebant monopolia in civitatibus . . .', but after dealing with the Bolognese masons, he exclaimed: 'Nec velit Deus, quod mihi contingat'.[19] Baldus reported that similar agreements existed between engineers and carpenters.[20] The jurists were unanimous in their condemnation of agreements whereby wheat and other necessary commodities could not be bought or sold under a certain amount. Salycetus complained about the monopolizing convention amongst the Bolognese tailors, cobblers and merchants in general. An interesting case of a clandestine monopoly was reported by Albericus de Rosciate. Citizens in possession of land were very much disliked by the farm labourers ('rustici'). These labourers therefore formed an association with the avowed aim that no member should inflict any damage on the land of certain wealthy citizens, under pain of being fined ten pounds. In fact, however, they had agreed not to work for those citizens singled out in their convention nor to render any assistance.[21] He, too, raised his protest against such obvious breaches of the law, but remarked that it is 'quasi impossibile' to take any action against those organizations because of the tremendous power and influence they wielded.

---

[17] Here again it is worth while quoting the whole passage, because its rendering by Gierke, *loc cit.*, was inaccurate: 'Et ista vera, quantum ad hoc, ut dicatur populus; quantum vero ad hoc, ut illa aedificiorum collectio sit civitas vel castrum seu villa, requiritur auctoritas superiorum. Nam in usu nostro non appellatur civitas, nisi episcopatum habens, sed episcopatum habere non posset sine superioris auctoritate: diceretur tamen castrum, terra seu communantia secundum modum diversum loquendi', Bartolus, D. 47, 22, 4, No. 5, fol. 148.

[18] It may be open to doubt whether those and the following organizations were monopolies in the strict meaning of the modern term.

[19] Odofredus in his lecture on C. iv, 59, fol. 255 *verso*.

[20] C. iv, 59, No. 3, fol. 131 *verso*.

[21] See his commentaries on C. iv, 59 *Rubrica*, fol. 228: 'Intelligebant, quod nullus debebat ei laborare nec juvamen aliquid praestare, quia sic clam perordinaverant inter eos in fraudem huius tituli.'

It was clear that associations, such as criminal societies, which pursued an evidently illegal aim were considered as illicit. So also, of course, were associations with seditious aims. Moreover, Paulus Castrensis went even so far as to declare that associations whose activities might lead to public scandal should be branded as illegal because of the danger to public order and discipline.[22]

This brings us to the illegal associations within the *jus gentium*. They were, above all, the leagues and confederations between city states and the 'barones', unless the cause of justice was to be promoted thereby. Bartolus was the first to draw attention to the illegal character of certain leagues. He advanced the argument that 'civitates' which already owed allegiance to one king or to some other overlord should not be permitted to form an independent federation. The reason for Bartolus's argument seems obvious. On the other hand, city states, such as those in Tuscany, which did not recognize any superior authority in temporal matters, were at liberty to enter into a confederation on a political basis. Bartolus returned to this subject in his tract *Qui sint rebelles*,[23] where he warned his readers against the danger of these leagues: he said that the leagues of the Perugians, Florentines and of the rulers in Lombardy were ostensibly founded for defence purposes, but were in fact only instruments for the advancement of unjustifiable political or ethical ends. They were, therefore, 'ipso jure nullae'. But if they were genuine federations for defence against activities of mischievous societies or against the encroachments of tyrant rulers—so frequently besetting Italy—they then were founded for a just cause and were permissible.[24] Baldus recalled the wholesale condemnation of all leagues by the canonist Guido de Baysio, who said that all political federations must be presumed to have been founded for an evil purpose. Baldus himself adhered to his own teacher's doctrine and stated that the aim which a league pursued decided its legality or illegality. Federations of cities for the purpose of ousting other cities in politics or economics should be regarded as illegal. Political emulation and strife were the professed aims of the Ghibellines and of the Guelfs. Consequently, by the unanimous consent of the doctors, these parties were classified as illegal. The hostility of the jurists towards these organizations was based on the conviction that they were disruptive of the political unity and stability within the body politic; that, in other words, they were factors disturbing the smooth and peaceful internal development and, consequently, might unduly upset the political and social balance within the State. That was, in particular, the well-considered view of Raynerius de Forlivio, who was consulted on this subject in Todi. He judged that both parties were illegal organizations. The controversy which he was called upon to decide resulted from the ejection from Todi of the Guelfs, who insisted that the city was under papal dominion. This declaration was considered by Raynerius as null and void, because if this declaration had been made by the Guelfs, not as a party, but as individual members, it

22 *Loc cit.*, No. 6.

23 *Versus* 'occulte'.

24 *Loc cit.*, No. 2: 'Non puto prohibitas tales societates seu collegiationes ad defendendum se ab impressionibus tyrannorum vel malarum societatum, quae saepe insurgunt in Italia ad depredendum alios. Fit enim ad justitiam servandam, ergo debet valere.'

was invalid, since individual declarations could not alter the status quo or affect the rights of a 'universitas', such as a city, and if it had been made by the Guelfs as a party, it could not be valid by reason of the illegal character of the whole organization.

The writings of the jurists provide ample testimony of the alarming growth of sectional organizations, and of the people's desire to found associations with more or less justifiable ends. At the same time the scholars raised their voices in protest against the laxity and leniency of public administration towards obscure, openly or clandestinely mischievous societies. The 'weakness of the Empire', its obvious inability firmly to handle and consistently to apply the law against illicit organizations together with the declining moral standards of public officials and the waning appeal of ethical principles to the population at large, were freely admitted to be the chief reasons for the exuberance of illegal associations. To counteract them the jurists demanded the full implementation of the sanctions which the law itself laid into the hands of its administrators. The type of sanction was to be dependent on the type of the illegal organization, or as Baldus lucidly expressed it: 'Imponuntur diversae poenae secundum diversos fines, ad quos istae congregationes fiunt'.[25] To take only a few examples, monopolizing organizations were to be punished with the expulsion of their members from the locality; seditious movements were to be stamped out by inflicting the death penalty upon their adherents; illegal political federations were to be suppressed by superior authority, whilst the members of criminal societies were to suffer death, and their illegally acquired property was to be confiscated. The conviction that it was particularly through the illegal political organizations that the safety of the Empire was jeopardized, haunted the minds of conscientious scholars. They made resolute, though in the end futile, attempts to stem the tide of those organizations which later contributed effectively to the break-up of the Empire. The internecine struggle brought about by the political organizations must be reckoned as one of the major causes of its downfall. The jurists as the upholders of the cause of law and order became the outspoken antagonists of those political organizations, but their purely verbal protests were too weak to convince the authorities of the seriousness of the danger.

---

[25] D. 3, 4, 1, No. 2, fol. 204.

XII

MEDIEVAL PRINCIPLES OF EVIDENCE.

IT cannot be denied that the knowledge of the principles and the structure of medieval proceedings, both criminal and civil, is somewhat obscured by a mist of prejudice and of consequent ill-informed criticism. Yet the writings of the medieval scholars of law on this topic not only show how detailed and elaborate their theory was in regard to the principles governing proceedings, but they also testify to the sound practical sense which was a characteristic feature of all their scientific investigations. It was, as Professor Esmein put it, 'the writings of the jurisconsults that brought criminal procedure to its perfect development'.[1] Averse as they were to all dogmatizing and theorizing for the mere sake of dogma and theory, the Postglossators had their eyes fixed upon the practical administration of the law. Moreover, before their ascent to the academic chairs in the various Italian universities, these Postglossators were, without exception, either judges or advocates themselves, and thus personally experienced the difficulties and problems which the practical administration of the law entailed. The principles, which they deduced from the daily application of the law, and which they cast into a workable system, were elaborated by them with the little assistance which they received from the few utterances of the Roman jurists. Justinian's codification formed, so to speak, merely the framework within which they worked. Judicial procedure and the judiciary with its function, organization and composition, had almost completely changed, since Justinian had codified Roman law. Furthermore, by the time of the classical period of the medieval jurists, that is in the fourteenth century, new ideas had been brought to bear upon the practice in the Courts, through the recognition of canon law as a source which, at least theoretically, had equal authority with that of the *Corpus Juris Civilis*. And, lastly, the practice of the ecclesiastical Courts evolved principles which were bound to react upon secular Courts, just as canonistic theory reacted upon the doctrines of the civilians. This theoretical and practical interplay resulted, then, in the establishment of certain fundamental principles which influenced Western legal thought to a very marked degree. We may well attempt to sketch briefly those principles laid down by the Postglossators, and we shall concentrate upon the evidence rendered by witnesses and by documents.

Whether in civil or in criminal proceedings, the judicial decision was to be based, not upon probabilities, let alone presumptions, but solely upon that degree of certainty of which the human mind was capable: the facts upon which the eventual legal decision was to rest, had to be proved so extensively that the opposite could reasonably be excluded and no reasonable doubt entertained. That kind of proof ('probatio') was at once considered necessary and sufficient 'circa quam non potest

[1] See A. Esmein, *History of Continental Criminal Procedure* (Continental Legal History Series), London, 1914, p. 291. It is, at the same time, unfortunate that this scholar devotes no more than four lines to the jurists of the fourteenth century; and still more unfortunate that he reckons the somewhat unoriginal, though prolific representatives of the fifteen and sixteenth centuries—Hippolytus de Marsiliis, Farinacius and Menochius—amongst those who 'shine with incomparable lustre', *loc. cit.*, p. 291–2.

Reproduced by permission of the publishers, Stevens & Sons Ltd.

intellectus errare, et ista est indubitata, quae nec elidi potest, sive loquimur in civili sive in criminali '.[2] But the jurists were unanimously agreed upon the requirement of more detailed evidence in criminal trials than in civil proceedings. ' Sed cur hoc tam varie ? ' asked Cynus,[3] discussing the differences between the two kinds of proceedings. The reply was that in criminal proceedings greater issues were at stake than in their civil counterparts, since the former concern the life, freedom and reputation of the accused.[4] That is why we read the stereotyped phrase in all lectures and commentaries that ' in criminalibus probationes debent esse luce clariores '. This difference showed itself in the demand for greater precaution, care, discretion and subtlety in criminal trials, or as Lucas de Penna expressed it: ' In criminalibus gravius est periculum, et ideo subtilius est consulendum '.[5] In short, a greater certainty of proof was demanded in criminal trials than in civil proceedings. In default of the greatest possible evidence against the accused he had to be acquitted: ' Sanctius est impunitum relinqui facinus nocentis quam innocentem damnare '.[6]

The idea that the reception of evidence was the principal means by which the truth relating to facts could be established, produced certain features characteristic of medieval proceedings. Perhaps the most characteristic feature was the function of the judge, especially in criminal trials, as the sole authority to determine the kind and amount of evidence. He alone was charged with the reception of evidence. This conception of the judge as a seeker after truth went hand in hand with the idea of the medieval jurists that judicial proceedings were conducted in the public interest. The public, they maintained, had an interest in the maintenance of law and justice, and the agency through which law and justice were to be materialized was conceived to be the judge: to achieve this aim, however, he was given complete liberty to determine which evidence and proof he considered necessary and adequate to establish the facts in dispute. The eventual decision was regarded as the concrete realization of justice which, in order to be true, had to be based upon fully established facts. Consequently, the judge was thought of as a seeker after truth who, in the performance of his judicial task, was to be free to weigh up the relative value of conflicting evidence, and also to be independent of the proposals by the parties. In his official capacity as a cognitional judge he was at liberty to hear those witnesses whose depositions he considered necessary for establishing the facts at issue. It is ' non in potestate partis ', Baldus taught, to examine the witnesses or to produce them: production and examination of the witnesses were the sole prerogatives of the judge who summoned those likely to assist him in his task.[7] Perhaps still clearer was the *dictum* of Bartolus who

[2] Baldus in his lecture on C. iv, 19, 25 no. 10, fol. 45.

[3] Cynus in his lecture on C. iv, 19, 23 no. 1.

[4] Cf. Cynus, *loc. cit.*: ' Quia de salute homis agitur, cautius est agendum '. Gomez, *Commentariorum Tomi Tres*, tom. iii, cap. 12, no. 25, fol. 552; ' Cum tractetur de vita et fama hominis '.

[5] Lucas de Penna in his commentaries on C. xi 65, 4 no. 6, fol. 276 *verso*.

[6] Bartolus on D. 48, 9, 5 no. 2, Lucas de Penna on C. x, 69, 2 no. 13, and the general opinion.

[7] Baldus on C. iv, 20, 19 no. 3, fol. 53: ' In examinandis testibus officium judicis debet esse curiosum, id est, judex debet esse solicitus et ad curam judicis pertinet hoc, scil. examinare, unde hoc non est in potestate partis '. See also Baldus on C. i, 3, 8 no. 8, fol. 37 *verso*: ' Pone, quod testes non sunt producti, sed judex ex mero officio

taught that, with or without a proposal by a party, 'judex tamen potest ex officio suo testes producere ad inquirendam veritatem'.[8] Therefore, the question as to whether the testimony of a witness was admissible was one to be answered by the judge *ex officio* in criminal proceedings, regardless of the proposal by a party, aiming at the exclusion of a particular witness.[9]

A corollary of the conception that judicial proceedings servc the public interest was the idea that every citizen concerned had the duty to appear as a witness before the Court. Unless this civic obligation was waived in certain cases by the law itself, nobody could rightfully claim to be exempted, on the grounds of some immunity granted in another respect. 'Nota', said Baldus,[10] 'quod ubi publica vertitur utilitas, infringitur singularis immunitas'.[11] And other jurists, such as Bartolus and Salicetus, maintained that giving evidence was an 'officium publicum' which even the unwilling person had to undergo.[12]

That the evidence to be given had to concern relevant facts was a principle which the medieval jurists readily grasped. The proposal of a party had to be investigated in order to ascertain whether the alleged knowledge of the proposed witness was pertinent to the facts to be established. All facts which had a bearing upon the legal interpretation of the case were considered relevant, even though they belonged only to 'appendiciis' as the Bolognese professor Nicholas de Mattarellis taught, because in connexion with facts or circumstances already proved, they, too, may assist the judge in establishing the truth relating to the facts at issue.[13] The whole weight of the testimony was conceived to lie in the source of the witness's knowledge.[14] In practical terms, the jurists said, the witness should not be asked whether Peter was the owner of a certain thing, or whether he was a drunkard or an irrascible person, for the answers to those questions constituted a conclusion from certain facts, a conclusion which it should be the office of the judge to draw. But if the witness should have stated that Peter was the owner of the contested thing, or was a drunkard, and the like, the judge should then have inquired further into the source of his knowledge, that is, into the 'causa scientiae'. It was sufficient, Lucas de Penna declared, when the witness stated that he saw Peter buying wool out of which he himself made the garment whose ownership was contested.[15] This jurist in summing-up his lengthy discussion said: 'Tota vis esse videtur in causa scientiae, quam testis in suo testimonio reddit, an sit sufficiens'.

The necessary prerequisite for a truthful reproduction of the 'causa scientiae' was the capability of the witness to register facts with one of

recipit eos. Quaeritur, an dictum eorum probet? Et dicendum est, quod non in civili causa, quia non potest judex in causa civili inquirere de facto ex mero officio . . . sed in criminali . . . potest ex mero officio recipere testes etiam post publicationem processus'.

8 Bartolus in his lecture on C. ix, 42, 2 no. 2, fol. 124. Baldus declared in his commentary on D. 22, 5, *Rubrica* no. 1, fol. 182: 'Nota, quod ad officium judicis spectat testem examinare et eius productionem'.

9 Gomez, *loc. cit.* no. 22, p. 551.

10 In his lecture on D. 22, 5, 8 no. 2, fol. 184.

11 In his commentary on D. 22, 5, 7 no. 1, fol. 183 *verso*, he said: 'Testes sunt compellendi ad ferendum testimonium'.

12 See Bartolus and Salicetus in their lectures on C. iv, 20, 19.

13 See the report of Baldus in C. iv, 20, 18 no. 8, fol. 51 *verso*.

14 Lucas de Penna on C. xii, 35, 13 no. 18.

15 *Loc. cit.*, no. 17.

the five senses. The witness was required to be an 'idoneus seu habilis testis'. The requirement of direct, sensual perception was insisted upon by all jurists. Thus Cynus, though still distinguishing between the registration of facts by the eye ('visus') and by the ear ('auditus') stated that the general term 'visus' embraced all sensual perception—'verbum "visus" seu "videre" largissime accipitur pro quolibet hominis sensu'[16]—and that truthful reproduction of external events depended upon their reliable registration in the human mind.[17] In short, the witness was required to reproduce facts registered 'de illo sensu, per quem rei veritas comprehenditur'.[18] And Baldus concisely summing up recapitulated that 'testis debet testificari per unum de quinque sensibus'.[19] This stipulation of reliably registering facts led necessarily to the exclusion of two main categories of witnesses, of whom the one category was prevented from giving evidence in any proceedings—we may call this an absolute incapacity—whilst the other category comprised individuals who were excluded as witnesses only in certain cases (so-called relative incapacity).

To the first category belonged, for understandable reasons, blind persons, who had not 'visum oculorum nec notitiam personarum et notitiae est testificatio visus et auditus'.[20] Children under fourteen years were inadmissible as witnesses because of their lowered faculties of perception and understanding: 'Quicquid talis aetas videt, ignorat', said Baldus.[21] Children were thought of as being incapable of giving testimony about the source of their knowledge. This presupposed, the scholars held, reasoning powers involving conclusions and other logical operations which could not be expected from persons under fourteen years of age.[22] Since criminal proceedings required a higher degree of reliability of the proofs than did civil trials, persons under twenty years of age were excluded as witnesses.[23] On the other hand, old age was not necessarily a reason of exclusion, although some of the jurists, such as Richardus Malumbra, maintained that this was so. Bartolus and Baldus rejected this opinion and pointed out that old age was only a bar to correct perception if the memory was disturbed, or if old age was characterized by infirmity which produced 'mental barrenness'.[24]

---

[16] Commentaries on C. iv, 20, 18 no. 7.

[17] 'Veritas proprie per visum percepta in mente tenetur'. He continued: 'Unde per qualemcumque sensum veritatem rei recipimus, sive gustu, ut in saporibus . . . sive odoratu, ut in odoribus . . . sive auditu, ut in verbis, quae audivimus . . . sive aspectu . . . videre ea dicimus, scil. per intellectum'.

[18] *Loc. cit.* In almost identical terms Bartolus on D. 22, 5, 3 (*Ideoque*) no. 1, fol. 155 *verso*: 'Testis debet testificare de his, quae percepit per aliquem sensum'.

[19] D. 22, 5, 3 (*Eiusdem quoque*) no. 2, fol. 182 *verso*. Innocent IV, *Commentaria super Libros Quinque Decretalium*, II, 20, 37 no. 3, fol. 262, declared a testimony invalid if the witness simply stated: 'Ego scio, quia nullus dubitat' or 'quia sic omnes dicunt'. It was, according to Innocent, sufficient, if the witness said: 'Ego scio, quia vidi', because this was sensual perception. All observations should be confirmed by one of the five senses. Thus the declaration of a witness that some food was sweet or bitter, must be corroborated by the statement: 'Quia ego gustavi', etc.

[20] Cynus on C. iv, 20, 18 no. 6, fol. 218.

[21] On C. iv, 20, 18 no. 8, fol. 51 *verso*.

[22] Lucas on C. xii, 35, 13 no. 17.

[23] This was the common opinion, see, *e.g.*, Bartolus on D. 48, 18, 20 no. 4, fol. 38 *verso*, Baldus on D. 22, 5, 19, fol. 184 *verso*, and Lucas de Penna on C. xi, 65, 4 no. 6.

[24] Baldus on D. 22, 5, 8 no. 1, fol. 184: 'Nisi sit talis senectus vel infirmitas, quae induceret mentis exilium vel faceret memoriam turbare'. There is a delightful description of old age in the philosopher jurist Lucas, C. xii, 3, 1 no. 5, where he discusses the value of the depositions of old people: 'Senes habent mores vituperabiles, nam sunt

The position of women was a controversial point. There was agreement amongst all scholars that pregnant women, if they wished to do so, might rightfully claim to be exempted—one of their privileges, Baldus declared.[25] Others would have extended this privilege to all women 'propter fragilitatem sexus'[26] or because they could not be considered as reliable on account of their unsteady character and their proneness to false testimonies. But, as far as we can gather, the general opinion did not accept this extreme antifeminist view. Thus, Gomez, the Spaniard, stated briefly: 'Vera et communis resolutio est, quod de jure civili indistincte mulier possit esse testis tam in civilibus quam in criminalibus'.[27] Other categories of inadmissible witnesses included perjurers, mentally deficient and imprisoned persons.[28] Baldus added monks and clerics to those incapable of giving evidence.[29]

The second category comprised individuals who were disqualified as witnesses only in certain cases. Cynus stated that witnesses who were moved by personal considerations for either party could not claim to command credibility: 'Non reputatur idoneus testis, qui gratia hominis moveretur ad dicendum'.[30] This applied to friend and enemy alike, for Cynus rightly saw that hatred and personal favour were apt to colour statements: 'Nam gratia et odio vacuus esse debet, qui testificatur'.[31] Cynus said, following Petrus de Bellapertica, his French master, that if it were necessary for a friend to be admitted, his testimony had not the same value as that of a personally disinterested individual.[32] If, however, the witness were an enemy to both parties, no reason could then be advanced to exclude him from giving evidence.[33] In practical terms, the wife was commonly considered inadmissible in all causes in which her husband was a party. The reason put forward was that she was 'under the husband's discipline',[34] or as Benedictus de Servia said: 'Maritus jus habet in ea'.[35] On the other hand, the position of the husband in causes affecting his wife was controversial. One group declared that he must be considered biased in these affairs: the husband, according to Paulus Castrensis, is a 'suspecta persona propter communem vitam et summam affectionem',[36] whilst others, such as Cynus and Bartolus, saw no reason to exclude him. Brothers were admissible in civil affairs, but not in criminal ones.[37] The statement of Paulus

---

nimis increduli, valde suspiciosi, timidi et pusillanimi, illiberales, difficiles aut malae fidei, non verecundi et inerubescitivi; item non sunt amativi, id est, ad amicitiam apti, sed potius severi, etenim raro gaudent delectatione'. But Lucas recognizes that youth alone is no guarantee for truthful observations, because they are often 'passionum insecutivi, de facili vertibiles et omnia quoddammodo pertinaciter asserentes, modum in suis actibus non habent'.

25 *Loc. cit.*, no. 1.

26 Angelus de Ubaldis on D. 22, 5, 18 no. 7.

27 *Loc. cit.*, no. 13, 547.

28 See Bartolus on D. 48, 18, 1 (*Item*) no. 5.

29 C. iv, 20, 11. 'Propter periculum irregularitatis, quod possent incurrere': see also Gomez, *loc. cit.*, no. 15.

30 Cynus on C. iv, 20, 5 no. 1, fol. 217.

31 *Loc. cit.*

32 'Istud tamen teneas, quod cum amicus admittitur, non facit tantam fidem sicut alius', *loc. cit.*

33 See Bartolus, *loc. cit.*

34 'Sub eius obedientia', Paulus Castrensis on C. iv, 20, 2 no. 3, fol. 187 *verso.*

35 See Cynus, *loc. cit.*

36 *Loc. cit.*

37 See, *e.g.*, Baldus on C. iv, 20, 5, fol. 188.

Castrensis that neither ascendants nor descendants should be heard as witnesses, seems to have been his individual opinion,[38] since a similar statement was not made by any other authority, although Spanish doctrine inclined to a similar view. Gomez said that the plaintiff's blood relations were to be excluded 'in infinitum' and his relations-in-law 'ad quartum gradum propter affectionem'.[39] If at the time of their depositions the witnesses actually belonged to the household of one party, their evidence was inadmissible.[40] Lastly, the position of a witness was incompatible with that of one of the parties. This was the common opinion: 'In causa propria non est quis idoneus testis'.[41] All those persons were excluded whose interests would have been affected by the final decision, or as Cynus put it: 'Propria causa dicitur, cuius commodum vel incommodum pertinet ad testem'.[42] That was the reason why the vendor could not be admitted as a witness in litigations concerning the transfer of the property.[43] The 'causa propria' also included litigations carried on by a tutor or a procurator on behalf of some individual, and consequently, the lawyer of a party was not an 'idoneus testis'. It was considered a breach of professional rules on the part of the lawyer to instruct the witness as to how and what to say. Odofredus, however, as usual little concerned with professional standards, maintained that the advocate may not instruct witnesses 'falso', but that he was allowed to inform them 'ut sciant veritatem'—a course which he himself had 'multotiens' adopted.[44] The mere fear of a witness that his testimony may possibly cause scandal, was not considered sufficient reason to exempt him.[45] The position of several co-defendants in criminal proceedings was not wholly clear. Bartolus would deny them the character of witnesses against each other,[46] whilst Cynus, following his teacher Jacobus de Arena, made the following distinction: if an acquittal of one accused automatically affected the others, co-defendants were not to be heard as witnesses; if this was not the case, Cynus said, there was no reason to deny them the character of witnesses.[47] In particular, robber bands were, strictly speaking, *societates lucri et damni*, their members were banded together for better or for worse, and therefore inadmissible as witnesses against each other. It should be emphasized once more that any disputed incapacity to appear as a witness, whether absolute or relative, fell within the competency of the judge to decide.

This point requires a closer examination of the function of the judge. The conception of the judge as a seeker after truth entailed that strict and binding rules of evidence were out of the question. The judge was

---

38 Castrensis on C. iv, 20, 5, fol. 187 *verso*.

39 Gomez, *loc. cit.*, no. 15, fol. 548. Innocent IV draws attention to the fact that in matrimonial causes parents should be allowed to appear as witnesses, because they know more about the true state of affairs in the family than strangers, *op. cit.* II, 20, 22 no. 1, fol. 258.

40 See Bartolus on D. 48, 18, 1 (*Item*) no. 2, and Salicetus on C. iv, 20, 8.

41 See Cynus on C. iv, 20, 10 no. 1, fol. 218, and Paulus Castrensis on C. iv, 20, 9 no. 1, fol. 188.

42 Cynus, *loc. cit.*

43 Cynus, *loc. cit.*, and the general opinion.

44 Odofredus on C. iv, 20, 18, and gleefully reported by Baldus in his lecture on D. 22, 5, 22 no. 1.

45 Baldus on D. 25, 5 *Rubrica* no. 11, fol. 182.

46 Bartolus on D. 48, 18, 1 (*Si servus*) no. 2, fol. 190.

47 Cynus on C. iv, 20, 11 no. 2, fol. 218.

considered to be entirely his own master, once the proceedings had reached the cognitional stage: he was at complete liberty in sifting and evaluating the evidence. In other words, the jurists would not allow this freedom to determine the relative value of conflicting evidence to be restricted by a straitjacket of fixed and rigid rules. Truth, they thought, is obtainable in many a way, and the discovery of truth would certainly not be furthered by forcing the judge to observe certain classes or rules of evidence. This profound thought was perhaps best expressed by Baldus: 'De fide argumentorum seu testium non potest tradi vera et certa regula propter hominum varietatem et negotiorum multiplicitatem et incognitam testium fidelitatem'.[48] This statement reveals a standard of legal and judicial culture which was far above that of many other countries in the fourteenth century.[49] 'Considera', Baldus counselled his hearers, 'ex omni genere probandi solvendam veritatem, non tamen arctandam ad unam probationis speciem, quia veritas, quae multis modis defensatur, opprimitur, et ideo mens judicantis non debet esse ligata'.[50] Therefore, this liberty of weighing up the respective value of testimonies made it impossible to lay down stringent rules as to when and how the statements of witnesses should be credited with trustworthiness. It was entirely left to the discretion of the judge—'arbitrio judicis' as the usual phrase ran [51]—whether he would accept their depositions as true or reject them. Bartolus declared: 'Nota, quod potestati judicis conceditur, utrum debeat adhibere fidem testi vel non'.[52] This principle of free evaluation of evidence was a cardinal tenet of medieval legal scholarship and practice. This same illustrious jurist, well acquainted with the intricacies of the actual proceedings and the problems frequently arising in the Courts of appeal, admonished the judges to give specific reasons in their decisions why they credited testimonies with trustworthiness or why they did not do so.[53] As a sequel to this cardinal tenet the jurists declared that quantity of evidence alone would not count, but solely the quality of statements: 'Virtus probationis non consistit in numero, sed in deponentibus magis'.[54] The scholars often pointed out that the testimonies of a small number of the aristocracy counted more than those of a multitude of farm labourers: 'Pauci nobiles testes multis rusticis et vilibus praeferendi sunt'.[55]

The indispensable requisite for the judge to form his opinion on the

---

48 Baldus on C. iv, 20, 18 no. 29, fol. 52.

49 And in certain European countries *Beweisregeln* were a characteristic feature as late as the end of the nineteenth century: the judge was bound to accept the statement of two witnesses as true, no matter how little he himself was convinced of the truth.

50 Baldus, *loc. cit.*

51 See Baldus on D. 22, 5, 3 (*Tu magis*) fol. 182: 'Judicis arbitrio committitur, quanta fides sit adhibenda testibus, et utrum sit adhibenda vel non'. See also Lucas de Penna, *loc. cit.*

52 Bartolus in his lecture on D. 22, 5, 3 no. 1, fol. 155 *verso.*

53 'Tamen', Bartolus continued in the same lecture, 'quia acta quandoque sunt examinanda in causa appellationis, tutius est, quod causam suspicionis propter quam fides testis minuitur, judex faciat apparere in actis'.

54 Baldus on D. 22, 5, 3 (*Eiusdem quoque*) no. 2, fol. 182 *verso.*

55 See Baldus on C. iv, 20, 18 no. 36, fol. 52; he continued: 'Quis autem dubitat magis credendum cardinalibus paucis quam multis pannosis clericis? Item quis dubitat minus credendum multis suspectis quam paucis omni exceptione marjoribus? . . . non enim ad multitudinem respici oportet'. See also Bartolus on D. 22, 5, 21 no. 1, fol. 156 *verso*: 'Statur enim potius dignitati quam numero, quod intellige nisi in numero sit magnus excessus'. This was the general opinion.

trustworthiness of witnesses was that they appeared before him personally. The jurists clearly realized the advantages of the personal interrogation by the judge. The personal impressions made upon the judge by the witnesses, their way of answering questions, their reactions and behaviour in Court, were the only means of ascertaining whether their statements were trustworthy or not.[56] It seems that at the time of Cynus the personal appearance of witnesses before the judge was only insisted upon in criminal proceedings: 'Testes debent in criminali coram judice venire', although another of his lectures contains the general statement that 'probatio vivae vocis est dignior quam vocis mortuae'.[57] At the time of Baldus, however, personal appearance before the cognitional judge was the ordinary procedure adopted in all trials: 'Dic, quod judex debet audire vivam vocem et sic qua constantia et qua trepidatione loquatur'.[58] Bartolus said that the judge should watch the witness carefully, 'qualiter se gerit'.[59] It was thought necessary, therefore, that the judge should not only take down the depositions of the witnesses, but also that he should put on record in the files any specific reactions, *e.g.*, that the witness stammered, hesitated in replying to a specific question, or showed fear during the interrogation: 'Ille, qui examinat testes', said Bartolus with an eye to the practice, 'hoc debet facere scribi in actis "hoc dicebat trepidando et balbutiendo"'.[60] All scholars emphasized that reliable records were a guarantee of an efficient administration of justice.

This principle produced three important consequences. Firstly, it was an illegality on the part of the judge to commission a notary with the reception of witnesses, a procedure sometimes apparently adopted by the less conscientious judges.[61] Secondly, a document made out by a notary in which a witness declared that he had seen the perpetration of a crime, could never be a substitute for the spoken word of the witness: if produced in Court, a document of that kind had no value as evidence.[62] Nevertheless, documents were adequate means of proof if the litigation concerned a point which was contained in a document, *e.g.*, forgery,[63] and furthermore, as means to establish auxiliary facts,

---

[56] Here again it should be pointed out that this principle—in the terminology of the nineteenth century it came to be called 'der Grundsatz der Unmittelbarkeit' (the principle of immediatcy)—was enacted in many continental codes of procedure not before the end of the century. Until then the written testimony of a witness was considered sufficient; hence the depositions of two witnesses tied the judge.

[57] I refer to Cynus's lectures on C. iv, 19, 23 no. 1, fol. 216 *verso*, and on C. iv, 20 *Rubrica*, fol. 217.

[58] Baldus on D. 22, 5, 3 (*Tu magis*) no. 2, fol. 182, repeated in many places, *e.g.*, C. iv, 19, 25 no. 13, fol. 46, and maintained by all scholars, see, *e.g.*, Paulus Castrensis on C. iv, 20, 2 no. 6, fol. 187 *verso*. See also Lucas on C. xi, 65, 4 no. 7: 'Ut magis scire valeat, quanta sit fides eius adhibenda . . . plurimum quidem in excutienda veritate etiam vox ipsa et cognitoris subtilis diligentia affert'.

[59] Bartolus on D. 48, 18, 10 (*Plurimum*) no. 2, fol. 192 *verso*.

[60] *Loc. cit.*, no. 3.

[61] See Bartolus and Baldus, *loc. cit.*, Lucas de Penna on C. x, 1, 2 no. 7.

[62] Cynus on C. iv, 19, 23 no. 2, fol. 216 *verso* gives us an example of a document of this kind: 'In nomine Dei, amen. In praesentia mei notarii et testium infra scriptorum, Sempronius percussit et vulneravit Titium cum una spata taliter, quod vidente me notario et testibus infra scriptis, dictus Titius in continenti cecidit in terra mortuus, ex dicto vulnere . . .'

[63] Baldus on C. iv, 19, 25 no. 13, fol. 45.

e.g., marriage certificates in cases of adultery.[64] And the third consequence of this principle was the right of the judge, if he was unable to form an opinion on the trustworthy character of the witness, to investigate *ex officio* the reputation of the witness and his past history.[65]

All testimonies were to be given on oath [66] which was administered in the presence of both parties before the witnesses proceeded to their depositions. The hearing itself was performed in the absence of the parties, only judge and clerk being present. But copies of the testimonies were handed over to the parties who could then propose further evidence. Even after the disclosure of the depositions the judge was entitled to hear the witnesses again, if this procedure was in his opinion likely to shed more light on the case. Bartolus stated: 'In qualibet criminali causa judex ex suo officio etiam post aperturam testium potest testes de novo recipere, tam ad offensam quam ad defensam'.[66a]

Documentary evidence, provided the dispute concerned the document itself, was fully admissible. A clear distinction was made between public and private documents. Public documents were those which were issued by some public official, especially by a notary. His documents made full proof 'quia notarius propter officium publicum et juramentum, quod praestat . . . non praesumatur scripsisse nisi veritatem'.[67] Private documents were all those which emanated from private persons and contained points relevant for the decision of the case. There were three kinds: acknowledgments of receipt of payments ('apochae'), commercial registers and minute books, and also private letters. The first kind constituted full proof, if the opponent admitted it to be written with his own hand [68]; if he denied it, the document could still make full proof, if his signature had been witnessed and attested by three other persons.[69] Similar rules were laid down for the other kinds of private documents. In general, Bartolus said, private documents had the same force as the spoken word of their writer: 'Privatae scripturae creditur tantum, quantum crederetur voci illius scribentis'.

Bartolus developed a very interesting theory of the various mental operations which could be distinguished in a judge when weighing up the evidence. Bartolus set out from the axiom that the judge must arrive at the conviction that certain facts could be taken as proved. Now the question arises, Bartolus said, as to how the judge reaches that mental state of being convinced that a fact had been proved. That mental state Bartolus called 'credulitas'.[70] This concept covers the

---

[64] Bartolus on D. 22, 5, 3 (*Idem divus*) fol. 155 *verso*; 'Possunt tamen produci instrumenta super his, quae pertinent ad adminicula maleficii, ut in causa adulterii, si produco instrumentum matrimonii'.

[65] See, *e.g.*, Baldus on D. 22, 5, 3 no. 1, fol. 182: 'Adverte, quod judex de omnibus conditionibus testis debet investigare ex suo officio ab hominibus bonae opinionis'.

[66] An example of an oath is given by Baldus, C. i, 3, 8 no. 4, fol. 37 *verso*: 'Juro dicere meram et puram veritatem pro utraque parte de his, super quibus sum productus et de quibus fuero interrogatus'. Cynus said that the witness could swear by the Gospels or by touching a statue of Christ or even by some saint. Petrus de Bellapertica taught Cynus that it was correct to swear by the prince: see Cynus on C. iv, 20, 18 no. 5, fol. 218: 'Item jure nostro juratur per principem, et istud juramentum est sufficiens secundum Petrum'.

[66a] D. 48, 5, 2 (*Si publico*) no. 15, fol. 167.

[67] Castrensis on C. iv, 19, 18 no. 1, fol. 184.

[68] Bartolus on D. 12, 2, 31 no. 25, fol. 33 *verso*.

[69] Bartolus, *loc. cit.*

[70] Bartolus in his lecture *loc. cit.*, fol. 33: 'Videndum est, qualiter judex ad istam fidem seu credulitatem adducetur'.

province which lies between 'scientia' and 'nescientia', since there can be no 'credulitas' in matters which cannot be known nor in those which are known.[71] In other words, 'credulitas' takes place, according to Bartolus, only in cases which are decided upon circumstantial or presumptive evidence. It is through logical operations that the judge arrives at this mental state which is preceded by three clearly distinguishable stages of mental operations. The first stage is that of doubt: the facts upon which the plaintiff or the prosecutor bases his claim, are denied by his opponent. The characteristic feature of doubt is, Bartolus continued, that the mind has not applied itself to either proposition: 'Est enim dubitare, quando quis non applicat magis animum suum ad unam partem quam ad aliam'. The second stage is that in which the judge is only *inclined* to accept a proposition as proved, and this stage Bartolus called 'suspicio', and in this stage a good deal of doubt remained: 'Jam incipit animus judicis adhaerere uni parti, licet remaneat dubium'. A weaker form of 'suspicio' is the 'opinio' of the judge which is still tinged with doubt. In neither of these three stages would the judge be justified in taking a fact as proved. He might accept the proof of a fact, if, according to the rules of logic, no reasonable doubt could exist, that is to say, if the arguments conclusively proved an actual event or fact. The argumentation, whilst not permitting of any other reasonable conclusion, must be natural and intelligent. When the judge arrived at this conclusion, he was said to be in the mental state of 'credulitas': the judge was then fully convinced. Its effects are identical to those of 'scientia', though both ends are reached by different channels, the one by argumentation and logical operations, the other by direct, sensual perception: 'Tamen est differentia in modo perveniendi ad istam adhaesionem, nam sciens perducitur ad hanc scientiam seu adhaesionem per sensum, credens per alia argumenta'. This doctrine of Bartolus was, as Paulus Castrensis testified, later generally accepted.[72] The influence of Bartolus' doctrine upon theory and practice can perhaps best be gauged from the treatment of one and the same case before and after his time. The accused was seen, with the sword drawn, fleeing from a house in which a man was found dead. Whilst Cynus, Bartolus' teacher, entertained no doubt that the accused should be condemned for murder, Gomez declared, expressly referring to Bartolus' doctrine, that 'per hoc non poterit condemnari', since the incriminating circumstances were capable of other interpretations, and the death might be explained in other ways: the accused might have acted in self-defence, or somebody else might have committed the murder, or the death was not caused by any illicit action at all.[73] The same Spaniard concluded

[71] 'Praemitto quaedam extrema, quae omnino sunt extra fidem et credulitatem et primo est nescientia, illud enim, quod homo nescit, de eo non est fides nec credulitas . . . secundo est scientia vera . . . et inter ista duo extrema, scil. nescientiam et scientiam, est quoddam medium, videlicet credulitas'.

[72] Paulus Castrensis on C. iv, 19 *Rubrica* no. 4, fol. 179. An interesting case of circumstantial evidence was reported by Cynus in his lecture on C. iv, 20, 18 no. 9, fol. 220 *verso*: 'Testis deponit, quod aliquid vidit, ex quo verisimiliter dicit se credere, ut quia deponens super adulterio vel copula carnali dicit, quod vidit nudum cum nuda facere, quod homines et mulieres faciunt in talibus, scil. crura agitare atque crissare, non tamen scit, si rem intrinsecam peragerent, et ex hac extrinseca visione deponit, quod credit firmiter, quod adulterium commiserunt. Certe istud tale testimonium credulitatis, quae venit in visione, de qua deponit testis, bene admittitur et valet'. Cynus made out a case of a 'vehement presumption', and in this way could justify condemnation.

[73] Gomez, *loc. cit.*, no. 25, fol. 552.

that 'ubicumque esset possibile rem aliter se habere, non statur indiciis'.[74]

A position identical to that of a witness was afforded to the expert. He was called upon to give information to the judge 'in rebus, quae sunt artis seu scientiae alicuius per rationes et demonstrationes'.[75] The testimony of obstetricians in sexual offences was particularly insisted upon by Baldus who preferred the expert statements to the well-meaning, but often unreliable testimonies of witnesses.[76] Although the jurists did not yet clearly distinguish, in terminology, between the expert and the witness, they nevertheless grasped the essential difference between the latter testifying a 'factum' and the former expressing an opinion by reason of his special knowledge 'artis seu scientiae'. It is to Bartolus that we owe the distinction between witness and expert.

We have briefly sketched the leading ideas and principles governing the reception of evidence which were propounded by the medieval scholars of law. Their writings, especially on this topic, reveal a standard of judicial procedure and of legal culture in general, which proved to be a model for the great European legal reform movements in centuries to come, until political and social upheavals in our own time temporarily threw European legal culture back to the days, before the Postglossators, the pioneers of the theory of law, bequeathed to the world their fundamental ideas of evidence based upon the twin conceptions of justice and truth.

---

[74] Baldus on C. iv, 19, 25 no. 5, fol. 45, recalled another case which referred to circumstantial evidence only, but which was not the same as the one mentioned in the text. The accused entered a house and after a while the screams of a woman were heard; immediately afterwards the accused was seen fleeing from the house, blood on his sword ('cum sanguinolento gladio') and the woman appeared to have cuts in her face. 'Unde dubitatur', Baldus asked, 'an esset probatum de vulnere contra illum et videbatur, quod non, quia non fuit visus in vulnerando'. But Baldus advised condemnation of the accused, because one cannot easily say that she herself inflicted the wounds: 'Quia non praesumitur ipsamet sibi vulnus inflexisse, sed passam esse ab inimico'.

[75] Bartolus on D. 12, 2, 31 no. 16, fol. 33.

[76] Baldus on C. iv. 20, 18 no. 36, fol. 52: 'Unde obstetricibus dicentibus cognitam magis credendum est quam dicentibus virginem . . .'

XIII

HONORIUS III AND THE PROHIBITION OF LEGAL STUDIES

THE famous decree of Pope Honorius III by which the clergy were forbidden to study or to teach Roman civil law, marks the end of a development in ecclesiastical and papal policy which had begun nearly a century before Honorius III issued the decree " Super Speculam ". The decisions of the Council at Rheims of 1131 contained a provision whereby monks were to be excluded in future from studying Roman law (and medicine).[1] This decree, though in the first place directed against monks only, breathed the spirit of St. Bernard : he it was who first raised his voice against the predominance of the laws of Justinian in the palace of the Popes, where not these, but the laws of the Lord should reign supreme. The prohibition to study the civil laws was repeated by the second Lateran Council (1139),[2] a little later by the Council held at Tours (1180)[3] and above all by Pope Alexander III. The latter's decree was incorporated in the *Compilatio Prima* by Bernardus Papiensis,[4] and thence made its way into the Gregorian collection (1234).[5] Whilst all these decrees concerned monks only, Honorius III, on November 22, 1219, extended the scope of the prohibition to all secular priests; moreover, the Civil Law School at the University of Paris

---

1 See Mansi, *Sacrorum Conciliorum . . . Nova et Amplissima Collectio*, tom. xxi, col. 459.

2 Mansi, *loc. cit.*, col. 528. To judge by his *Concordantia Discordantium Canonum* (the *Decretum*), Gratian, himself a Camaldunensian monk, was well versed in Roman law, see the penetrating analyses by A. Vetulani " Une suite d'études pour servir à l'histoire du ' Décret ' de Gratien " in *Revue historique de droit français et étranger*, 1936, pp. 343–58, 1937, pp. 461–79, 674–92, and 1947, pp. 11–48.

3 Mansi, col. 1179.

4 Lib. III, tit. Ne clerici vel monachi, c. 2.

5 *Liber Extra*, III. l. 3.

was abolished—a step that was not retraced until 1679, when the University was again empowered to resume the systematic teaching of the civil law.[6]

The decree of Honorius III consisted of three parts. Although Potthast [7] registers it as having been issued " to the archbishops, bishops, prelates and chapters in Sweden ", a MS. copy of the decree preserved in the Laurenziana in Florence,[8] to which Professor S. Kuttner first drew attention a few years ago,[9] heads the decree " Honorius III universis prelatis ". In this MS. the first part, beginning " Sane licet sancta ecclesia ",[10] appears under the heading " De Constitutionibus ", the second part, " Sane licet fallax ",[11] bears the title " Ne clerici vel monachi se negotiis se immisceant ", whilst the third part, " Volumus et mandamus ", is headed by the title " De Magistris ".[12] The decree was embodied in this tripartite form in the *Compilatio Quinta* (1225).[13] But this MS. is also noteworthy from another point of view, for it contains an *Apparatus* of glosses written by Guilielmus Vasco (or Guascus), a Gascon canonist, supplemented by glosses from the pen of Johannes Teutonicus. As regards the latter's canonistic activity we are fairly well informed, but we know practically nothing about the former, except that he was a master of canon law at the University of Padua in the year

---

6 See Savigny, *Geschichte des Römischen Rechts im Mittelalter*, vol. iii, p. 373.

7 Potthast, *Regesta Pontificum Romanorum*, No. 6165.

8 MS. S. Croce, Plut. V sin. 4, fly-leaf. I desire to express my thanks to the Librarian of the Laurenziana for his permission to obtain a photostatic copy of this MS.

9 S. Kuttner, " Bernardus Compostellanus Antiquus " in *Traditio*, vol. i, 1944, p. 337, note 43. Kuttner also discovered another copy in the National Library, Lisbon (Alcob. 381), but I was unable to obtain a photostat from this library.

10 *Extra*, V. xxxiii. 28.

11 *Extra*, III. l. 10.

12 *Extra*, V. v. 5.

13 *Comp. V*, V. xii. 3, III. xxvii. 1; V. ii. 1. The *Compilatio Quinta* was issued in 1225 and was the second official collection of decretals, the first being the *Compilatio Tertia* in 1210. On the exact date of its composition see now Kuttner in *Miscellanea Mercati*, 1946, vol. v, p. 621. The *Comp. V* did not enjoy the same popularity as the previous collections: the MSS. are very rare and the compilation was not the subject of intensive scientific enquiries. One *Apparatus* on the collection, written by Jacobus de Albengo, is in the British Museum, MS. Royal, 11 C VII, fols. 246r–271v. Further MSS. listed by Kuttner, *Repertorium*, pp. 383–5

1226 and that he had written glosses on the *Compilatio Prima* and *Quarta*.[14] His *Apparatus* on this Honorian decree must have been written shortly after its promulgation, since no useful purpose would have been served by the glossing of an individual decree after its inclusion in the fifth collection of decretals. As far as the present writer could establish, neither the glosses of William nor those of Johannes were referred to by later canonists.

The first three glosses of this *Apparatus* in the Laurenziana bear the siglum " Guil ", whilst all the others simply have " G ". The decretalist and teaching activity of William the Gascon seems to have begun in the last decade of the twelfth century, for in a *Summa Quæstionum* composed towards the end of the century by the Archdeacon of Richmond in Yorkshire, Honorius,[15] we find very numerous references to, and discussions with, a " Magister G ", and the possibility cannot be excluded that he had taught at one of the English schools of canon law : it is, however, a mere tentative suggestion based upon the equally numerous references by Archdeacon Honorius to a " Magister jo " who may have been a contemporary of William and identical with the " Magister jo " frequently referred to in the *Quæstiones Londinenses*, which are certainly a product of an English canonistic school.[16]

But let us return to the decree itself. This decree aroused interest and was much discussed in former times [17]

---

14 Kuttner, *art.cit.*, *loc.cit.*, at notes 38 and 42.

15 About his struggle for the archdeaconry of Richmond and his successful pleadings with Innocent III, see Roger of Hoveden, *Chronica*, R.S., vol. iii, p. 298, vol. iv, pp. 9, 52, 158, 159, 177, 181; A. Hamilton Thompson, " The Registers of the Archdeaconry of Richmond " in *Yorkshire Archæological Journal*, vol. xxv, 1920, pp. 131–5, and also *Early Yorkshire Charters* (ed. C. T. Clay), vol. iv, 1935, pp. xxv–xxvi.

16 The MS. of this *Summa Quæstionum* is in the Cistercian Monastery of Zwettl, Lower Austria, MS. no. 162, fols. 178r–213ra, although I think that this *Summa* in this MS. is incomplete. In this Codex there are also the *Generalia* of another English canonist, Richard de Lacy, fols. 73–82, as well as his *Ordo Judiciarius*, fols. 83–94, and his *Distinctiones*, fols. 105–122vb. The *Quæstiones Londinenses* are in the BM., MS. Royal 9 E. VII, fols. 191–198v, and were written between 1196 and 1198.

17 Cf. also Esmein, in *Mélanges Fitting*, vol. i, 1907, pp. 198–201, and Fournier in *Nouvelle Revue historique de droit français et étranger*, 1890, pp. 80 ff.

because of its prohibition of legal studies at Paris. And yet, the decree also bears a definite political complexion which emerges clearly from its first part,[18] and to which too little attention has been paid. Here in the first part the Pope drops all pretence of motivating his prohibition by a recourse to purely clerical, ecclesiastical or moral reasons. Quite bluntly he states that, on the one hand, lay people in France and other provinces do not use and apply the laws of the Roman emperors, and, on the other hand, that there are rarely ecclesiastical causes which cannot be decided on the basis of the existing canon law. In other words, Honorius's clearly expressed opinion was that the civil laws had become obsolete, at least as far as France was concerned : they were not necessary, firstly because the French people and others did not live according to them, and secondly because the canon law catered for all ecclesiastical exigencies.

This last statement, however, should not pass without comment. It should be borne in mind that at the time of the promulgation of this decree (1219) there was only one official collection of decretals, the *Compilatio Tertia*, consisting of decretals issued by its promulgator, Innocent III, during the first twelve years of his pontificate; this collection was published in 1210. None of the other collections bore any official imprint. The *Compilatio Prima* was the private work of Bernardus Papiensis (published 1192), the *Compilatio Secunda* was the work of the Welshman, Johannes Galensis, which he compiled on the basis of two previous and private collections (those of Alanus and Gilbertus), whilst the *Compilatio Quarta*, composed by Johannes Teutonicus contained the decisions of the fourth Lateran Council (1215) and a number of Innocentian decretals; it was published in the early summer of 1216,[19] but papal approbation was refused.[20] It was only through

---

18 *Extra*, V. v. 5.

19 See Kuttner in *Miscellanea Mercati*, pp. 626–7.

20 Johannes Teutonicus who himself presented his work to Innocent, left the curia " ira sucensus ", see the transcription of the report in MS. Vat.Borgh. 45, fol. 23r, § 13, by Kuttner, *loc.cit.*, pp. 626, 633.

the law schools that these collections were accorded, so to speak, an academic standing; even the designation Prima, Secunda, and so forth, were only names given to the compilations by the professors of canon law. Next to these academically recognized collections there were numerous other private collections which did not, however, enjoy academic favours. It was not until 1234 that Gregory IX officially published most of the decretals contained in the five previous compilations: the *Gregoriana* was therefore the first canonical and official law book. In view of this legal state of affairs it is a euphemism on the part of Honorius III to speak of existing canon law, since in the words of the bull of publication by Gregory IX (September 5, 1234) constitutions, decretals and letters of Popes were dispersed in so many different places: and the reason for the publication of the *Gregoriana* was precisely to put an end to the intolerable confusion.

The implications of Honorius's decree in the political sphere are not difficult to see. Just at that time papal political aspirations had reached their zenith—the pontificate of Innocent III had imprinted itself on nearly every European country, and in no other political unit had papal policy, ably stimulated and supported by canonistic doctrine, been felt more strongly than in the empire. Here the peculiar circumstances after Emperor Henry VI's death had enormously helped in actively promoting the aim of all medieval papal policy: the subjection of the Emperor to the Pope. Innocent III's *Registrum de negotio Romani imperii*[21] bears eloquent witness to the widely flung aims of the Roman curia. By the time Honorius had become Pope, the young Frederick II was still an obedient son of the Church; there was not the slightest indication that he would ever become the deadliest enemy of everything the papacy stood for. Now it was not, of course, the person of the Emperor that antagonised the papacy, but the political

---

21 Printed in Migne, *Patr.Lat.*, vol. ccxvi, and now newly edited by W. Holtzmann, *Das Register des Papstes Innozens III*, vol. i, Bonn, 1947–8, on the basis of the facsimile of the Vatican MS.

ideas as they were enshrined in the *leges*, that is to say, in the Roman law which not only made the Emperor the *dominus mundi*, but made also his laws *universally* applicable. The conflict between empire and papacy was one for the predominance of the one body of law over the other: the conflict concerned the supremacy of Roman law or Canon law. More than any other single factor, it was the law of the Emperor which, according to curial designs, had to give way to the law of the Pope. The *leges* coming down from ancient Rome formed the ideological backbone of the imperialist claims, and proved the strongest ideological barrier to the advancement of papal aims. Hence, it was a matter of secondary importance whether or not there was a personal ruler of the empire. According to the papal plans, then, the target of the attack was not so much the Emperor as his laws demanding as they did universality of application and supported as they were by the myth of veneration that radiates from an ancient and especially Roman institution. But when it could be established that these laws were no more obeyed, when therefore they had become obsolete, and this above all in a vital country such as France, the imperial claim was bound to lose much of its inherent force. Nor should we forget the fact that when Honorius III issued his decree " Super Speculam ", Frederick II was still a mere king of the Romans, and not yet an emperor crowned by the hands of Pope Honorius III. The coronation did not take place until the following year.

In this decree, then, we may plainly see a dangerous, because so much tucked away, manifestation of the perennial papal design to deprive the Roman civil law of its universal character. The decree formed a not unimportant link in the deployment of papal arguments which were to weaken the cause of the Empire and to strengthen its own. Perhaps the foremost political Pope of the Middle Ages, Innocent IV, also recognised in the study of the *leges* a continual threat to the advancement of papal aims. It is not therefore surprising to find that this Pope in 1253, extended the prohibition of Honorius III to England, Scotland, Hungary, Spain and the whole of medieval France.[22]

The political implications of Honorius's decree were dimly conceived by the Gascon canonist in his glosses. Firstly, according to Justinian himself, says William, the civil laws do not consider themselves unworthy followers of the canon law [23] and those civil laws which do not pursue this line may safely be disregarded,[24] the implication being that there is really no *raison d'être* for the civil laws, especially as they are not used. And this brings the glossator to the second point. He praises Honorius for employing the term " leges ", because the Pope thereby did not mean to exclude the Lombard laws which, William maintains, are still in use [25] and which, together with customary law, have the force of law.[26] These laws, then, are harmless, because they can never be anything else but territorially restricted laws : they lack precisely the offensive feature which the imperial laws so blatantly exhibit. Moreover, as Johannes Teutonicus says, s.v. " raro ", the rare cases which cannot be decided on the basis of canon law, certainly would

---

22 See Bulæus, *Historia Universitatis Parisiensis*, tom. iii, pp. 265 f, Savigny, *op.cit.*, vol. iii, pp. 369–70, Denifle, *Chartularium Universitatis Parisiensis*, vol. i, no. 235, and Matthew Paris, *Chronica Majora*, vol. vi (Addidamenta), pp. 293–5; this Innocentian bull is also printed by Fournier, *loc.cit.*, pp. 118–9. Denifle, *loc.cit.*, doubts the authenticity of this bull " Dolentes " (which is addressed to "omnibus prælatis in regno Franciæ, Angliæ, Scotiæ, Walliæ, Hispaniæ et Hungariæ constitutis), but Fournier, with good reasons, dispelled these doubts, pp. 98 ff. In this context it should also be borne in mind that Innocent IV who had founded the University of the Roman Court (1244–1245) and who had so much inveighed against the study of Roman law (in this bull he maintained that it was through the study of Roman law that " affliguntur liberi, et servi obtinent principatum "), nevertheless especially encouraged the study of Roman law at *his* University. Innocent IV was too great a jurist not to know the value of Roman law for the development of a legal mind, and he fully recognized that canon law without Roman law was but an empty shell. But the study of Roman law was to be carried on within the protected walls of the Roman University.

23 *Authenticum*, collatio VI, xii, 1; see also v. 9.

24 " Dic . . . secundum eas posse judicari, si concordant cum canone . . . sed si contradicant, non . . . "

25 s.v. " leges ": " Bene dicit ad differentiam lombardæ, qua utuntur ".

26 " Utuntur etiam jure consuetudinario sive generali sive speciali, quod pro lege accipitur."

not justify a further recognition of the civil laws, just as it would be idle to deduce a rule from very rare events, such as the resurrection of Lazarus or the birth of a monstrous child, and the like. Hence, on the strength of this consideration, too, the *raison d'être* of the civil laws is in abeyance, and therefore the implication is quite plain : the Roman civil laws had become obsolete.

An attack on Roman civil law in more or less veiled form was, however, only one of the reasons which motivated Honorius III to issue the bull " Super Speculam ". The other and equally important reason is no less political, namely, to give papal support to the French monarchy, so as to secure a vigorously ascending nation as a capable ally in the contest against the Empire ; and in this second reason we may well find an anticipation of the policy pursued a century later during the pontificates of Clement V and John XXII. The late Hastings Rashdall [27] already hinted at this genesis of " Super Speculam " when he said that the Pope " was seconded by the French king's suspicion of a legal system which endangered the supremacy of the customary law of his country in the courts of his capital ". And Sir Maurice Powicke draws attention to an ordinance of Philip IV which shows that Philip Augustus was instrumental in procuring the decree, in order to emphasize the validity and independence of the French customary law.[28] In discussing the extent and scope of the term used in the bull, " parisiis, civitatibus seu aliis locis vicinis ", in which the study and teaching of civil law was to be prohibited, the Gascon canonist asserted that through this prohibition " crescit regia " (*scil.* potestas).[29] This interpretation by William is not weakened by his explanation of the term " vicina " which, he says, means a distance to be covered within two days. " Sed quae loca dicis esse vicina? Forte usque ad duas dietas." William here simply adopts the terminology

---

[27] *The Universities of Europe in the Middle Ages*, ed. F. M. Powicke and A. B. Emden, vol. i, p. 323.

[28] *Ed.cit.*, *loc.cit.*, p. 322, note 2, and Fournier, *loc.cit.*, p. 106.

[29] s.v. " parisiis ".

of a " not too remote place " which had been given by Innocent III in the fourth Lateran Council a few years before (1215).[30] But it was not some remote place, but the capital of France that mattered and where Philip Augustus was vulnerable. No danger could accrue to him, if somebody were to set up a school of law three or four days' journey from Paris. Nevertheless, the Gascon was careful enough to say that this prohibition was territorially restricted and that it would be absurd to maintain—as conceivably it might—that Honorius's terms should be applied to the whole world : it is necessary to give this definition of a vicinity, William says, " alias sequeretur, quod una civitate vel loco interdicto totus mundus esset interdictus, quod esset absurdum ".

The further contents of this *Apparatus* are of little interest today and do not touch upon the political aspects of the decree. The two glossators point out that those who disobey this prohibition are on an equal footing with the murderers of clerics and monks[31] ; that particular care should be taken concerning the secret teaching of civil law, so that " omnis fraus evitetur " ; that no bishop is allowed to grant a dispensation from this prohibition[32] whose violation entails automatic excommunication ; and so forth. However much both these canonists backed the Honorian decree forbidding all clerics to study Roman law, their *Apparatus* does not give an example worthy of imitation by their canonistic brethren : their glosses have at least as many references to the Roman law as they have to the canon law. Nor should we omit to refer to the somewhat unfavourable reception with which Alexander III's decree[33] was met by the earlier generation of canonists. Although Alexander merely forbade monks to frequent the universities in order to study the civil laws and medicine

30 c. 37, and *Comp. IV*, I. De Rescriptis, c. Nonnulli.

31 With a reference to the *Decretum*, C.XVII, q. iv., c. 29, and C.XXIV, q. viii, c. 30.

32 "Dico episcopum non posse dispensare quantum ad leges et physicam, secus circa alias facultates non prohibitas . . . G."

33 *Extra*, III. 1. 3.

—and this for reasons quite different from those which prompted Honorius—some canonists, if we can believe the Englishman Alanus, tried to interpret it in such a way that monks who went to a university with the intention of studying laws (or medicine), in order to be useful to their monasteries afterwards, would not violate the Alexandrian prohibition. " Hanc prohibitionem non intelligunt (*scil.* quidam) in casu, ubi in tali intentione audire volunt." [34] As in so many other respects the pontificate of Innocent III had considerably contributed to stiffening the attitude of the canonists, even towards such narrow-minded and illiberal decrees as " Super Speculam ".

---

[34] This gloss of Alanus is incorporated in Tancred's *Apparatus* on the *Compilatio Prima*, III Ne clerici, c. Non magnopere (c. 2), s.v. " leges ", fol. 38vb, of the MS. C. III 4, Durham Cathedral Chapter Library. Alanus introduced this passage: " Quidam tamen dicunt, quod pro necessitate . . . monasterii liceat eis physicam et leges sæculares audire ". It is noteworthy that this report of Alanus was not repeated by any of the later canonists whom the present writer consulted.

XIV

MEDIEVAL VIEWS CONCERNING PAPAL ABDICATION

IN a rather inconspicuous manner modern canon law lays down (can. 221) that the validity of the abdication of the Pope does not depend on its submission to a consistory or to any other body. Modern canon law, therefore, quietly takes for granted the constitutional possibility of the abdication of a Pope. Medieval canonistic theory, on the other hand, though continually touching upon this point, was by no means unanimous in its verdict. On the contrary, the medieval canonists were very much at loggerheads on this purely constitutional issue, and the whole problem received a fresh impetus by the abdication of Pope Celestine V on 13th December, 1294. This Pope's abdication was by no means accepted as valid by all the canonists, and it was only after the promulgation of Boniface VIII's decree in his *Liber Sextus* (I., vii. 1) that the question received some authoritative ruling and was answered in the affirmative. As we can gauge from Boniface's introductory remarks to his decree, Celestine's step was certainly viewed with some apprehension by a number of ecclesiastics.[1] The fundamental question confronting the consistory was this : was it constitutionally in order for a Pope to resign his office once he had consented to the election by the cardinals ? Celestine V himself, his successor assures us in his decree, had presided over the fateful consistory in which the unanimous decision was reached that the Roman Pontiff was at liberty to resign from his office. By way of exemplification the alleged or admitted inability of the Pope to govern the Church was adduced, but only as one out of many reasons for the Pontiff's step. The specific mentioning of this motive of abdication, although clearly intended to be no more than an indication of a number

[1] See specially the First Manifesto of the Colonna Cardinals against Boniface VIII, printed by H. Denifle in *Archiv f. Literatur u. Kirchengeschichte*, vol. v., pp. 493 ff.

of possible motives, somehow seems to have detracted from the general applicability of this decree. For the canonists continued debating the problem whether, apart from any self-confessed inability to rule as a supreme pontiff, he could abdicate on other grounds. As far as it is possible to determine, this interesting constitutional problem was not settled until 1918 when the new *Codex Juris Canonici* was promulgated. In this, as in so many other instances, the somewhat matter-of-fact legal announcement appears to the modern mind as the direct result of constitutional theory, and the passage (can. 221) would not convey to the student of canon law the very heated and profound arguments of former times which attempted to find an answer to the question : ' Is there anything in the divinely instituted office of the Papacy, established by Christ Himself, which renders that office inabdicable ? ' The modern canon law is a particularly good example of the influence of theory upon the mind of the legislator, and it may not therefore be without interest to review briefly the arguments for and against the constitutional right of the Pope to resign his office.

One of the chief reasons adduced to show the invalidity of the Pope's abdication was connected with the unique position which his consecration by the cardinal-bishop of Ostia was alleged to entail. By this consecration the elected candidate was made a bishop and therefore automatically became Bishop of the universal Church. Chiefly following the doctrines of the Master of the Sentences, Peter Lombard,[1] canonistic doctrine maintained that the universal episcopate of the Pope could not be compared with any other sacerdotal power : hence any regulations specifically applying to bishops and their rights to resign their offices were found to be inapplicable to the case of the universal Bishop at Rome.[2]

[1] *Liber Sententiarum*, iv. 24.

[2] Bishops were given the right to renounce their episcopal dignities, see Alexander III in *Decretales*, I., xiii. 1. It will be recalled that the resignation of bishops gave rise to some delicate ecclesiastical questions, particularly the problem of the so-called re-ordinations; on this cf. R. Saltet, *Les Réordinations*, 1907, and A. Schebler, *Die Reordinationen in der altkatholischen Kirche*, 1936, against Sohm's Protestant presentation and strongly supporting Saltet's Catholic explanation.

Now, the consecration of a Pope was said to bestow upon him an 'indelible character' which could not be separated from the personality of the occupant of St. Peter's throne. Even if the Pope wished, he could not divest himself of this specific adjunct. For, were one to allow this, the antagonists of papal abdication maintained, the whole function of the papal office would be jeopardized. The Pope held the power of the keys, that is to say, the very same power which was given to St. Peter by Christ Himself. St. Peter could not conceivably have given up this power of the keys, and the same must be said of St. Peter's successors. Owing to the 'indelible character' of the episcopal office the power of the keys would not be lost, even if the holder wished to lay it aside. Now if abdication were conceded, the abdicated Pope would still have the same power of the keys as his possible successor. And obviously having the distasteful aspects of canonically invalid ordinations in mind, these canonists, logically enough, denied all validity to the abdication.

The second argument adduced by the opponents of papal abdication was the character of the special obligations into which a Pontiff entered by reason of his so-called spiritual marriage with the Church. By consenting to the election the candidate was tied by the bonds of marriage to the universal Church in general and to the Roman Church in particular. But a spiritual marriage could not be dissolved by *renuntiatio*, unless this *renuntiatio* was made into the hands of a superior. But who was to act as the superior of the Pontiff ? He had no superior except God, and one could not reasonably assert that the Pope had the right to resign his office into the hands of God. But apart from all that, a spiritual marriage produced far stronger ties than its carnal counterpart : when even the latter was indissoluble, how much more was the former. The Pope as God's vicar on earth would, by the simple act of resignation, violate one of the most fundamental principles of Christian doctrine.

The theory of the Pope's being the vicar of God on earth prompted the canonists to inquire into the origin of the Pope's powers. Antagonists and protagonists of papal abdication were unanimously agreed that the Pope received his powers from God. The former, however, qualified this derivation by the insertion of an 'immediate,' that is to say, they claimed that the Pontiff received his powers from God directly, without any human intermediary. Consequently, God alone was in a position to accept the abdicatory declaration of a Pope. 'Ea, quae a Deo solo immediate sunt, non possunt tolli per aliquem nisi per Deum ipsum.'[1] In other words, the dissolution of a spiritual marriage as well as the release from the specific obligations imposed by God, were to be reserved to God alone. And the retort that the Pope as God's vicar could act like God on earth, and hence could dissolve his own marriage with the universal Church, was brushed aside by the consideration that the Pope *in re sua* could not legitimately be the judge—and the dispenser.

In regard to the legislative question as to whether any Pope—or anybody else—could lay down in an enactment that a papal abdication was valid, this antagonistic section of the canonists reminded their opponents—and probably also the legislator himself, Boniface VIII—that the papal office was instituted by divine ordinance: whatever was thus instituted could not be put aside by human law. The *lex creaturae* had no share in the establishment of this office, and therefore it was beyond the scope of any human law, however much consented to by high ecclesiastics, to interfere with any obligations imposed by divine law. Moreover, by consenting to the election the Pope made a binding promise to God Himself and a solemn vow to govern the Church and to guide the souls of mortals. No human law could possibly grant a dispensation from this vow.

However much Boniface VIII might have tried to mock at those who questioned the constitutional legitimacy of Celestine V's step, it is nevertheless worth noticing that his own decree did little to convince his canonistic opponents who continued to hold to their doctrines, though with diminishing fervour. At the same time, it should be pointed out that the protagonists of papal abdication never based their

[1] This was usually deduced from 2 Tim., 1. 13–14.

views on this Bonifacian decree. The very fact of Celestine's abdication was bound to be explained by the canonists, and hand in hand with this explanation there developed the new theory of the constitutional right of a Pope to abdicate. Although Boniface's decree would have furnished the most appropriate basis for this doctrine, I do not know of one single canonist of the fourteenth century who would have contented himself with a mere reference to this decree. The new theory appears far more a theoretical justification of a *fait accompli* and an implicit act of acceptance of the Bonifacian law than an elaboration of the latter. The right of a Pope to abdicate was admitted, not because Boniface VIII as supreme legislator had said so, but because there were compelling reasons for ascribing this right to a Pontiff. Parenthetically we may remark here that this instance provides one more proof of the profundity of medieval canonistic scholarship : in order to be acceptable, a law must be justifiable on theoretical grounds. The mere reliance on a papal decree by a medieval canonist would have been an unusual feature. This critical spirit of the canonists was, of course, a direct outcome of an intelligently understood freedom of scholarship.

How did the new theory justify the constitutional right of the Pope to abdicate ? The reasons advanced may conveniently be classed under three headings, viz. :

(1) *Ex parte ipsius renuntiantis.*—The first and foremost duty of a Pontiff was to the multitude of Christians. It was he who directed their lives morally and spiritually. By his teaching and by his example he had to show them the paths that led to eternal salvation. The very name of pontiff implied this function, that is, *pontem facere :* he was a bridge-builder between this life and the next. But, and this is an important point, the fourteenth-century canonists did not conceive any substantial difference, so far as their spiritual functions went, between the Pontiff and the ordinary priest. No greater power was attributed to the Pope than to a parish priest. The difference between the two lay in the field of administration and jurisdiction : in this field the Pontiff surpassed the power of any other mortal and was truly God's

vicar on earth, but as regards purely sacerdotal functions there was no difference within the ecclesiastical hierarchy.

In a number of specific cases Church practice had allowed the abdication of a Pope.

(*a*) In the case of criminal behaviour on the part of a Pope. The classic and often repeated example was that given by Pope Marcellinus.[1] This Pope had confessed his own crimes to his bishops. It was quite true, the protagonists declared, that Marcellinus's action did not lead to an abdication, but to a deposition. But the effect was exactly the same. Pope Marcellinus could have abdicated because of his self-confessed crimes. For it was considered a mere playing with words to draw a distinction between deposition and abdication. Moreover, canon law itself in *Distinctio* lxiii., cap. 23, laid down that a Pope could submit himself to the judgment of others and hence he voluntarily faced an adverse verdict which could be no other but deposition. If a Pope could be deposed for crimes, why, these canonists asked pertinently, should he not be allowed to resign for the very same reason? Then, canon law again as bluntly as possibly decreed in *Distinctio* xl., cap. 6, that a Pope could be deposed for committing heresy. The antagonists could not possibly deny the force of these canonical regulations, or of the arguments deduced from them.

(*b*) In the case of physical or intellectual incapacity of a Pope. The advocates of papal abdication correctly referred to the already mentioned Alexandrian decretal and, on the basis of the foregoing considerations, maintained that, there being no fundamental spiritual difference between a Pope and a bishop, the former must be conceded the same rights as the latter already possessed. It was the established practice that bishops could resign their office on account of some physical defect or because of the lack of proper intellectual equipment. There was all the more compelling reason to attribute this right to a Pontiff who, as head of the universal Church, could inflict far more damage on his flock than a bishop whose powers were territorially limited. It was this sort of inability that prompted Celestine V to abdicate. His beatification by

[1] *Decretum Gratiani, Distinctio,* xxi. cap. 7.

the Church was taken as a particularly convincing proof of the legitimacy of his step.

(*c*) Another case that justified the abdication of a Pontiff was considered to lie in his causing grave scandal. Writers towards the end of the fourteenth century, and especially during the fifteenth century, saw in the Great Schism one such example in which a Pope, in order to avoid scandal to the whole of Christendom, was constitutionally entitled—and bound, if we follow Antonius de Rosellis[1]—to resign. This way of avoiding scandal must be chosen if there was no other.

(2) *Ex parte papatus*.—The office of the Pope did not prevent his abdication. Once again it was stressed that as regards sacerdotal functions there was no difference between a Pope and any other priest. For St. Peter as successor of Christ was not invested with more powers than the other apostles: they all, including St. Peter, were made priests, and St. Peter was merely a *primus inter pares*. It was true that the Pope was the successor of St. Peter, but he was just as equal to bishops and priests as St. Peter had been an equal of the other apostles. The term *papatus*, therefore, was not a name of any specific sacerdotal order, as the adversaries would have it, but merely designated the height of dignity within the ecclesiastical hierarchy. The advocates of papal abdication accordingly denied that the consecration of a papal candidate bestowed any distinct character upon him, let alone any indelible character. If the antagonists were right, how could they explain the possibility of deposing a heretical Pope? The theory of the protagonists asserted that the papal office was merely a particular status that was superimposed upon its holder. If a layman were to be made Pope, these canonists said, he would assume the papal office immediately after giving his consent to the election. From this it could easily be deduced that no specific sacerdotal order was attached to the papal office, but that all this office implied was the supreme jurisdictional power over everyone. But jurisdictional power could be increased and decreased—a phenomenon in juristic thought with which everyone was

[1] Antonius de Rosellis, *De Monarchia*, in Goldast, tom. i., fol. 340.

familiar and with which everyone agreed—and hence in a particular instance this power could also be abolished altogether. The deposition of a Pope on account of some heresy committed meant nothing else but the loss of supreme jurisdictional powers. In other words, the consecration by the cardinal-bishop of Ostia did not confer any sacerdotal order, but merely bestowed the right to exercise supreme jurisdiction and administration. The arguments derived from the alleged 'indelible character' of the papal office therefore fell to the ground.

(3) *Ex parte ipsius renuntiationis.*—In contrast to their adversaries the advocates of papal abdication asserted that papal power was only indirectly derived from God, through the medium of the cardinals. And just as the duties of the office itself were accepted by the simple assent of the candidate, in the same way, by a simple act of renunciation, he could divest himself of them. 'Sicut potest eius consensu papatus haberi, ita videtur eius dissensu posse tolli.' The force of the very plausible and attractive argument of the spiritual marriage between the Pope and the Church was destroyed by the consideration that the indissolubility of a carnal marriage rested upon its sacramental character: one could not reasonably maintain that a spiritual marriage constituted a sacrament in the meaning of the term. The study of the title *De translatione episcopi* in the Gregorian *Decretales* would convince the antagonists of papal abdication that the spiritual marriage of a bishop could be dissolved by a simple declaration. Other reflexions, too, lent force to the reasoning of the advocates. The spiritual marriage between a prelate and the Church considered primarily the public good, but if this marriage were indissoluble, enormous harm might accrue to the Church. How much more would this apply to the Pope who, by his inability to rule the universal Church, would inflict untold harm upon the whole of the Christian body. A carnal marriage, on the other hand, considered the private good only of the spouses. Hence the criteria applicable to the two kinds of marriage were quite different. Nothing militated against the dissolution of a spiritual marriage, whilst

every consideration was against the dissolution of a carnal marriage. The dissolubility of the latter kind would entail grave moral upheavals, whilst the dissolubility of the former could only be beneficial. The canonists made, however, one important condition. The marriage between the Pope and the Church should be dissolved without the consent of the cardinals : they were not to be parties to the dissolution. Since God alone could bring about this dissolution, it was the Pope himself who would have to effect it: he as the vicar of God on earth was constitutionally entitled to end his union with the Church. When the adversaries of the new doctrine retorted that in this case the Pope would be judge in his own affairs and that therefore a fundamental legal principle was violated, the advocates of papal abdication had no difficulty in pointing to the erroneous premiss of this argument : this legal rule was a positive human law, to the constrictions of which the Pope was not subjected.

To the initiated student of canon law the regulation of canon 221 of the *Codex Juris Canonici* must appear as the faithful reflexion of the canonistic doctrine prevalent since the middle of the fourteenth century, with one apparent exception, however, and that is that this canon does not insist on the requirement of a just cause for the abdication of the Pope. Medieval canonistic doctrine insisted on the fulfilment of this condition, although the abdicating Pope alone was in a position to judge whether or not the cause was sufficiently just to warrant his step. And yet too much weight should not be placed upon this omission in canon 221, because the framers of this canon quite obviously desired to lay down not so much the constitutional right of papal abdication as the supremacy of papal power. The declaration of abdication on the part of the Pope does not depend for its validity on the consent of the college of cardinals. In this, as in every other aspect of Church government, the Pontiff is supreme.

XV

THE DEFENCE OF THE ACCUSED IN THE MEDIEVAL INQUISITION

THE current misconceptions of the medieval inquisition are chiefly due to the neglect of the canonistic literature on this topic. It is, indeed, remarkable that some of our modern historians, notably Lea and, largely following him, the late Dr. G. G. Coulton, hardly ever refer to the canon law, and if they do, the relevant Bull or decree of a pope or of a council is quoted in a manner which is apt to convey a totally misleading impression. In these historical productions one will look in vain for any reference to a medieval canonist. The accused is usually depicted as the victim of a sadistic black-robed clique: the fairly high standard of the defence in Anglo-Saxon countries is smugly compared with what was held to be the helpless position in which the accused found himself in the network of the inquisitors. Let us, therefore, briefly review the fundamental principles which governed the defence in medieval inquisitorial proceedings.

The summary character of the inquisition ordered by Pope Boniface VIII left all possibilities of legal aid untouched. Canonistic scholarship was unanimous in its demand that the accused must not be deprived of legal aid. For the canonists recognized that inquisitorial proceedings, deciding as they did life and death and possibly the salvation of the accused, should be conducted in such a manner that all possible legal objections, remedies and defences might be employed to save an individual from the not infrequently harsh sanctions of the law. But what defendant charged with the crime of heresy was conversant with the legal subtleties and niceties that might prevent him from being delivered to the executioners? The rule was that, if after careful admonition the defendant had pleaded guilty, he was considered to have forfeited his right to legal help: but if he denied committing any heretical action, which was, of course, the normal reply to the charge, the inquisitor was bound to grant him legal aid in the person of a qualified advocate, even if there were no explicit petition for his help: *Si autem post tres monitiones reus negat se unquam haereticum fuisse, tunc advocatus ei dandus est, etiam non petenti.*[1] The defence was looked upon as an integral part of the proceedings: *Judices providere debent, ut advocatus adsit, ne reus defensionis careat.* For the inquisitors ought not only to be judges in the strict meaning of the term, but also the *patres reorum.*

To be eligible for this role, the advocate had to be an *idoneus vir*, that is to say, a man equally versed in legal and religious knowledge; he himself, of course, had to be above all suspicion of heresy. Before the proceedings started he was made to take an oath to the effect that he would defend the accused to the best of his ability and in good faith and that he would submit those *exceptiones* (legal objections) which he deemed expedient and in the interest of justice and of the accused; the advocate had to promise, furthermore, that he would 'desert' the cause, as soon as he felt that his position was irreconcilable with the dictates of justice: he was to communicate his intention of resigning

[1] See, for instance, Jacobus Simancus, 'De Catholicis Institutionibus' in *Tractatus Universi Juris*, tom. xi. pars. 2, fol. 12lvo, titulus V, No. 2. But a confession of the advocate on behalf of the accused could be revoked, see the *glossa ordinaria* of Bernardus Parmensis on *Gregoriana* (Liber Extra), III. xxxix. 20, s.v. 'non revocata.' For the purpose of showing the position of the accused, the 'Handbook for Inquisitors' of the Dominican, Bernard Gui (*Practica Officii Inquisitionis Hereticae Pravitatis*, ed. by G. Mollat under the title *Manuel de l'Inquisition*, 1927), is of little avail, as it is exclusively designed for the use of the inquisitors themselves, and hence gives a one-sided picture. Cf. Mollat, ed. cit., p. vii: it is 'un traité composé à l'usage exclusif des inquisiteurs, afin de leur faciliter la recherche de l'hérésie. . . .' On the question of the participation of the State in inquisitorial proceedings see P. Havet, 'L'hérésie et le Bras Séculier au Moyen Age' in *Bibliothèque de l'Ecole des Chartes*, vol. xli. pp. 492 ff. (mainly for France) and J. Ficker, 'Die gesetzliche Einführung der Todesstrafe für Ketzerei' in *Mitteilungen des Instituts für oest. Geschichts-forschung*, vol. i. pp. 177 ff. (comprehensive). Cf. also G. Schnurer, *Kirche und Kultur im Mittelalter*, Paderborn, 1927, pp. 14 ff, 315 ff, J. Guiraud, *Histoire de l'inquisition au Moyen Age*, 1935, 1938 (purely historical), and the recent work by Father A. C. Shannon, *The Popes and Heresy in the 13th Century*, 1949, who investigates the growth of the procedure on the basis of the papal Registers.

from the defence to the accused and the inquisitor beforehand, and was to give his reasons for doing so.

The chief function of the advocate lay in the assistance he was to render in the elucidation of truth and in the promotion of justice. If the charge were true, he would therefore urge the accused to confess his crime and to plead for mercy. If the accused deemed himself innocent, he would have to inform his advocate which of the witnesses were likely to be hostile to him, and what other means he had at his disposal to disprove the allegations made against him.

There was no salary fixed for this office, but a honorarium was to be paid to the advocate from public funds, especially if the defendant were poor. The defence of the poor was dictated by the injunctions of the law of charity and should not therefore be evaded.[1] But if the defendant had means of his own, he should be compelled to pay the costs of his defence, even if it were unsolicited ; in this case the proper fee was to be the object of the inquisitorial sentence.[2]

Which objections could the advocate raise ? In short, all those which were connected with the essence and substance of any crime. Heresy, however, had some features which distinguished it from the ordinary crimes. Above all, this offence was characterized by the concurrence of two features, that is, by the *error intellectus* as well as by the *pertinacia voluntatis* : only when both these elements were co-existent, the inquisitor was entitled to proceed to a condemnation. And the legal objections to the charge of heresy emanated naturally from these two aspects of the crime. Consequently, the defence was to concentrate on attempting to prove that the accused was either wholly mentally deficient or not fully accountable for his actions ; into this category fell those accused persons who were considered fanatics or obsessed by some demoniacal powers, for one could

[1] 'Stipendium ex bonis fisci datur advocatis, ut pauperum causas defendant . . . Adde, quod advocati lege charitatis tenentur, pauperum causas gratuito defendere,' Jacobus, loc. cit. No. 6.

[2] Cf. Lucas de Penna, *Commentaria in Tres Libros Codicis*, C. XII. 6, 1 : 'Si rei pauperes non sint, merces advocatis ex bonis eorum tribuenda est.'

hardly speak of those persons as committing an error of judgment or pertinaciously clinging to their errors.[1] Children under fourteen years of age were, of course, outside the scope of punishment altogether. The reverse side was old age: on the basis of Platonic reasoning[2] old people were put on a footing equal to that of children, as they too *suae mentis non fuerint compotes.* The consultation of two medical specialists was advisable.[3] Heretical utterances during sleep were also not within the compass of punishable offences[4] nor so-called *lapsus linguae.*[5] Heretical expressions or deeds committed by people in a state of drunkenness were not punishable either, *nesciunt enim ebrii, quid loquuntur.* Illiteracy was another reason for exculpation, and it is interesting to note that offences against even the most fundamental articles of faith were not considered punishable, if *nimia rusticitas* (otherwise unpardonable ignorance) gave birth to heretical opinions. The same exculpating condition was attributed to heretical expressions directed against articles of faith which were not fundamental, if these expressions were the result of faulty or defective teaching.[6] For, following the doctrine of St. Augustine, all crimes were classified as sins resting either on human weakness or on inexperience or on malice. The first two categories were

[1] 'Hinc est, quod haeresis a furioso dicta, impunita esse debet; idemque erit, si ab insano, fanatico et furiis seu daemonibus agitato—hii nec errorem intellectus habent nec pertinaciam voluntatis.'

[2] *De Legibus*, lib. ix.

[3] Jacobus Menochius, *Consilium* 82. The general principles of medieval criminal proceedings were outlined by the present writer in 'Reflections on Medieval Torture' in *Juridical Review*, 1944; 'Medieval Principles of Evidence' in *Law Quarterly Review*, 1946; and 'Some Principles of Medieval Criminal Procedure' in *Juridical Review*, 1947, where the attempt was made to show the reason for the growth of inquisitorial proceedings. On the canonical inquisition in particular see the *Glossa Ordinaria* of Bernardus Parmensis on *Gregoriana*, V. i. 24, and P. Hinschius, *System d. Kathol. Kirchenrechts*, vol. v. pp. 481–92.

[4] *Clementines*, V. iv., and the gloss of Zenzelinus de Cassanis.

[5] *Decretum*, C. XXII. qu. ii. cap. 3, was usually the legal basis for this type of defence. See, for instance, Guido de Baysio, ibid.

[6] 'Is enim haereticus non est, qui errat sine pertinacia contra aliquam veritatem catholicae fidei, quam explicite scire non tenebatur, et eo magis, si ab aliquo deceptus fuit, cui credere tenebatur': *Decretum*, C. XXIV. qu. iii. cap. 29. 'Nimia rusticitas excusare potest ab haeresi, etiam si in iis rusticus erret, in quibus nulla esset prudentium defensio.'

offences against virtuous or wise living, whilst the third category was the domain of crime proper, directed as it was against *bonitas*. In the previously mentioned cases, according to the doctrines of the medieval canonists, one could not perceive any premeditated attack against virtuous or wise living, and therefore these cases deserved acquittal.

This was also the reason why heretical utterances made during a state of great emotional strain and excitement were outside the sphere of punishment.

Compulsion, when it amounted to a threat to life, had only extenuating, but not exculpating, effects.[1] The total denial of the Catholic faith in face of mortal danger was an offence entitling the offender to exculpation or extenuation. But inquisitors were warned that externally heretical opinions might be misleading, as those might be uttered by weak individuals who, despite their expressed statements, might at the bottom of their hearts adhere fully to every article of faith.[2] For not the same degree of fortitude and resistance can be expected from all individuals: bowing before some threat by *graves et sapientes viri* assumes an aspect quite different from that when *humiliores et fragiliores* yield: *nec exigitur eadem virtus in hiis et in illis*. Heavier punishment should therefore be meted out against princes, clerics, monks, aristocrats, theologians and philosophers than against the *plebei*, women—and the rest. Bishops, however, could not claim any extenuation in the face of threats, as this would have meant a betrayal of their position as *bonus pastor*. Women as a rule were considered to deserve lighter punishment than men, because their minds were those of adolescents and their judgment therefore of little value.[3]

The best line of defence was considered to be proof that

[1] 'Sed cum aliquid metu mortis vel alterius mali impium dicit, aut facit, is quidem puniendus est pro modo culpae, sed mitius. Nam etsi id facere noluisset, maluit tamen facere quam talia pati.'

[2] 'Quinimo, qui tali metu lapsus est, et corde non discessit a fide catholica, is nec haereticus est.'

[3] 'Mulieres levis sententiae sunt et mitius puniri debent quam viri.'

the accused did not say or commit the incriminated offence. But in this context it may be profitable to destroy a very popular misconception. It is usually maintained with an air of superiority that in canonical proceedings—and hence in nearly all modern Continental proceedings—the accused is held guilty unless he is able to prove his innocence. This is a complete distortion of the position in canon law and nothing but a malignant attack on ecclesiastical proceedings. For the innocence of the accused was always taken for granted, so long as the prosecutor did not bring forth convincing proof of the defendant's guilt. The great canonist at the end of the thirteenth century, Cardinal Johannes Monachus (Jean le Moin), said: *Quilibet praesumitur innocens, nisi probetur nocens ; et jus est promptius ad absolvendum quam ad condemnandum.*[1] It was, therefore, the business of the prosecutor to prove the guilt of the defendant, and the latter's task to prove his innocence. It was, nevertheless, better for the accused if he were in a position to disprove the factual correctness of the charge : *Ea optima defensio fit, si reus probare poterit, se nihil eorum, de quibus accusatur, dixisse vel commisisse.* To achieve this end, his advocate was to summon those witnesses who could bear out the statements of the accused.[2] Blood relatives of the accused, his wife and members of his household, were not admitted as witnesses for the defence, because they were not considered *integri et fidei digni.* The defence was successful if animosity or open hostility on the part of the incriminating witnesses were proved by the defendant. Moreover, if he could prove that they were bribed or had conjured against him, his acquittal followed.

Closely allied with the topic of defence is the problem of custody as a preparation for the trial itself. Imprisonment can have two functions : either the prevention of flight of

[1] Johannes Monachus, in his gloss on *Extravagantes Communes*, II. iii. cap. un. (Boniface VIII). This view was clearly supported by two decrees of Innocent III, i.e. *Gregoriana*, II. xxiii. 16, and I. xii. 1, for criminal proceedings, and by Lucius III for civil proceedings, ibid. II. xix. 3.

[2] See, e.g. Philipus Decius, *Consilium* 94.

the defendant before the trial, or punishment after sentence had been passed. Whilst the civil laws permitted imprisonment only as a means of custody, the canon law also allowed it as a form of punishment.[1] The normal procedure in the case of custody before trial was that the inquisitor issued a writ or a warrant to his officials—the so-called *executores*—to apprehend the accused and to take him into custody. This warrant was issued after a summary trial in which sufficiently good cause must have been shown that there existed reasonable suspicion for the flight of the accused, or for his attempting to influence witnesses, and the like.[2] A reference to this decision had to be made in the files of the case. A controversial point in canonistic literature was as to whether private individuals were allowed to deliver a notorious heretic—*haereticus manifestus*—into the hand of the 'executor,' or whether the latter alone was entitled to effect the incarceration. The older doctrine, such as Hostiensis (Cardinal-bishop Henricus de Segusia) and Goffredus de Trano, maintained that any private individual could apprehend a notorious heretic, because he was a *communis hostis*.[3] But the younger generation of canonists thought this procedure too dangerous, not only because of the easy opportunity of creating public scandal, but also because the accused was perfectly entitled to resist the attempted apprehension by a private individual. The accused could be apprehended by private persons, however, if he were fleeing or if he had escaped the 'executor.' A bishop was entitled to incarcerate a suspected heretic, but the inquisitor in this case had to consult the bishop before

[1] 'Carcer jure pontificio non solum ad custodiam, sed etiam ad poenam habetur.' Cf., on the one hand, the lecture of Baldus on *Cod. Just.*, 9, 47, 6, and, on the other, *Extra*, V. vii. 12 and the *gl. ord.* ibid.: life imprisonment was remitted, if the prisoner recanted, 'quia ecclesia non claudit gremium redeuntibus ad ipsam.' See also *Les Reg. de Greg. IX*, nos. 539, 1416.

[2] 'Caeterum pro crimine haeresis nemo mittendus est in carcerem absque sufficienti ad eam rem probatione,' Bartholomaeus Salicetus, *Commentaria in Codicem*, lecture on C. IX. 3, 2.

[3] Hostiensis, *Summa Aurea*, tit. De haereticis, § 'Qualiter devenitur'; Goffredus de Trano, *Summa Decretalium*, De haereticis, Rubrica.

sentence was passed.[1] The most frequent form of imprisonment was a kind of 'house arrest,' that is to say, the accused was confined to his dwelling-place or to the locality within which he lived, or to the whole district.[2] In some provinces, notably in Sicily and France, the custom had grown up to set aside a special building for the custody of prisoners.[3] They were made to work for their own support; female and male wards were separate.

Food and other amenities might, with the permission of the inquisitor, be brought to the prisoners by relatives. Permission was also necessary if they wished to speak to him, in which case the two warders had to be present. Each prison—where there was a special building—had to have two warders, one appointed by the bishop, the other by the inquisitor. They should be *industri, fideles et boni viri.* The growing tendency to appoint less suitable supervisors was challenged by a reference to Aristotle's famous saying: *Quis autem custodiet malos custodes?* In order to supervise the administration of the prisons themselves, the inquisitors were bound to pay two visits a month. There the prisoners, whether in custody or undergoing punishment, were allowed to state their complaints and grievances as regards any prison matter, especially the treatment by warders and the provision of adequate food.

A nice legal problem concerned the alimentation of his wife by the imprisoned heretic. A number of jurists considered that no such obligation rested upon the husband, as he was not living with his wife, nor was he in a position to earn a sufficient amount.[4] Others impugned this opinion by referring to the divine, natural and civil laws,

[1] Cf. *Clem.* I. i. and V. iii. 1, § Sane, quia.

[2] 'Pro qualitate criminum et personarum possunt judices jubere, ut reus domum suam vel alterius vel civitatem (ut plerumque solet) cum suburbiis pro carcere habeat,' Jason de Mayno, *Commentaria in Digestum Vetus,* lecture on D. 12, 4, 5, 4.

[3] Andreas de Isernia, *In Usus Feudorum,* tit. De Statu, cap. Credentes, fol. 134 vo.

[4] Ludovicus Romanus, *Consilium* 517; Alexander Tartagnus, *Consilium* 133, lib. iv.

all of which made the husband's support of his wife obligatory, especially if he were wealthy.[1]

This extremely brief sketch of some fundamental principles in medieval inquisitorial proceedings may have shown that a vast and practically unexplored field of medieval history offers itself to unbiased research. Modern historians have taken far too little account of the writings of medieval canonists[2]—and what would one think of historians six or seven centuries hence, if, in trying to depict twentieth-century administration of justice, they relied on second or third rate sources, such as the popular press or exotic films, instead of on the writings of the competent authorities? What is needed is a balanced picture of the medieval inquisition, and this can only be obtained if the competent authorities, that is, the canonists, are given first place.

[1] Matthaeus de Afflictis, *Decisiones Neapolitanae*, decisio X, and Raphael Cumanus, *Consilium* 175.

[2] For a recent forceful plea for the restoration of canonistic studies in the Universities see Prof. St. Kuttner's address to the Medieval Academy of America in *Speculum*, October, 1949, pp. 493 ff.

XVI

HISTORICAL INTRODUCTION
to H.C. Lea,
The Inquisition of the Middle Ages

I

Historians and general readers of the older generation probably need no introduction to the three-volume work on the history of the medieval Inquisition that established Henry Charles Lea's reputation. But as is so often the case with literary and historical productions, after a time they are read less and less, until indeed they themselves belong to history. This not uncommon fate is shared by Lea's pioneering work that was acclaimed a classic in its own right in its time.

Lea was a man of many interests, endowed with an astonishing vitality, energy and tenacity. Born on 19 September 1825 [1] in Philadelphia, he received private tuition from a teacher whose interests appear to have been directed towards the incipient natural sciences, whilst at the same time Lea's mother seems to have provided a corrective by stimulating in her son a very lively interest in literature and poetry. Still only in his teens Lea published a number of papers on biological and botanic subjects, contributed to literary journals articles on literary criticism, published poems and translated Greek poetry. The civil war and its aftermath caused an enforced idleness which Lea used to widen his literary interests by delving into history: he began reading Froissart's *Chronicle*, Villehardouin's *Conquest of Constantinople*, the *Chronicle of St Denis*, and at the same time made efforts to build up his own historical reference library. One should not forget that in the mid-nineteenth century

[1] For all biographical details I am very much indebted to E. S. Bradley, *Henry Charles Lea* (Philadelphia, 1931).

historical studies were still in their infancy. In a biographical note Lea himself explained how he gradually came to realize three factors that were to influence his future historical work: (1) that the study of the sources is indispensable if a period or a movement or an institution is to be properly understood: the reliance on secondary authorities is to be discouraged, because they in one way or another have succumbed to purely subjective assessments; (2) that in order to see and explain and understand an institution or the actuality of living in an historical period or in a particular country, there is no better guide and no more reliable mirror than the law enacted and practised: in this realization Lea was far ahead of all his contemporaries and of many historians in later decades; (3) that in the medieval period it was the Church which dominated the social and political life both by its practices and its laws; its sources were on the whole well preserved; its canon law was the best possible guide to an understanding of medieval institutions, at least in the predominantly ecclesiastical field.

What apparently led Lea to medieval studies was his quest for an understanding of nineteenth-century civilization: what factors gave birth to "modern civilization", how was it moulded, what had retarded its evolution? These and similar questions seem to have engaged Lea from the time when the American civil war prompted reflective thinking. Throughout his life Lea was intensely preoccupied with the idea of justice and liberty. The choice of subjects on which he wrote and on which his reputation as an historian rests, is not therefore without significance. But few nowadays would realize what enormous obstacles a searching mind had to overcome in order to delve into matters which so far had not been recognized topics of scholarly pursuit. Not only was Lea himself untrained as an historian and had to acquire the necessary skill and training by hard work, but there were also in his time no compendia such as those with which any research student today is familiar, giving exhaustive and up-to-date bibliographies, nor were there bibliographical periodicals which would have presented recent literature in systematic form. To this handicap must be added the other great difficulty confronting any serious historical scholar at that time: the location of the original materials. Many libraries and archives had not yet even begun to publish catalogues of the materials in their charge: nor was historical scholarship as yet in the fortunate position of having access to first-class editions of medieval authors, writings, tracts, laws, and so forth – again, the modern researcher has an incomparably easier start, since every good library is stocked with reliable modern editions of medieval works. It was, in actual fact, in precisely this period of the mid-nineteenth century that the great labours of the Abbé Migne resulted in the indispensable *Patrologia Latina* and its 217 volumes. At the same time the *Monumenta Germaniae Historica* had only just got over its initial impetus and experienced one of its periodical crises. It was also in the mid-nineteenth century that the first tangible steps were taken to initiate what later became known as the Rolls Series. These are but a few examples to show with what difficulties a conscientious scholar had to contend: the tools which every young researcher today takes for granted had not yet been forged.

These difficulties to a great extent explain Lea's achievements and deficiencies. Nevertheless, true historical scholar as he was, Lea by sheer pertinacity and industry overcame the obstacles as best he could. Before the publication of his first book, he had written a number of review articles on subjects on which he himself was engaged; for instance, on Palgrave's *History of Normandy and England*, on canonical compurgation and the wager of battle, on judicial ordeals, on slavery in the early Church, and so on, mostly in the *North American Review*. These articles are by no means small fare: they show a combination of critical acumen with an almost uncanny insight into the historical texture and a remarkable evaluation of the available source material. Lea's first substantial book was *Superstition and Force*, published at Philadelphia in 1866, which went through several editions. In reviewing the fourth edition a no lesser man than Maitland had to say this:

> When such a book as Dr Lea's reaches a fourth edition, our first compliments are due rather to the public whose good taste has surprised us than to the author. Dr Lea has nowhere

> courted a great public . . . we can here only speak of it as a well-known book . . . Dr Lea still pursues his policy of ignoring, if not German erudition, at all events German theories and German controversies. Of course there is something to be said against this policy, even when it is pursued by one so learned and so circumspect as Dr Lea . . . But a little more criticism of current theories might have been very dearly purchased at the cost of originality . . . We trust him thoroughly because he keeps his gaze fixed on the Middle Ages and never looks for opinions to be refuted or for quarrels to be picked. This is not exactly the policy that we could recommend to any but a strong man. Dr Lea, however, is strong, and sober, and wary.[1]

This work, as also the one immediately following,[2] was translated into Italian.

Meanwhile, Lea continued his labours on the subject on which his fame was to rest – the Inquisition in the Middle Ages – wrote numerous reviews and articles on related topics and published his *Studies in Church History* (Philadelphia, 1869) of which again an Italian translation appeared later. With the launching of our own *English Historical Review* Lea entered the distinguished company of its contributors: in the very first volume he appears as a reviewer and was to be a faithful contributor for many a year, not only of reviews, but also of articles.[3] When the *American Historical Review* was started, Lea again appeared in its pages as a frequent contributor, right down to the twilight of his life. In 1890 he published his *Chapters from the Religious History of Spain connected with the Inquisition* which contained preliminary studies to the four-volume work of *A History of the Inquisition of Spain* (New York and London, 1906–7), shortly to be translated into French and German. A work that had engaged him for a long time and was in some ways linked both with the medieval and the Spanish Inqusition, was published separately by Lea in three volumes: *A History*

[1] F. W. Maitland, in *E.H.R.*, viii (1893), pp. 755–6.

[2] *A Historical Sketch of Sacerdotal Celibacy in the Christian Church* (Philadelphia, 1867); several times edited and revised.

[3] Cf. *E.H.R.*, ii. 235 ff.; iv. 229 ff.; viii. 424 ff.; x. 86 ff.

of Auricular Confession and Indulgences in the Latin Church (Philadelphia, 1896), of which there appeared within a few years a French and an Italian translation. It was of this work that Acton, soliciting a contribution from Lea for the *Cambridge Modern History*, wrote to him: "Your last work contains almost all I am asking for, ten times told, and full measure running over." [1] That the question of property was a very topical problem in the medieval Church and that it was of vital concern to the papacy, Christendom at large and theology, has now been recognized by most historians, but Lea was one of the first to have made this subject the central theme of his book *The Dead Hand: a brief sketch of the relations between Church and State with regard to ecclesiastical property and the religious Orders* (Philadelphia, 1900) which within a year was translated into French and Dutch. The four volumes on the Spanish Inquisition were followed by one volume on the Inquisition in practice within the Spanish dependencies (Sicily, Naples, Sardinia, Mexico, Peru, etc.) in 1908. Lea's main work of the Inquisition was, after his death, reprinted in a uniform edition of eight volumes in 1922 comprising the three volumes on the medieval Inquisition, the four volumes on the Spanish Inquisition, and the one volume on the Inquisition in the Spanish dependencies. Lea accepted Lord Acton's invitation to contribute to the *Cambridge Modern History* an article on the "Eve of the Reformation" which appeared in its first volume in 1902.

This very brief sketch of Lea's chief works cannot convey the many vicissitudes with which the historian and scholar had to contend. Because of his innate and healthy distrust of secondary literature, his supply of material was to him a constant anxiety. In order to have available the original source material, he had to engage in lengthy and weary correspondence with librarians, archivists, scholars, had to enlist the good services of the United States representatives in numerous European capitals, had to instruct his copyists and to purchase documents at considerable expense. Sometimes he had the originals on loan, but mostly he relied on the transcripts made by copyists whom foreign scholars had engaged. Nearly 200 bundles of transcripts

[1] E. P. Cheyney in Bradley, op. cit., p. 364.

from the Bodleian are still preserved in the Lea Library at Philadelphia.[1] So as to secure the best available materials and the best copyists, Lea entertained a wide-flung correspondence which brought him into contact with the historical luminaries of the time. And this correspondence was to last until the very end of his life. Both Creighton and Lecky were frequently approached and most readily put their help at Lea's disposal; with Migne, Reinach, Paul Sabatier, Edouard Montet, Charles Molinier and Paul Frédéricq, Lea had regular contact, whilst in Germany it was Döllinger, Hinschius and Preger who came to Lea's help; in Italy it was Ugo Balzani and Felice Tocco who were instrumental in securing the co-operation of archives and libraries. This lively correspondence brought Lea not only into close touch with the foremost historical scholars of the time, but also very largely contributed to his own development. An historian who has the good fortune of being in touch with such a galaxy of glittering names can indeed call himself happy: it was this personal contact which enabled Lea to receive stimulus, appreciation and encouragement as well as constructive criticism from precisely those who were his peers. Recognition in the form of honorary degrees and honorary fellowships of numerous learned academies and societies followed in due course: Harvard, Princeton and Giessen were amongst those which conferred honorary doctorates on Lea, whilst the British Academy, the Bavarian Academy, the Accademia dei Lincei in Rome, the Società Romana per la storia di patria, the Società internazionale di studi Francescani (Assisi), the University of Moscow, and scores of other learned bodies made him an Honorary or Corresponding Fellow. He was also President of the American Historical Association and of the Wycliff Society. He died after a short illness on 24 October 1909.

II

In 1887 the first of the three volumes of the *History of the Inquisition of the Middle Ages* was published by Harpers. It may perhaps be advisable to quote a few statements from the Preface: they will allow us a better insight into Lea's mind and

[1] Bradley, op. cit., p. 154.

aim than any lengthy disquisition: they will also show with what unfailing historical sense he fixed attention on medieval jurisprudence as the most reliable and informative source for obtaining knowledge and understanding of the actuality of living in the Middle Ages.

> The Inquisition was not an organization arbitrarily devised and imposed upon the judicial system of Christendom by the ambition or fanaticism of the Church. It was rather a natural, one may almost say an inevitable evolution of the forces at work in the thirteenth century, and no one can rightly appreciate the process of its development and the results of its activity without a somewhat minute consideration of the factors controlling the minds and souls of men during the ages which laid the foundation of modern civilization.

In a more personal way Lea also wrote the following statement, which should be quoted in full, because of its intrinsic importance. For there were then no historians who had taken the route pursued by him and there are still very few today who orientate themselves in the manner suggested by him: nothing demonstrates better the superb historical sense and above all the medieval flair with which Lea was endowed than the statement he made in the Preface to another book: "The history of jurisprudence is the history of civilization." And in the Preface to the *History of the Inquisition* he wrote:

> At the commencement of my historical studies I speedily became convinced that the surest basis of investigation for a given period lay in an examination of its jurisprudence, which presents without disguise its aspirations and the means regarded as best adapted for their realization. I have accordingly devoted much space to the origin and development of the inquisitorial process, fully convinced that in this manner only can we understand the operation of the Holy Office and the influence which it exercised on successive generations.

There is so much truth, so much profundity of insight in these few lines that it seems superfluous to comment on them. Indeed, the law is the mirror of any civilization – it reflects the aims and underlying ideas of any society, because only through the law and its application can the end of organized society be translated into practice. The focal attention which Lea gave to this vital axiom is and remains one of the great merits of an historian, self-made and self-taught, but endowed with a rare historical sense.

It is consequently in pursuit of this jurisprudential line that, with admittedly limited sources and resources at his disposal, Lea depicted for the first time in a coherent manner the working of the medieval Inquisition. This is preceded by some preliminary chapters on the intellectual and theological state of affairs in the twelfth century: without disparagement one may say that these chapters are not entirely satisfactory. They move too much on the surface and whatever merits they may have had at the time of publication, they cannot demand much attention today, when so much detailed work has been done on these topics. It is quite otherwise with the chapters here reprinted, which form the main part of the first volume devoted to the organization of the Inquisition. In them Lea shows with an enviable command of the sources the mechanics of the inquisitorial process, from the first suspicion cast upon a person, through the tortuous and long-winded machinery of the trial, to the day on which the victim was marched to the stake. The reader is made familiar with the buildings and prisons, the personnel of the Inquisition, the records taken at the interrogations, the application of torture, the numerous official pronouncements widening or restricting means of extracting confessions, the kinds of evidence taken, their value, the defence and its limitations, modes of sentences, penalties, abjurations, relapse, and so on.

Whilst the first volume deals with the principles of the Inquisition, the second attempts to elucidate the inquisitorial procedure and its actual working in the different countries, notably in France, Germany, Hungary, Bohemia, Italy, and above all in Languedoc. This volume of the work suffers from many limitations, not the least of which is the fragmentary nature of the sources at Lea's disposal. Since then a number of detailed monographs have appeared which deal with the individual countries and which, though not radically upsetting the picture drawn by Lea, nevertheless permit a more realistic appraisal of the Inquisition at work. This applies with particular force to the manifestations of Catharism, a subject which has received special attention in recent years.[1] Similar observations may be made about the Beguines and Beghards and above all the Waldenses and their activities in different countries. Wycliff and Huss and the effects of their teachings, too, have been made the subject of penetrating studies. But despite all these defects and considering the state of historical research at his time, there is no gainsaying that Lea's second volume presents a very remarkable achievement.

From the geographical treatment of the Inquisition in the second volume Lea turns in the third to the topographical presentation, that is, he shows in what spheres the Inquisition was particularly active. The spheres singled out are the different heretical movements, including what might be called political heresy as well as the manifestations of sorcery, witchcraft, and other occult arts. It is the spiritual Franciscans, the Fraticelli, the expansion of the concept of heresy in the service of both the Church and the royal governments, the manifestations of certain doctrines, such as Averroism, beatific vision, immaculate conception, and so forth, which form the backbone of the third volume. In some respects this volume is an attempt at a history of sects and doctrines, and therefore the criticisms directed against the second volume are here applicable with still greater force. Above all, the presentation is rather uneven, the information scrappy and perhaps for no other volume has Charles Molinier's statement that the treatment of the Inquisition in all its forms and varieties might well transgress the ability of any one author greater relevance than here: on hearing that Lea had attempted a work of such vast scope, Molinier said that this undertaking "*serait à notre sens une entreprise à peu près chimérique*". And now after many years of detailed research into doctrinal and dogmatic history, into the emergence and

[1] Cf., for instance, A. Borst, *Die Katharer* (Schriften der Monumenta Germaniae Historica, vol. xii, Stuttgart, 1953). See also Steven Runciman, *The Medieval Manichee: a study of the Christian dualist Heresy* (Cambridge, 1947).

development of medieval doctrines, theories and views, the picture drawn by Lea here has been radically altered. No doubt, these departments of learning were barely recognized as proper objects of study by the time Lea had begun his work and one can hardly be surprised that the fierce searchlight of modern research has exposed the untenable character of a number of views which three generations ago may have appeared perfectly plausible. The history of medieval philosophy and theology has in actual fact only in the last few decades made great strides forward.

But all this is very largely hindsight, and we ought now to see what sort of reception Lea's work had when it first appeared. As was only to be expected, it was widely reviewed, particularly as an English edition was published at the same time. The sheer weight of learning condensed in the three volumes, the mass of information, the ever-topical problem of whether the Church was justified in using the methods described in the work, the equally topical problem of the protection of minority views in the face of a swollen and seemingly all-powerful organization, the gruesome details depicted – all these circumstances brought forth a variety of judgements. But if the variety of judgements – the lot of every pioneer at all times – is to be properly appreciated, the historical background itself should also be borne in mind. The work appeared in the heyday of Liberalism; some seventeen years after the Vatican Council which, in proclaiming the pope's infallibility, caused so much stir; at a time when the civilized world still knew that the Inquisition had been in force in Italy where the events of 1870 swept it away; at a time when, especially in England and Germany, the Catholics were making determined efforts to display greater activity in political and public life. When all these factors are properly assessed, the enthusiasm on the one hand welcoming the appearance of the book, and its fiery condemnation on the other, will be more easily understandable. For the one, the book was a warning of what might be in store if conditions came about again which resembled the domination of Europe by the one and undivided Church governed by the infallible pope; for the other, the book presented a challenge and contained an equally strong warning that no conclusions could be drawn from the work, because it was based on a serious misunderstanding of the sources and of the teaching of the Church. Lea himself anticipated the mixed reception of his work when in the Preface he spoke of the subject as one "which has called forth the fiercest passions of man, arousing alternately his highest and his basest impulses". Nevertheless, he also continued: "I have not paused to moralize, but I have missed my aim if the events narrated are not so presented as to teach their appropriate lesson." What he wished to do was to present pure history, but if this history were to convey a moral, it was the topic itself which might teach a lesson. There is here no need to go into the numerous reviews which the book excited, but so much may be said that the scholars who were experts in this field, gave the work unstinted approval: scholars, that is to say, who were names – and still are – with an international reputation. The detractors on the whole seem to belong to a minority whose vociferousness and shrillness was equalled by their unhistorical mind and their inability to attack more than peripheral matters. Still spellbound by the late Pio Nono, they were writing blissfully unaware that the views of the Roman Church on vital issues touching public, political and social life were just about to undergo some radical changes entailing a modern orientation towards awkward features of medieval history. Perhaps we may select one reviewer from each camp.

None other than Lord Acton accepted the invitation to review the book for the *English Historical Review*.[1] In a very long and perceptive review of some fifteen closely printed pages he subjected the book to a searching criticism, in which all of Acton's massive erudition, true humanity, profundity of reflection and sublimity of observation shine forth. The topic of the medieval Inquisition was, of course, one that was very close to Acton's heart. He did not give unqualified approval – how could this be expected from a man of Acton's stamp and on a work of such dimensions? – and criticized a number of individual points which have, however, little bearing on the theme itself: these points were wholly concerned with the doctrinal parts of the

[1] See *E.H.R.*, iii (1888), pp. 773–88.

book. But as far as the substance of the work was concerned it received warm praise from its reviewer. "The work which has been awaited so long has come over at last, and will assuredly be accepted as the most important contribution of the new world to the religious history of the old. Other books have shown the author as a thoughtful inquirer in the remunerative but perilous region where religion and politics conflict . . . he is armed at all points. His information is comprehensive, minute, exact and everywhere sufficient, if not everywhere complete." On the perusal of Lea's sources Acton had to say this: "He is exceedingly careful in rendering the sense of his informants, and neither strains the tether nor outsteps his guide." Nor was Acton sparing in his laudatory commendation on Lea's proposal not to point to a moral: "He starts with an avowed desire not to say what may be construed injuriously to the character or feelings of men. He writes pure history and is methodically oblivious of applied history. The broad and sufficient realm of fact is divided by a scientific frontier from the outer world of interested argument. Beyond the frontier he has no cognisance . . . for the erring and suffering mass of mankind he has an enlightened sympathy; for the intricacies of speculation he has none." Acton bestowed particular praise on Lea's treatment of the Templars: "The deciding test of his critical sagacity is the masterly treatment of the case against the Templars"; and for the treatment of the general principles of the Inquisition Acton had nothing but unfeigned commendation: "The design and organization, the activity and decline of the Inquisition constitute a sound and solid structure that will survive the censure of all critics."

From the opposite camp we may select the review by the Jesuit J. Blötzer in the *Historisches Jahrbuch*.[1] His review runs to over twenty pages and strikes some very harsh and dissonant chords. Scholarly value cannot be attributed to this sort of review: it is highly polemical, coloured, hairsplitting, captious, misrepresents the author (after having mistranslated his texts), studiously avoids any discussion of substantial points, operates, in a well-known fashion, with the *petitio principii* and

[1] See *Hist. Jb.*, xi (1890), pp. 298 ff.

the very tergiversations so severely criticized by Lea himself in picturing the Inquisition at work, and relies on authorities, such as Hurter, who had long been discredited, even by 1890. But in the din of all these attacks even this reviewer had to point out that Lea disposed of rich material, that the presentation of the affair of the Templars belonged to the best parts of the work (not, however, without mollifying this praise by insinuating that there was a remarkable similarity between Lea and a recent German work on the subject) and that the juristic questions were dealt with particularly fully, though the reviewer, after awarding marks for the presentation of the essential procedural points and after paying tribute to Lea for "at least" having seen their relevance, cannot abstain from employing a hackneyed stratagem by concluding: "I do not wish to investigate how successfully the author has discharged his task." [1]

The great importance attached to Lea's work by the most eminent scholars and the grudging admission by his detractors that the work had some value, ensured that a new edition became necessary seven years after the original publication, and in 1906 it was re-edited uniformly with the four-volume sequel of the History of the Spanish Inquisition. Meanwhile in France and Germany translations were put in hand. The French translation by the excellent Sal. Reinach appeared in two volumes between 1900 and 1902 and was prefaced by a penetrating historical introduction by Paul Frédéricq.[2] Summaries of individual chapters were separately published in the form of brochures by Alexandre Bertrand. A new French edition of the whole work became necessary in 1910. After some vicissitudes besetting the German translation this, too, got eventually under way, and the three volumes appeared between 1905 and 1913, the first volume also carrying the German translation of Frédéricq's Introduction to the French edition. Both the French and German

[1] loc. cit., p. 312. A very appreciative review in Germany appeared just before Blötzer had published his, by W. Bernhardi in the *Historische Zeitschrift*, lxii (1889), pp. 116–21.

[2] When Reinach asked Lea for permission to translate, he received an affirmative reply in which Lea characteristically enough said also this: "My only request would be that the tone of calm impartiality which I have endeavoured to impress upon the work be retained", Bradley, op. cit., p. 270.

translations were authorized and revised by the octogenarian himself.[1] A one-volume abridgement of the work, mainly dealing with the foundation and the procedure of the Inquisition, was published in Italy in 1910, and another one in 1914. Considering the swift succession of editions and translations, one may well share the satisfaction of the author at the great – and deserved – success of his work. And one should, I think, also realize that the editions and translations came after the most scurrilous attacks by admittedly historical ignoramuses who nevertheless did their best to poison the atmosphere. Lastly, to appreciate Lea's success one should bear in mind that American historical scholarship had not yet achieved any great standing, and that there was detectable a certain prejudice in the old world against an American who, moreover, was no academic historian: perhaps nothing illustrates the value of the work better than the fact that its translations were sponsored and welcomed by the most severe and reputable historical scholars at the time. In a number of ways the indefatigable worker and searcher after truth achieved that crowning of success which is the envy of the many, but accorded to so few.

III

An over-all assessment of Lea's *History of the Inquisition* in the mid-twentieth century will have to stress that the work still forms today the basis of research into the subject. Were it necessary to bring forward witnesses for this assertion, it would suffice to mention two of very disparate inclination and orientation: neither the Abbé E. Vacandard [2] nor the late A. S. Turberville [3] could have produced their admirable works without Lea. Even such a stern critic as Jean Guiraud,[4] despite all his reservations on Lea, could hardly have written his work without his

[1] Cf. also the review by H. Haupt in *Historische Zeitschrift*, xcvii (1906), pp. 440 f.

[2] E. Vacandard, *The Inquisition: a critical and historical study of the coercive powers of the Church*, transl. by B. L. Conway (London, 1908).

[3] A. S. Turberville, *Medieval Heresy and Inquisition* (London, 1920); cf. also idem in *Cambridge Medieval History*, vi (1936), pp. 699–726.

[4] J. Guiraud, *The Medieval Inquisition*, transl. by E. C. Messenger (London, 1930).

assistance, and he freely acknowledged this. In fact, it would only be tedious to enumerate the long list of authors who are indebted to the basic researches of Lea. This dependence on him has, however, only limited application: it applies almost exclusively to that part of the first volume that is reprinted here, that is, the organization of the Inquisition, the proceedings and sentence. Undoubtedly, they are the best worked parts of the whole *opus*: they have done what no other work had done before, that is, to present the principles of the Inquisition on the basis of the rich source material, notably the manuals and instruction books of some noted (or notorious) inquisitors, the official statements made by provincial and general councils concerning the modes of inquiry, and lastly, the numerous papal laws modifying, enlarging, deepening, refining and restricting the powers of the inquisitors, laying down the assistance which secular governments, magistrates, municipalities, etc., were obliged to render to the inquisitorial personnel, and dealing with the multitude of contingenicies which emerged as a result of the rapidly increasing spread of the Inquisition. There was no critic who could bring forward any substantial criticism against this part of the work: it has stood the test of time.

But, though suffering less than other parts of Lea's work, this, too, does exhibit some of Lea's shortcomings which may well be due to the immensity of the subject itself. The individual parts are not knitted together as well as they might be; there is some looseness of construction; there is – even in this part – a very noticeable tendency to focus attention on the individual case instead of making it merely illustrative of a general theme. In other words, the construction is not as firm and tight as the subject might have warranted.

Of more serious concern is another deficiency, and this concerns the literary apparatus with its references to the sources. It was Lea's habit not to break up his presentation within a paragraph, but to relegate all references to the sources to the end of the paragraph. From the point of view of the cursory reader this may be quite a good plan, because he does not wish to interrupt his reading after every sentence or even within a sentence, by looking at the bottom of the page. But even the general reader might wish to verify or to pursue a particular point, and it certainly is troublesome to ascertain which of the dozen or so sources cited in the one footnote, is relevant. Moreover, Lea is sometimes loose in giving bibliographical details: exactness is particularly demanded in the kind of literature which he quotes, otherwise the reader inevitably experiences a sense of frustration.

But when compared with the substance of the pioneer work itself, these deficiencies are of minor importance and do not in the least detract from its substantive value. They concern technicalities rather than the essence. And the essence is, as already pointed out, firmly based on the sources: it is true that since the first publication a number of original sources have been made available in better editions than Lea could obtain and, moreover, sources were published of which he could have had no knowledge. For instance, C. Douais, P. Frédéricq and J. M. Vidal published collections of documents relative to the Inquisition.[1] Further, the papal Registers of the thirteenth century and the early fourteenth century have now at last been fully edited: these Registers with their hundreds of letters and decrees for the inquisitors provide, of course, a mine of information for the actual law which governed the workings of the Inquisition.[2] Nor is there any shortage of modern works on the Inquisition which have appeared since Lea. Only a few need be mentioned for those who would wish to pursue the subject further. Still indispensable for the understanding of the procedural aspects are L. Tanon as well as Paul Fournier,[3] whilst in Esmein's book [4] the student will find many topics relating to the inquisitorial procedure treated within the wider framework of criminal procedure. Of works dealing specifically with the

[1] C. Douais, *Documents pour servir à l'histoire de l'inquisition dans le Languedoc* (Paris, 1900); P. Frédéricq, *Corpus documentorum inquisitionis haereticae pravitatis Neerlandicae*. 5 vols. (Ghent, 1889–96); J. M. Vidal, *Bullaire de l'inquisition française au xive siècle et jusqu'à la fin du grand schisme* (Paris, 1913).

[2] An attempt to utilize the papal Registers for the purpose of elucidating the constitutional problems of the Inquisition was made by A. C. Shannon, *The Popes and Heresy in the Thirteenth Century* (Pennsylvania, 1949).

[3] L. Tanon, *Histoire des tribunaux de l'inquisition en France* (Paris, 1893); P. Fournier, *Les officialités au Moyen Age* (Paris, 1889).

[4] A. Esmein, *A History of Continental Criminal Procedure* (Boston, 1913).

Inquisition mention should be made, apart from Vacandard and Turberville, of H. Maisonneuve;[1] G. G. Coulton;[2] della Veneria;[3] and J. Guiraud.[4] The latter work is a very detailed historical account of the Inquisition in the important Western countries, but does not specifically deal with procedure and organization.[5]

Although not distinguished, Lea's writing is free from all ambiguities, clear, concise, exact and forthright. Only here and there a certain nineteenth-century ponderousness and heaviness emerges, but apart from this, his style is polished and refined, even in those passages in which his sense of justice appears to have been particularly taxed. Here and there, too, his manner of writing rises to dramatic heights, as is evidenced, for instance, in his presentation of some of the tragic moments in the affairs of the Templars. Indeed, Lea amply fulfilled his promise in the Preface not to moralize and not to point to a lesson. It is this detachment which had made the first volume so valuable and which cannot fail to appeal to the reader in the twentieth century who, indeed, has been forced to witness, and sometimes to experience himself, the revival of inquisitorial procedures on a scale not within the vision of man in the late nineteenth century.

IV

This reprint provides an opportunity of offering some reflections on the institution of the Inquisition itself. There is perhaps no other topic that provokes so much abhorrence of anything medieval as does the Inquisition, with the consequence that irrationalism easily conquers calm and detached reasoning. Indeed, the virtually limitless expansion of the concept of heresy,[6]

[1] H. Maisonneuve, *Études sur les origines de l'inquisition* (Paris, 1942; second edition, Paris, 1960).

[2] G. G. Coulton, *Inquisition and Liberty* (London, 1938).

[3] C. della Veneria, *L'inquisizione medieovale* (Milan, 1939).

[4] J. Guiraud, *Histoire de l'inquisition au Moyen Age*, 2 vols. (Paris, 1935–8).

[5] Some years ago a pupil of mine, Miss Patricia Dodds, worked on the canonistic treatment of the Inquisition; cf. her dissertation in the University Library, Cambridge.

[6] For this cf. also L. Buisson, *Potestas und Caritas: die päpstliche Gewalt im Spätmittelalter* (Tübingen, 1958), and my review in *E.H.R.*, lxxxvi (1961), pp. 324 ff.

its ramifications into virtually every department of social and public life, the inability of those charged with heresy to defend themselves adequately in the face of the tortuous and involved casuistry practised by the inquisitors, the – on the whole – low educational standard of the defendants when compared with the highly professional skill and training of the inquisitorial interrogators, the severe restrictions placed upon the defence during the trial, the secrecy of all proceedings, the fact that neither those who laid information nor those who supported it as witnesses, were made known to the accused, that not knowing the precise facts constituting the charge nor his hostile witnesses he was given no opportunity to call rebutting evidence, the liberal employment of torture – its actual mechanics left ample margin to the fertile imagination of the torturers, the economic aspects of the Inquisition, especially in regard to the wealthier victims, with the consequences of wholesale confiscation of the victims' property, the cruel administration of the death penalty – all these features are indeed apt to engender an irrepressible feeling of disgust. This utter revulsion is only accentuated when the circumstances accompanying the final stages of the proceedings, particularly the sentencing and the paraphernalia of the stake, are properly appreciated, when indeed a detached spectator may have been seized with a rebellious feeling against what might well have appeared to him as sheer hypocrisy.

There is some justification in asking whether the repression of heresy by such methods was not a sign of the brittleness and feebleness of the system itself which demanded and warranted their employment. Would it not be a justifiable assumption to say that the very fact of instituting procedures of this kind proves conclusively and implicitly that the government that used them could no longer hope to work effectively with the ordinary means against those who were alleged to attack the bases of society? That extraordinary procedural means had to be devised to deal with rather ordinary occurrences? That, in other words, the conviction in large sections of the population had been corroded by doubt and the only means of combating doubt appeared to be those of the torture chamber, perpetual imprisonment, confiscation of the culprit's goods, or in the worst case the spectacle of being burned at the stake? Is it not at all times a sign of the weakness of governments when they have to have recourse to force against those who doubt or who impugn one or other of the tenets upon which the government stands, no matter how little this in actual fact may affect the working of the government? Is it not also the case that the result of persecution is usually not the end intended, that is, conversion and strengthening of the faith, but fear and terror, purely external acceptance of rulings by the government without the necessary inner participation or consent or fervour, leading in the end to loss of vitality and resilience, to arrested development and pure, if not meaningless, formalism?

These are some of the questions which an historian is bound to ask himself and to answer as best he can. Another facet that confronts him is the crying divergence between theory and practice. The inquisitors were men trained in the law, trained in that science that had as its core the implementation of justice. There is hardly one item in the whole inquisitorial procedure that could be squared with the demands of justice; on the contrary, every one of its items was a denial of justice or a hideous caricature of it. If this were not so, the papacy would have had no need to institute that whole apparatus, because the episcopal courts would have been quite sufficient to deal with the matter: this would at least have left open an appeal against sentence to the papal court, but even this primitive legal means did not exist in the case of the inquisitors, because they constituted an exceptional court that derived its powers, not from the common canon law, but from the pope himself, who invested the inquisitors with an authority by far transcending the authority and power of the bishops. The inquisitorial tribunal was a papal court and the inquisitors functioned "by apostolic authority" (*ex auctoritate apostolica*) because their jurisdiction was wholly papal. The term employed, *appellatione remota* (no appeal allowed), made it impossible to seek redress by legal means in a higher court, because there was none: all that remained was a special plea to the pope with a view to invoking his special favours in an individual case. That the sentence passed on a convicted defendant also affected his born and unborn descendants

– although innocent, they were declared dead in civil life and incapable of holding ecclesiastical or civil offices – is well known, and the punishment was no doubt conceived to have deterrent effects, though how far this tallied with the most primitive and natural notion of justice, or for that matter with natural law, is again difficult to understand. The invariable designation of the Roman Church as the *sedes justitiae* appeared, in these circumstances, somewhat paradoxical.

Nevertheless, there are two factors which must be borne in mind here. The first is that few of the items which characterized the Inquisition were the invention of the papacy. They have a long though undistinguished pedigree, reaching back to the imperial legislation in late Roman times. Further, the more pronounced the theocratic nature of royal or imperial governments in the Middle Ages was, the more they themselves demanded severe measures against those who might be suspected of attacking the basis of their own societies. The imperial legislation of Frederick II, preceding the papal-inquisitorial legislation, is an eloquent testimony to a pronounced theocratic-imperial government;[1] and so is the legislation and practice of the French kings in the thirteenth century. The motives prompting secular governments and the papal government to exterminate heresy and the heretics were identical.[2] Lastly, the feature that is so repulsive to modern observers, the death penalty for deviationism, was not a papal invention at all: Justinian decreed the burning of "heretical" books, and the stake for the "erring" Christian was a measure devised by the humanity of the early Capetian kings, long before the papacy had envisaged a special tribunal.

The second factor concerns the popular demand for inflicting the death penalty for "aberrations from the faith", and the popular insistence on executing it in public. This is why Frederick II in decreeing death for the heretic laid down that

[1] Cf. especially G. de Vergottini, *Studi sulla legislazione imperiale di Frederico II in Italia: le leggi di 1220* (Milan, 1952). For some general principles relating to medieval criminal procedure cf. W. Ullmann in *Juridical Review*, lix (1947), pp. 1 ff., and on torture in general idem, ibid., lvi (1944), pp. 123 ff.

[2] For some observations on this point cf. W. Ullmann, *Principles of Government and Politics in the Middle Ages* (London, 1961), pp. 195 ff., 223 f.

the execution must be public.[1] No doubt, a mixture of motives contributed to this demand for a public spectacle: an appetite for sensationalism, a desire to get rid of vociferous "cranks" and "eccentrics" within a community, personal enmity and revenge, a rationalized wish to be rid of unpleasant and disturbing elements who might upset the traditional and conservative way of living, and so forth.

The importance of these factors should not be minimized, but when all allowance for contemporary medieval conditions has been made, the responsibility of the papacy for the horrors of the Inquisition remains large enough. It is true that the crime of heresy constituted the most serious offence medieval man (or woman) could commit: it was constructed as the crime of *lèse majesté*, that is, high treason,[2] and as such demanded the most rigorous treatment, high treason at all times being the most dangerous of all public crimes. This is not the place to argue how far the construction of heresy as high treason was correct, but assuming that no juristic flaw can be detected in this construction – and both from the medieval ecclesiastical-political point of view as well as from the strict juristic angle a good deal can be said in favour of this reasoning – the methods adopted by the papacy cannot command respect. No other European power had made the law so much its own domain and its special prerogative as the papacy had – from the time when the papacy reflectively entered the historic scene it was anxious to see pure *justitia* distilled into the concrete and tangible rule of law. This legalism of the Roman Church was its strength, a strength derived from applying biblical, and especially Pauline, themes to concrete situations; a strength also derived from a conservatism that is nurtured by the easy availability of former decisions, judgements, decrees, etc., in the shape of the archives.

Instead of carrying over into the sphere of prosecuting

[1] Cf. Frederick's constitution in *Monumenta Germaniae Historica: Constitutiones*, ii. 210, p. 283: "ut vivi in conspectu hominum comburantur, flammarum commissi judicio." The statutes in the North Italian cities show a great variety in the treatment of heresy. Some did not punish it at all, others adapted Frederick's laws, others again left it to the ecclesiastical courts. For some details, cf. G. Dahm, *Das Strafrecht Italiens im ausgehenden Mittelalter* (Leipzig, 1931), pp. 39, 41, 279 f.

[2] See the decretal of Innocent III in *Liber Extra*: V. vii. 10 (*Vergentes*).

heretics the basic principles of jurisprudence which the papacy had hitherto so loudly and so successfully proclaimed, which it itself had constantly applied and by which it had thereby made itself a model for contemporary governments, thus potently influencing the development of orderly and constitutional government, now in the thirteenth century it was the papacy that became unfaithful to its own history, its own principles, its own proclamations, its own practice. Instead of utilizing for the proceedings against heretics the channels which in any case existed and which only needed to be modified and adapted, the papacy left this path and adopted principles which were the very denial of the demands made by the most primitive concept of natural justice. Whilst in the ninth century Pope Nicholas I strongly condemned the use of torture, because it violated both divine and human law,[1] in the mid-thirteenth century Pope Innocent IV made torture part of the legal machinery to be employed against defendants, merely charged with suspected heresy. Principles of evidence relating to the character and quality of witnesses in ordinary proceedings were set aside and their place was taken by the very opposite principles, otherwise harshly condemned by the papacy itself: the testimony of convicted perjurors, of excommunicate persons, even of other heretics, of children, of servants, of spouses against each other – all this was sanctioned by the Roman Church in its function as the *sedes justitiae*; none of these witnesses was admitted if their testimony was in favour of the prisoner. In a word, when a man (or a woman) was suspected of, or charged with, heresy, he or she had no hope that the elementary rules of procedure were employed: on the contrary, the dice was heavily loaded against them. And when due consideration is given to the expansion of the concept of heresy, which came to include also sacrilege, blasphemy, sodomy, refusal to pay tithes, sorcery, the assertion that usury was no sin, and so on – this kind of proceedings has no longer any semblance to a judicial trial, but is

[1] See *Mon. Germ. Hist.*, *Epistulae*, vi. 595, no. 99, cap. 86 ("*Responsa ad Bulgaros*"): "*Quam rem nec divina lex nec humana prorsus admittit, cum non invita, sed spontanea debeat esse confessio, nec sit violenter elicienda, sed voluntarie proferenda.*"

rather its systematic and methodical perversion. Instead of being the *magistra* of civilized means of trials, the Roman Church became the *ancilla* and instrument of practices which it would have had all the powers in its possession to condemn: but with its accustomed skill the Roman Church made the practices of other governments its own and with equally consummate skill shaped them into a perfect system.

The result of the widespread use of inquisitorial proceedings was what could be foreseen: terror and fear, partly because the lines of demarcation between orthodoxy and heterodoxy, between faith and heresy, were in any case rather fluid, and an aberration from the faith could without great efforts be detected in some verbal expressions or even in some unaccustomed actions; partly because the inquisitors were nowhere and everywhere, roaming about the countryside, so that one was never quite sure whether or not their vigilant ears and eyes were not attracted by suspected heresy; partly because it was the legal duty of everyone, including husbands and wives, children and servants, in order to avoid any suspicion of heresy on their own part, to report suspicious views to the inquisitors, so that there was plenty of opportunity to stir up trouble and create mischief – the bigoted were no less numerous then than they are now, and equally dangerous; partly because the secrecy which surrounded inquisitorial proceedings was apt to underline the seriousness of the whole business and enveloped it with an awe-inspiring aura, which was an excellent means of increasing the already latent fear. These factors would go a long way to explain why we read of only sporadic outbreaks of resistance against the doings of the inquisitors. Resistance was not only a highly dangerous undertaking, but also in some ways quite impractical, because the inquisitors were so elusive, and because they had an almost perfect organization, whilst the resisters could in the most favourable circumstances merely attack the local machinery, as, for instance, was the case in Narbonne, where the citizens destroyed the records of the Inquisition. Resistance was severely hampered by lack of organization, lack of knowledge, lack of co-operation.

To expect the secular authorities to give a lead would be

quite unjustifiable. As has already been hinted at, governments based on the theocratic premisses were not only not hostile to the Inquisition, but positively furthered it, because in the long run their own government would have suffered from the "heretics" as much as the faith itself: and after all, these theocratic governments were based on the faith, on the thesis that the kings had derived their power from God. The heretics' attack on some article of faith would no doubt eventually have redounded to the detriment of all theocratic rulership. The assistance and lack of resistance to the inquisitors in this quarter is therefore easily explicable. Moreover, papal legislation had in any case made it a legal duty of the secular governments to exterminate heretics within their domains; in case of negligence the secular ruler himself was threatened with the deprivation of his ruling powers and with the occupation of his country by orthodox Catholic princes; that he himself was to incur a charge of suspected heresy, and that the ecclesiastical interdict could be brought into action, should also be mentioned. Lastly, the coronation oath of the king was to include the promise to exterminate the heretics, a legal demand which was as eagerly fulfilled by the pronouncedly theocratic French kings as it was persistently rejected by the English kings.[1]

On the other hand, civil magistrates or municipal authorities could not very well be envisaged as leaders of organized resistance partly for the same reason which applied to the kings, and partly, because special papal legislation existed which in great detail regulated the local authorities' duties to establish, maintain and put at the disposal of the inquisitors, prisons for the heretics, and which also forbade local magistrates to release prisoners without the approval of the inquisitors, however much the magistrates themselves may have been convinced of the innocence of the prisoners in their charge.[2] In these cir-

[1] For some details cf. *Principles of Government and Politics in the Middle Ages*, cit., pp. 80 f., 202 ff.; and for the practical application of the papal law against secular rulers, ibid., pp. 83 ff.

[2] The civil authorities had also to denounce to the inquisitors persons suspected of heresy, to take them into custody in the meantime, to abstain from any interference with the work of the inquisitors and to give the latter all possible assistance – under threat of the civil power itself becoming suspected of heresy. The papal

cumstances it was difficult to entertain any hope for a successful and organized resistance, because the long arm of the inquisitors would surely have reached the individuals who had initiated any resistance. And what civil magistrate would have – in the thirteenth and fourteenth centuries – taken upon himself the charge of being at least a fautor of the heretics or of having been responsible for the interdict over his locality? And especially if he himself was possibly quite disinterested in the purely dogmatic or what might well have appeared to him abstruse quarrel? The answers to these questions suggest themselves when one cursorily glances at the highly efficient work of the secret police in otherwise civilized modern States.

The historian anxious to understand and to explain the Inquisition is, however, faced with the perturbing problem of why the papacy with its record of insistence on justice, on law, on regularized procedure, and so on, so easily turned aside from its past and was so largely instrumental in giving inquisitorial procedure a complexion which resembled a judicial trial only in name. How is one to explain this? The explanation is all the more difficult as the inquisitorial measures decreed by the papacy came at a time when, after centuries of inculcating and refining the ideas of justice and right, the papacy had to all intents and purposes reached its goal and achieved on the European scene a veritably commanding position. Motives belonging to the economic sphere can hardly have influenced the papacy: for the most part, the heretics were poor, ill-educated, illiterate, though with the spread of "heresy" wealthy individuals, too, became its victims, and the confiscation of their property and of their possessions offered no doubt some lucrative inducements, but not to the papacy itself. In his famous

---

legislation is in *Liber Extra*: V. vii. 8; 13; *Liber Sextus*: V. ii. 11; 18; etc. Further, Innocent IV's *Ad extirpanda* (in *Bullarium Romanum*, iii. 552–8).

But quite apart from the immediate issue, resistance to the inquisitors would have been resistance to lawfully constituted authority (and one appointed by the pope for the sake of safeguarding the faith) and would have created a multiplicity of offences, i.e. at least a charge of heresy (or of favouring heretics), disobedience to a lawful command, dereliction of duty, misuse of official position, etc. Within a theocratic framework it is impossible to construct a *right* of resistance, cf. *Principles of Government*, pp. 22, 81, 97, 131.

decree *Ad extirpanda* Innocent IV minutely regulated the sharing out of the confiscated property, and no part went to the papacy.[1] Where the papacy might have found a source of revenue might have been in the granting of the *litterae de gratia* as a substitute for an appeal from the court of first instance. But this certainly did not develop until the latter half of the thirteenth century, when the Inquisition was already firmly entrenched.

Economic reasons as determining and primary factors can safely be dismissed. The answer to this, as will readily be admitted, crucial problem may lie in a different field which touches the very core and nerve-centre of medieval Christianity. The difficulty in explaining the papacy's inquisitorial legislation is that modern man is apt to concentrate on the rights – sometimes also called natural rights – of the individual: the view that the individual had a natural right to a fair trial was not held, if issues were at stake which touched the fundamentals of medieval Christian society. Differently expressed, the primary, if not exclusive concern lay in maintaining the whole entity of society itself, and not in upholding the rights of individuals. It is this which for want of a better name may be called collectivist thinking which stands in so marked a contrast to the modern individualist kind of thought. The very idea that the *publica utilitas* must be preferred to the *privata utilitas* is merely a symptom of this thinking: society was one whole, was indivisible, was one *totum* and the individual was no more than a part of the whole. But what mattered was the well-being of society, and not of the parts constituting it. When the individual was seen as merely functioning for the good of society, when he was conceived merely as an infinitesimally small element of the whole, the medieval emphasis on the whole and not on the individual will be easier to grasp.[2] Whilst earlier *libertas ecclesiae* signified freedom of the Church from lay control, it

[1] Except, of course, for goods confiscated within the Roman diocese, cf. Alexander IV on 24 September 1260, in *Bullarium Romannm*, iii. 672.

[2] In actual fact this is the organic viewpoint which was already fixed by St Paul: I Cor. xii. 14 ff., and which was given its classic medieval presentation by Hugh of St Victor, cf. W. Ullmann, *Growth of Papal Government in the Middle Ages* (London, 1955), pp. 442 f. Cf. also below for the quotation from St Thomas Aquinas, p. 42, n. 3.

now in the thirteenth century meant freedom of the Church from the infectious disease of heresy. To this demand all other considerations had to be subordinated. The reproach that the papacy did not uphold the dignity of man (his body and soul) is not based on papal conceptions.[1]

Conversely, the individual as a being endowed with indigenous, autonomous and independent rights was a thesis for which we shall look in vain in the Middle Ages. To begin with, man as mere *homo*, as a being that by nature had inborn rights, was not yet seen. What there was, was the Christian, and by virtue of his baptism he stood on a level quite different from mere man. Further, the Christian as such was never held to be endowed with indigenous rights: as St Paul had said, By the grace of God I am what I am.[2] The Christian was considered to be merely the recipient of rights eventually originating in divinity: it was the latter which conferred rights (and duties) on the former, and could also take them away. But inalienable and inborn rights the Christian had not: this theory did not come about until very much later. In particular, papal theory in the Middle Ages did not operate with any rights which were not conceded or which pre-existed before they were given.[3] The Christian's mode of living was directed by principles and norms which flowed from the fact of his being a Christian, that is, a member of the Church. And just as the Church was no mere human institution or a product of nature, so was the member of the Church not a mere human or natural person, but took part – by virtue of baptism – in the divine attributes themselves. The presupposition for this was the faith of the Christian: and the mouthpiece of divinity, the exponent of Christian doctrine, the organ which pronounced the individual articles of faith, was, as a result of the historical and doctrinal process, the papacy. It

[1] Nor would this reproach accord with St Thomas Aquinas: in his *Summa Theologiae* (ii–ii, qu. 64, art. 2 ad 3) he does speak of the dignity of man, but maintains that this dignity can be attributed only to the virtuous man and must be denied to the bad man: the latter may be killed, which violates his dignity as little as killing of an animal does: "Peior enim est malus homo quam bestia."

[2] "*Gratia Dei sum id quod sum*" (I Cor. xv. 10) which was always taken in the Middle Ages to mean that the Christian had no inherent *right* to anything.

[3] For some observations on this point cf. *Principles of Government*, pp. 54 f., 58, 75 ff., 131 (principle of concession).

would indeed have been an inconceivable enormity to have asserted that a Christian had the right to dispute articles of faith, let alone to set aside doctrine defined by the papacy, and to put something else in its place. This aberration from the faith constituted a veritable denial of the basic principles of established Christianity in the Middle Ages: it was nothing but rebellion against the most fundamental thesis that only he could be a Christian who was a member of the Church, and only he was a member of the Church who accepted unquestionably the faith expounded by the appropriate organ. In the final resort this rebellion was a denial of Christ's being the source of the Christian's life; it was an open challenge to the divinity of Christ. The juristic construction of heresy as high treason can, on this admittedly narrow basis, be understood.[1]

The essential point is that by asserting differently from the accepted doctrine the individual forfeited any rights which as a Christian he might otherwise have enjoyed or which otherwise might have given him some protection. An opinion or assertion which *aliter sentiat quam ecclesia catholica* [2] entailed the automatic loss of any rights which might have been conferred on him. Hence faith could not be kept with him who himself had no faith in God.[3] In short, the Christian holding heretical opinions or even suspected of holding them, was considered to have wilfully divested himself of that grace which had raised him to the level of a Christian and which had given him rights: he ceased to be a Christian. He who doubts is an "infidel", the law had declared,[4] and is therefore a heretic.[5] Consequently, he

[1] See also below, pp. 39 f. and 50.

[2] Or as Gerhoh of Reichersberg had it in the twelfth century: "Haereticum esse constat qui a Romana ecclesia discordat": *De edificio Dei*, cap. 69 (in *Mon. Germ. Hist., Libelli de Lite*, iii. 174). See already Gregory VII in the eleventh century, in his *Dictatus Papae*, cap. 26 (*Reg*. ii. 55a), and his model, the Dictatus of Avranches, cap. 3: "*Qui decretis sedis apostolicae non consenserit, hereticus habendus est*" (*ca*. 1070).

[3] Cf. Innocent III in his *Reg*. xi. 26 (in *Patrologia Latina*, ccxv. 1357 A).

[4] Originally this came from Pseudo-Isidore. The passage is in *Liber Extra*: V. vii. 1: "*Dubius in fide infidelis est.*"

[5] This is still the law today, cf. *Codex Iuris Canonici*, can. 1325 (2); the tribunal today is also the Holy Office which is one of the three congregations of cardinals presided over by the pope himself (can. 247) assisted by the Commissar, always a Dominican.

had put himself outside the protection which only a "faithful" (*fidelis*) was entitled to enjoy.

There is one more consideration which may contribute to a better understanding of the steps the papacy took in its inquisitorial legislation, though this is a consideration which for some inscrutable reason has not entered the horizon of medieval historians. It was one of the most cherished and guarded axioms that without the institution of the papacy Christian society would neither have come into being nor could it continue to exist. The papacy considered itself, to use Innocent III's expression, the *fundamentum totius christianitatis*, the very rock upon which Christendom was founded. Without the papacy there would be no Church, no Christian society, no salvation. But the cementing bond of this society was faith, that is, the faith as expounded by the very organ which constituted the base of the society. An essential ingredient of the faith was, however, the function of the papacy itself. Aberration from the faith as laid down by the papacy was in itself a rebellion against constituted authority, because only the Roman Church was qualified to expound and define faith; no individual Christians or groups of Christians could with impunity set themselves up as expounders or interpreters of the faith: this was considered as a sign of intellectual arrogance, because they had relied upon their own judgement – "*ad semetipsos recurrunt*" – instead of believing what authority had laid down.[1] A heretic contumaciously and persistently resisted the exposition of the divine word by the very authority which was instituted precisely in order to make known the divine word, i.e. the papacy. Doubt or deviation in matters of faith therefore was an implicit attack on Christ as the *stabile et perpetuum fundamentum*,[2] and because in the pope Christ was present in a corporeal form – Christ's *presentia corporalis*[3] – this implicit attack was in actual fact directed against the vicar of Christ, the pope. After all, the pope's

[1] See Gratian, C. XXIV, qu. iii, cap. 30 (Leo I): teachers of errors are those "qui ad cognoscendam veritatem aliquo impediuntur obscuro, non ad propheticas voces, non ad apostolicas litteras, nec ad evangelicas auctoritates, sed *ad semetipsos recurrunt*".

[2] Cf. Innocent IV in his *Quia tunc* (in *Bullarium Romanum*, iii. 584).

[3] See *Growth of Papal Government*, cit., p. 444, n. 1.

plenitude of power embraced, like Christ's, everything and everyone: the Lord, Urban IV declared, had put everything at the feet of the popes [1] and Gregory IX stated that the pope alone could open the gates to paradise.[2] The pope was, in short, the point of intersection between heaven and earth. Because of the closely woven texture of doctrine infringement of one of its elements was tantamount to attacking the whole system.[3] In the last resort every aberration from the faith attacked the foundation of the whole Christian edifice, the Roman Church. It is not without coincidence that because the maintenance of the Catholic faith was the overriding consideration of the papacy, so many of its laws dealing with the Inquisition referred to it as a *negotium fidei catholicae*.

The fierce determination of the papacy in eradicating heresy is less of a puzzle if sufficient weight is attached to the consideration that every aberration from faith was capable of being constructed as an attack on the function of the Roman Church, that is, on its supreme magisterial office. This consideration also explains why a person excommunicated for merely suspected heresy, if not released from excommunication within a year, became automatically a heretic who had then to face the full rigour of heretical punishment: he was obstinately and defiantly disregarding, not only the teaching of the Roman Church, but also its law. In no other sphere did the concatenation of faith and law [4] produce such profound public effects as in that of heresy and in the measures adopted to combat it. The extent and scope of the faith could at the same time be fixed by the only authority which was held to be divinely instituted to regulate matters of faith, that is, the papacy. Hence the assertion that the pope was not entitled to issue this or that law, constituted in itself heresy, because thereby the pope's plenitude of legislative power, an essential part of the medieval Christian's

[1] "Subjecit omnia sub pedibus nostris . . . contulit nobis dominii potestatem;" for the full text see *Principles of Government*, p. 53. Cf. Ephes., i. 22.

[2] Ibid., p. 41. Cf. also for some recent papal statements pp. 39, n. 1, 41, n. 1, 52, n. 1.

[3] The biblical justification for this was found in I Cor. v. 6; Gal. v. 9; cf. also Matt. xiii. 33; James ii. 10.

[4] About this cf. *Principles of Government*, pp. 95 ff., 105 f., 295 f.

faith, was impugned.[1] By striking at the root of medieval Christendom the "heretic" was held to be assaulting Christendom itself. Seen thus, the efforts made by the papacy through the inquisitorial machinery were efforts dictated by the demand for self-preservation: if heresy were not halted, the result would be the collapse of the papacy and herewith of Christendom.

Admittedly, these are considerations which strike no familiar chord in modern readers unaccustomed as they are to medieval ways of ecclesiastical reasoning. But both the collectivist or totality view of the papacy and the medieval concept of a Christian seem sufficiently to explain the setting aside by the papacy of the usual safeguards surrounding a criminal trial. One can hardly charge an institution with disregarding natural rights and the like when the institution itself was not even aware of the existence of such natural rights as the accused's right to a fair trial. These rights grew on a soil vastly different from that on which the medieval papacy prospered. That within the wholly ecclesiastical setting the medieval inquisitorial proceedings must not be judged or measured by the yardstick of modern ethical and wholly unecclesiastical norms, should be clear by now. A similar observation can be made in respect of the question of tolerance and intolerance, freedom of thought and the suppression of free thought, topics so frequently brought into play in this context,[2] in which they have, however, little

[1] For some interesting remarks on this point cf. most recently M. J. Wilks in *Bulletin of the John Rylands Library*, xliv (1962), pp. 489 ff., at pp. 504–11, 514, with copious illustrations.

[2] Both St Augustine and St Thomas Aquinas considered the question of tolerance in connexion with I Cor. xi. 19. For the former cf. his *Ep.* 93 (in *Patr. Lat.*, xxxiii. 321, 322, 329, etc.) where he declares that steps taken against heretics are taken "*non odio nocendi, sed dilectione sanandi*" (col. 324); his principle is that what matters is not that someone is compelled to do something, but what it is he is compelled to do: "*Non considerandum est, quod quisque cogitur, sed quale sit illud, quo cogitur, utrum bonum an malum*" (col. 329); the basis of this view is Luke xiv. 23: "Go out . . . and *compel* them to come in that my house may be filled." For the latter cf. his *Summa Theol.*, ii–ii, qu. 10, art. 8: because heretics (and apostats) are infidels, they are to be compelled physically, so that they do as they had promised: "*Tales sunt etiam corporaliter compellendi, ut impleant quod promiserunt.*" It is interesting to see that the fourteenth-century Statutes of Bologna, though prohibiting disputation attacking the faith, nevertheless exempt from this prohibition disputations in the service of scholarship: see G. Dahm, op. cit., p. 39, n. 112.

meaning, for freedom of thought implies a choice of accepting one of several alternatives,[1] each equally valid and true; that this would have been a wholly unacceptable supposition in the Middle Ages needs no stressing. Medieval Christendom ruled by the papacy knew neither freedom of thought nor a natural right to a fair trial by a defendant accused of heresy. When it was held – and held it was for centuries – that the only true doctrine emanated from the pope as successor of St Peter and vicar of Christ, any doctrine not in agreement with it or casting some doubt upon it, was bound to be considered untrue and detrimental, because subversive,[2] to the fabric of the whole society. The aberration was held to be a disease of an infectious nature, and hence its victim had to be cured or, if incurable, destroyed.[3] The papacy was perfectly aware that the path it trod deviated from that which it had trodden so long: the very designation of heresy as an exceptional crime[4] is revealing. Exceptional crimes require exceptional measures. Whether the view on the exceptionality of the crime could still be maintained in the fourteenth century may well be doubted: the enormous legislative output of the papacy dealing with heresy and the Inquisition would militate against it; and so would the ubiquitousness of the inquisitors and their plain records testifying to the frequency of the exceptional crime. Nonetheless, the Inquisition was considered to be an answer to the problem of how to preserve the Christian order of things believed to be

[1] See St Jerome in Gratian, C. XXIV, qu. iii, cap. 27.

[2] This view of the subversive character of heresy goes back to St Paul's letter to Titus (iii. 10–11), who calls the heretic himself *subversus*.

[3] The comparison of heresy with a physical and infectious disease may make the understanding of the medieval treatment of heretics easier: a medieval inquisitor when reproached with intolerance by modern man might have replied that modern society segregates and isolates persons infected with dangerous diseases in special hospitals and would never tolerate the victims to be a source of danger to the public. St Thomas distinguished between the heretic and the Church: the heretics, he declared, had merited (*meruerunt*) not only excommunication, but also their exclusion from the world by death and could therefore lawfully be killed; the Church after two admonitions (cf. Tit. iii. 10) and for the sake of salvation of other Christians had the right to hand the heretic to the secular power for dispatching him to the other world: *Summa Theol.*, ii–ii, qu. 11, art. 3.

[4] See *Liber Sextus*: V. ii. 8 (Alexander IV).

divinely ordained and fixed by the organ specifically instituted for this purpose, the papacy.

If one tries to view the matter from the contemporary medieval angle, one will perhaps also understand why the inquisitors themselves were overwhelmingly characters leading blameless and devoted lives; they were well-trained jurists and theologians, quick-witted, alert and circumspect. Above all, in the overwhelming number of cases they had no personal advantages and profits. They were men who saw in their activities perhaps the highest task which could be thrown on any man, that is, to excise from the Christian body politic cancerous and lethal growths. Devotion to their office and the conviction that without their activities Christendom would face collapse was as characteristic of them as was their selflessness and absence of personal ambitions. They bore their responsibilities well – after all, they were papal delegates with extensive powers including the grant of indulgences, and were virtually a law unto themselves: they were in the possession of an authority which amounted to a decision of life and death. To judge the medieval inquisitor by modern ethical standards would again be unhistorical.[1]

The need to preserve the basis of medieval society on the one hand, and the "heretic's" own contumelious assertions resulting in the loss of protection otherwise afforded to him on the other hand, appear to make the procedural measures decreed by the papacy understandable. In order to appreciate this fully, one should realize that in concrete circumstances faith was a somewhat elusive quality: being so much internal, it was a difficult matter to prove or to disprove its existence. From this follows that as often as not recourse had to be made to statements, expressions, gestures, actions, and so on, which in one

[1] Nevertheless, the more recent period would offer some remarkable parallels in the secret police. For instance, one of the most feared bloodhounds during the early stages of the Bolshevik Revolution and head of the secret police (the G.P.U.), Ian Dzershinsky, carried out the functions of his office above reproach without any personal gain or ambition; cf. I. Deutscher, *The Prophet Unarmed* (Oxford, 1959), p. 85 ("incorruptible, selfless, intrepid"). Similar observations can be made about Heinrich Himmler and Reinhard Heydrich as respective heads of the German Gestapo and of the Security Service. For inquisitors' qualifications cf. *Clem.* V. iii. 1.

way or another could serve or could be interpreted as an *indicium*, as circumstantial evidence, for an aberration from faith. Direct proof was, considering the nature of the crime of heresy, not easily obtainable. Hence the resort to hearsay evidence and, above all, to the *fama*, that is, common talk and general report in a locality or community. The witnesses appearing before the inquisitors were not therefore witnesses of fact, but witnesses of rumour, of the general reputation of the accused. Presupposing the character of the crime of heresy it is difficult to see what other means of evidence could have been devised. On the other hand, the very fact that rumours or bad repute were current about a particular person, made him already virtually guilty, because thereby he became at least suspected of heresy and because there was – and is – no effective defence against such elusive means of proof as rumour and hearsay evidence. Rebutting evidence against a charge based on rumour – however much testified by honest and upright men – is not easily conceivable, and in view of the interrogating skill of the inquisitors and the absence of any corresponding skill on the part of the accused, an acquittal was very difficult to achieve. It is no doubt interesting to see that this inquiry without any specific accusing individual was based – rather tenuously – on two passages in the Bible: Innocent III made the point very clearly when he declared that the canonical sanctions concerning inquisitorial proceedings were derived from *Luke* xvi. 1–4 and from *Genesis* xviii. 21.[1] Furthermore, the need to preserve

[1] Innocent III in his *Reg.* viii. 200 (in *Patr. Lat.*, ccxv. 777–81): "*Debeat praelatus procedere ad inquirendum et puniendum subditorum excessus; ex auctoritatibus novi et veteris testamenti colligitur evidenter, ex quibus super hoc processerunt canonicae sanctiones;*" follows text of Luke xvi. 1 ff. and of Gen. xviii. 21. The last-mentioned passage was already adduced for the purpose of justifying an official enquiry by Gregory I in his *Moralia*, xix. 25, no. 46 (in *Patr. Lat.*, lxxvi. 126–7), whence with some alterations the argument was taken over by the Council of Aix-la-Chapelle in 816, cap. 37 (in *Mon. Germ. Hist.*, *Concilia*, ii–1, p. 359, lines 13 ff.). Pseudo-Isidore foisted the latter decree on to Pope Evaristus (who was said to have lived at the end of the first century), *Ep.* 2, cap. xi (in P. Hinschius, *Decretales Pseudo-Isidorianae* (Leipzig, 1863), p. 92). The canonical sanctions mentioned by Innocent III were: Gratian, C. II, qu. v, cap. 6, and qu. vii. cap. 46, both from Gregory I. The *inquisitio* in ancient Rome was an extraordinary procedure, the ordinary being that of *accusatio*, cf. Th. Mommsen. *Römisches Strafrecht* (Leipzig, 1899), pp. 347 f., but even when in late imperial times the *inquisitio* became more

the basis of society also accounted for the introduction and lavish use of torture against the accused. The employment of torture did not aim at obtaining the truth, but at a confession: no legal regulations existed for the actual use of torture, except that it could not be repeated against the same accused, a regulation which was easily circumvented by simply continuing the torture, if the accused chose to retract his confession "voluntarily" made after an administration of torture. When even after several applications of the instruments of torture the accused did not confess, he was to be released, but no acquittal followed.[1] The *favor fidei* explained not only the employment of torture, but also the recourse to such other means of evidence which in any other proceedings were illicit: the testimony of perjurers, excommunicate persons, convicted criminals, wives and children, no less than the aiders and abetters, fautors and all those who in one way or another had assisted the accused and knew of his "heresy", was legitimate, provided that they were hostile to the defendant; the presupposition for admitting these as witnesses was that they testified "out of zeal for the Catholic faith" – *zelo catholicae fidei* – and that the inquisitors could presume that these witnesses would not give false testimony.[2] In order to protect witnesses testifying as they did out of this zeal, their names were withheld from the prisoner, who, being in custody, had, of course, no means of testing their statements. Only when the accused could prove that the witnesses were motivated by personal enmity against him, was their testimony to be rejected [3] – a legal possibility, no more, because not knowing who they were, he was hardly in a position to prove their malignity.

It is the same consideration of the *favor fidei* which explains

---

prevalent, hearsay evidence, rumour, and the like, were never admissible, see Mommsen, pp. 440 f. Innocent III himself gave only very broad and general instructions to inquiring officers, *Liber Extra*: V. i. 17.

[1] See P. Hinschius, *Kirchenrecht der Katholiken und Protestanten* (Berlin, 1895), v. 485, n. 4. The employment of torture in the case of witnesses seems to have aimed at obtaining the truth.

[2] *Liber Sextus*: V. ii. 5.

[3] Ibid., V. i. 19.

that for a condemnation mere suspicion was sufficient: the judgement in the case of a slight or vehement suspicion demanded abjuration of the suspected heresy from the accused and imposed a variety of penalties; if he should relapse into the same or some other heresy, he was automatically and without further proceedings treated as a relapsed heretic and to be handed over to the secular magistrate for special treatment.[1] If the suspicion was grave (*suspicio violenta*), the accused was not given an opportunity of disproving any allegations, and he was treated as a heretic: the judgement demanded abjuration of the heresy – which was thereby taken as proved – whereupon he was absolved from excommunication by the inquisitor and sentenced to wear the blue-striped outer garment with its yellow crosses in front and at the back or to imprisonment for life or to a number of years. If the accused should refuse abjuration, there was nothing else to be done for him but to deliver him to the civil magistrate for the special treatment. The confession of the accused entailed his abjuration and the imposition of a number of punishments, including lifelong imprisonment with bread and water.[2]

There remains to be faced the question of why the Inquisition as a permanent institution came to be confined to Southern, Central and Western Europe or, which is the same question, why Northern and Eastern Europe as well as the British Isles were spared the Inquisition. The fact has often enough been stated, but the reason why this was so has not been asked, let alone answered. Why was this so? It is a very large question, for the full answer of which the present context does not allow sufficient space. It must therefore suffice to state that perhaps in no other field of its public activity was the papacy so dependent upon its prolonged arm, the secular power, as in the sphere

[1] Alexander IV, ibid., V. ii. 4: "*Sine ulla penitus audientia relinquendi sint judicio saeculari*" adding, however, that if the accused should repent, the sacraments, if he should humbly ask for them, are not to be denied to him before meeting his death, because the Church welcomes those who return to her: "*Ecclesia nulli claudit gremium redeunti.*"

[2] If he confessed at the commencement of the proceedings, Boniface VIII gave discretionary powers to the inquisitors in regard to mitigating the rigours of the imprisonment, its duration and the kind of food allowed, see *Sextus*: V. ii. 12. In Roman law imprisonment was custodial, not punitive, *Dig*. 48.19.8.9.

of bringing heretics to book. One might go as far as to say that the whole papal governmental scheme was epitomized in the relations between the papacy and its own tribunal, the Inquisition, on the one hand, and the civil magistrates, including the kings, on the other hand. It is assuredly no coincidence that the Inquisition could gain a firm foothold in some parts of Europe, whilst in others the work of the inquisitors was made impossible. And when we look at, say, Eastern Europe, we would find that, for instance, Manichaeism, Catharism, and so on, were infinitely better organized, far more widespread and their adherents far more numerous than in other parts of Europe, so much so that they virtually invited the inquisitors, and yet, we hear so little about the Inquisition there: large fields were not covered by it at all, and the persecution of heretics in these territories would have been indubitably rewarding, both from the doctrinal and the disciplinary point of view. A possible explanation may be that the papacy itself displayed far less authority in Eastern Europe, especially in the Balkans, than in Western Europe, and hence the exuberance of heresies affected the papacy to a much lower degree than the more or less isolated expressions of a heretical character in Central or Western Europe. The papacy, unable to establish its own governmental scheme in Eastern Europe, could not for understandable reasons evince much interest in destroying heresies there. The authority of an institution can be affected only where it is established, and when this presupposition is wanting, one cannot reasonably expect the institution to show much interest.

But this is at best only a partial explanation. The firm hold which the Inquisition had in some parts of Europe can perhaps be better explained by the kind of government which prevailed in these parts. It is certainly not coincidental that the Inquisition flourished in precisely those countries in which a fully-fledged and unimpeded theocratic form of government was at work. This at once explains the efficacy of the papacy's rulings and the services which the governments themselves rendered to the Inquisition. As we have tried to say, the motives for the pronounced theocratic governments and for the papacy in persecuting heresy, were identical: in either case heresy was in the final resort an attack upon the very bases upon which society rested.[1] On the other hand, Scandinavia and England exhibited a far weaker theocratic complexion of government than can be witnessed in, say, France or Germany. In the former the populist kind of kingship had never died out, whilst in England the theocratic and feudal elements in kingship were rather delicately blended and balanced, with the result that in neither country the full deployment of papal governmental principles could be effected. In contrast to his French colleague, the English king never incorporated the ruling of the Fourth Lateran Council concerning the extermination of heretics, into his coronation oath. But above all else, the law itself militated against the display of papal-inquisitorial forces in England: the protective shield which the common law afforded can be seen in this context. The law obtaining in England in the late thirteenth and in the fourteenth centuries was not the law of the theocratic king; it was not the *voluntas regis*; it was not the one-sided will of the king that created this or that law, but the law was arrived at by consent and agreement of the king and, for brevity's sake, of the barons. It was this law, so strongly impregnated with feudal elements, which operated with the accusatorial principle, with no secrecy attached to its proceedings, with the clear delineation of the functions of the accuser, judge and witness, which knew of no torture against the accused, which knew of a condemnation that was based on the verdict of a jury representing the neighbourhood, which had not familiarized itself with the characteristic elements of Roman-canonical procedure – and so forth. This common law entailed that the wings of the theocratic king were considerably clipped and resulted, as far as law-making and its application were concerned, in some quite drastic restrictions of the king's power. Admittedly, being of feudal origin, the common law did not exhibit all the stream-lined and gleaming attractiveness and logical consistency which the royal-theocratic law so bountifully

[1] Hence also the designation of heresy by Frederick II as the crime of *lèse majesté* in his own legislation (barely four weeks before his second excommunication): *Mon. Germ. Hist.*, *Constitutiones*, ii. 210, p. 283, line 25, and no 213, p. 286, line 28; etc. His reasons for defining heresy as high treason were, of course, the same as the papacy's.

manifested, but, embodying essential feudal ingredients, it focused attention more on the unsophisticated needs of the country than did its royal-theocratic counterpart. There was a realistic and unspeculative approach to the real and natural needs of the kingdom. And amongst them the protection of the theocratic character of kingship against the implied attacks of heretical views did not count: the feudal elements of kingship were a perfect barrier and protective shield against both ecclesiastical and heretical attacks. In these circumstances the inquisitors could not expect help from the king, the barons, and the law: it was the law which prevented the introduction of torture, and that law was not of the king's making, but was the result of a joint effort incorporating the element of consent. Important presuppositions therefore were lacking in the case of England: kingship was by no means constructed on the single pivot of theocracy; and the law itself did not conceive of a special papal tribunal operating in the country and thereby setting aside *legem terrae*.[1]

No assessment of the Inquisition can be complete or balanced or approach any degree of fairness, if the peculiar conditions of the European Middle Ages are not properly evaluated and taken into account. Amongst these the complexion of medieval Christianity must rank high: it was a tightly knit and closely woven basis which, because of its comprehensiveness, could indeed serve vastly different aims and ends. But as this medieval Christianity was merely a synonym for the descending-theocratic form of government, it reached deep into the texture of public life and affected virtually every department of it. The

[1] For an elaboration of the general theme cf. my *Principles of Government*, cit., Part II: The King. Without prompting, Louis IX introduced the inquisitorial proceedings into the French legal system, ibid., pp. 195 f., 200, 225 f. Only once, during Edward II's reign in England, were inquisitors active, and this was in connexion with the suppression of the Templars. The inquisitors, however, seem to have encountered difficulties hitherto unknown to them: like Clement V, they urged the use of torture, but in the Southern province apparently nobody was found who was trained in the art of its administration, whilst the bishops of the Northern province retorted that torture was not known in England and asked whether torturers should now be imported from the Continent. Cf. Greenfield's *Register*, cited by M. McKisack, *The Fourteenth Century* (Oxford, 1959), p. 292, n. 2.

concern of the papacy, and to a lesser extent of the episcopacy, as well as of the theocratic governments for the maintenance of the Christian faith is not difficult to understand. In particular, the papacy would have been unfaithful to its own *raison d'être* if it had allowed the propagation of views which it considered hostile to the faith: the institution and authority of the papacy was in the last resort, if not openly attacked, at all events implicitly impugned. No government worth its name can tolerate the dissemination of opinions and views opposed to it, if this opposition aims at the diminution, even if not the abolition, of the government's authority. Disobedience to a papal command, epitomized in the denial of the power of the keys (the *contemptus clavium*) was schism and the first concrete step to heresy, because it effectively attacked the unity and peace of the Church and of Christendom, guaranteed solely by the function of the pope as monarch. Boniface VIII was quite logical when he declared that denial of the true monarchic position of the pope manifesting itself in his possession of plenitude of power was heresy. Specially and uniquely charged as the popes considered themselves they were with the government of the *Respublica christiana* by the divine words of the Founder of the Christian Church, they would have abysmally failed in the discharge of their duties had they not taken upon themselves the task of eradicating what they conceived to be evil and subversive of that very society over which they were set in order to direct it to its proper end. That in so doing the popes disregarded the most fundamental demands of natural law, natural justice, natural rights, is a reflection based upon conceptions which have gained currency after the power and authority of the papacy had been reduced: these conceptions are not medieval, but owe their validity to the unecclesiastical, liberal, modern spirit. And yet, it has been the tragic experience of the present generation to have witnessed in a number of modern States a baffling recrudescence of the very spirit of the medieval Inquisition under more or less euphemistic nomenclatures and institutions, all, however, having in common police character and secrecy of its proceedings; the only difference from its medieval predecessor is the highly efficient, methodical and coldly calculated persecution of "the opponents of the régime". The results of both the medieval and the modern Inquisition are identical. But whilst the medieval Inquisition was the unadulterated offspring of the prevailing ideas and views, no such explanation will suffice for its modern successor – or is perhaps the much exalted modern liberalism nothing but a thin veneer? This is a perturbing question for a medieval historian, but fortunately not one which he is called upon to answer in the present context.

XVII

REFLECTIONS ON MEDIEVAL TORTURE

THE institution of torture is commonly regarded as a blot on medieval civilisation in general and on medieval criminal proceedings in particular. To the modern mind, the very name implies brutality and savagery arising out of perverted ingenuity. This reaction is the outcome of an uncritical acceptance of certain stereotyped invectives against the Middle Ages rather than of a well-balanced judgment. In our present-day attitude towards this and similar institutions we are only too apt to forget that torture was not the invention of the perverted minds in the Middle Ages, but an institution taken over from the otherwise highly valued Roman Law. The acceptance of Roman Law in theory and practice from the twelfth century onwards necessarily entailed the adoption of torture, which played an important rôle in Roman Law. It is misleading to assume that the twelfth century enthusiasm for this newly discovered body of law was tempered by a highly critical approach. Roman Law was axiomatically held to be the perfection of everything legal, the embodiment of the highest legal culture which man was able to contrive, and, as such, far superior to any other existing law. Roman Law was considered to be the complete crystallisation of the virtue of justice and the highest manifestation of reason, which no nation claiming to be civilised could afford to leave aside. It would indeed have been a strange phenomenon in the history of law, if medieval man had entertained doubts about the justice, soundness, or humanity of certain legal institutions, embodied in this *summum jus,* and established in this *summa ratio,* as Roman Law came to be called.

In view of the many current misconceptions of medieval

torture, it may be of interest to sketch briefly the leading ideas as they appear in the voluminous writings of medieval jurists; their lectures and commentaries convey a reliable and vivid picture of the conditions prevalent in medieval proceedings. The medieval doctors of law were not only outstanding theorists, but were also thoroughly familiar with all questions which the practical application of the law involved. As a rule, they themselves were judges before they entered upon their academic careers in the various Italian universities, and as professors they never lost touch with practical problems. Moreover, they were frequently consulted in difficult questions by both judges and advocates, and no conscientious judge could afford to disregard their expert opinions recorded in the *Consilia*. The perusal of their writings reveals the true medieval state of legal affairs.

The object of torture, according to the medieval jurists, was purely supplementary: torture was to supplement that evidence which had accumulated against the defendant during the trial and which threw grave and reasonable suspicions upon him. It was the very last step in medieval criminal proceedings and was only used when all other possibilities of fully proving a suspected defendant's guilt were exhausted, and when there were yet reasonable grounds for doubt. It was this last remainder of doubt which made a condemnation of the defendant impossible, for a condemnatory sentence had to be based, not upon presumptions and suspicions, but upon proved facts: "In criminalibus non est quis damnandus ex suspitionibus, sed ex probationibus luce clarioribus," Cynus de Pistoja taught.[1] If therefore no reasonable doubt could possibly exist, such as in the case of a publicly witnessed crime, the defendant would be convicted without

---

[1] Cynus, C. iv. 19, 23, no. 2, fol. 216 *verso*. That was common opinion, see, *e.g.*, Baldus de Ubaldis, in his lecture on C. iv. 19, 25, no. 1, fol. 45: "Nota ergo, quod lex in maleficiis probandis requirit claritatem probationis in quadam excellentia, hoc est per amplius quam in civilibus."

recourse to torture and without confession: "In notorio non habet locum tortura, quia tortura non adhibetur nisi in defectum probationis." [1] On the other hand, when the evidence presented to the judge was too weak even to arouse suspicion against the accused, the trial had to be brought to an end and the defendant had to be acquitted. Acquittal and condemnation were pronounced in a *sententia definitiva*, which ended the trial in the first instance. The trial did not close, however, if the judge considered the case as not yet fit for judgment, that is to say, when he arrived at the conclusion that the evidence so far presented would neither justify acquittal, because of the suspicion which still surrounded the accused, nor condemnation, because the possibility of the defendant's innocence could not wholly be excluded. In this case the judge passed a *sententia interlocutoria* by which he decreed the torture of the accused. The trial thus far was only preliminary and had to be continued after the torture.

In recognition of the possible abuses of the tremendous discretionary powers which the law laid into the hands of the judges, and in appreciation of the great moral and physical dangers which torture entailed for the individual concerned, the jurists were at great pains to restrict the powers of the judge to a minimum, so as to protect the accused, often illiterate and undefended, against unjustifiable methods of over-zealous and over-ambitious judges. The doctors laid down restrictive rules which the judge was bound to adhere to, if he did not want to become liable to punishment in the *sindicatus* process: it was here that the opinion of the *doctores legum* decided the issue.[2]

At this first part of the trial both parties had to submit all available evidence. Witnesses were summoned, sworn in and heard in the presence of both parties, who were

---

[1] Baldus on C. ix. 41, 8, no, 3, fol. 225.

[2] On the importance of this process, see W. Engelmann, *Die Wiedergeburt der Rechtskultur in Italien*, 1938, pp. 204 *seq.*, and J. W. Jones, *Historical Introduction to the Theory of Law*, 1940, pp. 19 *seq.*

entitled to put questions to them; any other evidence was to be taken and both parties were given an opportunity to examine statements and results. The counsels and advocates of either party could bring forward their pleas.[1] If the judge was unable to arrive at a decision, he pronounced the interlocutory order which decreed the torture. But this decree was by no means dependent upon the proposal of the prosecuting party. The jurists conceived the judge as a seeker after truth, who was permitted to use all lawful means to arrive at the truth, regardless of a proposal by a party. The doctors avowed that criminal procedures were introduced for the sake of the public good, in order to free society from the danger of criminals: the pursuit of this aim of criminal proceedings called for the powers of the judge to decide upon any lawful means which might further this aim. Consequently, the judge had to take care of the interests of society, even if no special plea to this effect was submitted to him. Lastly, it was held as an axiom that in criminal proceedings the explicit declaration of a party to renounce a right, such as the right of the prosecutor to propose torture, had no practical consequences: "In criminalibus expressa remissio partis non valet in prejudicium rei publicae." [2]

A fundamental requisite for the validity of the interlocutory order of torture was the full proof that the crime had been committed. Probability was considered insufficient; there was to be certainty that the crime in dispute was committed.[3] "Debet prius constare," said Bartolus succinctly, "quod maleficium est commissum." [4] And perhaps still clearer was the dictum of his great pupil, Baldus: "Tortura fit ad liquidationem personae, non ad

[1] Bartolus, D. 48, 1, 12, no. 1, fol. 154; Clarus, *Opera Omnia*, lib. v. quaestio 64, no. 35, fol. 321.

[2] Gomez, *Commentaria*, tom. iii. cap. 13, no. 22, fol. 566. He continued: "In his, quae concernunt publicam utilitatem, potest et debet judex procedere sine aliqua petitione . . . potest judex supplere defectum partium et advocatorum."

[3] Cynus in his lecture on C. ix. 41, 18, no. 2, fol. 565.

[4] D. 48, 18, 1 (*qui quaestionem*), no. 1, fol. 191; see also D. 48, 18, 22, no. 2, fol. 195 *verso*.

liquidationem facti."[1] The jurists laid greatest emphasis upon this requisite, though cases seem to have occurred in which the probability of the commission of the crime was deemed sufficient. Thus Clarus did not conceal his amazement at the decision of the Milanese Senate on 17th February 1555 to torture a Jew on account of a charge of raping and subsequently murdering a Christian girl, although her corpse was never recovered.[2] Torture could not be decreed for every crime, but only for capital offences, that is for those which were to be punished with death or with mutilation. The subjection of the accused to torture for minor offences would have been a greater evil than the real punishment which would have consisted of some fine.[3]

Another requirement for the validity of the interlocutory decree was that no other means should have been unexplored in an attempt to find out the truth about the perpetration of the crime. This requisite was insisted upon with equal firmness. The subsidiary or auxiliary character of torture emerged quite clearly in this requirement. Cynus said that torture could be ordered only when "veritas aliis probationibus illuminari non possit, cum quaestiones sint introductae in subsidium."[4] Bartolus was equally outspoken on this point when he taught that "ad tormenta pervenitur in subsidium, cum aliter veritas explorari non potest."[5] As long as any other evidence was available, torture must not be resorted to. The judge who, in spite of the clear and convincing proof of the defendant's guilt, ordered torture was held liable to punishment in the *sindicatus* process. For it was considered as illegal to extort confessions of guilt by torture, which was, by unanimous agreement, to be employed "ut amplius constet de delicto" and not "ut reus fateatur

---

1 Baldus on D. 22, 5, 3 (*Sed et divi*), no. 15, fol. 183.
2 Clarus, *loc. cit.*, no. 2.
3 See Gomez, *loc. cit.*, no. 2.
4 Cynus, *loc. cit.*, no. 2, fol. 565.
5 D. 48, 18, 8, no. 1, fol. 192.

delictum," as the Neapolitan Paris de Puteo maintained.[1] Judges who adhered to this method were called "malitiosi." They were to be punished after the expiration of their office, and had to pay indemnity to the defendant.[2]

The third and most important requisite concerned the sufficiency and adequacy of those facts which incriminated the accused and made him gravely suspected. It was, in other words, presumptive evidence, which spoke against the defendant. These facts would have been a very insecure basis for his condemnation, but they were so urgent and grave as to lead to a presumption of guilt. In his usual lucidity Bartolus stated: "Ex suspitionibus quis torquetur ad eruendam veritatem, non tamen ex suspitionibus quis damnatur."[3] These circumstances had to be of a certain and well-defined character and had to make the defendant's guilt probable, if they were to form a valid basis of the interlocutory order. Their premises had to satisfy the demands of sound reasoning; the arguments had to accord with each other. The conclusion to be drawn from the circumstances taken together should have made the perpetration of the crime by the accused a likelihood. Thus Baldus declared when consulted on the quality of *indicia* in this way: "Argumenta debent esse verisimilia et probabilia, quae in consideratione intellectus appareren t omnibus vel saltem sapientibus probabilia."[4] An *indicium* was considered to be a circumstance which, having been properly evaluated in relation to the particular situation, was able to shed more light upon as yet hidden matters. "Omnia indicia faciunt ad illuminandam veritatem."[5] The extraordinary variety of circumstances, which were bound to occur in any legal proceedings, pre-

[1] In his tract *De sindicatu*, fol. 462, no. 9. [2] See Clarus, *loc. cit.*

[3] In his lecture on D. 48, 18, 22, no. 1, fol. 195 *verso*.

[4] Baldus, *Consilia*, vol. iii. cons. 78, no. 2, fol. 16 *verso*. In his lecture on C. ix. 41, 8, no. 1, fol. 225, he said with a reference to Jac. Butrigarius, who was the teacher of Bartolus: "Ad hoc, ut procedatur in tortura in criminalibus, debent praecedere indicia certa et probabilia."

[5] Bartolus on D. 48, 18, 10 (*Plurium*), no. 4, fol. 192 *verso*.

cluded the establishment of certain fixed rules as to which *indicia* were apt to produce in the judge's mind the presumption of the defendant's guilt. Everything depended on the structure and the setting of the individual case itself. Consequently, the jurists introduced their lectures on this topic with the stereotyped remark that no definite ruling could be given and that the evaluation of the strength of the incriminating circumstances must be left to the individual appraisal and discretion: the judge should decide as a wise and virtuous man would have decided in his place. "In materia indiciorum non potest dari certa doctrina, sed totum relinquitur arbitrio boni viri, scilicet judicis," was the doctrine of Jacobus Butrigarius, later to be adopted by all jurists. Nevertheless, they tried to facilitate the task of the judge by laying down some general principles by which he should be guided. We may well discuss some of the more important circumstances which were held incriminating enough to justify torture.

In general, the jurists demanded full proof of the incriminating circumstance by the testimony of at least two witnesses. There was only one exception to this rule. The statement of an eye-witness, whose reliability, good character and capacity for correct observation were beyond doubt, was held to be an adequate basis for the interlocutory decree, but not for condemnation.[1] But in all other cases the incriminating circumstance had to be fully proved by two witnesses. Thus the statement of one witness that he saw the defendant at night time in the neighbourhood of the house which was broken into, would have been without avail had it not been corroborated by at least one other witness.[2] Both witnesses had to refer to one and the same fact: "Tale indicium debet probari per duos testes contestes, qui deponant et concludant de eodemmet indicio," Paulus Castrensis declared.[3] Their

---

[1] Bartolus on D. 48, 18, 20, no. 5, fol. 195.
[2] Bartolus on D. 48, 18, 22, no. 7, fol. 196.
[3] In his lecture on C. ii. 59, 1, no. 7, fol. 107.

depositions would have been insufficient, if they referred to different circumstances.[1]

Another important incriminating circumstance capable of forming the basis of the interlocutory decree, was the extrajudicial confession of the accused.[2] Vague hints about the crime were not considered sufficient. He had to refer to it in very specific and detailed terms; his confession had to be voluntary, convincing and clear.[3] A confession made by the defendant to a priest in the confessional was not conceived as an extrajudicial confession, even if the priest had divulged its contents: "Talis confessio fuit facta tamquam soli Deo et non tamquam soli homini." [4] Moreover, if the priest had communicated the penitent's confession, be it in court or otherwise, it was without any legal effects.[5] A different aspect opened up when a confession was made to the priest in his private capacity, and not in that as a confessor: this confession could have been made use of in the proceedings.

Of great practical importance was the value of hearsay evidence. The jurists recognised the dangers inherent in this kind of evidence and tried to lay down precautions so as to ensure that the common talk of the people, rumours, and the like, did not exert an undue influence upon the judge. Bartolus defined *fama* as common opinion, which was founded on concrete facts, which had originated with creditable, reliable, and sensible individuals and was the rational judgment about certain concrete facts.[6] Bartolus and all others after him demanded a *justa causa* as the source of this common opinion, and this *justa causa* was made the object of testimony.[7] Without it,

---

[1] Alciatus, *Consilia*, cons. 455, no. 1, fol. 243; Marianus Socinus, jun., cons. 45, lib. iii. no. 2, fol. 115 *verso*.

[2] Lucas de Penna in his commentary on C. xii. 50, 1, no. 7, fol. 823, and all other writers.

[3] See, above all, Clarus, *loc. cit.*, quaestio 2, no. 25, fol. 151.

[4] Ludovicus Romanus, on D. 29, 5, 3, no. 6, 7, fol. 58 *verso*; Gomez, *loc. cit.*, no. 9.

[5] Gomez, *loc. cit.*, fol. 561.

[6] *Loc. cit.*, fol. 192 *verso*.

[7] Bartolus, *loc. cit.*, no. 16: "Ista est proprie fama ex suspitione proveniens, quando justa causa suspitionis praecessit istam famam et istum rumorem."

that common opinion was merely foolish gossip ("vana vox populi") having no legal effects whatsoever. The majority of respectable people within the locality in which the crime was committed, had to entertain that common opinion.[1] The witnesses were to declare that they heard this common opinion expressed by the majority in public.[2] This circumstance had merely confirmatory value in criminal proceedings—that is, it only corroborated other incriminating circumstances already fully proved.[3]

Flight of the defendant from the locality of the crime immediately after its perpetration constituted another incriminating circumstance. He had to be seen fleeing from the place of the crime by at least two witnesses. Breaking out of prison without the use of force was not incriminating in itself, but violence and force—the accused struck a warder down or escaped after breaking the bars—threw grave suspicions upon him and formed a valid basis for the interlocutory order.[4] Enmity between the accused and the victim of the crime was not sufficiently incriminating, nor the declaration of a wounded or dying individual.[5]

The possession of stolen goods incriminated the defendant, unless he proved their legitimate acquisition or was a salesman.[6] The fact alone that the defendant was a habitual criminal with a bad reputation, only incriminated him on two conditions: firstly, that the crime with which he was charged was of the same type as that which he previously committed ("in eodem genere"), and, secondly, that he was unable to prove that he

---

[1] *Cf.* also Baldus in his lecture on C. iv. 20, 18, no. 30, fol. 52: "Non debet (scil. fama) esse rudis et indiscreta, sed etiam apud bonos et graves viros, qui non praesumuntur loqui, nisi id, quod credunt verum et quod credi debent."

[2] Bartolus, *loc. cit.*, no. 21: "Debet ergo dicere 'audivi publice dici a majori parte hominum huius civitatis.'"

[3] Baldus, cons. 77, vol. iii. no. 15, fol. 16: "Sola fama non est sufficiens ad torturam." Paulus Castrensis on C. iv. 19, 4, no. 7, fol. 180 *verso*: "Regalariter vero nec plenam nec semiplenam facit, sed factam probationem coadjuvat."

[4] Clarus, *loc. cit.*, no. 18.

[5] Clarus, *loc. cit.*

[6] Bartolus, *loc. cit.*, no. 4, and all other writers.

had been leading a blameless life for the last three years.[1]

A strong protection against arbitrary decisions of judges afforded the right of the defendant to demand from the judge a detailed statement concerning all *indicia* upon which he had based his decree. This statement had to be presented in the form of a documentary copy.[2] Furthermore, if the judge had heard the witnesses by summary methods, their depositions were invalid—as far as torture was concerned—and he was compelled to hear them again "in plenario judicio," [3] so that the accused had an opportunity of cross-examining them. Lastly, the defendant had the right of appeal against the interlocutory order, in which case the judge had to postpone the performance of torture. The accused or his counsel could point out in the appeal that the incriminating circumstances were not sufficient to warrant torture or that he was an exempted person. There were several classes who were exempted from torture. They were, above all, members of universities, persons in high authority, such as public officials, then knights and barons, members of the aristocracy, persons under 20 and over 60 years of age,[4] pregnant women and nursing mothers. The position of clerics was somewhat undecided. Some jurists maintained that they were exempt altogether, whilst others declared them to be in no way privileged. In fact, Paris de Puteo, the fifteenth-century professor, reported that he himself saw the torture of clerics for various kinds of crimes, such as for murdering relatives with poison, or for violation of tombs.[5] It was

---

[1] Salycetus in his lecture on C. ii. 22, 4, no. 2, fol. 38 *verso*: "Sed si talis diffamatus probaret, quod per triennium proximum bene vixisset et fuisset bonae vocis, conversationis et famae, illa mala fama contra eum probata nihil ei noceret, sed censeretur in totum purgata."

[2] Bartolus, *loc. cit.*, no. 8.

[3] Gomez, *loc. cit.*, no. 21, fol. 565.

[4] Though this requirement did not always seem to have been adhered to. Clarus reported a case in which the Milanese Senate decreed the torture of the 65-year-old Aloisius de Lorto on 17th September 1547, because he was of a robust physique; see the report of Clarus, *loc. cit.*, no. 22.

[5] *Loc. cit.*, fol. 474, no. 7.

frequently pointed out that the torture of clerics appeared necessary in order to check delinquency: it was the secular judge who performed it and this was, Clarus declared, "non mala consuetudo, alias saepenumero delicta clericorum remanerent impunita, quia si non essent laici, qui torquerent, clerici numquam torquerentur."[1]

Since the law did not lay down stringent directions, the determination of the kind of torture to be administered was left to the discretion of the judges. They were emphatically urged by the professors to abstain from any severity or brutality against the accused; they should by no means strive after a confession or employ savage methods: "Tortura debet adhiberi cum moderamine" was the watchword.[2] The most effective protection was the right of the defendant to charge the judge through the agency of the *sindicatus* process. Consequently, the jurists advised judges—especially the younger and more ambitious generation [3]—not to invent new torturing methods or to deviate from the customary way of torturing which was performed by binding the defendant on a tree in some elevated position and by striking him across his bare back with a cord. Over-severity causing bodily harm or even death entailed punishment of the judge. The case of Bartolus himself was only too vivid in the memory of the judges and jurists. When still a somewhat inexperienced judge, he tortured a young and seemingly strong and healthy man who nearly died during the procedure. Rumour had it that Bartolus had to flee from Pisa where he was a judge at the time of that incident.[4]

Several precautions had to be taken to ensure that no

---

1 *Loc. cit.*, no. 25.

2 Gomez, *loc. cit.*, no. 5, fol. 558.

3 See Gomez, *loc. cit.*: "Clamandum est contra judices severos et crudeles vanam et inanem gloriam affectantes et propter hoc majora officia in re publica appetentes, qui nova genera tormentorum miseris reis imponunt et moderatum modum a jure dispositum excedunt."

4 Bartolus, D. 48, 18, 7, no. 1, fol. 192. But this rumour was ill-founded, see Woolf, *Bartolus of Sassoferrato*, p. 396.

undue harm could be inflicted with impunity. A medical expert had to be present during the whole of the proceedings.[1] An official notary was commissioned to record the proceedings in greatest detail, so as to exclude any subsequent doubt or distortion; questions and answers had to be recorded verbatim. But by unanimous consent of the jurists the defendant's counsels were not allowed to be present.

In itself the confession made during torture had little value, because it could not serve as the basis for a conviction. That was common opinion amongst the jurists.[2] The defendant had to be taken away from the place of torture, so that he was removed from the direct impressions and influence which the sight of the locality was bound to exert upon his mind. He had to be kept isolated in a prison cell for one clear day, and it was only then in public session and in the presence of counsels and the notary, that the judge was allowed to question him as to whether he still adhered to his confession made under torture.[3] If the defendant confirmed it, the judge would pass sentence. Revocation of the confession in this session usually led to a repetition of torture, because the confession was considered as a new *indicium* against him; but torture could not be repeated more than twice, and if after the third torture the accused again revoked his confession, he had to be acquitted.[4] It is interesting to observe that some jurists

---

[1] Baldus, cons. 77, vol. iii. no. 3, fol. 16.

[2] See, *e.g.*, Cynus in his lecture on C. ix. 41, *loc. cit.*, no. 6, fol. 565: "Numquid confessio facta in tormentis extorta fidem faciat? Distingue: aut ultra perseverat in confessione, aut non. Si non perseverat ultra, non valet."

[3] Bartolus on D. 48, 18, 1 (*Divus Severus*), no. 3, fol. 189 *verso*: "Post confessionem factam in tormentis reducatur in loco publico judicii, ubi coram notario et personis publicis confiteatur." *Cf.* also Cynus, *loc. cit.*, fol. 565 *verso*: "Quando dicatur ultra perseverare in confessione? Respondeo, quod non territus in tormentis hoc facit. Et hoc est, quando est extra locum tormentorum, ita quod non videat, alias si est prope et videat tormenta, semper praesumitur in tormentis confiteri."

[4] Baldus on C. ix. 41, 8, no. 4; Clarus, *loc. cit.*, quaestio 21, no. 36, fol. 158: "Non est procedendum in infinitum, sed crederem sufficere, quod tormenta repeterentur usque ad tertiam torturam, et ubi deinde ductus ad ratificandum semper negaret, *absolveretur rebus sic stantibus.*"

put a confession under torture on an equal footing with that made under the mere threat of torture. Bartolus went even so far as to declare that a confession made whilst the defendant was in prison, was not voluntary and had to be confirmed with the usual precautions taken.[1] In all cases, however, the condemnation was based, not on the defendant's confession as such, but rather on the combination of his confirmed confession with the incriminating circumstances which led to his torture. Neither confession alone nor incriminating circumstances alone could have procured a condemnation.[2] Accordingly, if torture was decreed without incriminating circumstances, a confession made under torture even if subsequently confirmed had no value.[3] If the defendant had not confessed he was to be acquitted.[4] A repetition of torture could only be decreed when entirely new circumstances of an incriminating nature were produced against him.[5]

These were the leading ideas and principles concerning the use of torture. Space prevents the closer examination of details, the presentation of actions taken against over-severe judges, and fuller quotations from the lectures and *Consilia* of the jurists. The perusal of their voluminous writings leaves no room for doubt that they as the upholders of the cause of law and order tried with all their might to humanise torture, as far as the inhumanity of that institution allowed. The jurists were fully convinced of the moral and social dangers which the use of torture entailed. Moreover, they knew the harshness and unscrupulous attitude of some judges who were entrusted

---

[1] Bartolus, *loc. cit.*, fol. 190 *verso.*

[2] Baldus, C. iv. 19, 25, no. 2, fol. 45: "Simul collecta inducunt indubitabiliter veritatem, et est exemplum in confessione in tormentis extorta, quae non per se, sed perseverantia vel fama vel verisimilitudine facti vel aliis adminiculis inducat veritatem."

[3] Joannes de Imola: "Nota, quod aliquis confiteatur in tormentis non praecedentibus indiciis, quod numquam ex illa confessione debet damnari."

[4] Clarus, *loc. cit.*, quaestio 64, no. 37, fol. 326.

[5] Albericus de Rosciate, C. ix. 41, *Rubrica* no. 8: "Non possunt repeti tormenta, nisi superveniant nova indicia."

with criminal proceedings. It was precisely for this reason that the scholars laid down stringent rules, the transgression of which inevitably made the judge liable to be brought to account by the *sindicatus* process. This humanisation of torture lasted as long as legal scholarship was destined to play a decisive rôle in the actual application of the law. The progressive decline of legal studies at the universities in later centuries brought forth a lower standard of the lawyers who were called upon to serve the cause of law. The authority of the scholars diminished likewise, and their influence upon the practical administration of the law gradually faded away. The law itself was no longer regarded with that respect which was characteristic of previous centuries: lawlessness in social life and a laxity in the application of the law went hand in hand. The standard of public administration, like that of public and private morality, deteriorated considerably. The public administrators were no longer imbued with that spirit of responsibility, that sense of loyalty towards the law, and that respect for the individual which distinguished the judges of previous centuries. Instead of regarding themselves as restricted in their discretionary powers by the law, the judges largely ignored it in the age of transition from medieval days to modern times. The law had lost its sacrosanct character. Mainly on account of the deterioration of moral standards in social and public life, the protection and interests of the individual counted far less than in the heyday of medieval culture. The low standard of legal training, the loss of the humanising influence of the universities on the lawyers, the disregard of moral principles and the resulting lack of respect for the interests of the accused, largely explain the lamentable over-severity and brutality with which torture came to be used in the sixteenth and seventeenth centuries. The recourse to the *sindicatus* process was of no avail any more, since universities and scholars had ceased speaking with authority. And the idea of protecting the individual against judicial violations of the law did not seem to appeal to those authorities who were entrusted with the supervision of inferior judicial organs. Yet all these deficiencies of the legal and public administration must be considered against the background of contemporary civilisation. The brutality with which torture was employed, was but a concomitant feature of the cultural crisis which resulted from the disintegration of medieval civilisation and society. The sixteenth and seventeenth centuries were transitional ages and the upheaval caused by the turmoil of transition was bound to lead to aberrations, of which the detestable use of torture was only one instance. It needed the stirring and powerful appeals of Voltaire and Beccaria to abolish this inhuman institution.

INDEX

5-50